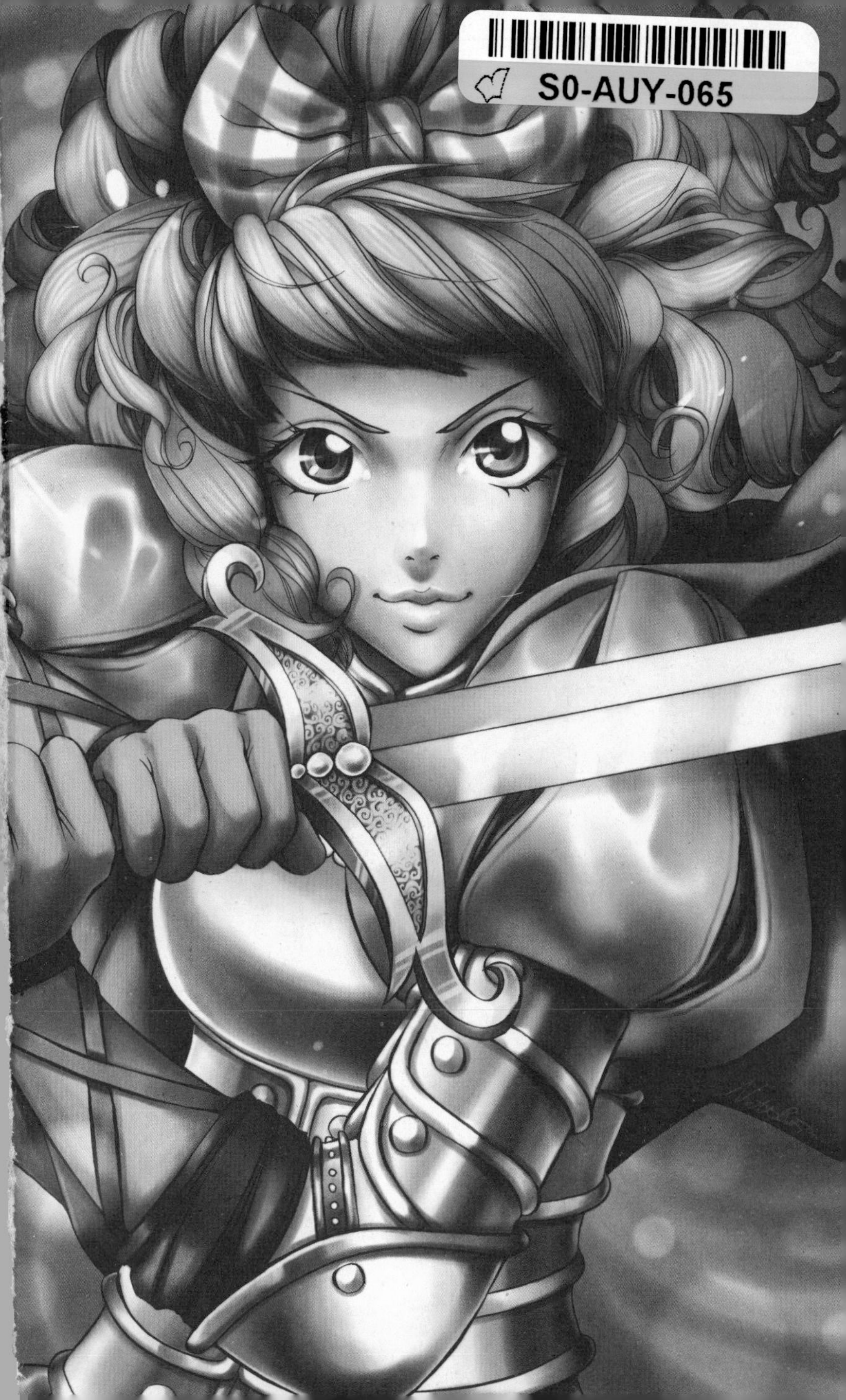

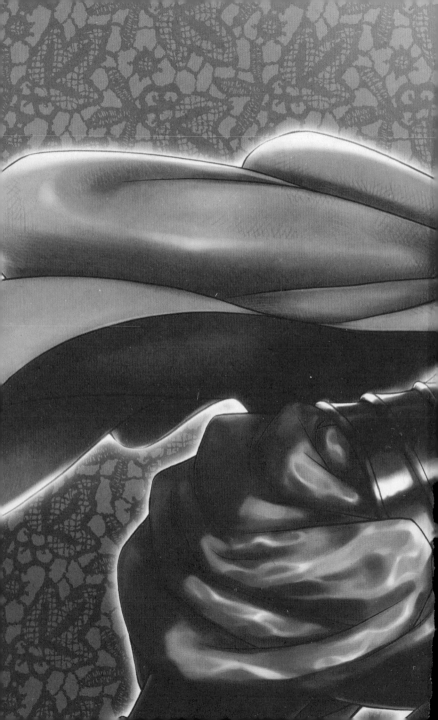

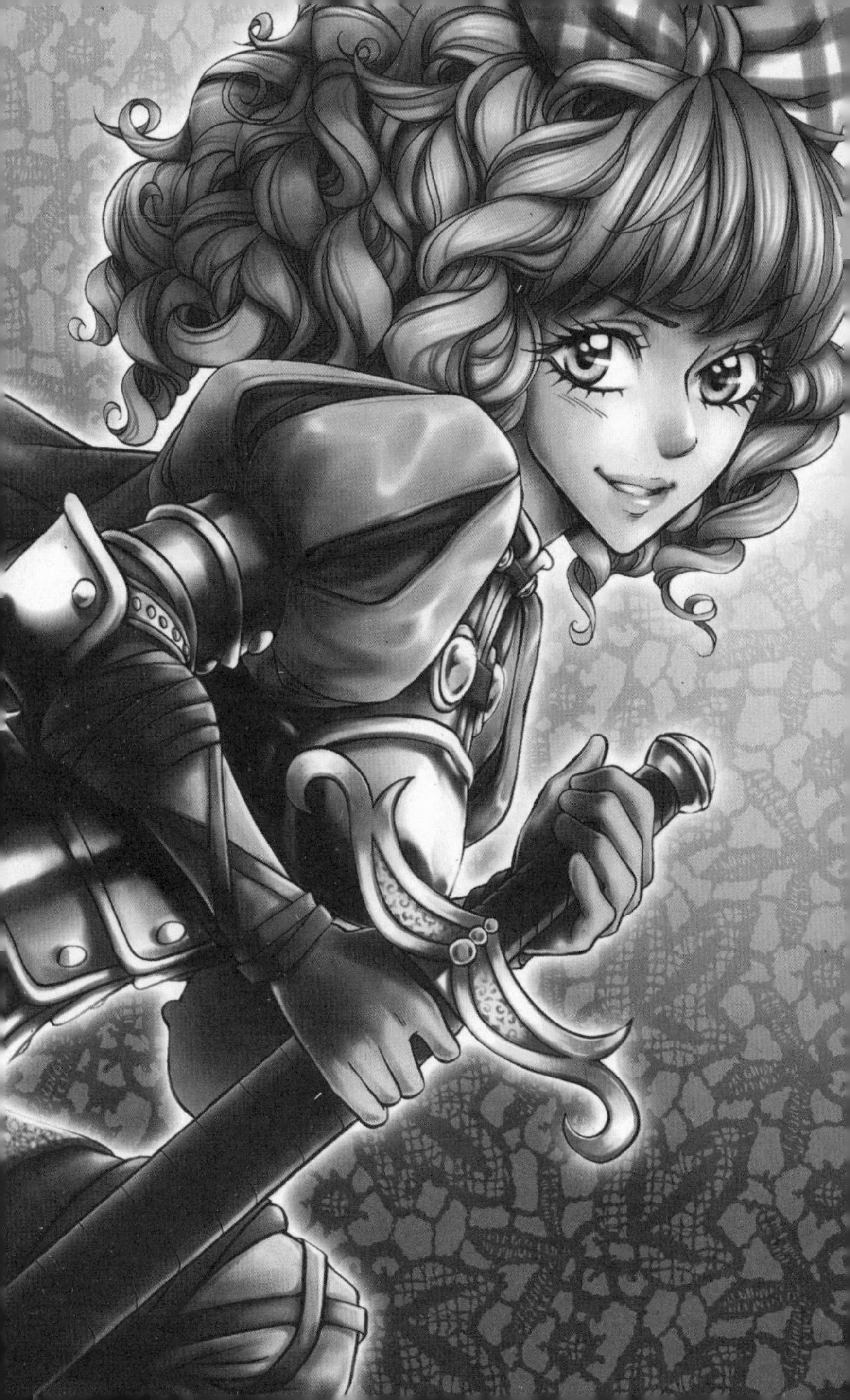

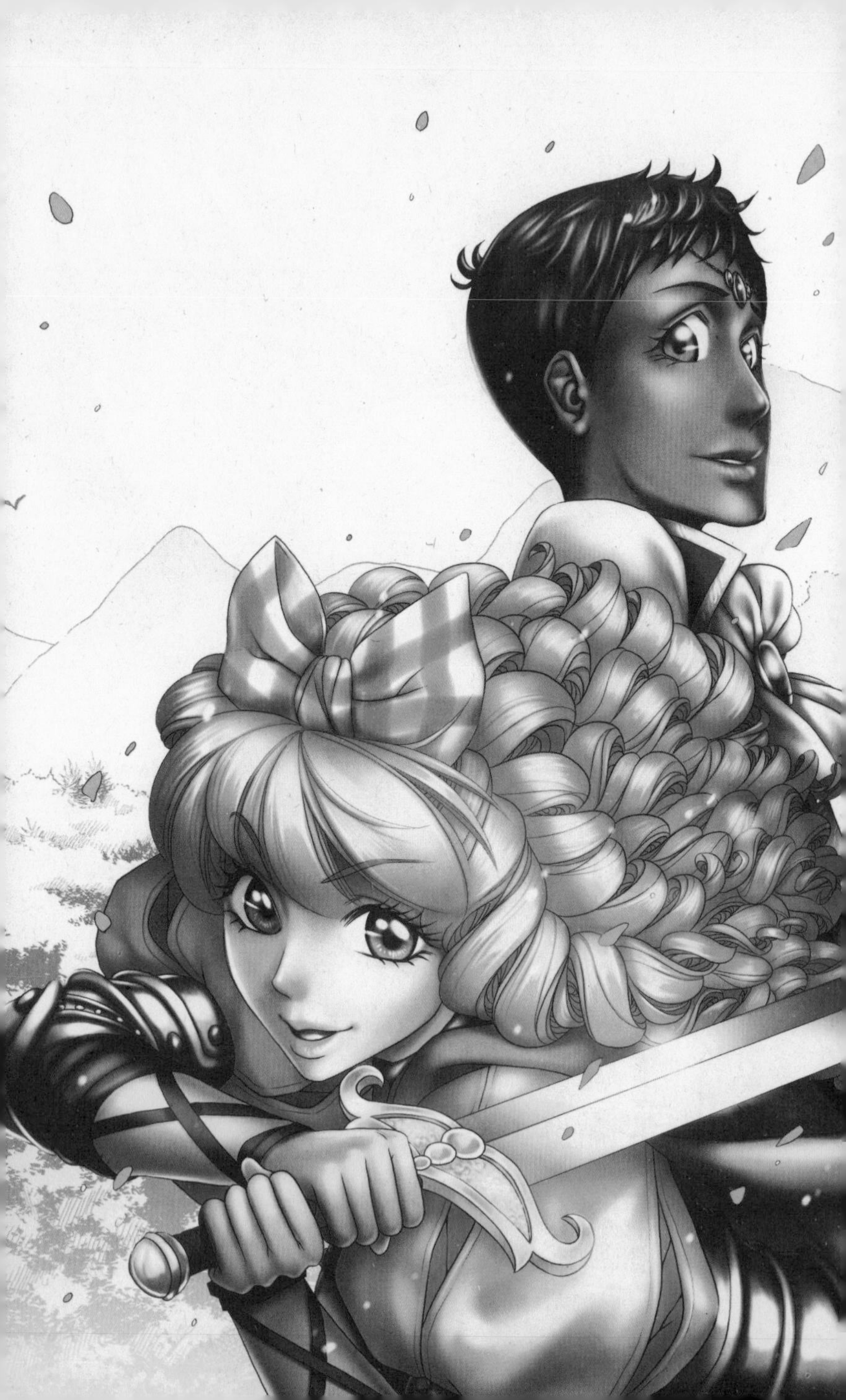

Sword Princess Amaltea

I

Natalia Batista

TOKYOPOP®

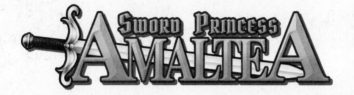

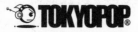

Characters In Book One:

Princess Amaltea

Princess Dorotea

Queen Galatea

King Theodor

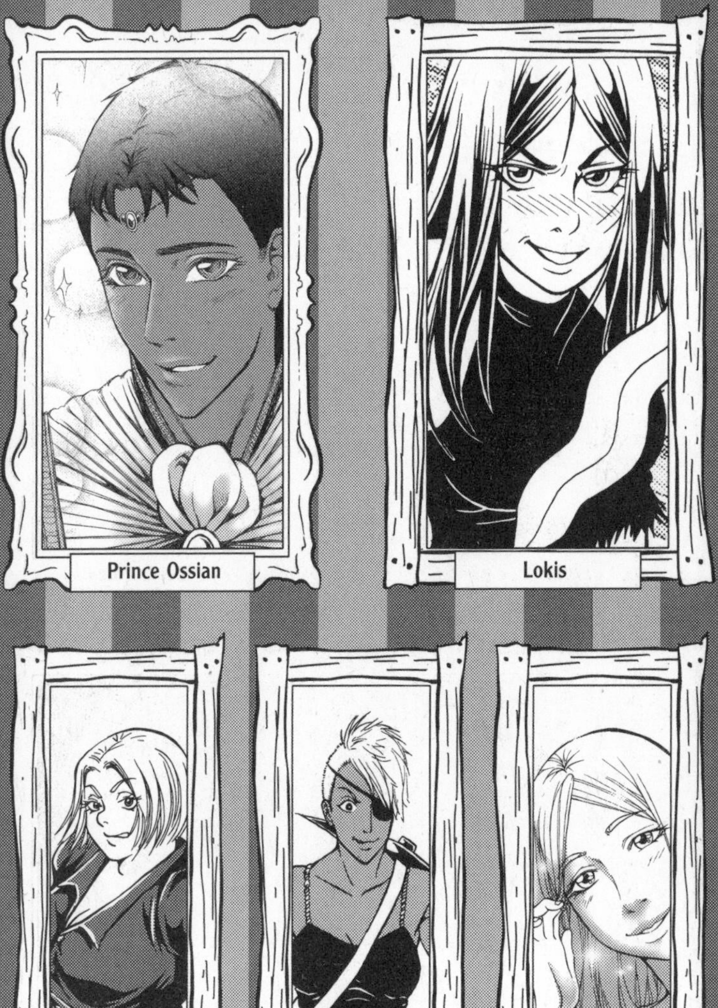
Prince Ossian
Lokis
Sanada
Are
Tibus

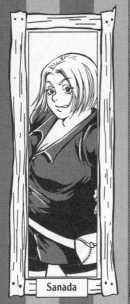

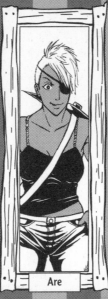

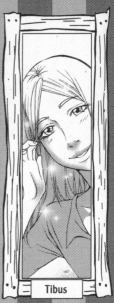

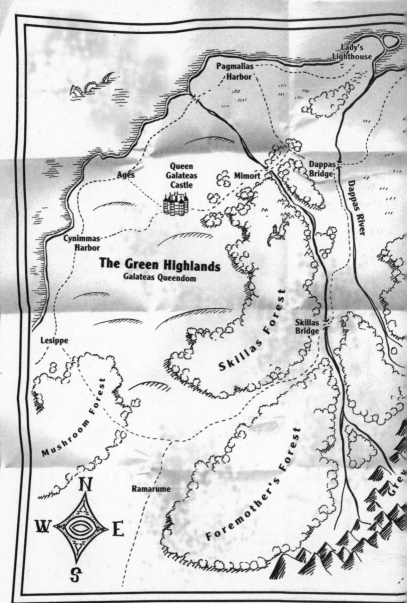

Lady's Lighthouse

Pagmalias Harbor

Agés

Queen Galateas Castle

Mimort

Dappas Bridge

Dappas River

Cynimmas Harbor

The Green Highlands
Galateas Queendom

Skillas Forest

Skillas Bridge

Lesippe

Mushroom Forest

Ramarume

Foremother's Forest

Grev

N
W   E
S

This map is produced

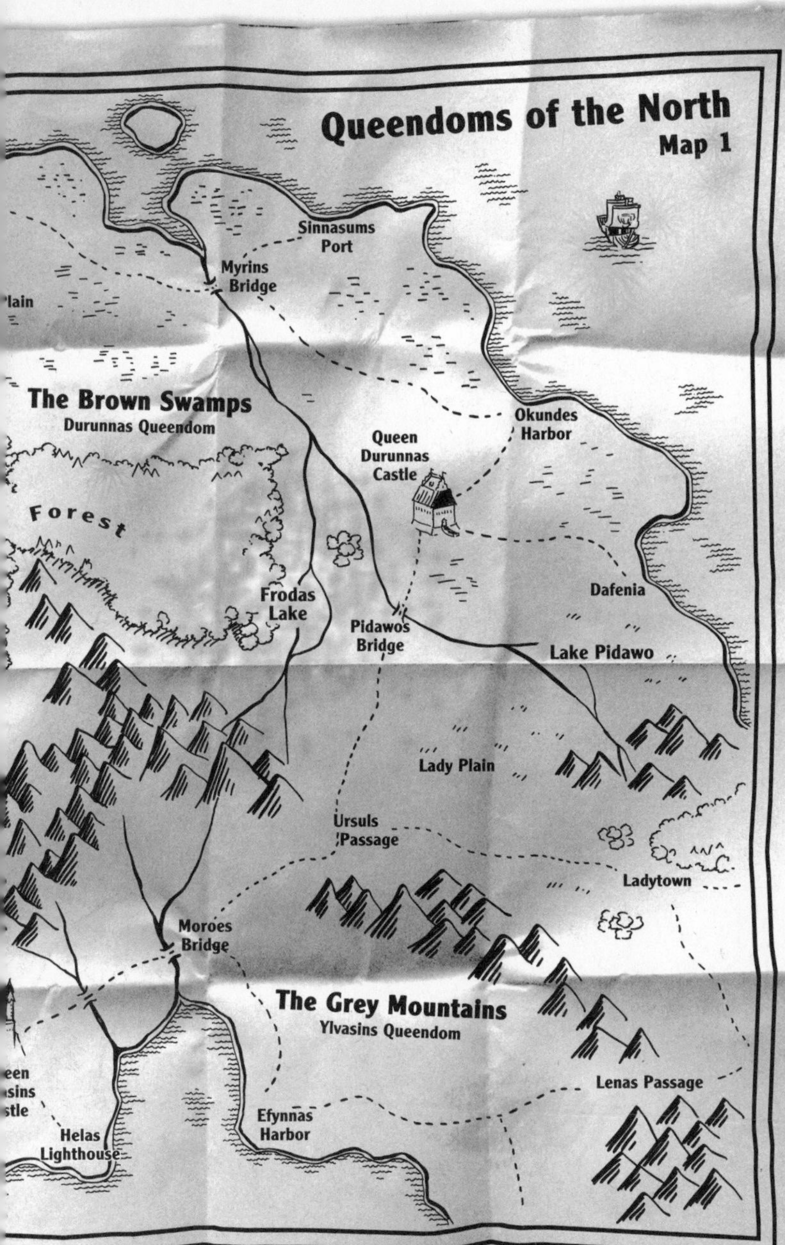
Queendoms of the North
Map 1
Sinnasums Port
Myrins Bridge
lain
The Brown Swamps
Durunnas Queendom
Okundes Harbor
Queen Durunnas Castle
Forest
Frodas Lake
Dafenia
Pidawos Bridge
Lake Pidawo
Lady Plain
Ursuls Passage
Ladytown
Moroes Bridge
The Grey Mountains
Ylvasins Queendom
een
sins
stle
Lenas Passage
Efynnas Harbor
Helas Lighthouse

Maps and Scripts in Ages - we make maps so ladyship can come find us, to buy more maps and scripts.

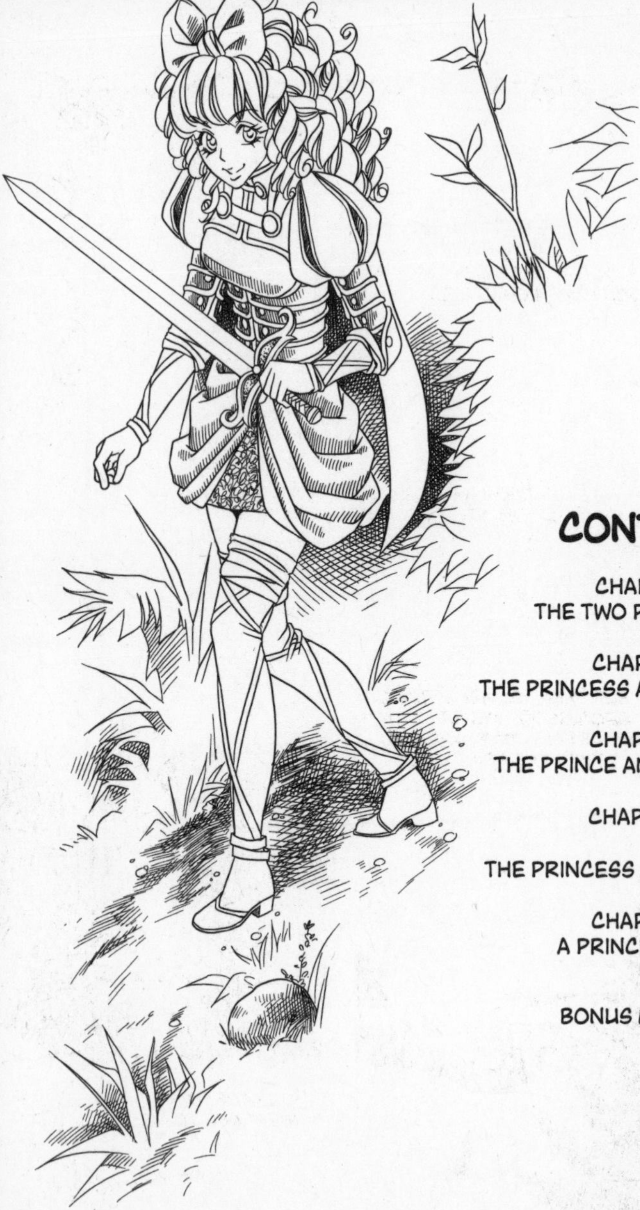

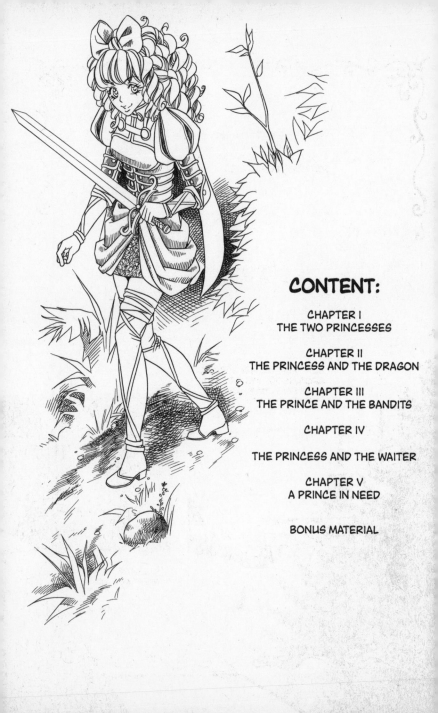

CONTENT:

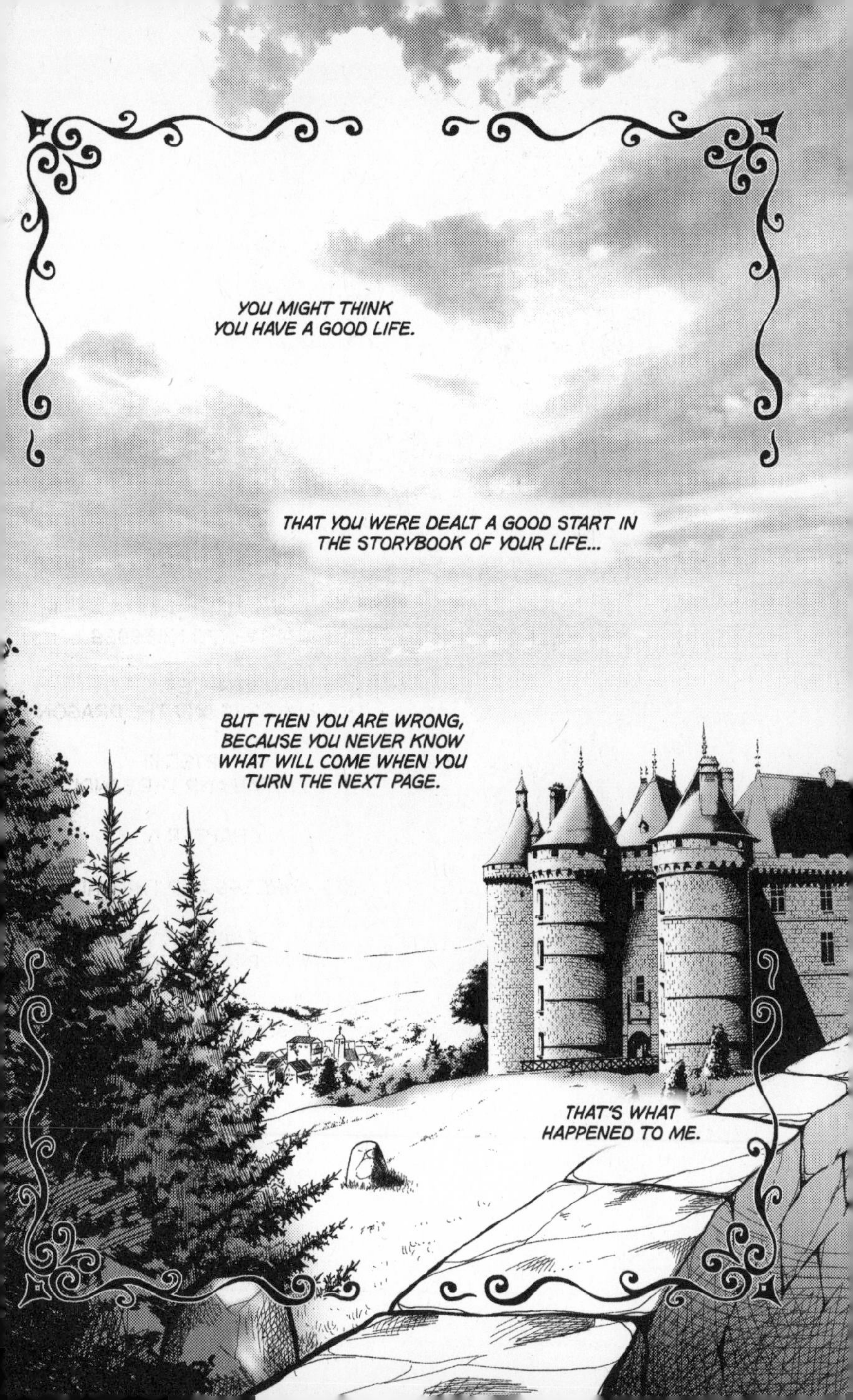
YOU MIGHT THINK YOU HAVE A GOOD LIFE.
THAT YOU WERE DEALT A GOOD START IN THE STORYBOOK OF YOUR LIFE...
BUT THEN YOU ARE WRONG, BECAUSE YOU NEVER KNOW WHAT WILL COME WHEN YOU TURN THE NEXT PAGE.
THAT'S WHAT HAPPENED TO ME.

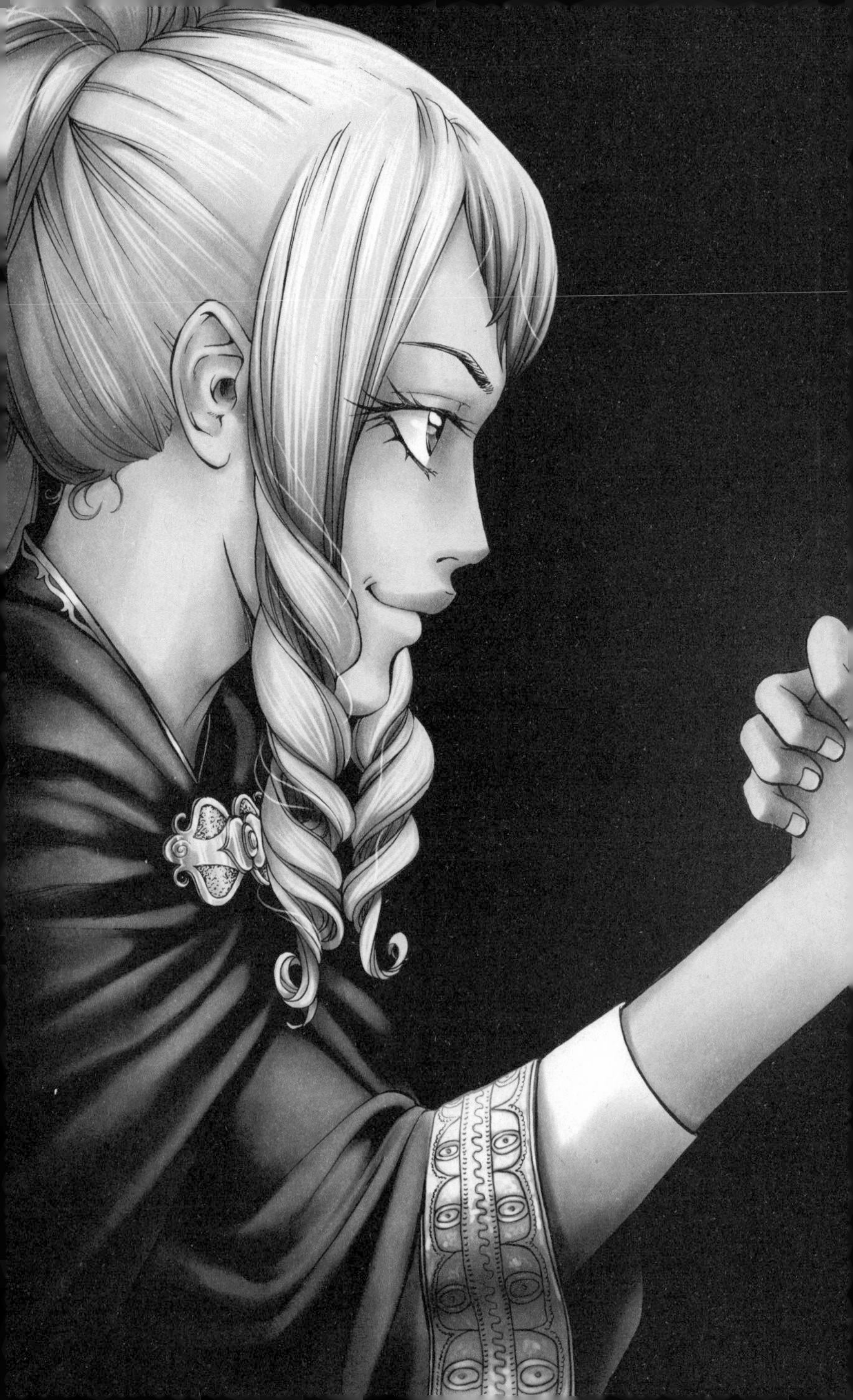

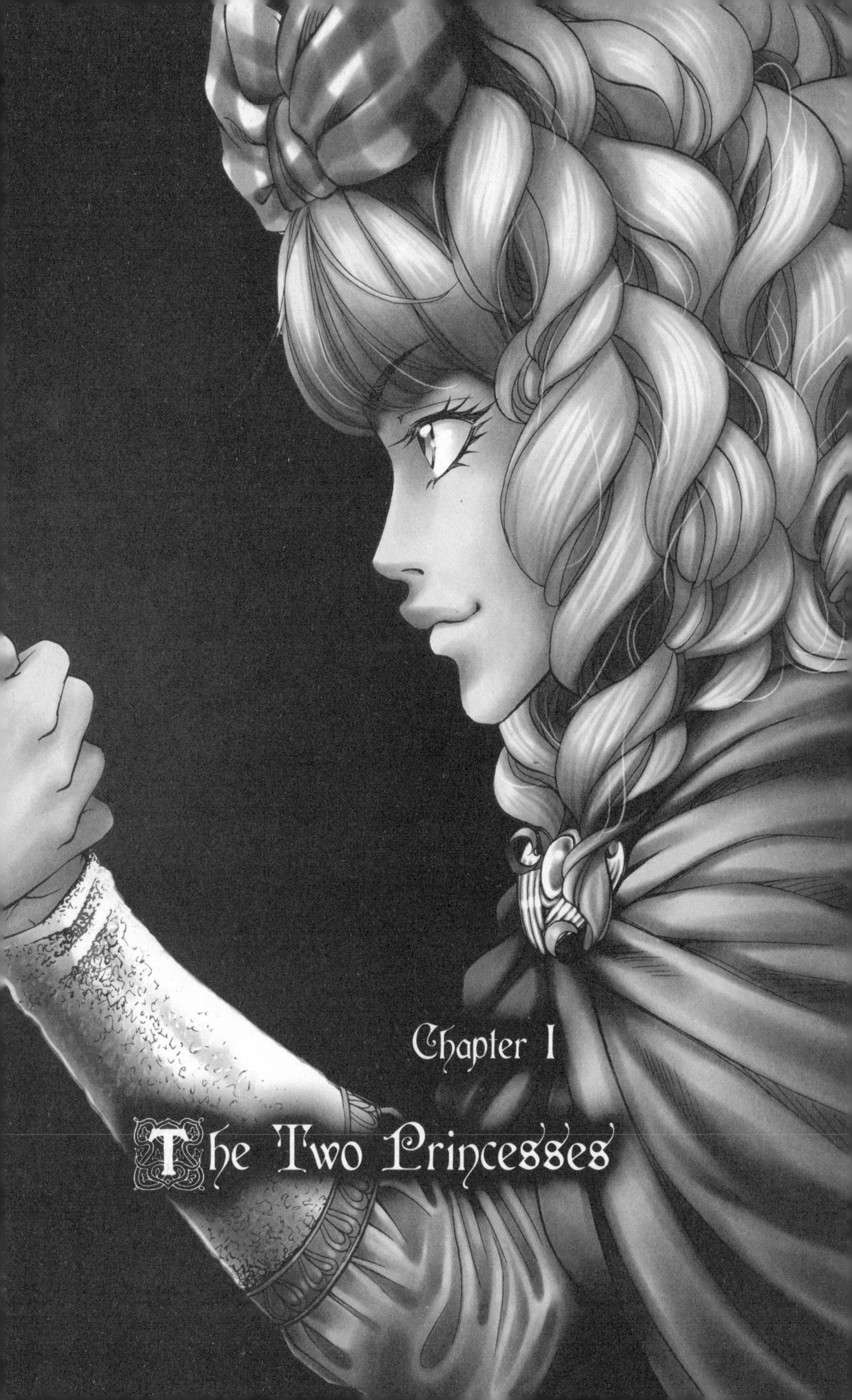

Chapter I

The Two Princesses

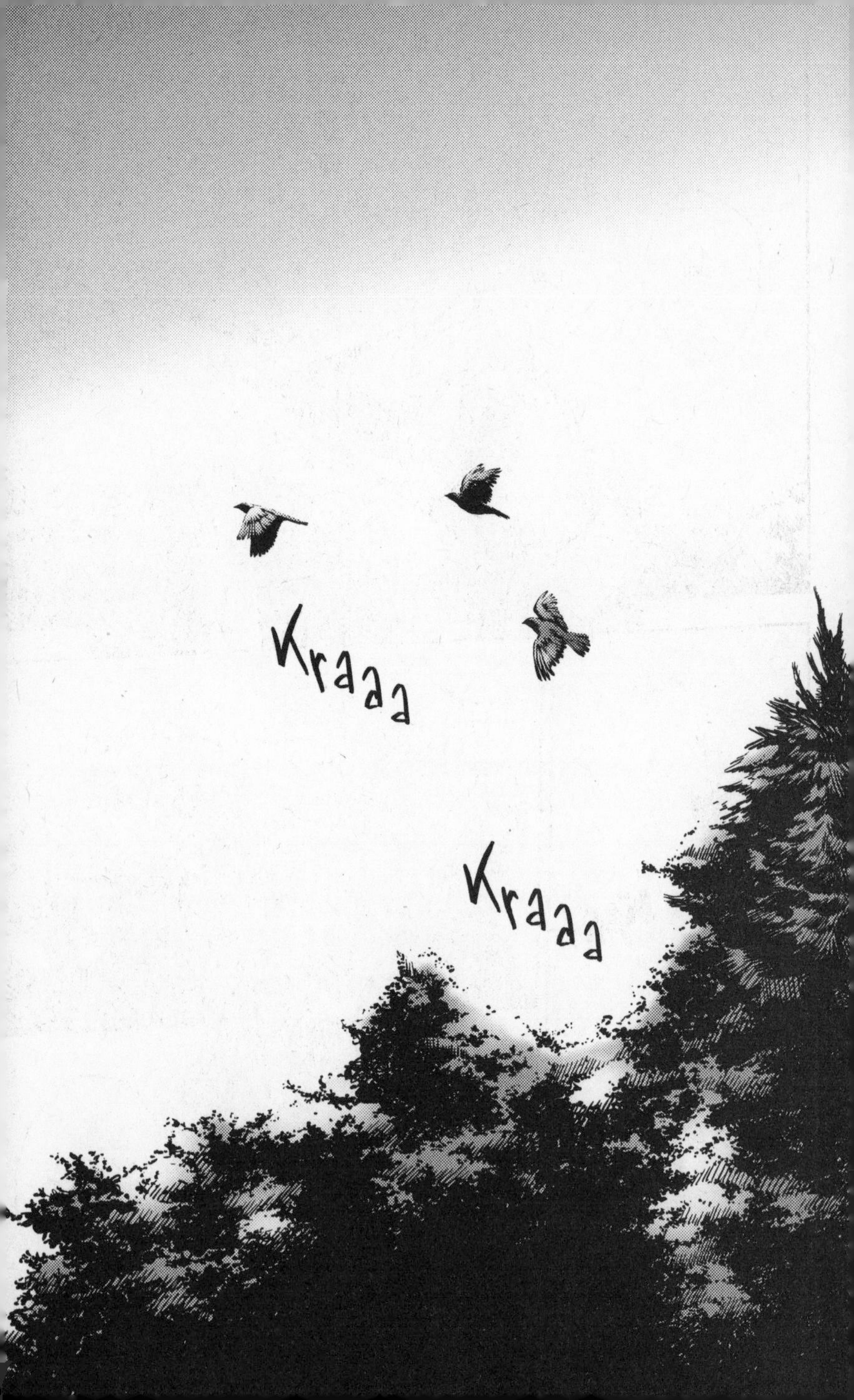
Kraaa
Kraaa

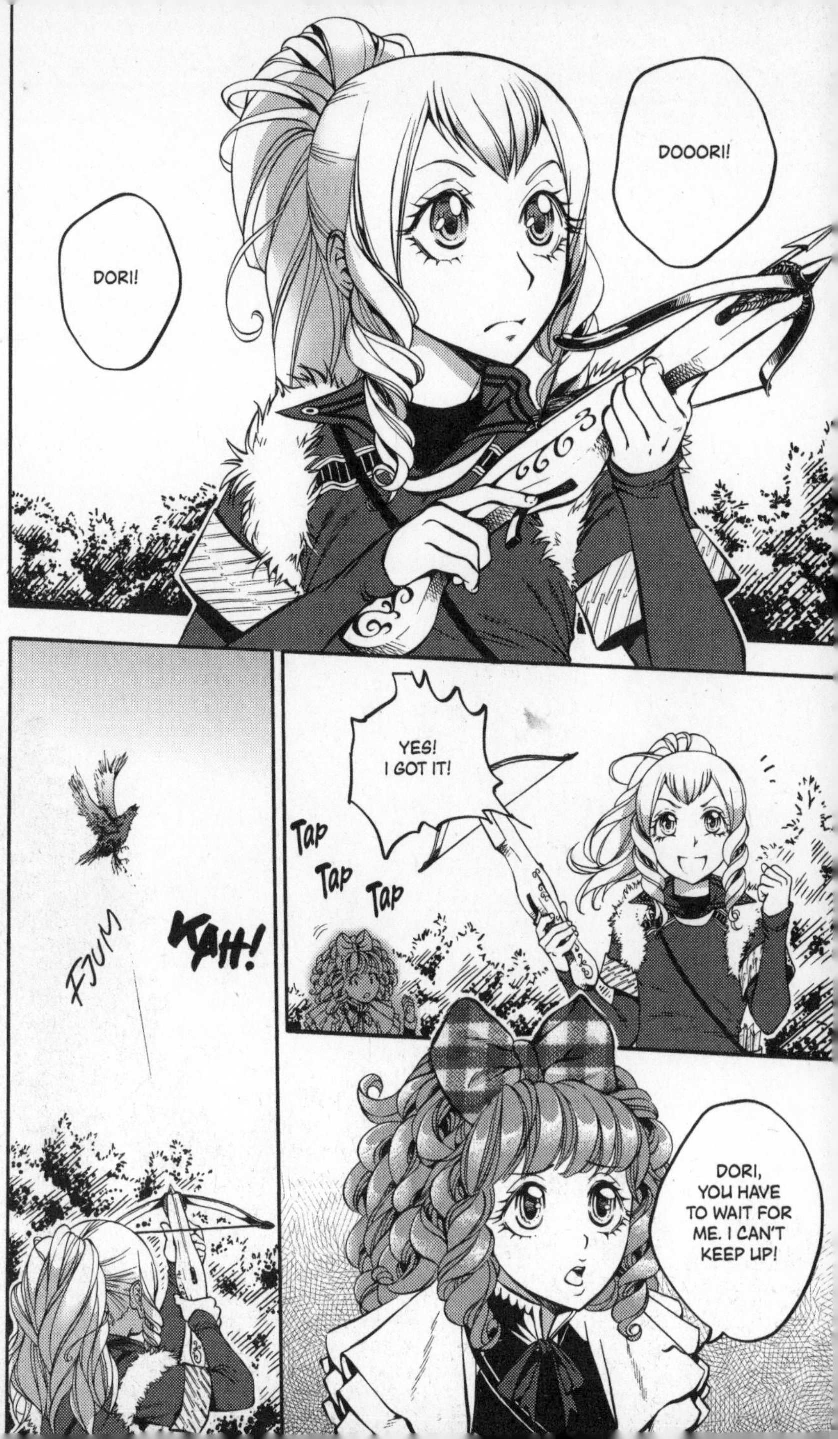
DORI!
DOOORI!
FJUM
KYAH!
YES! I GOT IT!
Tap
Tap
Tap
DORI, YOU HAVE TO WAIT FOR ME. I CAN'T KEEP UP!

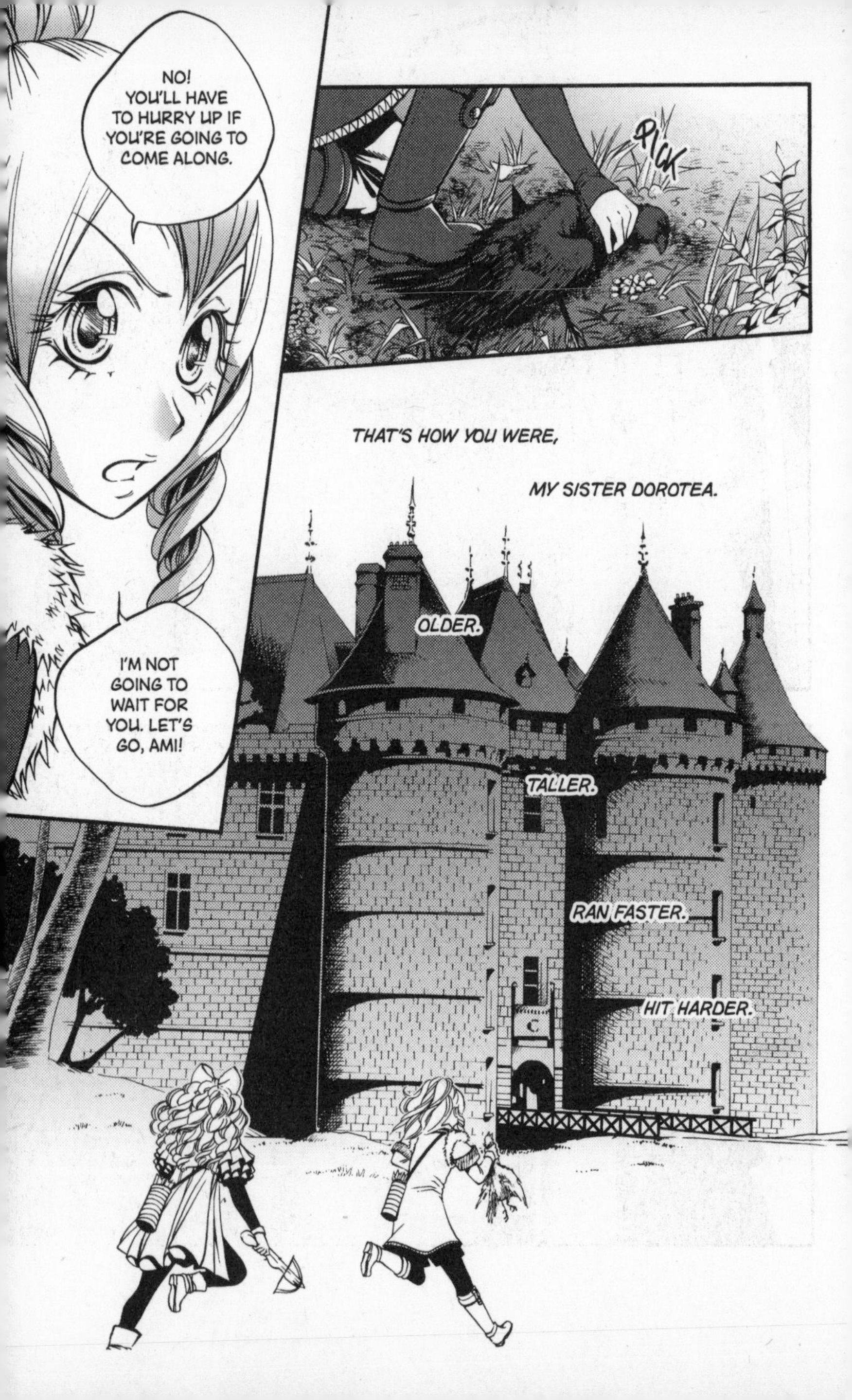
NO! YOU'LL HAVE TO HURRY UP IF YOU'RE GOING TO COME ALONG.
I'M NOT GOING TO WAIT FOR YOU. LET'S GO, AMI!
PICK
THAT'S HOW YOU WERE,
MY SISTER DOROTEA.
OLDER.
TALLER.
RAN FASTER.
HIT HARDER.

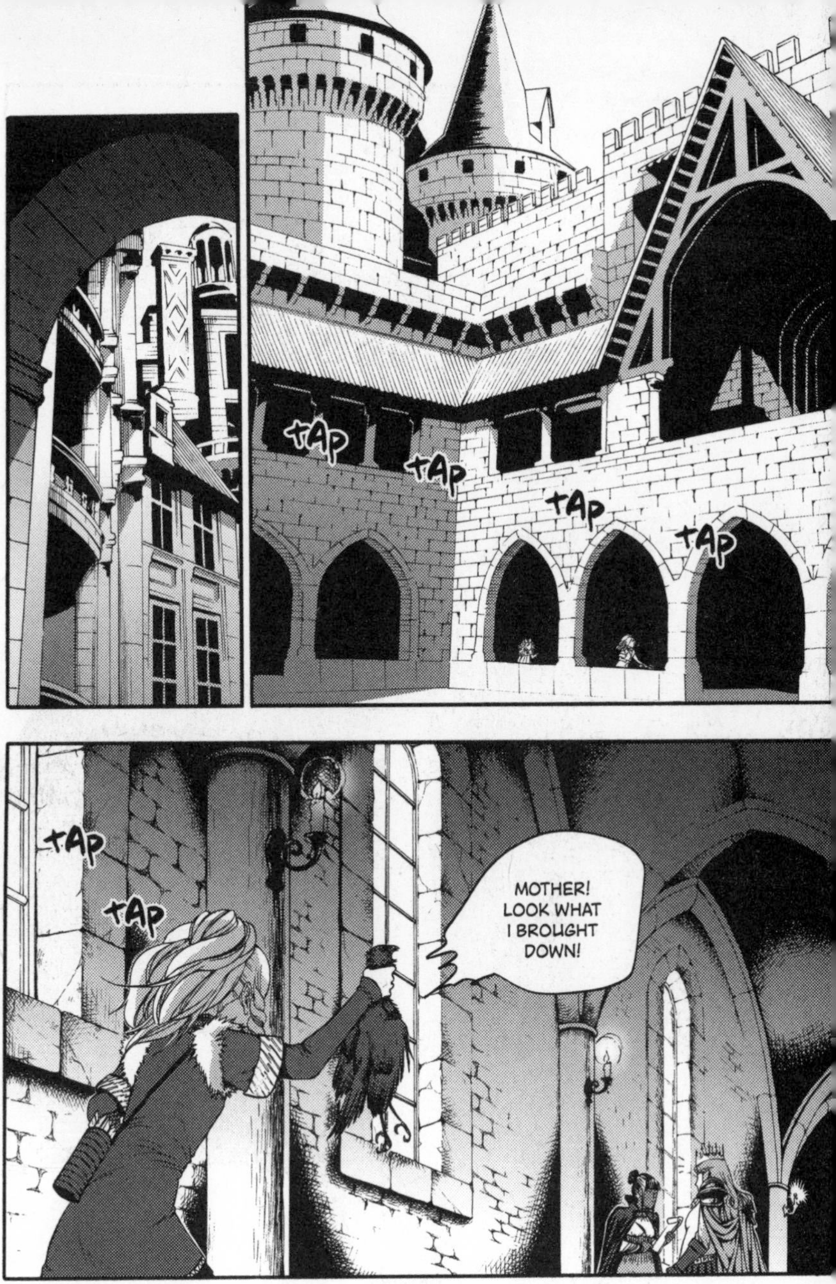
TAP
TAP
TAP
TAP
TAP
TAP
MOTHER! LOOK WHAT I BROUGHT DOWN!

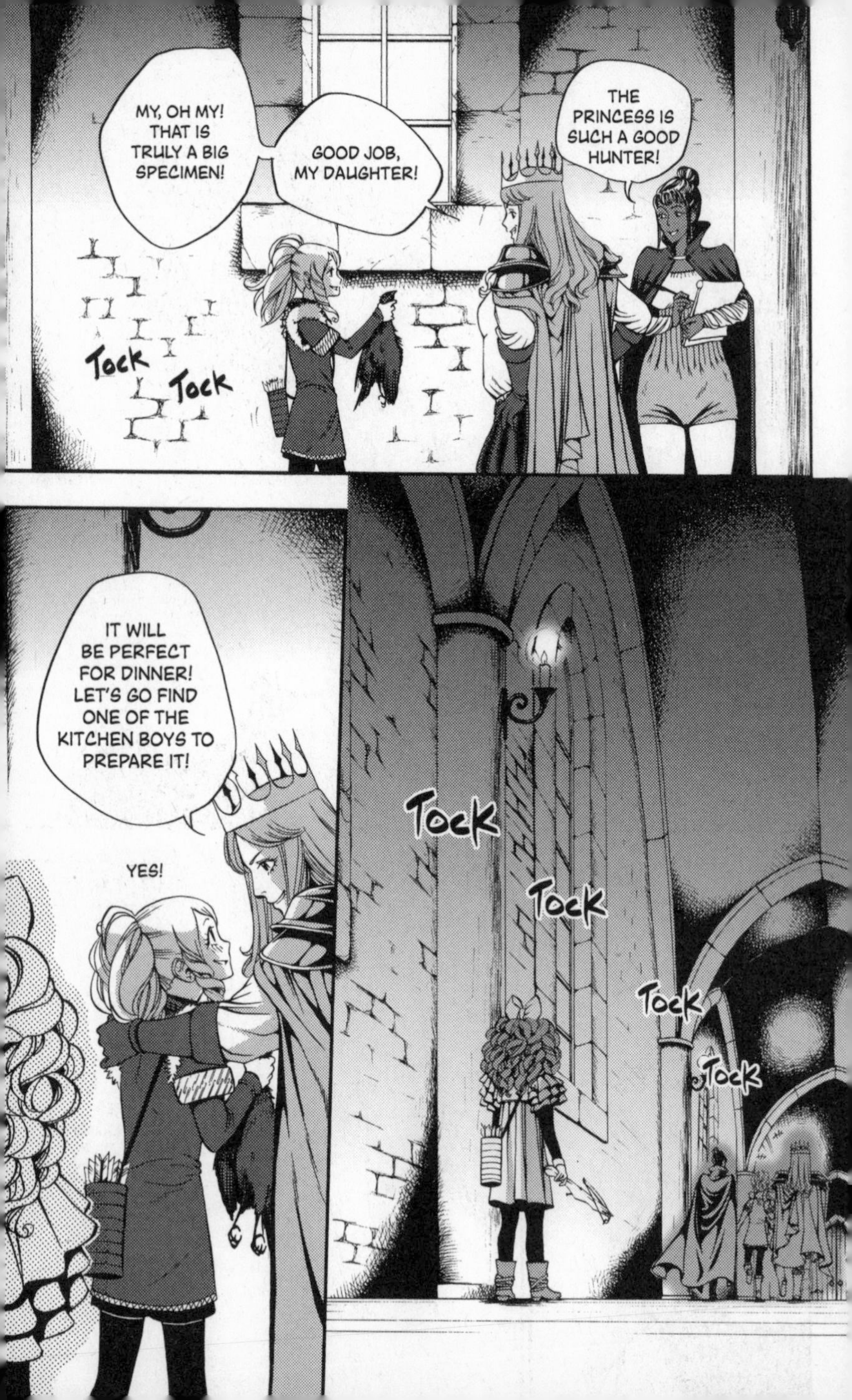

MY, OH MY! THAT IS TRULY A BIG SPECIMEN!
GOOD JOB, MY DAUGHTER!
THE PRINCESS IS SUCH A GOOD HUNTER!
Tock
Tock
IT WILL BE PERFECT FOR DINNER! LET'S GO FIND ONE OF THE KITCHEN BOYS TO PREPARE IT!
YES!
Tock
Tock
Tock
Tock

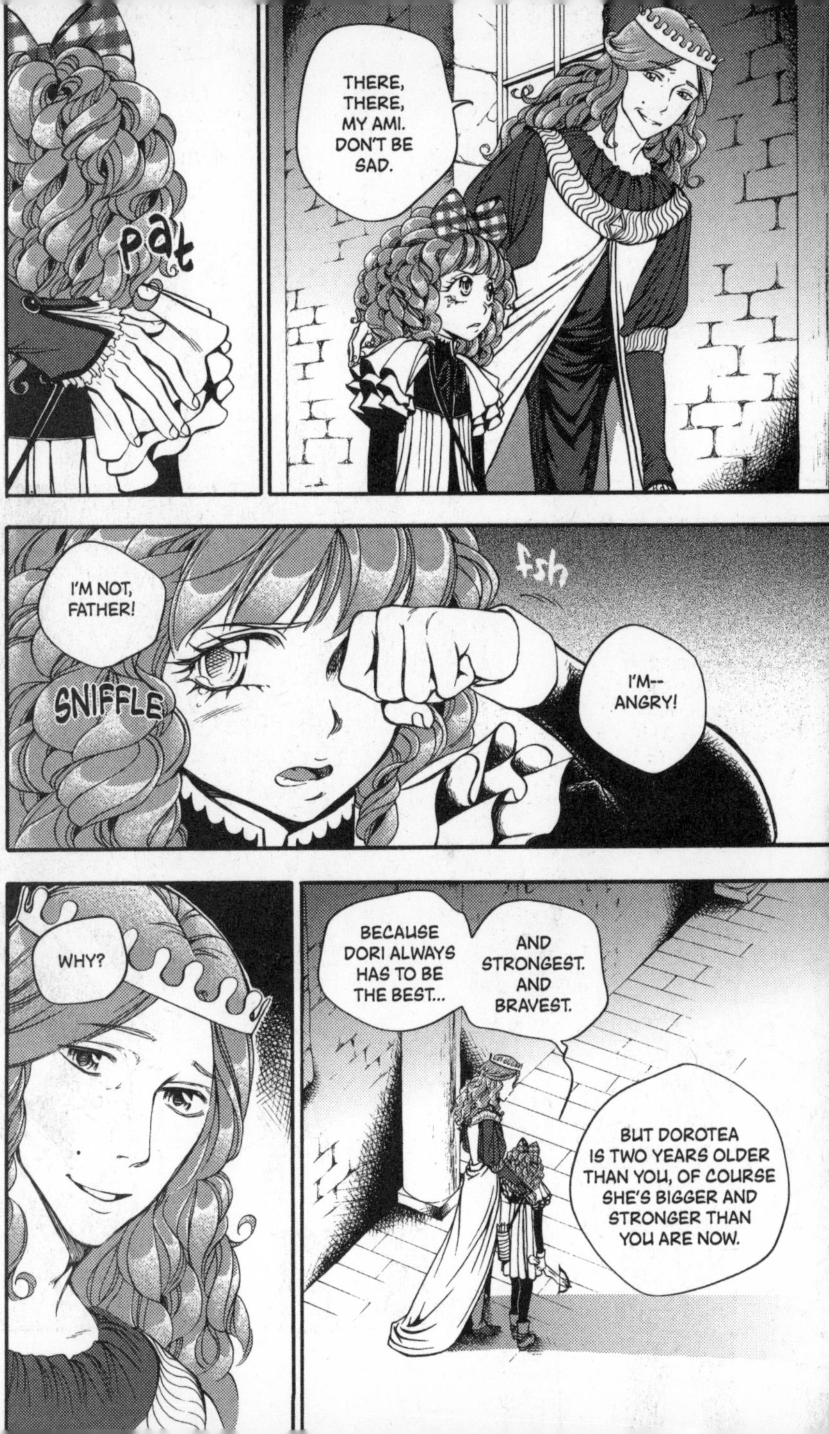
pat
THERE, THERE, MY AMI. DON'T BE SAD.
I'M NOT, FATHER!
SNIFFLE
fsh
I'M-- ANGRY!
WHY?
BECAUSE DORI ALWAYS HAS TO BE THE BEST...
AND STRONGEST. AND BRAVEST.
BUT DOROTEA IS TWO YEARS OLDER THAN YOU, OF COURSE SHE'S BIGGER AND STRONGER THAN YOU ARE NOW.

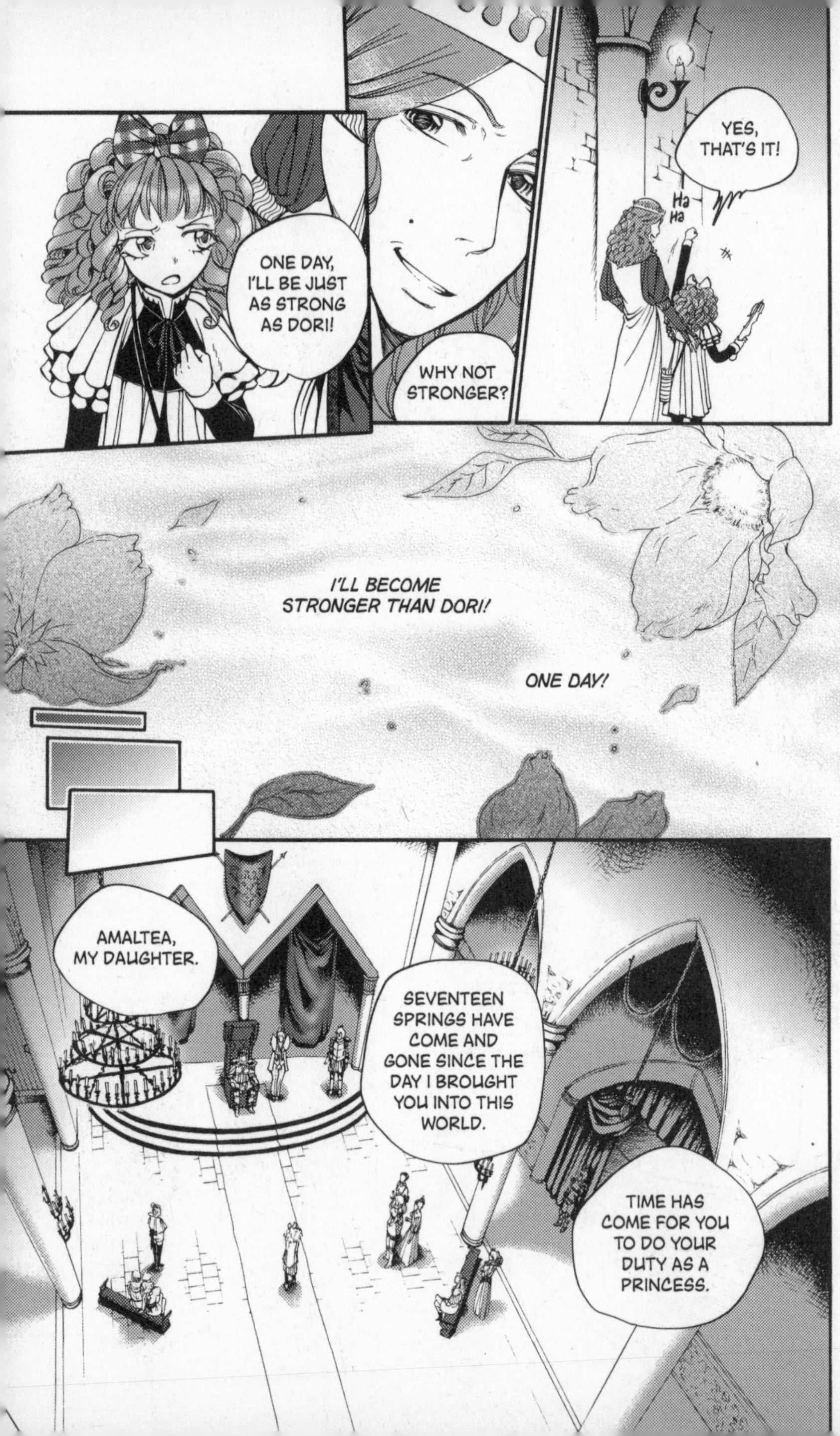
ONE DAY, I'LL BE JUST AS STRONG AS DORI!
WHY NOT STRONGER?
YES, THAT'S IT!
Ha Ha
I'LL BECOME STRONGER THAN DORI!
ONE DAY!
AMALTEA, MY DAUGHTER.
SEVENTEEN SPRINGS HAVE COME AND GONE SINCE THE DAY I BROUGHT YOU INTO THIS WORLD.
TIME HAS COME FOR YOU TO DO YOUR DUTY AS A PRINCESS.

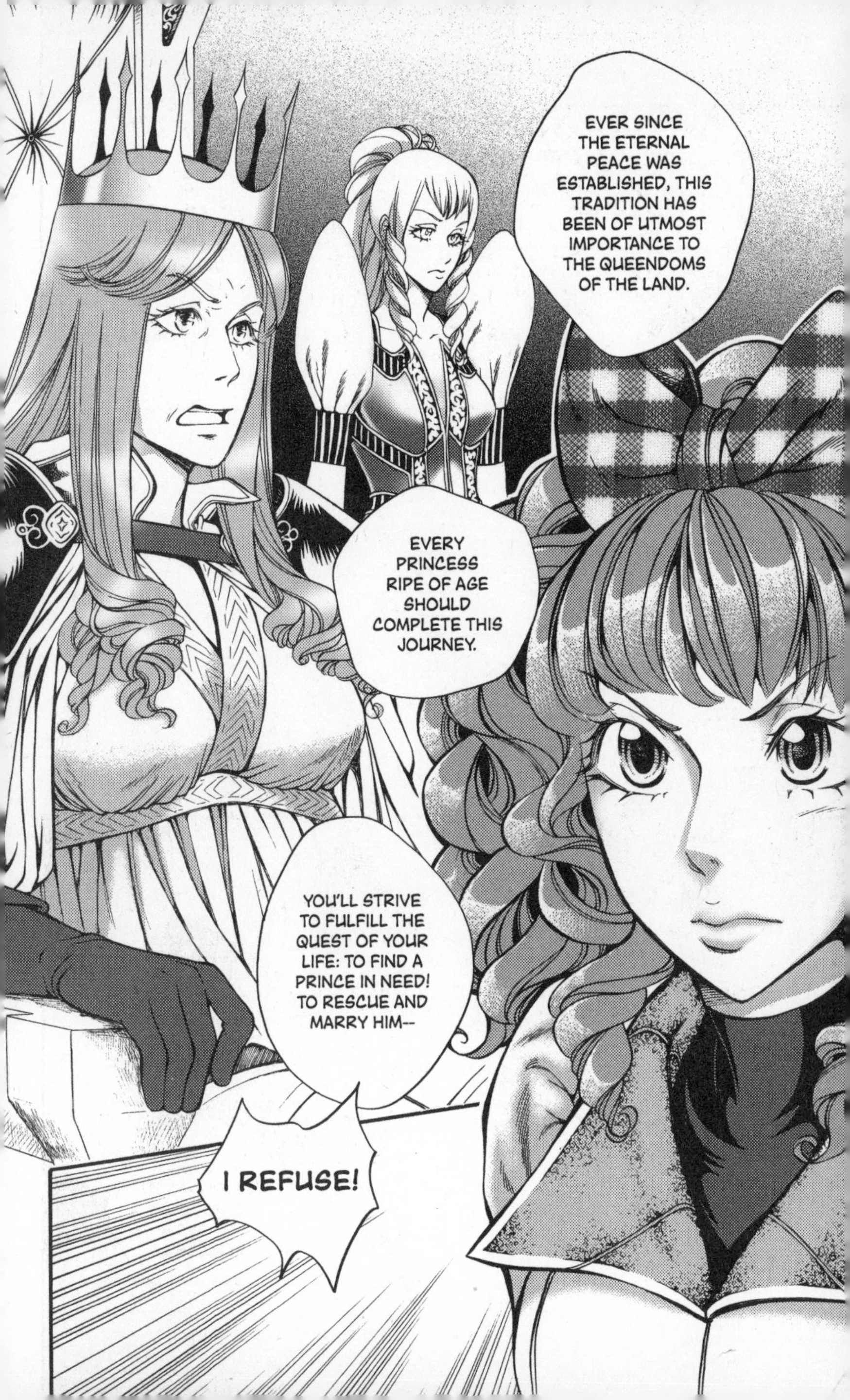
EVER SINCE THE ETERNAL PEACE WAS ESTABLISHED, THIS TRADITION HAS BEEN OF UTMOST IMPORTANCE TO THE QUEENDOMS OF THE LAND.
EVERY PRINCESS RIPE OF AGE SHOULD COMPLETE THIS JOURNEY.
YOU'LL STRIVE TO FULFILL THE QUEST OF YOUR LIFE: TO FIND A PRINCE IN NEED! TO RESCUE AND MARRY HIM--
I REFUSE!

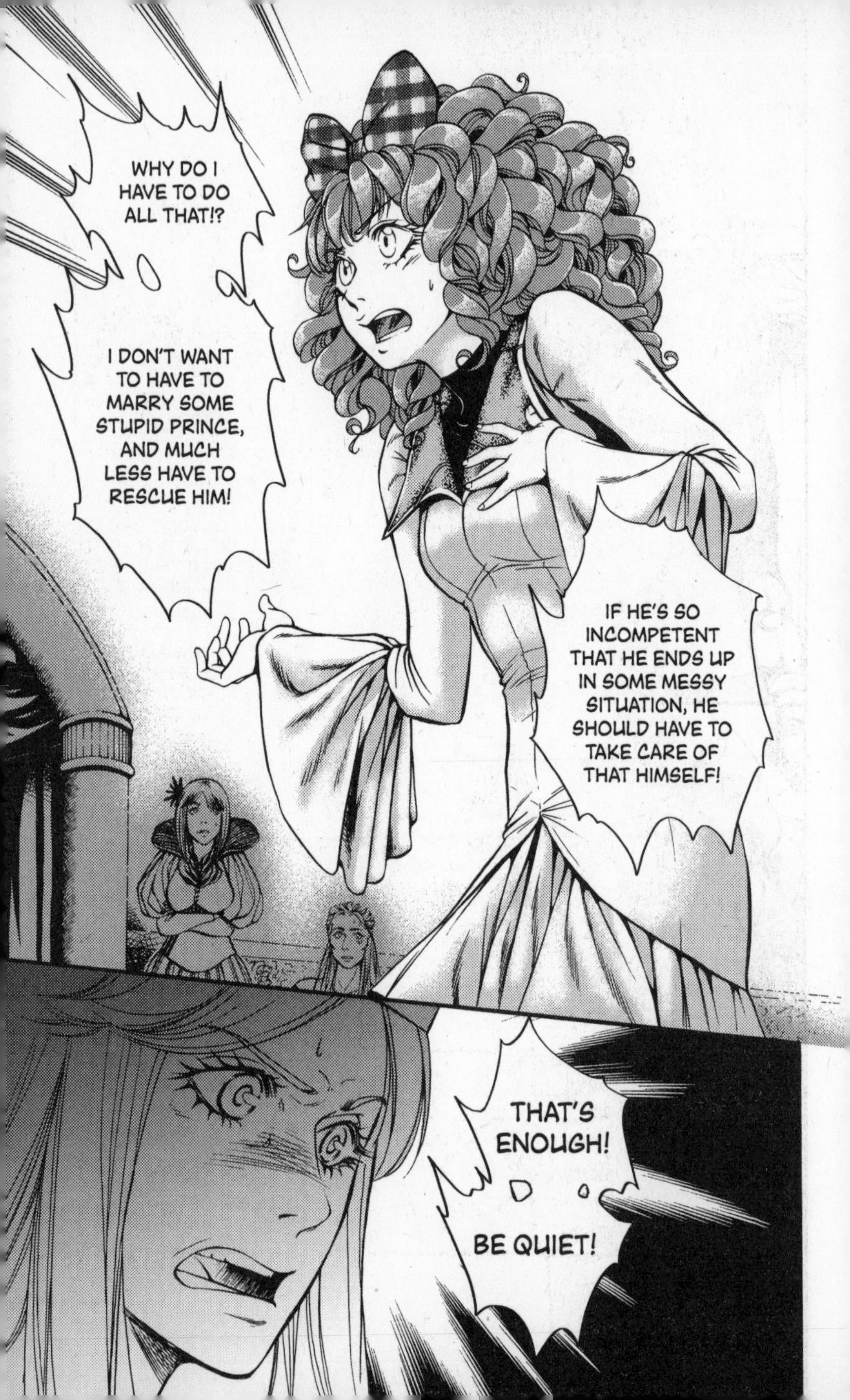
WHY DO I HAVE TO DO ALL THAT!?
I DON'T WANT TO HAVE TO MARRY SOME STUPID PRINCE, AND MUCH LESS HAVE TO RESCUE HIM!
IF HE'S SO INCOMPETENT THAT HE ENDS UP IN SOME MESSY SITUATION, HE SHOULD HAVE TO TAKE CARE OF THAT HIMSELF!
THAT'S ENOUGH!
BE QUIET!

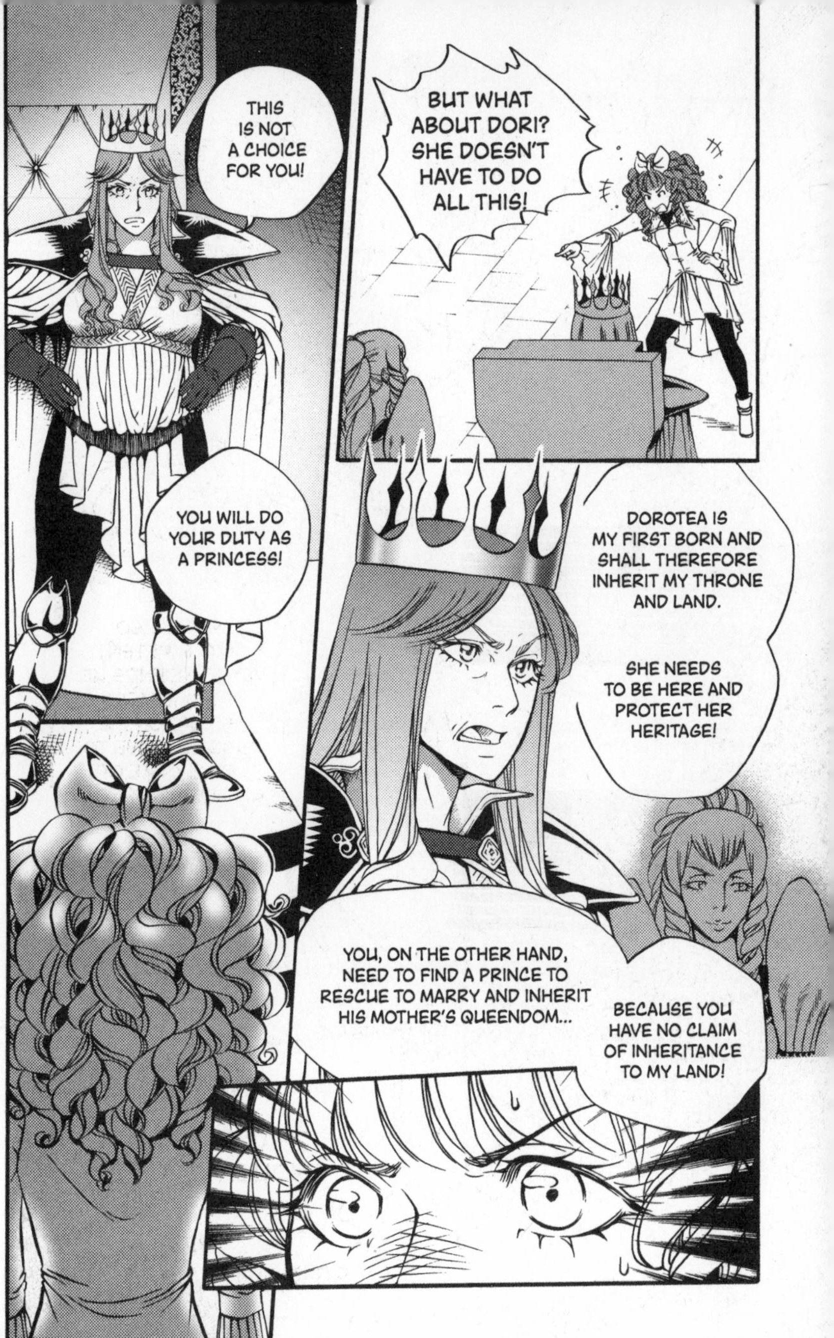
THIS IS NOT A CHOICE FOR YOU!
BUT WHAT ABOUT DORI? SHE DOESN'T HAVE TO DO ALL THIS!
YOU WILL DO YOUR DUTY AS A PRINCESS!
DOROTEA IS MY FIRST BORN AND SHALL THEREFORE INHERIT MY THRONE AND LAND.
SHE NEEDS TO BE HERE AND PROTECT HER HERITAGE!
YOU, ON THE OTHER HAND, NEED TO FIND A PRINCE TO RESCUE TO MARRY AND INHERIT HIS MOTHER'S QUEENDOM...
BECAUSE YOU HAVE NO CLAIM OF INHERITANCE TO MY LAND!

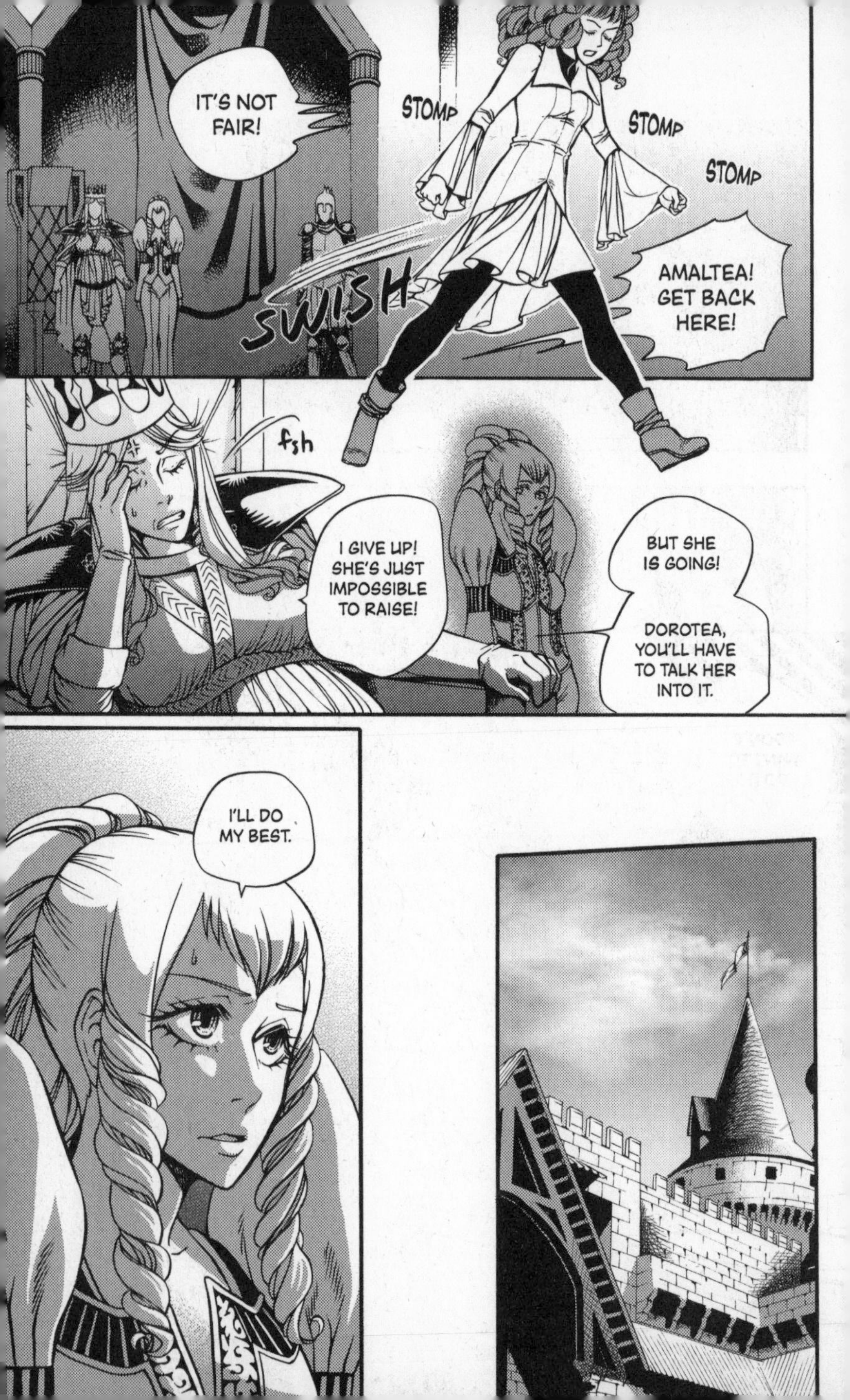
IT'S NOT FAIR!
STOMP
STOMP
STOMP
SWISH
AMALTEA! GET BACK HERE!
fsh
I GIVE UP! SHE'S JUST IMPOSSIBLE TO RAISE!
BUT SHE IS GOING!
DOROTEA, YOU'LL HAVE TO TALK HER INTO IT.
I'LL DO MY BEST.

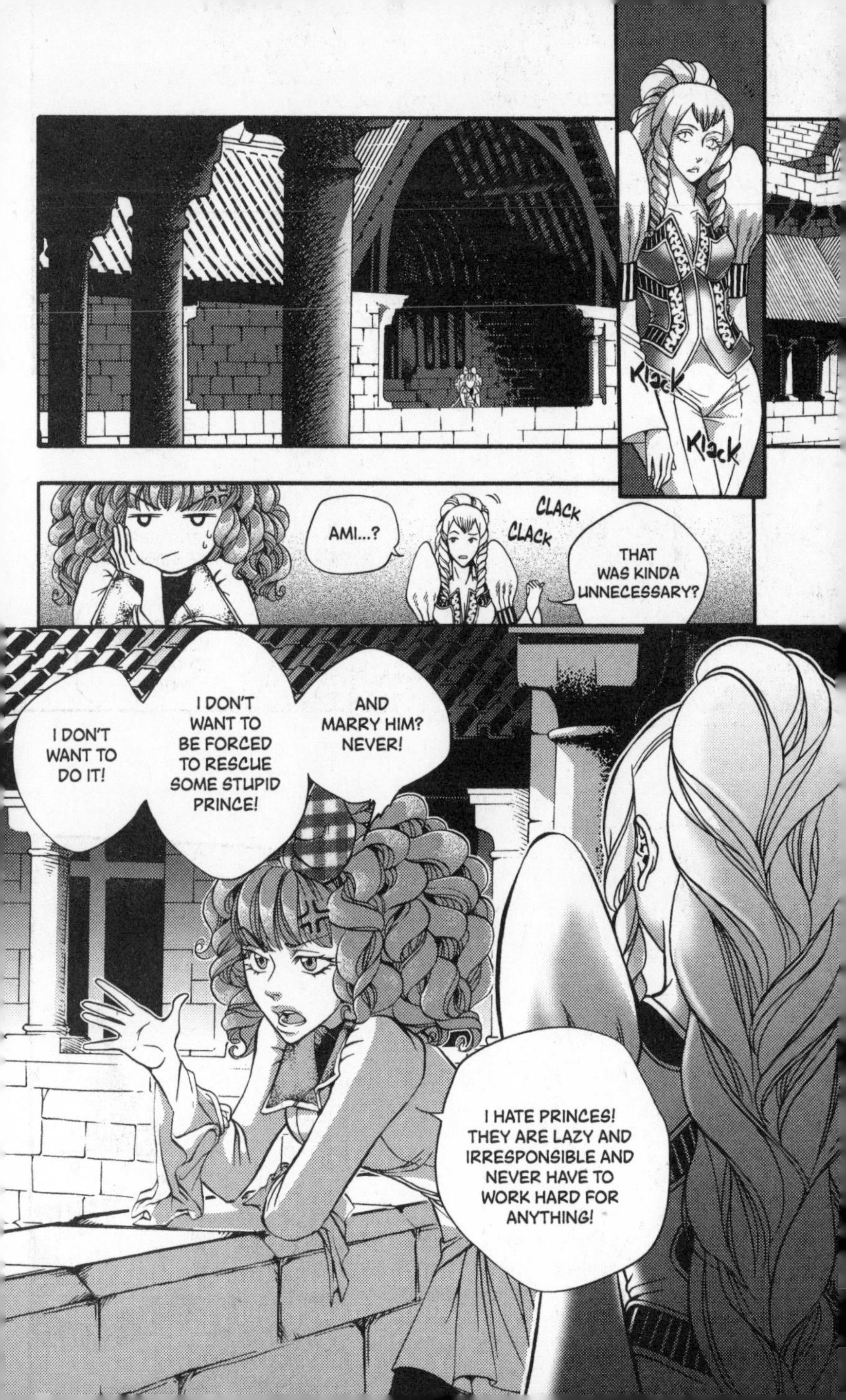
KLACK
KLACK
AMI...?
CLACK
CLACK
THAT WAS KINDA UNNECESSARY?
I DON'T WANT TO DO IT!
I DON'T WANT TO BE FORCED TO RESCUE SOME STUPID PRINCE!
AND MARRY HIM? NEVER!
I HATE PRINCES! THEY ARE LAZY AND IRRESPONSIBLE AND NEVER HAVE TO WORK HARD FOR ANYTHING!

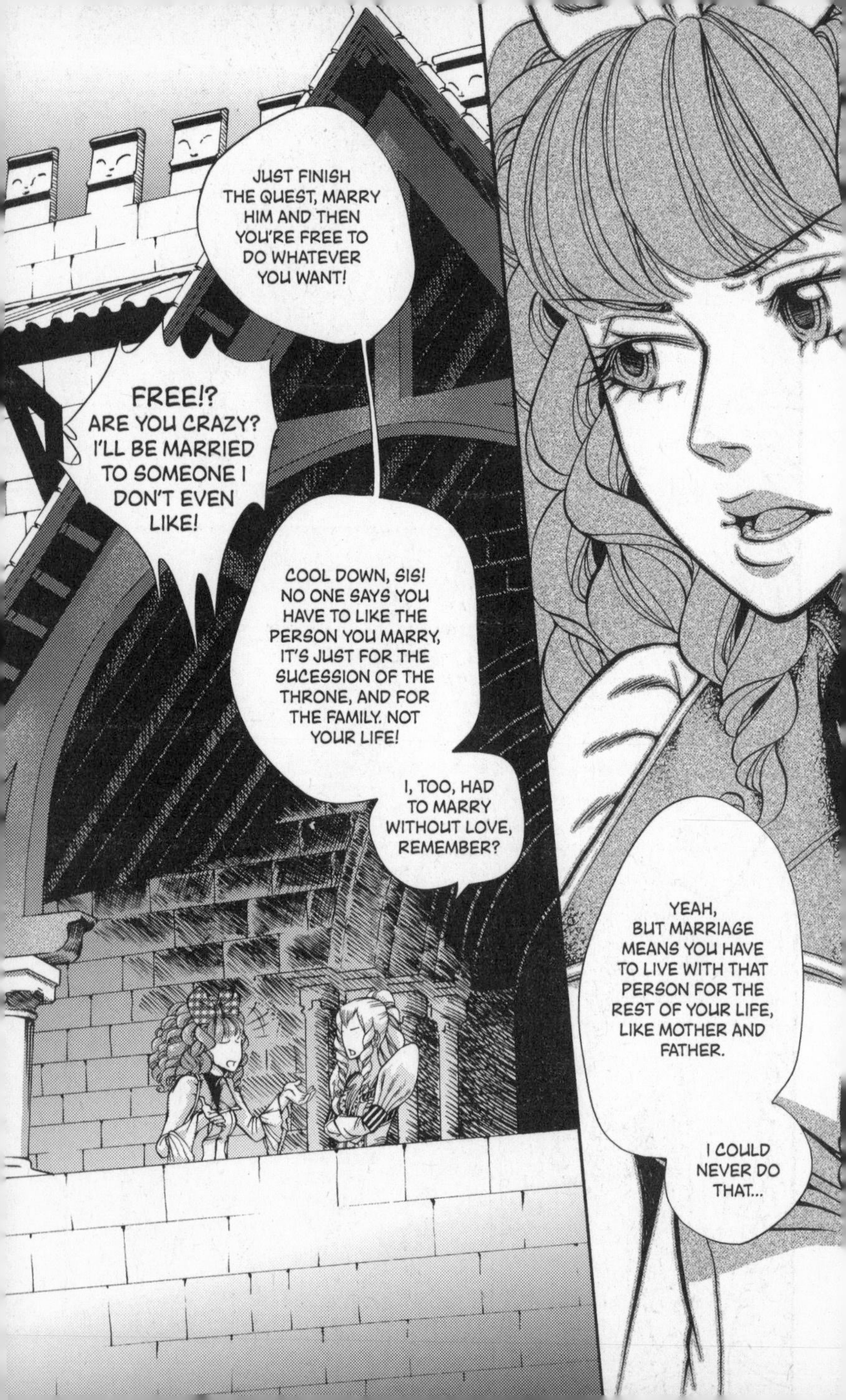
JUST FINISH THE QUEST, MARRY HIM AND THEN YOU'RE FREE TO DO WHATEVER YOU WANT!
FREE!? ARE YOU CRAZY? I'LL BE MARRIED TO SOMEONE I DON'T EVEN LIKE!
COOL DOWN, SIS! NO ONE SAYS YOU HAVE TO LIKE THE PERSON YOU MARRY, IT'S JUST FOR THE SUCESSION OF THE THRONE, AND FOR THE FAMILY. NOT YOUR LIFE!
I, TOO, HAD TO MARRY WITHOUT LOVE, REMEMBER?
YEAH, BUT MARRIAGE MEANS YOU HAVE TO LIVE WITH THAT PERSON FOR THE REST OF YOUR LIFE, LIKE MOTHER AND FATHER.
I COULD NEVER DO THAT...

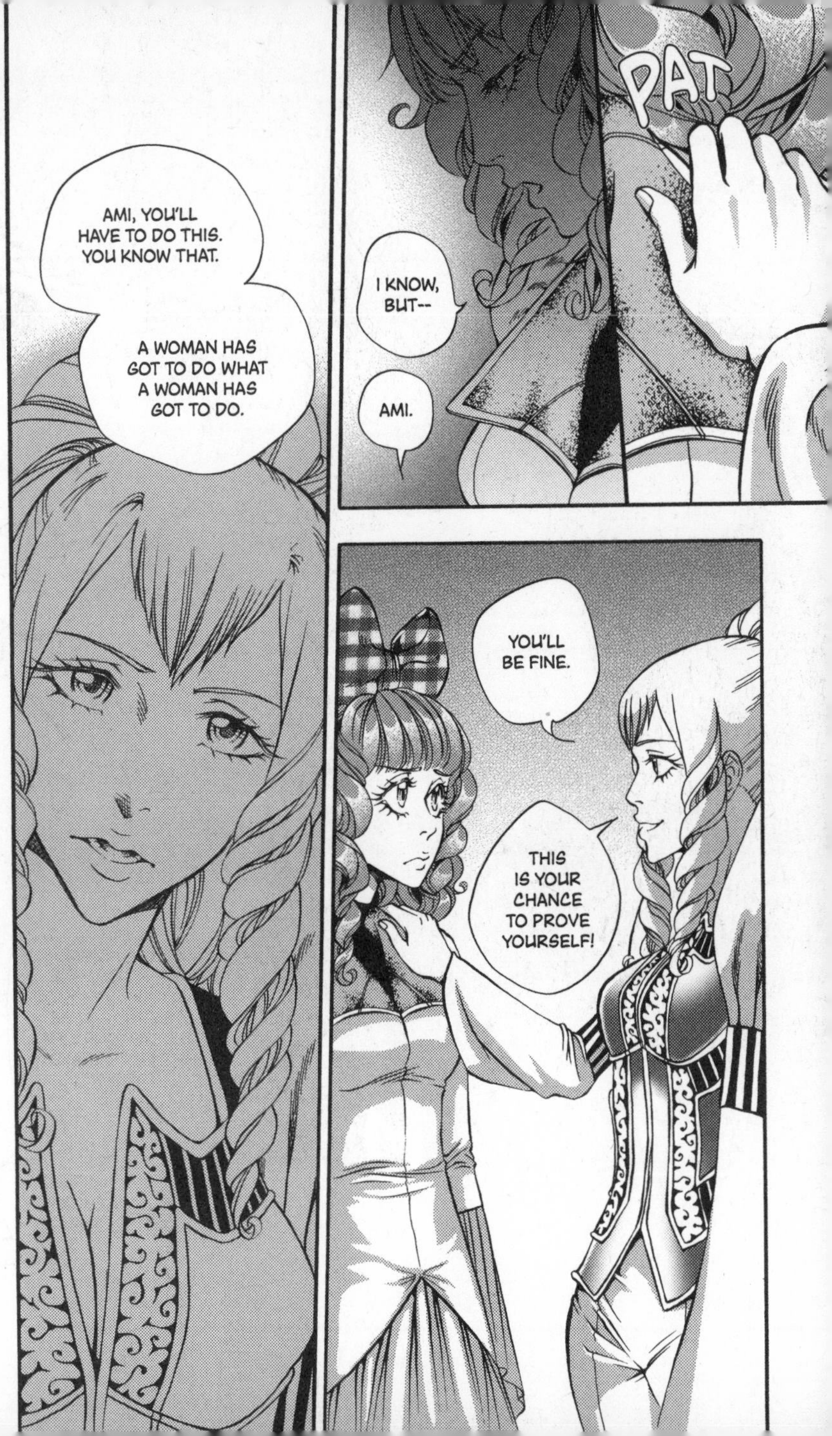
AMI, YOU'LL HAVE TO DO THIS. YOU KNOW THAT.
A WOMAN HAS GOT TO DO WHAT A WOMAN HAS GOT TO DO.
I KNOW, BUT--
AMI.
PAT
YOU'LL BE FINE.
THIS IS YOUR CHANCE TO PROVE YOURSELF!

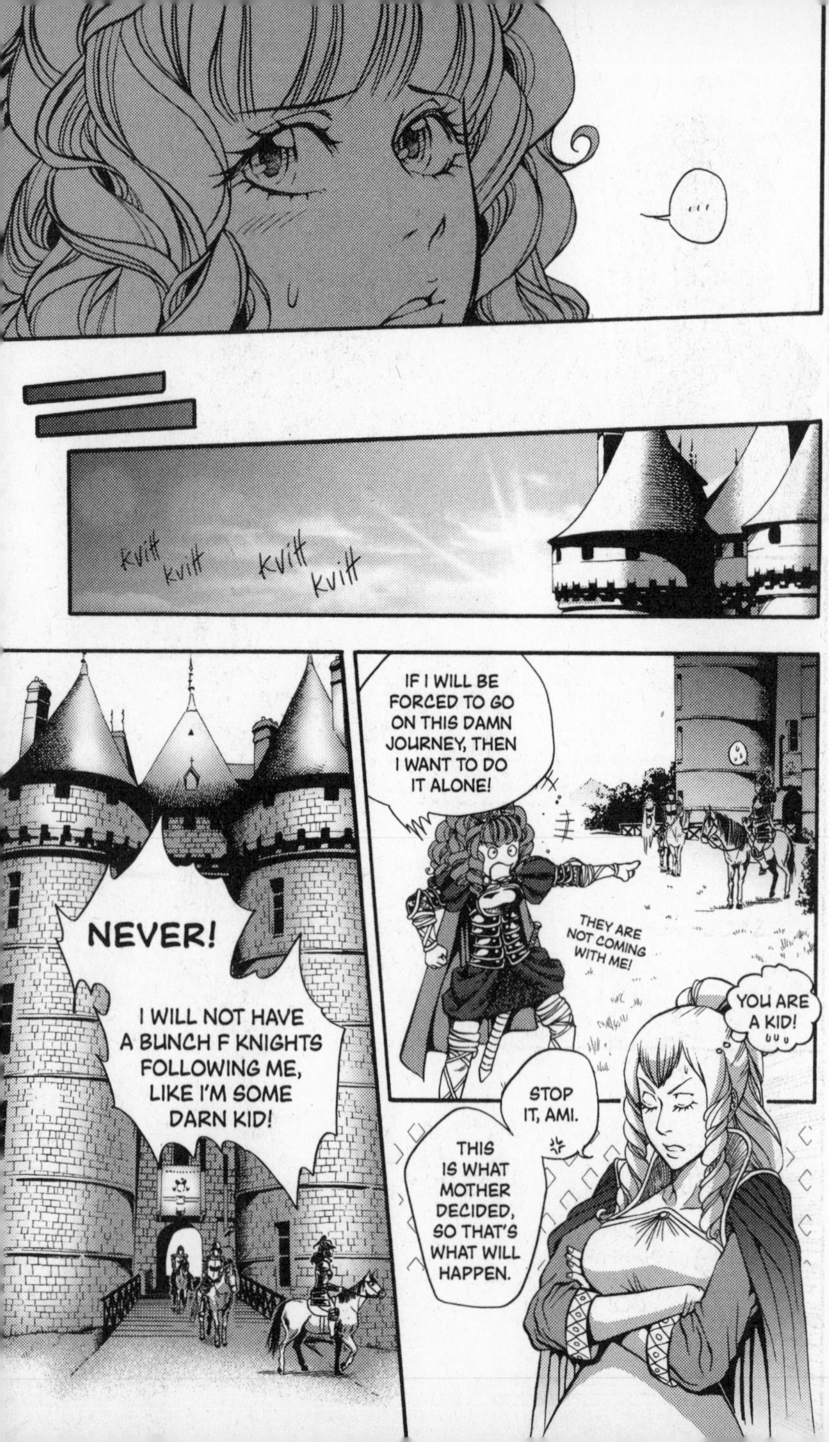
...
kvitt kvitt kvitt kvitt
NEVER!
I WILL NOT HAVE A BUNCH F KNIGHTS FOLLOWING ME, LIKE I'M SOME DARN KID!
IF I WILL BE FORCED TO GO ON THIS DAMN JOURNEY, THEN I WANT TO DO IT ALONE!
THEY ARE NOT COMING WITH ME!
YOU ARE A KID!
STOP IT, AMI.
THIS IS WHAT MOTHER DECIDED, SO THAT'S WHAT WILL HAPPEN.

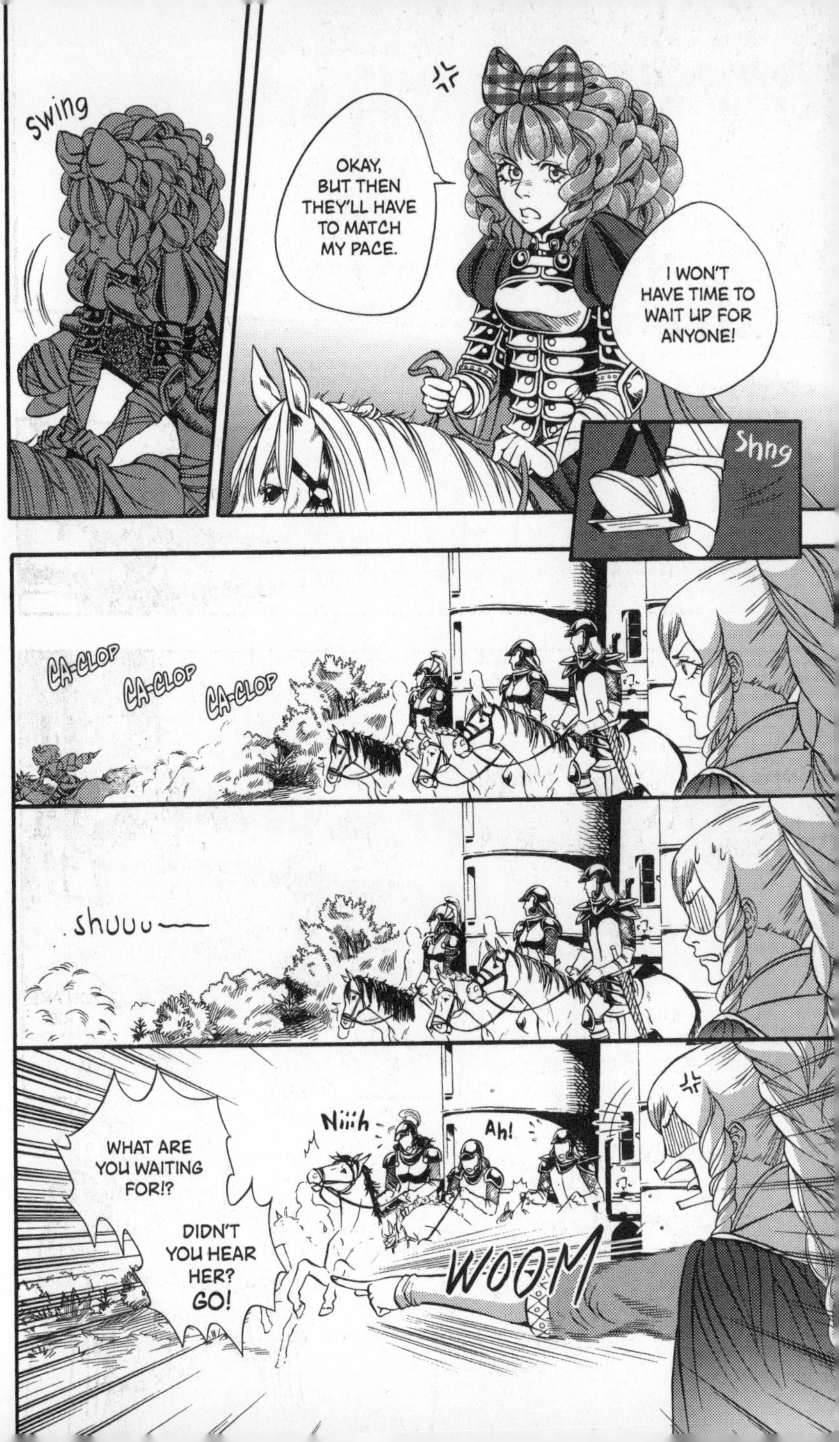
Swing
OKAY, BUT THEN THEY'LL HAVE TO MATCH MY PACE.
I WON'T HAVE TIME TO WAIT UP FOR ANYONE!
Shng
CA-CLOP
CA-CLOP
CA-CLOP
shuuu—
WHAT ARE YOU WAITING FOR!?
DIDN'T YOU HEAR HER? GO!
Niiih
Ah!
WOOM

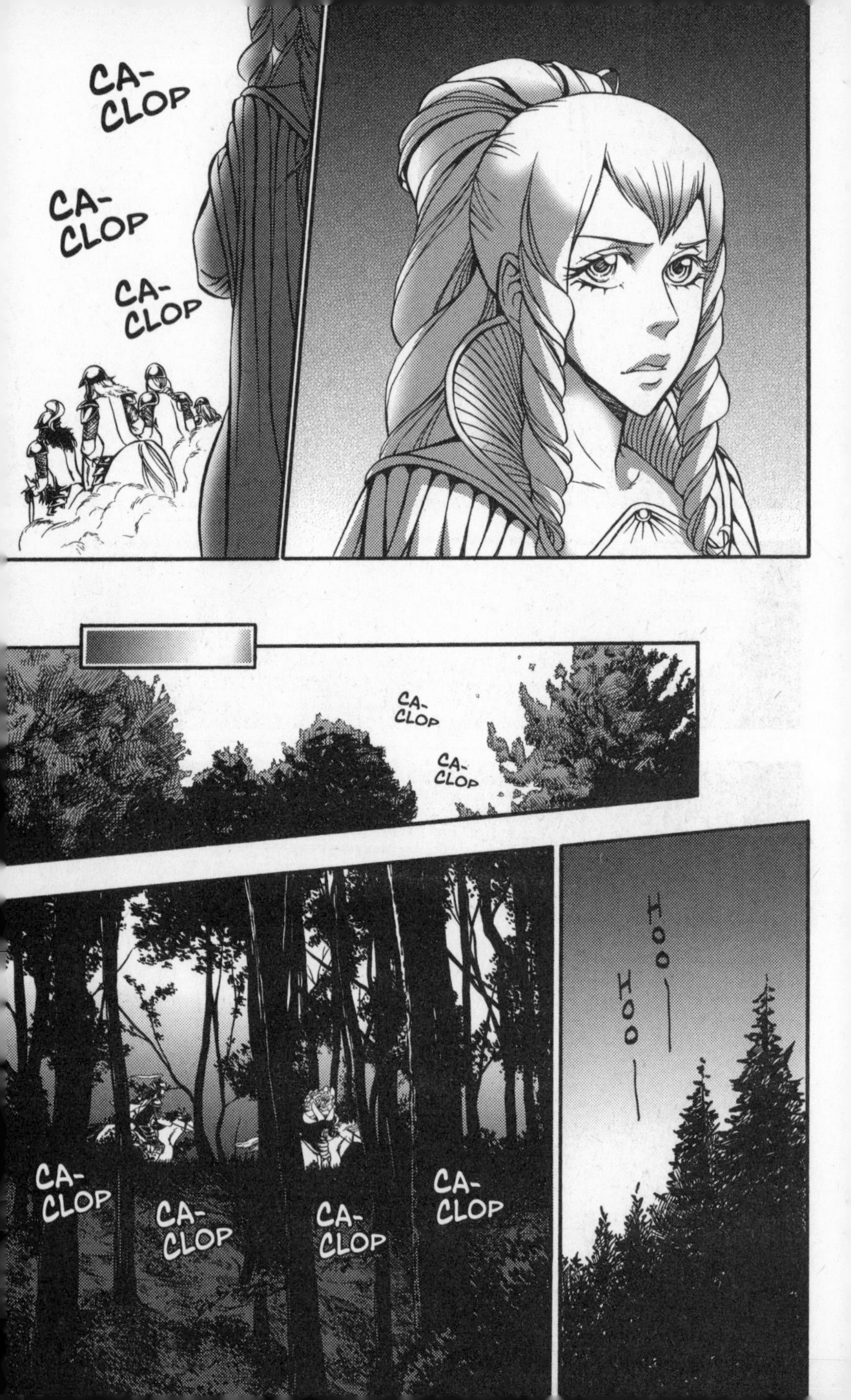
CA-
CLOP
CA-
CLOP
CA-
CLOP
CA-
CLOP
CA-
CLOP
CA-
CLOP
CA-
CLOP
CA-
CLOP
CA-
CLOP
HOO—
HOO—

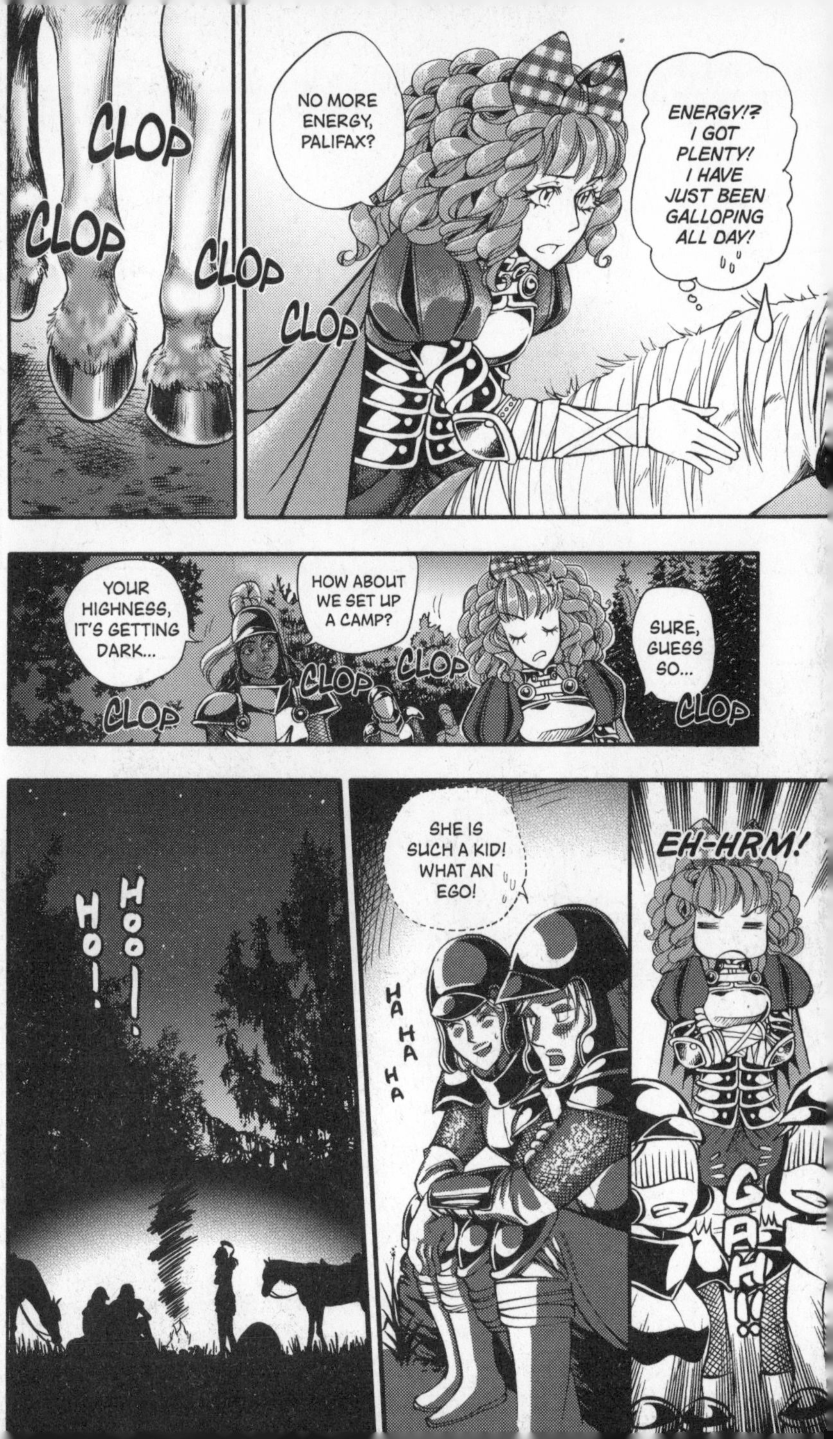
CLOP
CLOP
CLOP
CLOP
NO MORE ENERGY, PALIFAX?
ENERGY!? I GOT PLENTY! I HAVE JUST BEEN GALLOPING ALL DAY!
YOUR HIGHNESS, IT'S GETTING DARK...
HOW ABOUT WE SET UP A CAMP?
CLOP
CLOP
CLOP
SURE, GUESS SO...
CLOP
HOO!
HOO!
SHE IS SUCH A KID! WHAT AN EGO!
HA HA HA HA
EH-HRM!
GAAH!!

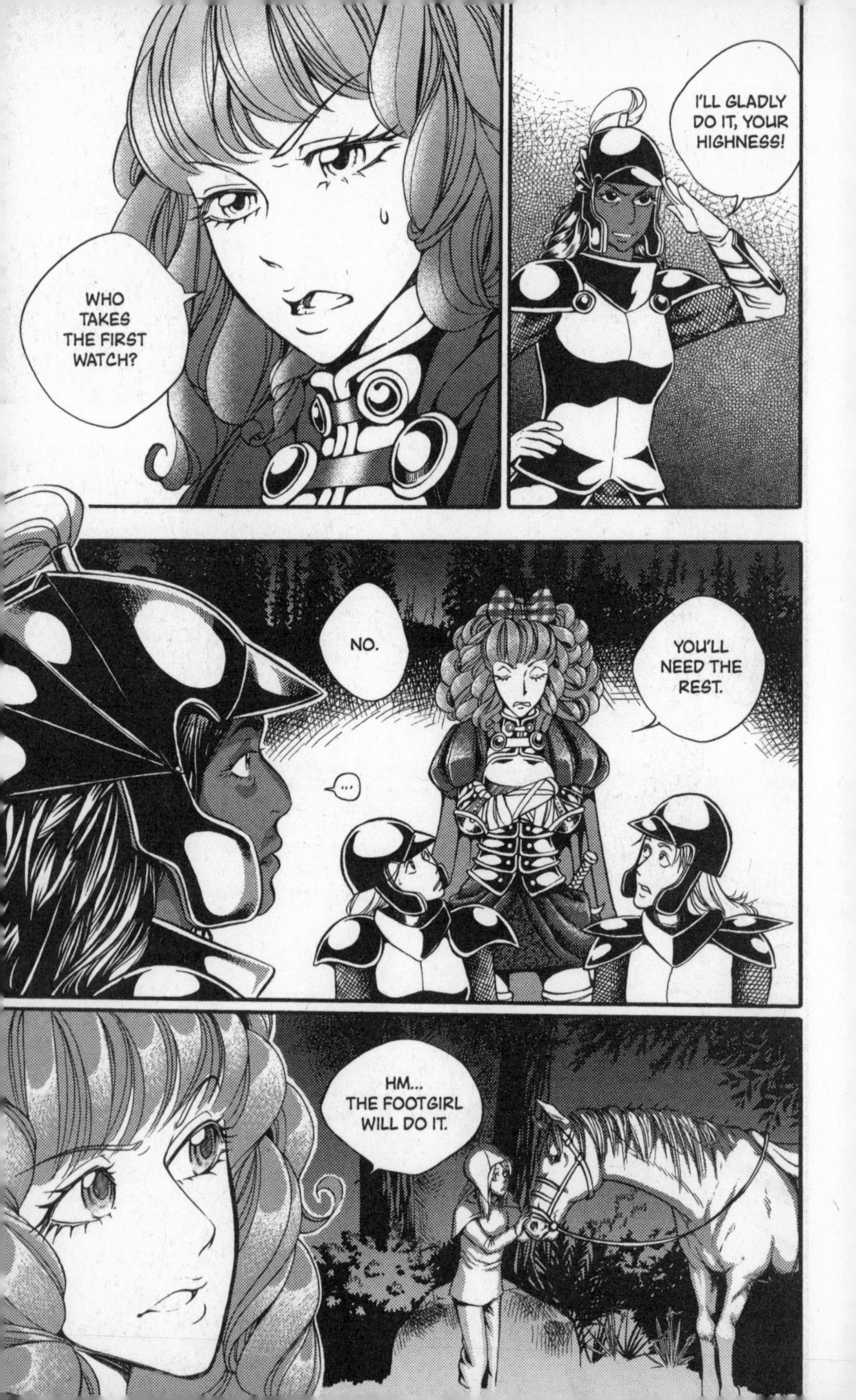
WHO TAKES THE FIRST WATCH?
I'LL GLADLY DO IT, YOUR HIGHNESS!
NO.
...
YOU'LL NEED THE REST.
HM... THE FOOTGIRL WILL DO IT.

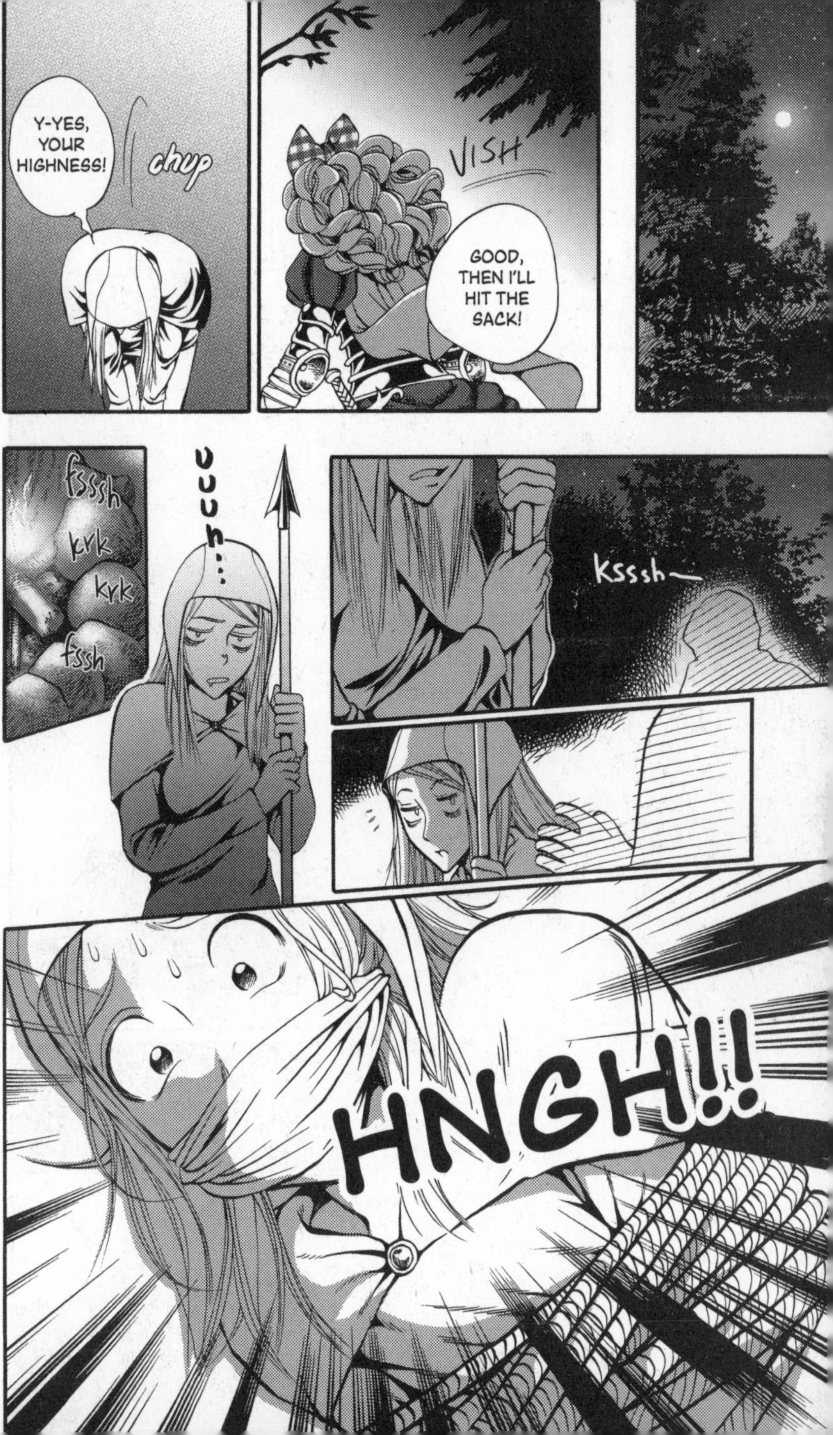
Y-YES, YOUR HIGHNESS!
chup
VISH
GOOD, THEN I'LL HIT THE SACK!
fsssh
krk
krk
fssh
uuuh...
ksssh~
HNGH!!

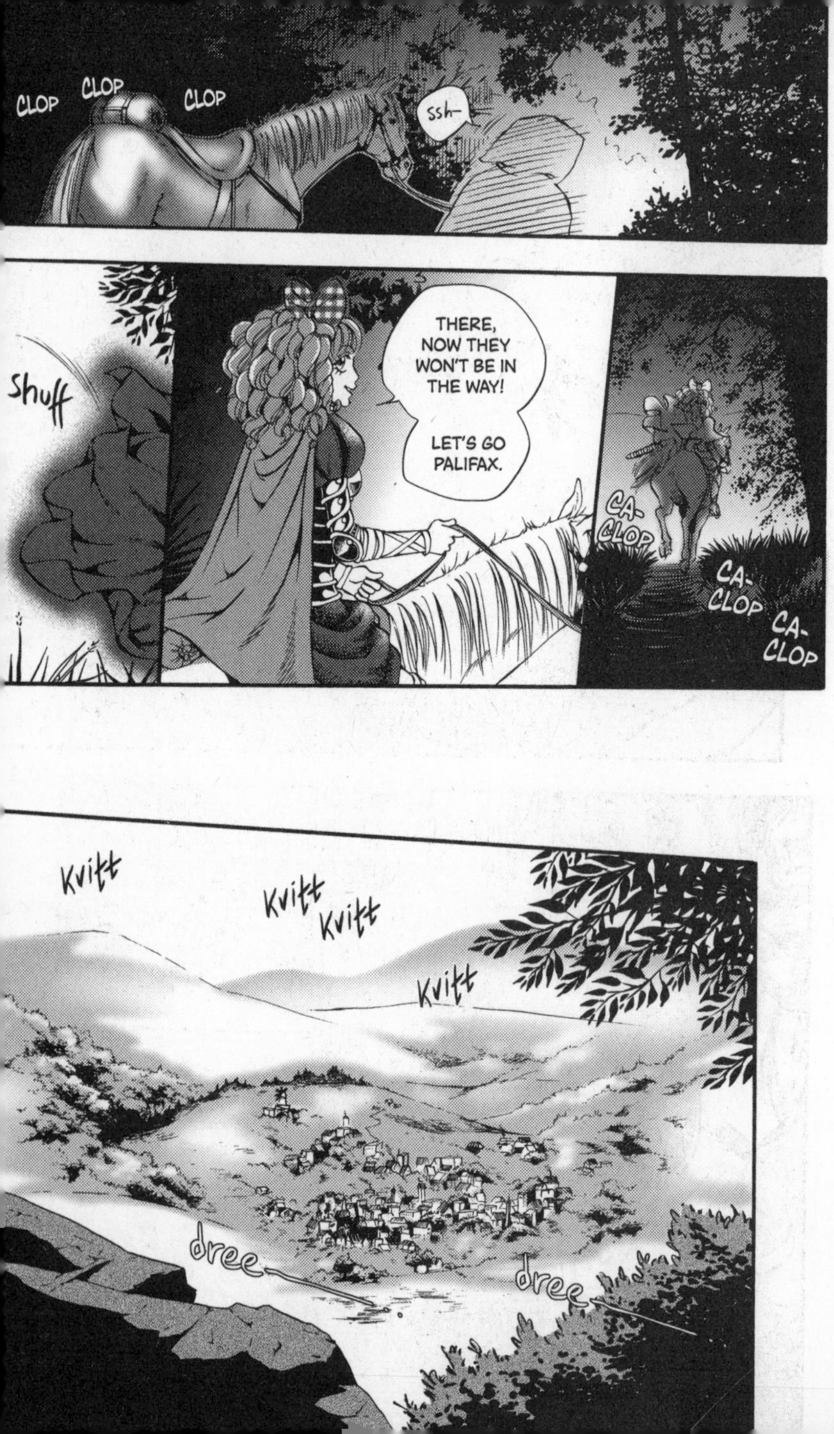
CLOP
CLOP
CLOP
ssh-
Shuff
THERE, NOW THEY WON'T BE IN THE WAY!
LET'S GO PALIFAX.
CA-CLOP
CA-CLOP
CA-CLOP
Kvitt
Kvitt
Kvitt
Kvitt
dree—
dree—

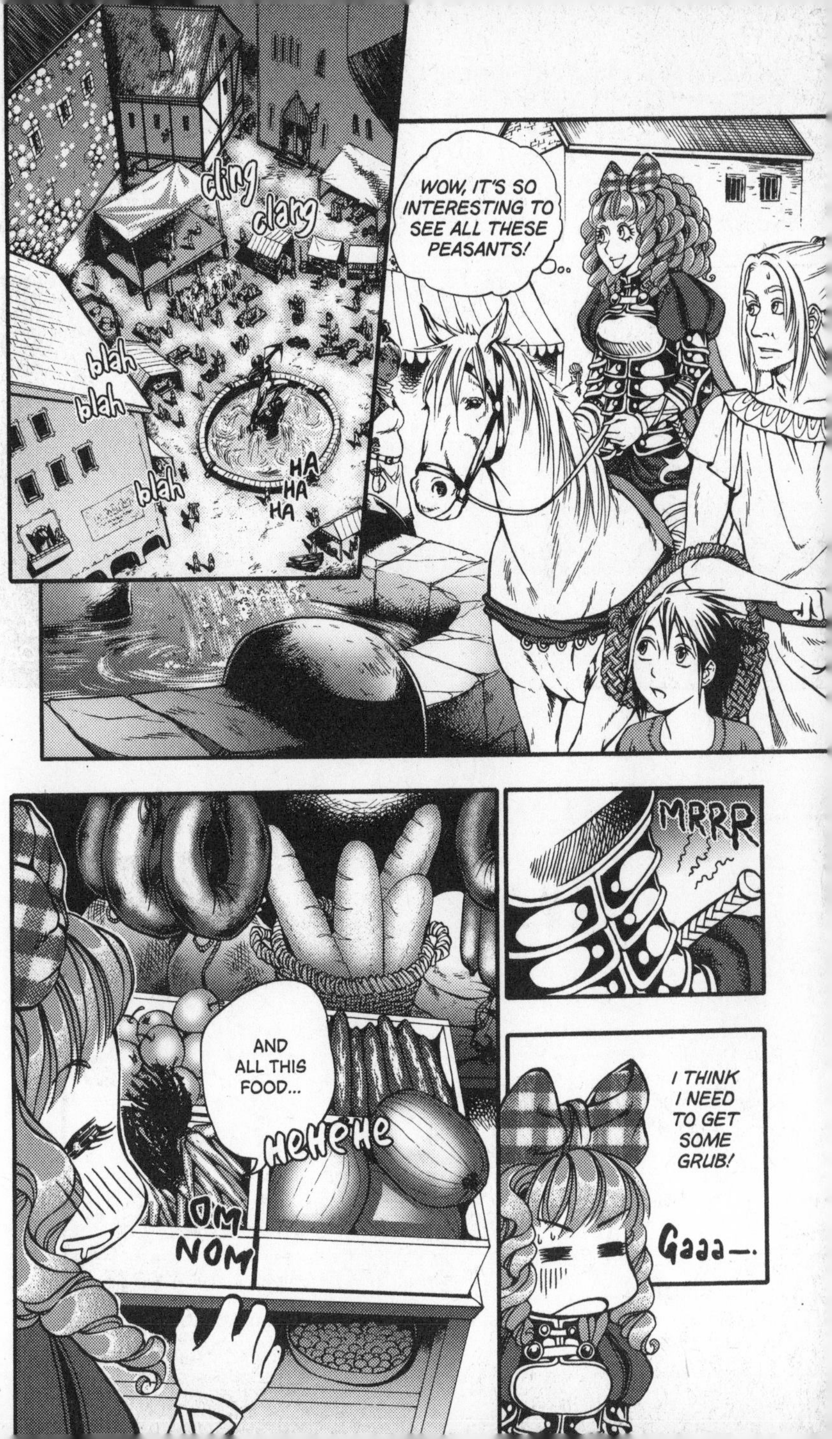
cling
clang
blah
blah
blah
HA
HA
HA
WOW, IT'S SO INTERESTING TO SEE ALL THESE PEASANTS!
AND ALL THIS FOOD...
HEHEHE
OM
NOM
MRRR
I THINK I NEED TO GET SOME GRUB!
Gaaa—.

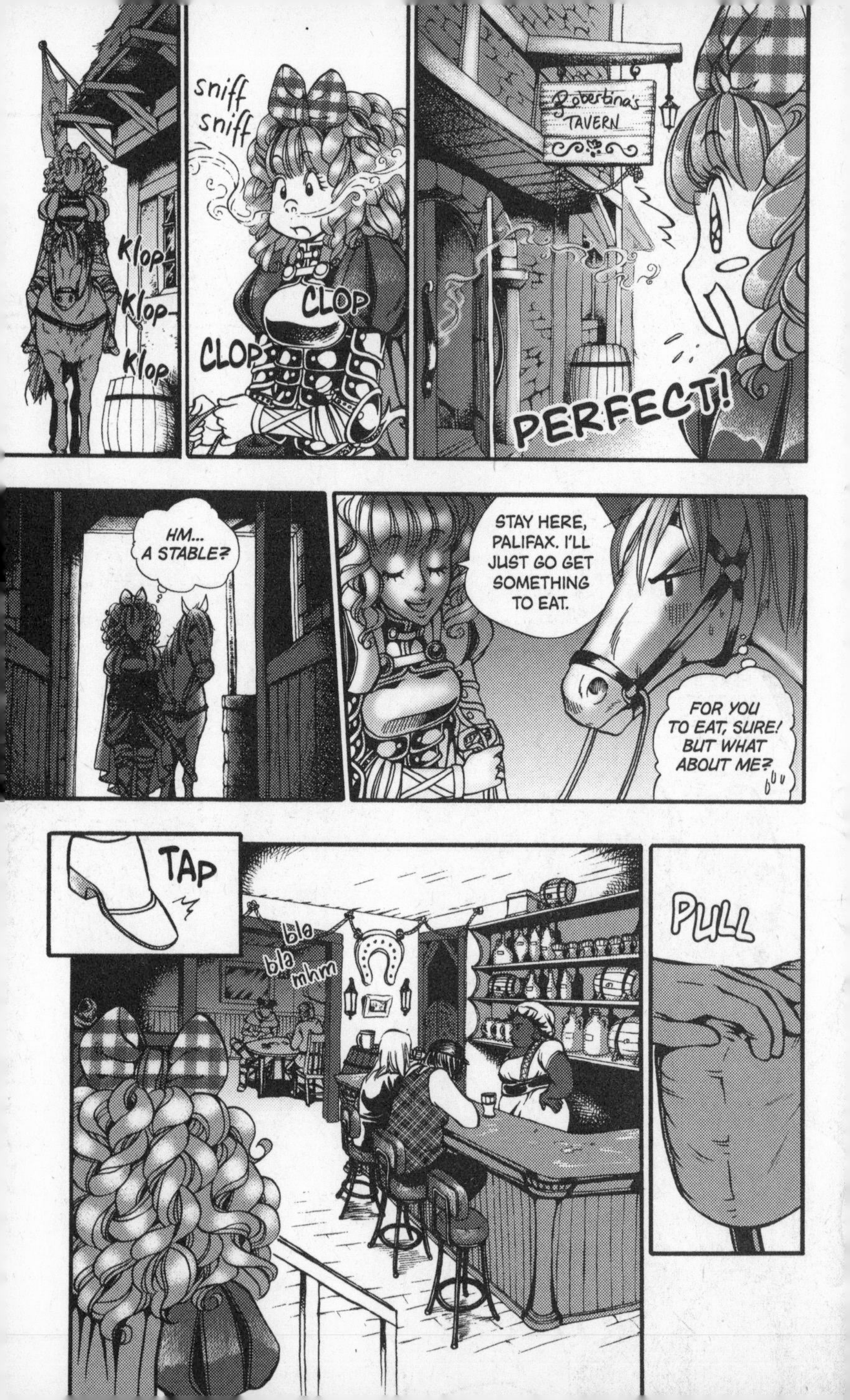
Klop
Klop
Klop
sniff
sniff
CLOP
CLOP
Robertina's
TAVERN
PERFECT!
HM...
A STABLE?
STAY HERE, PALIFAX. I'LL JUST GO GET SOMETHING TO EAT.
FOR YOU TO EAT, SURE! BUT WHAT ABOUT ME?
TAP
bla
bla
mhm
PULL

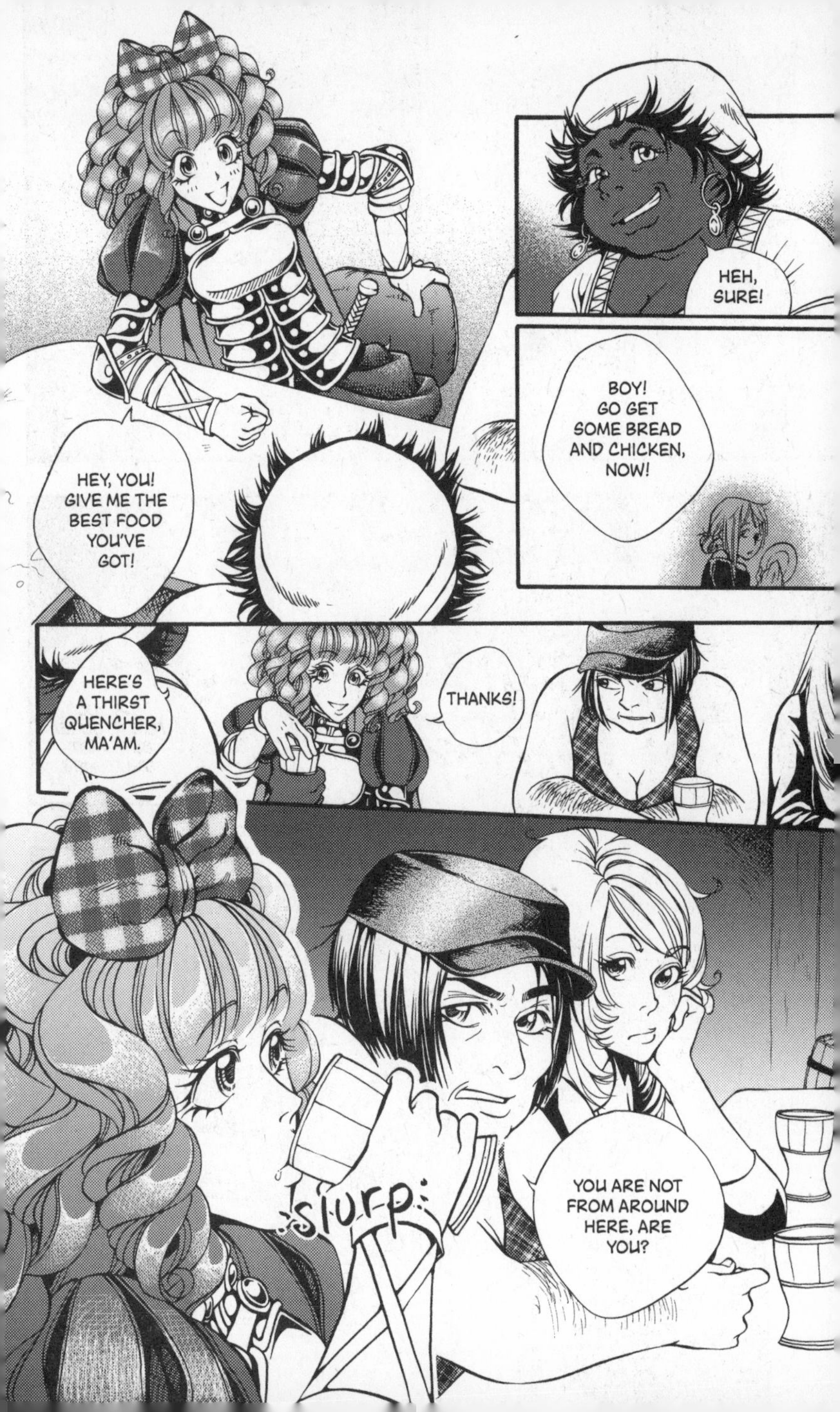
HEY, YOU! GIVE ME THE BEST FOOD YOU'VE GOT!
HEH, SURE!
BOY! GO GET SOME BREAD AND CHICKEN, NOW!
HERE'S A THIRST QUENCHER, MA'AM.
THANKS!
SLURP
YOU ARE NOT FROM AROUND HERE, ARE YOU?

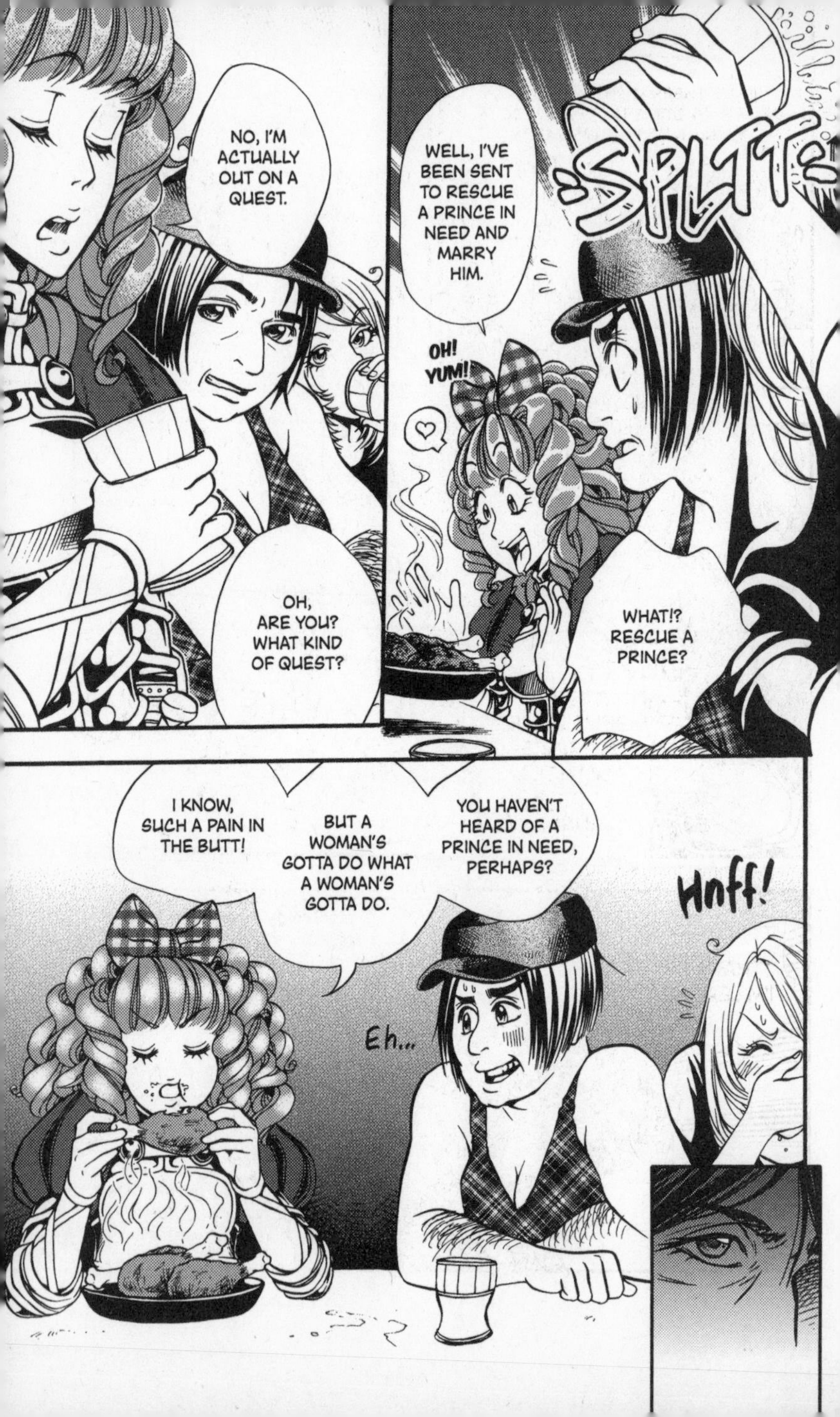
NO, I'M ACTUALLY OUT ON A QUEST.
OH, ARE YOU? WHAT KIND OF QUEST?
WELL, I'VE BEEN SENT TO RESCUE A PRINCE IN NEED AND MARRY HIM.
SPLTT
OH! YUM!
WHAT!? RESCUE A PRINCE?
I KNOW, SUCH A PAIN IN THE BUTT!
BUT A WOMAN'S GOTTA DO WHAT A WOMAN'S GOTTA DO.
YOU HAVEN'T HEARD OF A PRINCE IN NEED, PERHAPS?
Hnff!
Eh...

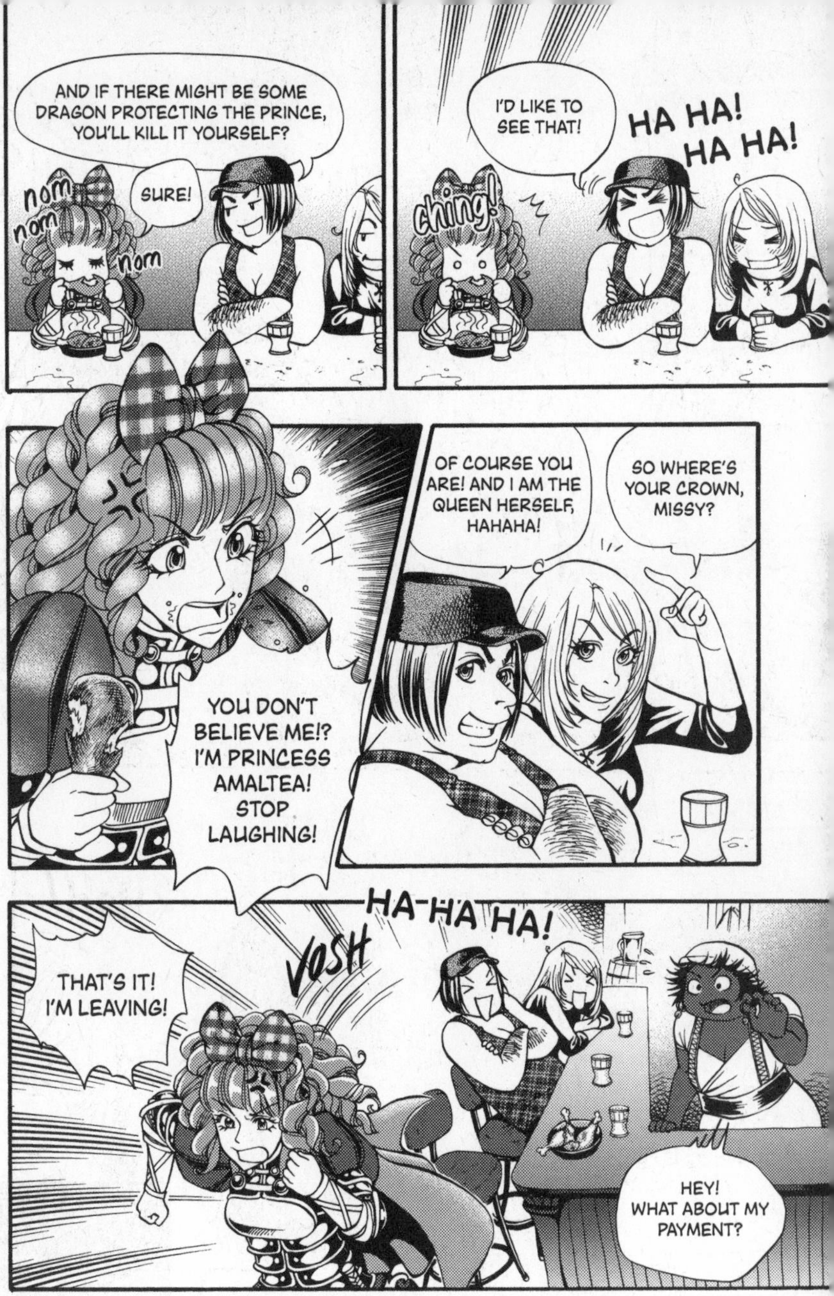
AND IF THERE MIGHT BE SOME DRAGON PROTECTING THE PRINCE, YOU'LL KILL IT YOURSELF?
nom nom nom
SURE!
I'D LIKE TO SEE THAT!
HA HA! HA HA!
ching!
YOU DON'T BELIEVE ME!? I'M PRINCESS AMALTEA! STOP LAUGHING!
OF COURSE YOU ARE! AND I AM THE QUEEN HERSELF, HAHAHA!
SO WHERE'S YOUR CROWN, MISSY?
THAT'S IT! I'M LEAVING!
VOSH
HA HA HA HA!
HEY! WHAT ABOUT MY PAYMENT?

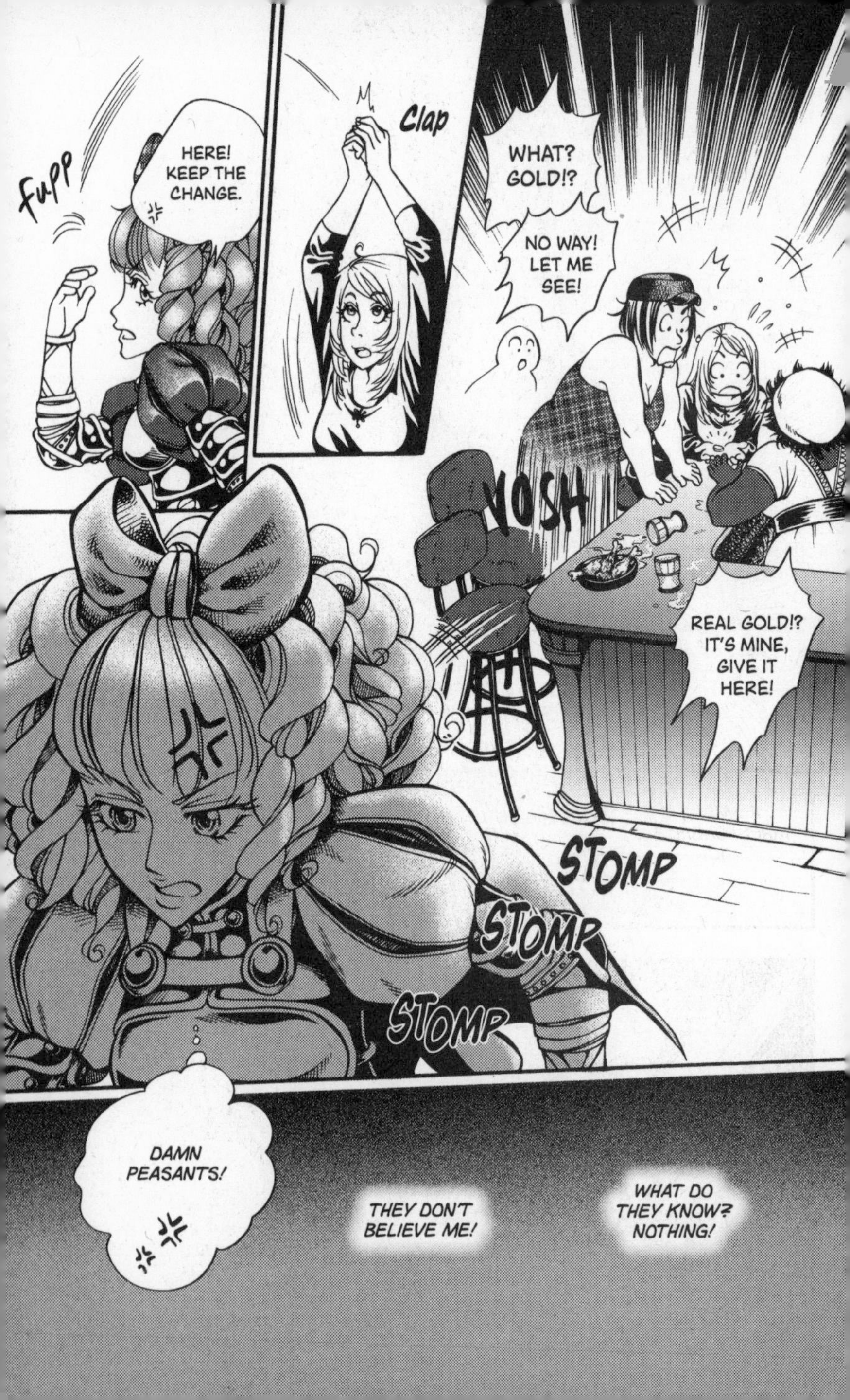
FUPP
HERE! KEEP THE CHANGE.
Clap
WHAT? GOLD!?
NO WAY! LET ME SEE!
NOSH
REAL GOLD!? IT'S MINE, GIVE IT HERE!
STOMP
STOMP
STOMP
DAMN PEASANTS!
THEY DON'T BELIEVE ME!
WHAT DO THEY KNOW? NOTHING!

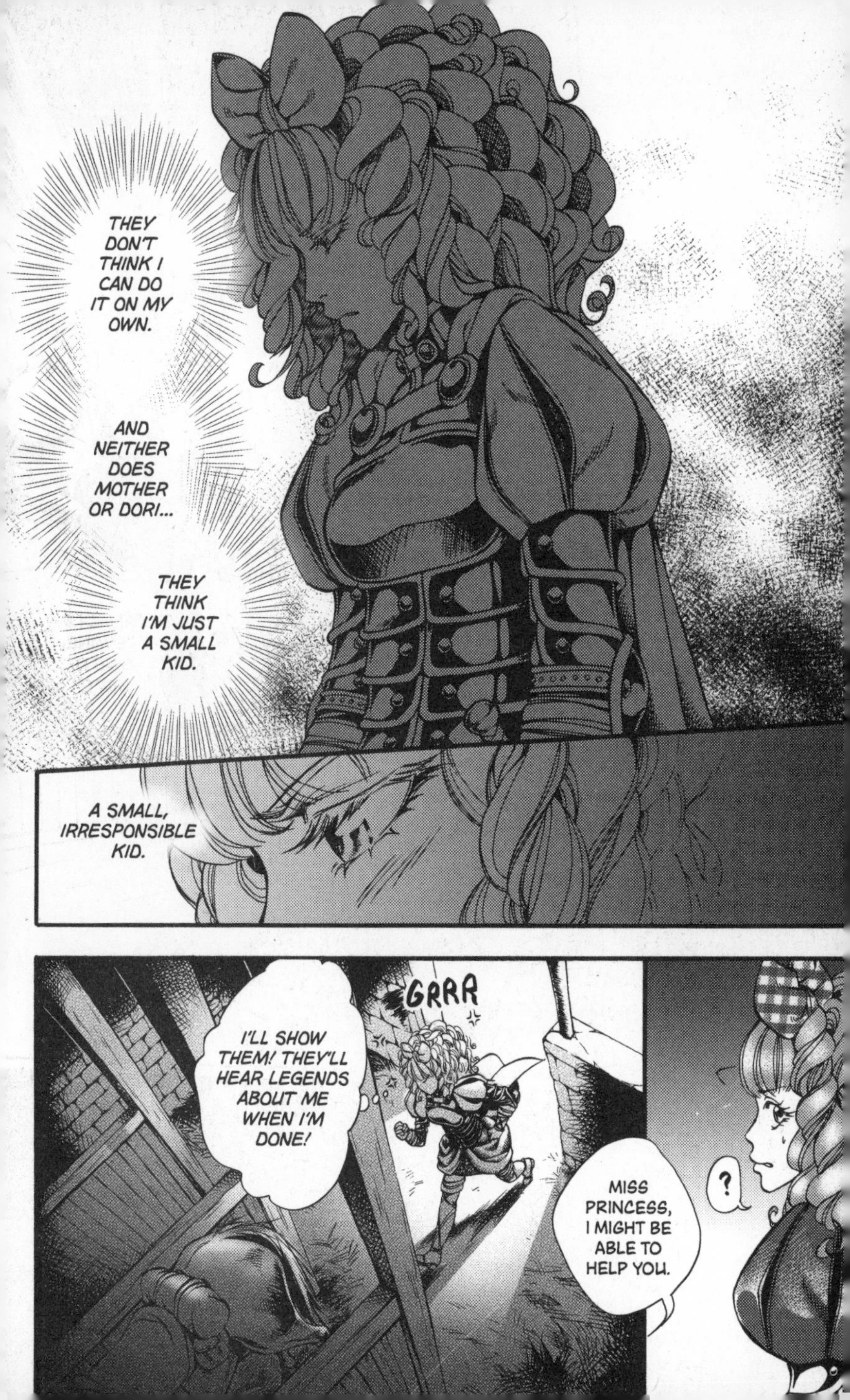
THEY DON'T THINK I CAN DO IT ON MY OWN.
AND NEITHER DOES MOTHER OR DORI...
THEY THINK I'M JUST A SMALL KID.
A SMALL, IRRESPONSIBLE KID.
I'LL SHOW THEM! THEY'LL HEAR LEGENDS ABOUT ME WHEN I'M DONE!
GRRR
MISS PRINCESS, I MIGHT BE ABLE TO HELP YOU.
?

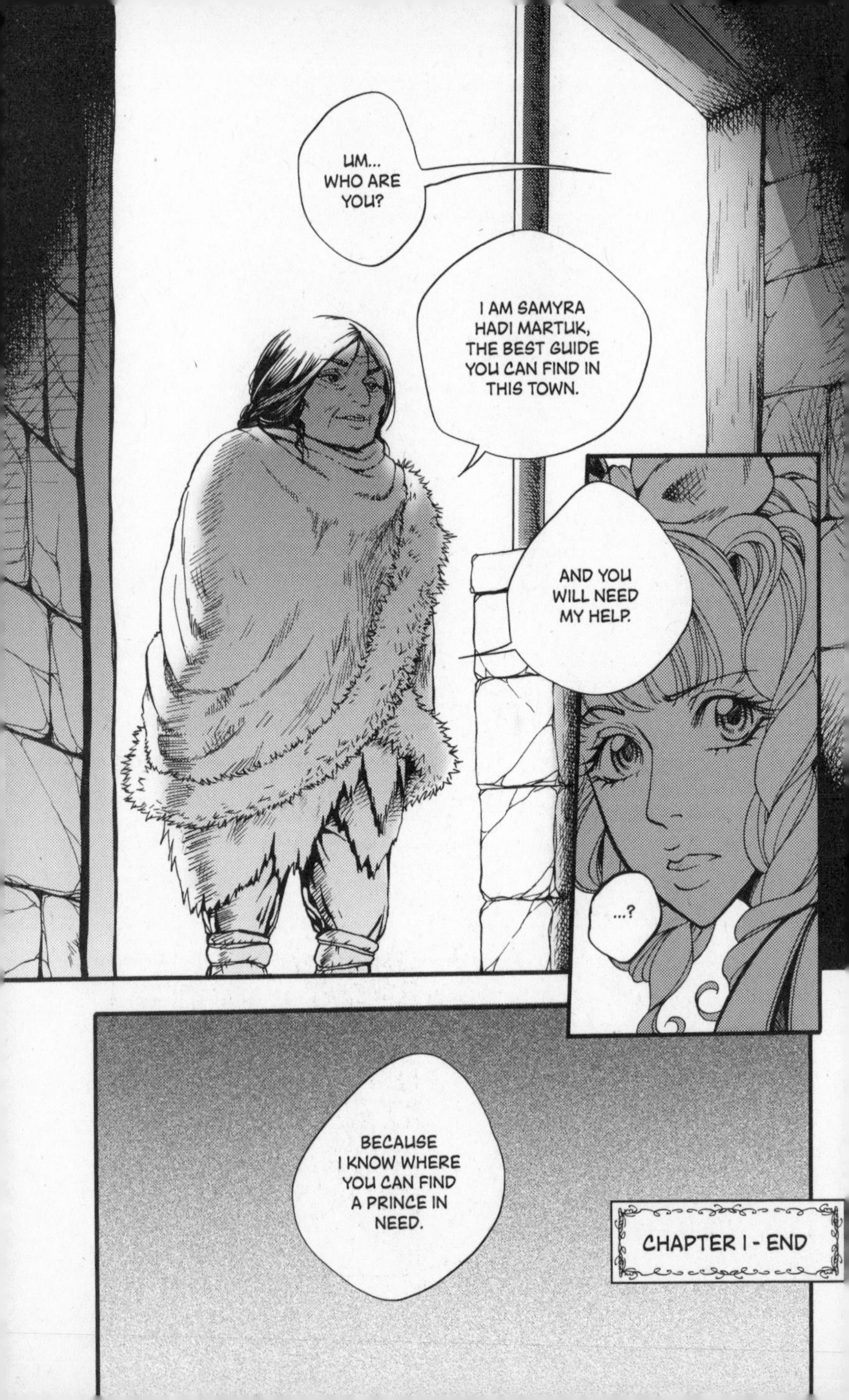
UM... WHO ARE YOU?
I AM SAMYRA HADI MARTUK, THE BEST GUIDE YOU CAN FIND IN THIS TOWN.
AND YOU WILL NEED MY HELP.
...?
BECAUSE I KNOW WHERE YOU CAN FIND A PRINCE IN NEED.
CHAPTER I - END

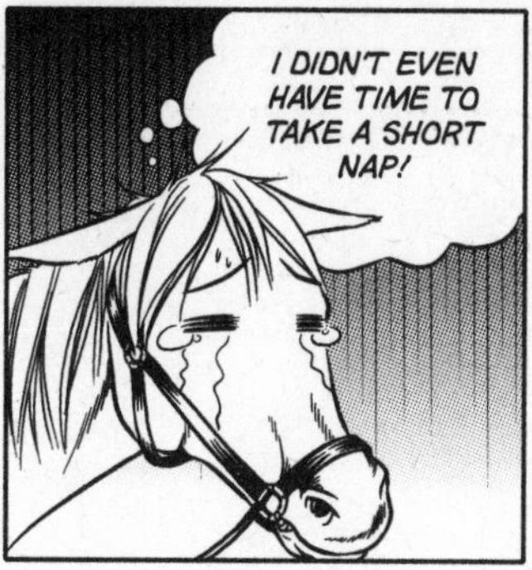
I DIDN'T EVEN HAVE TIME TO TAKE A SHORT NAP!

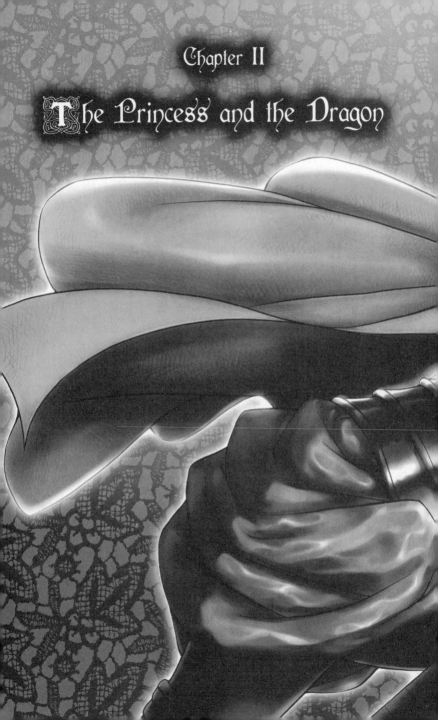

Chapter II

The Princess and the Dragon

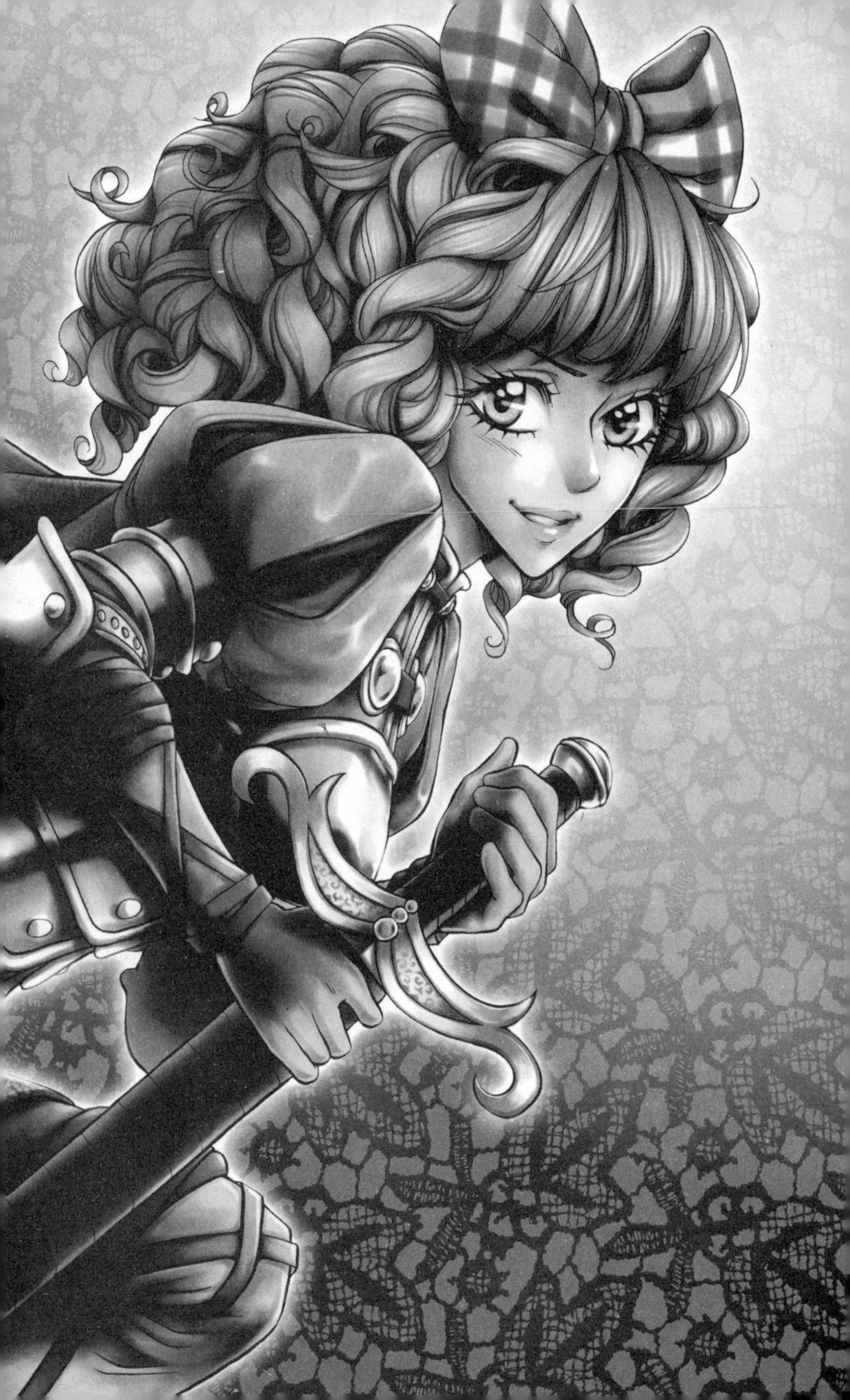

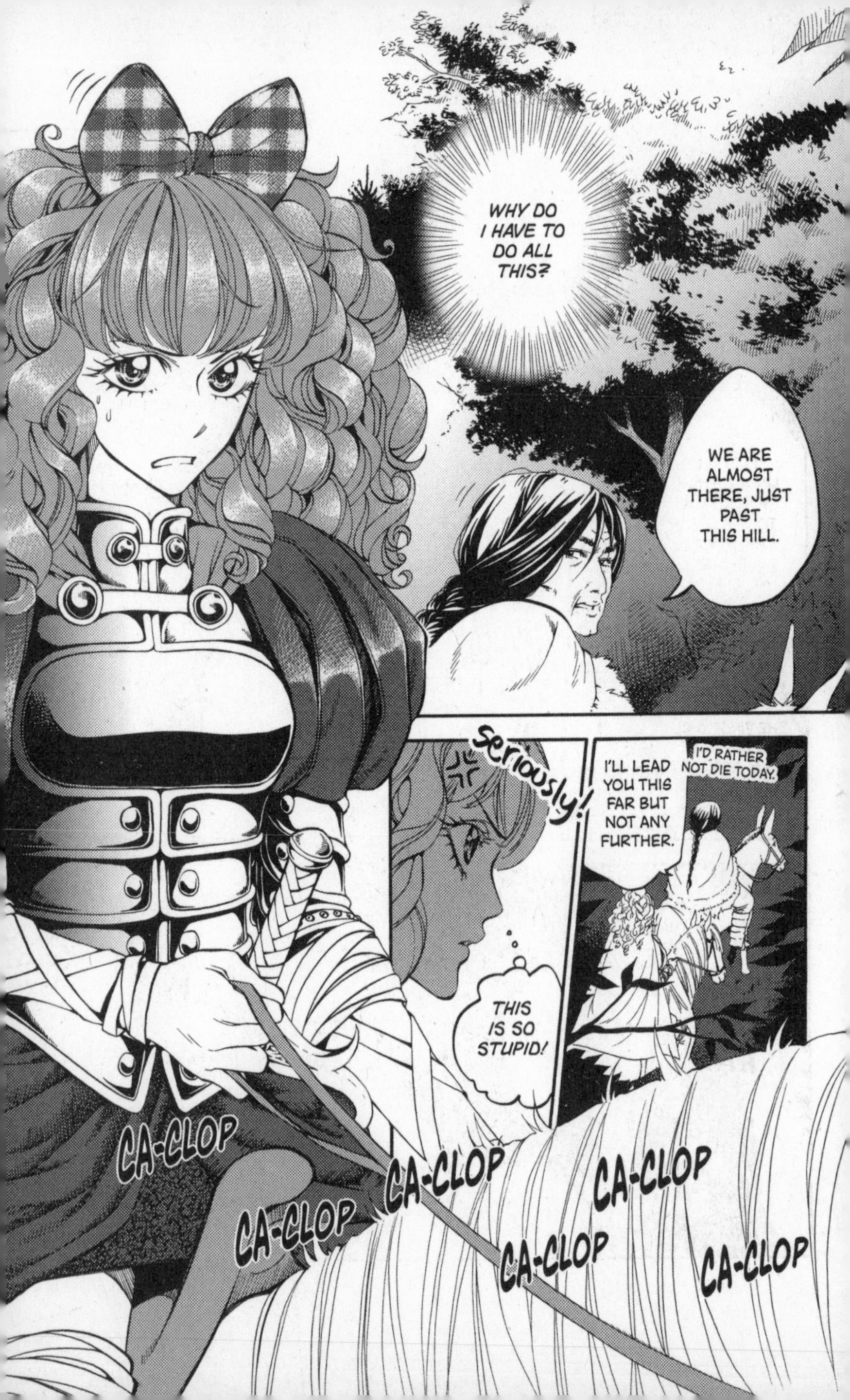
WHY DO I HAVE TO DO ALL THIS?
WE ARE ALMOST THERE, JUST PAST THIS HILL.
Seriously!
THIS IS SO STUPID!
I'LL LEAD YOU THIS FAR BUT NOT ANY FURTHER.
I'D RATHER NOT DIE TODAY.
CA-CLOP
CA-CLOP
CA-CLOP
CA-CLOP
CA-CLOP
CA-CLOP

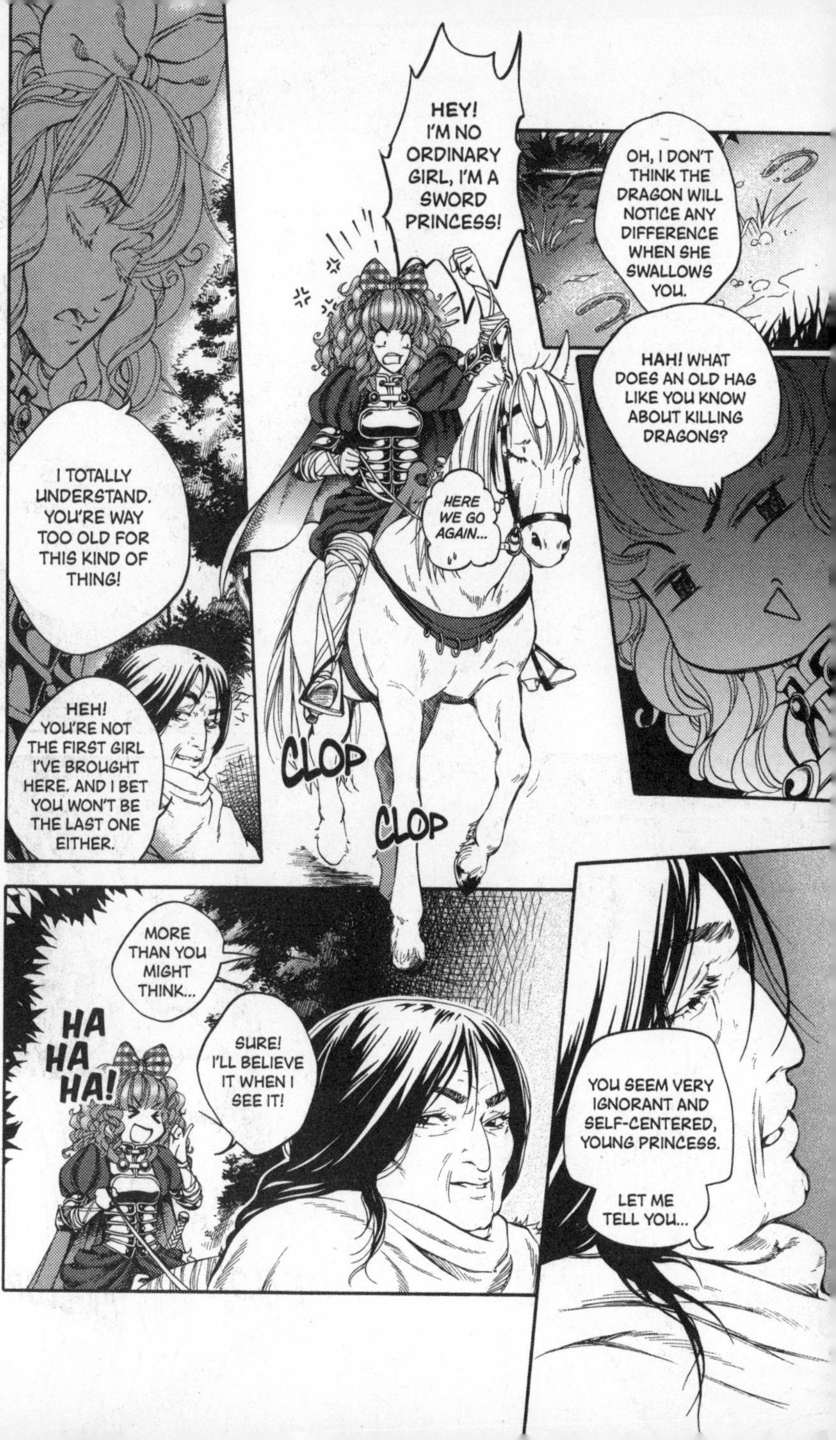
I TOTALLY UNDERSTAND. YOU'RE WAY TOO OLD FOR THIS KIND OF THING!
HEH! YOU'RE NOT THE FIRST GIRL I'VE BROUGHT HERE. AND I BET YOU WON'T BE THE LAST ONE EITHER.
HEY! I'M NO ORDINARY GIRL, I'M A SWORD PRINCESS!
HERE WE GO AGAIN...
CLOP
CLOP
OH, I DON'T THINK THE DRAGON WILL NOTICE ANY DIFFERENCE WHEN SHE SWALLOWS YOU.
HAH! WHAT DOES AN OLD HAG LIKE YOU KNOW ABOUT KILLING DRAGONS?
MORE THAN YOU MIGHT THINK...
HA HA HA!
SURE! I'LL BELIEVE IT WHEN I SEE IT!
YOU SEEM VERY IGNORANT AND SELF-CENTERED, YOUNG PRINCESS.
LET ME TELL YOU...

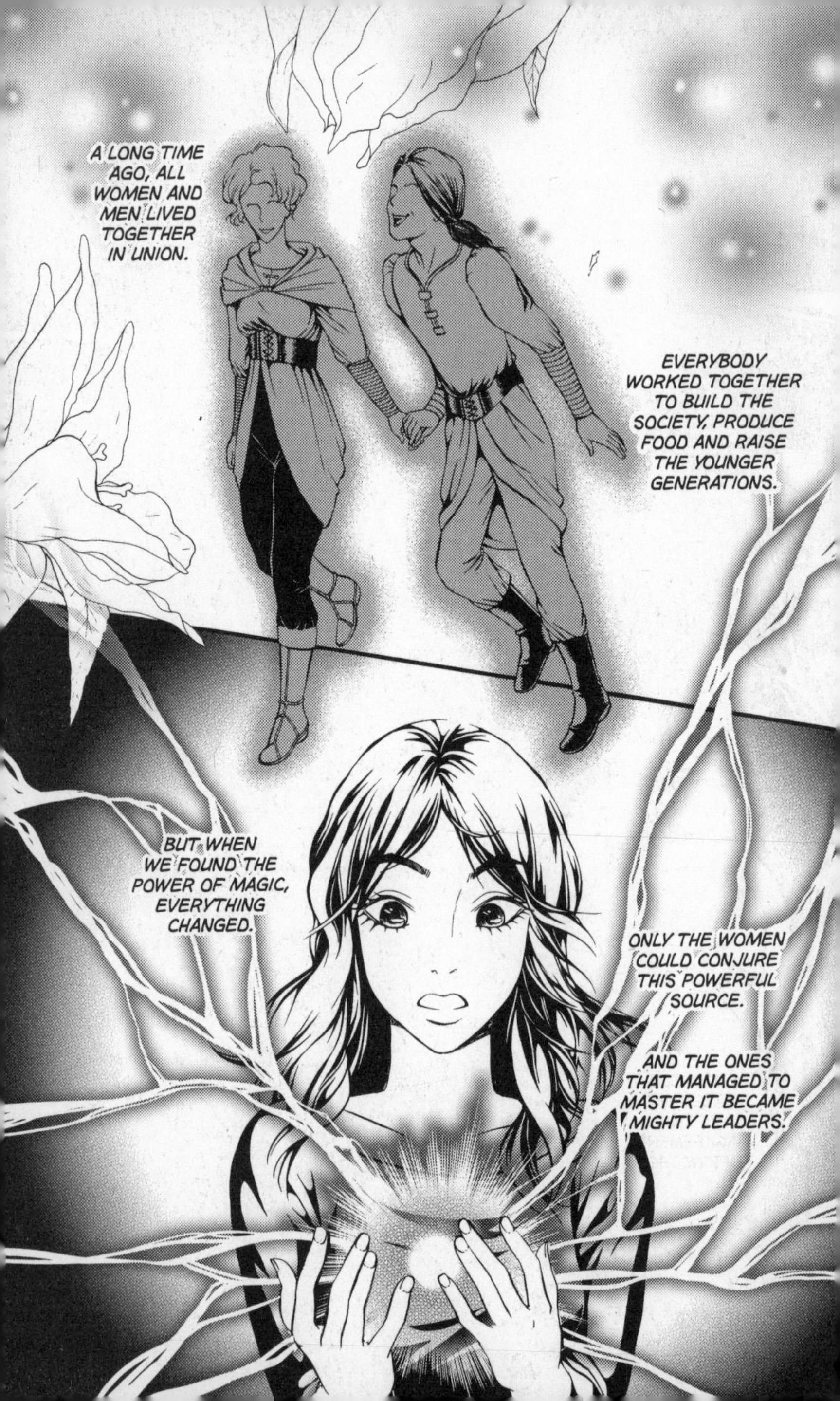
A LONG TIME AGO, ALL WOMEN AND MEN LIVED TOGETHER IN UNION.
EVERYBODY WORKED TOGETHER TO BUILD THE SOCIETY, PRODUCE FOOD AND RAISE THE YOUNGER GENERATIONS.
BUT WHEN WE FOUND THE POWER OF MAGIC, EVERYTHING CHANGED.
ONLY THE WOMEN COULD CONJURE THIS POWERFUL SOURCE.
AND THE ONES THAT MANAGED TO MASTER IT BECAME MIGHTY LEADERS.

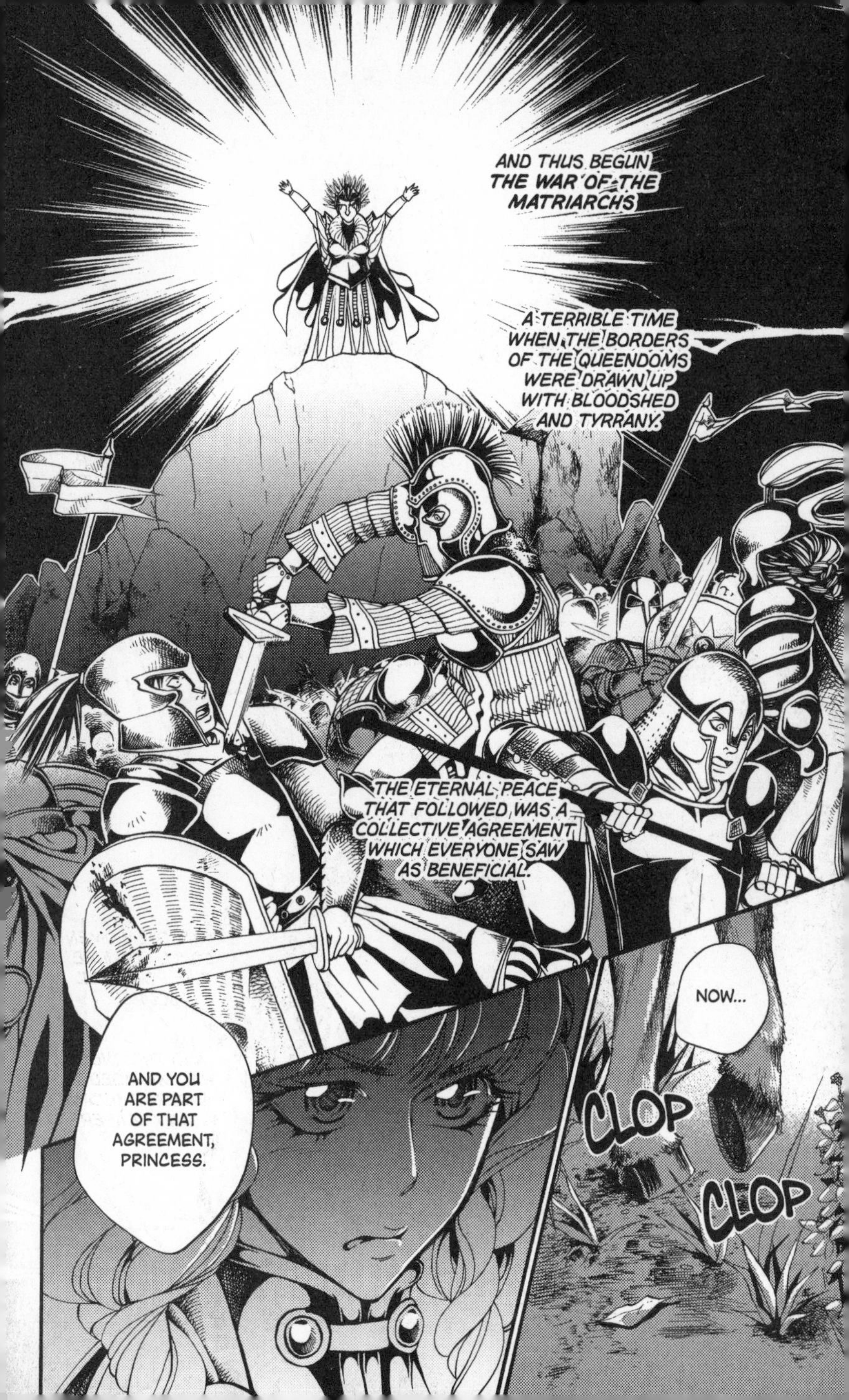

AND THUS BEGUN THE WAR OF THE MATRIARCHS
A TERRIBLE TIME WHEN THE BORDERS OF THE QUEENDOMS WERE DRAWN UP WITH BLOODSHED AND TYRRANY.
THE ETERNAL PEACE THAT FOLLOWED WAS A COLLECTIVE AGREEMENT WHICH EVERYONE SAW AS BENEFICIAL.
AND YOU ARE PART OF THAT AGREEMENT, PRINCESS.
NOW...
CLOP
CLOP

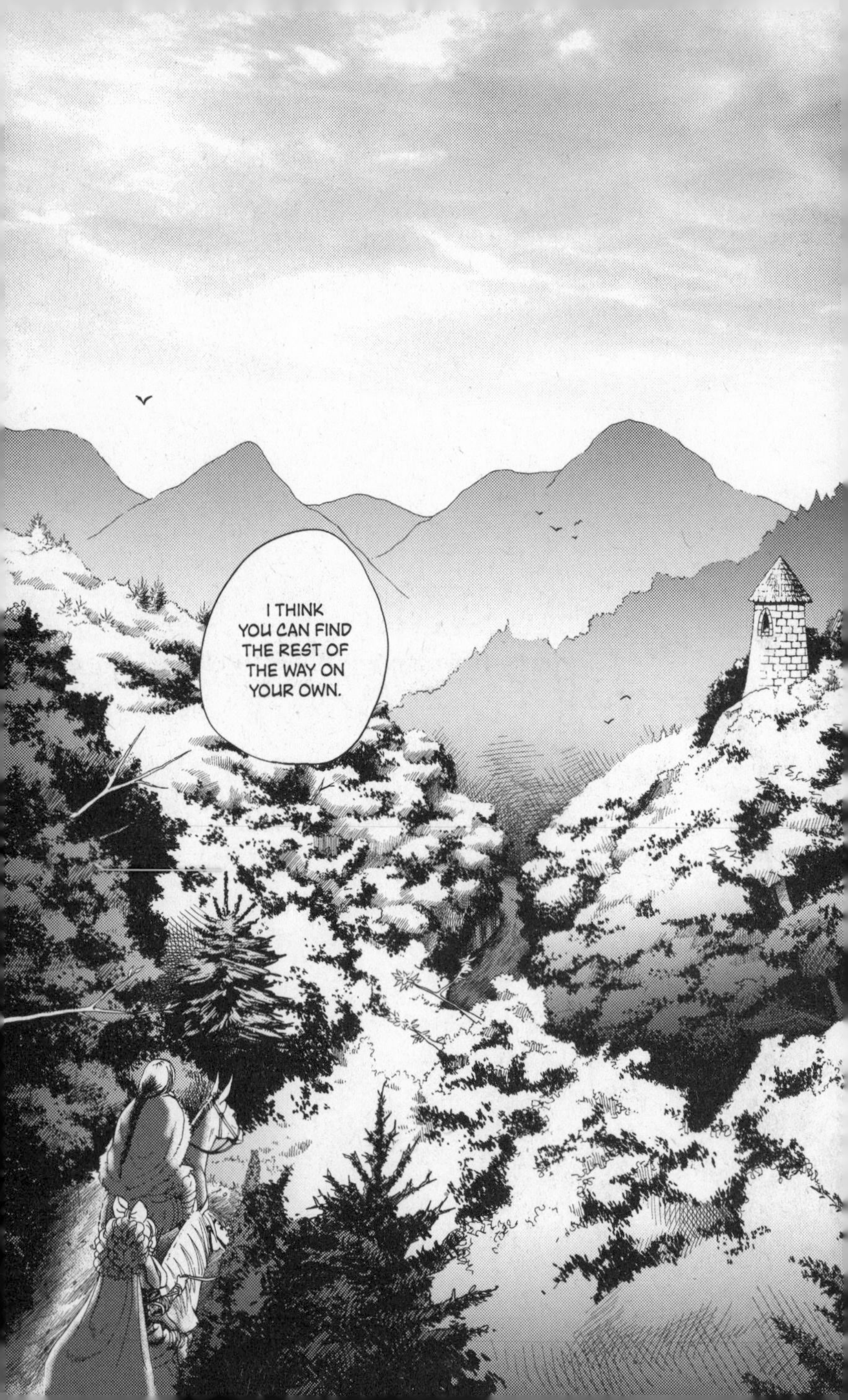
I THINK YOU CAN FIND THE REST OF THE WAY ON YOUR OWN.

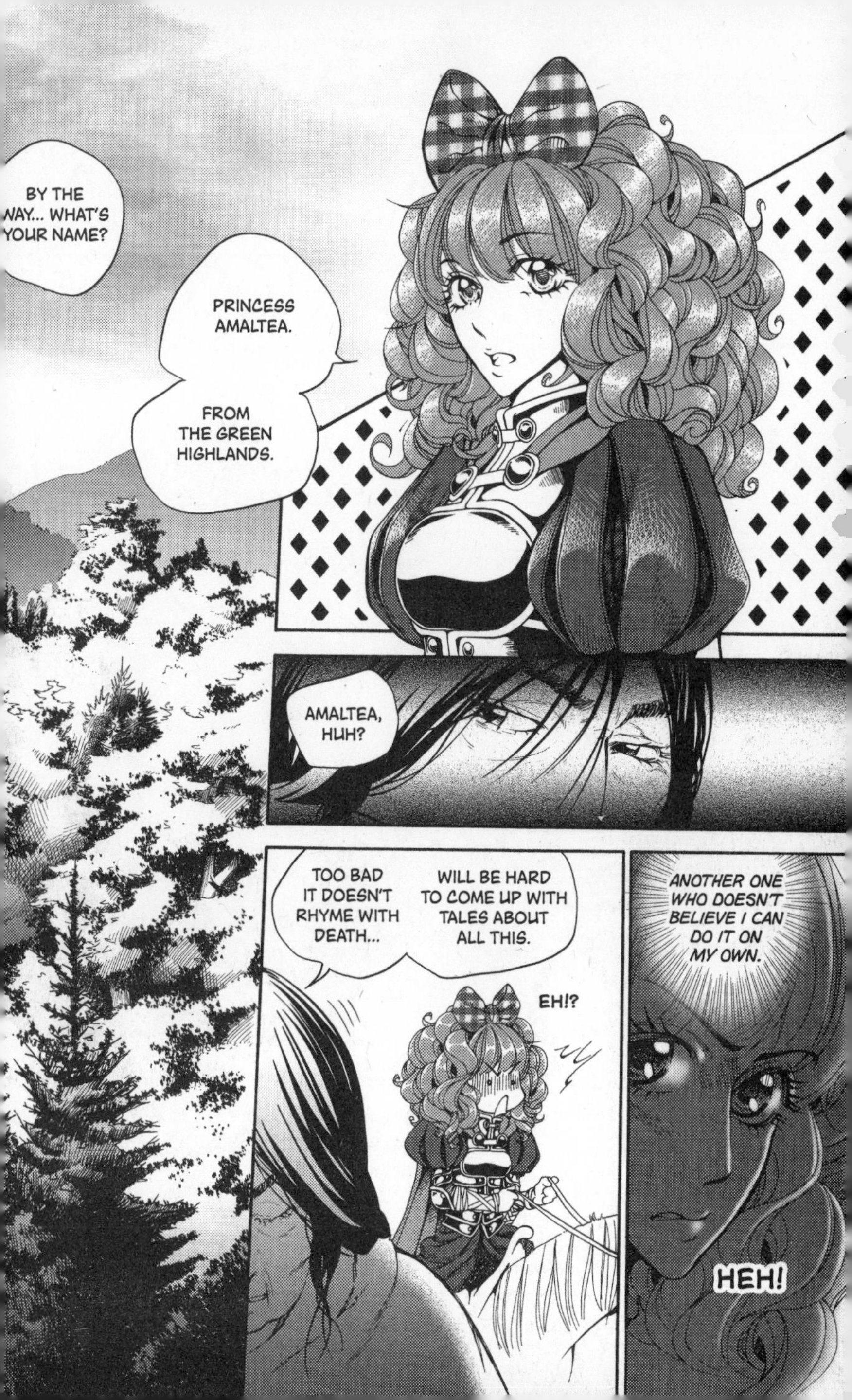
BY THE WAY... WHAT'S YOUR NAME?
PRINCESS AMALTEA.
FROM THE GREEN HIGHLANDS.
AMALTEA, HUH?
TOO BAD IT DOESN'T RHYME WITH DEATH...
WILL BE HARD TO COME UP WITH TALES ABOUT ALL THIS.
EH!?
ANOTHER ONE WHO DOESN'T BELIEVE I CAN DO IT ON MY OWN.
HEH!

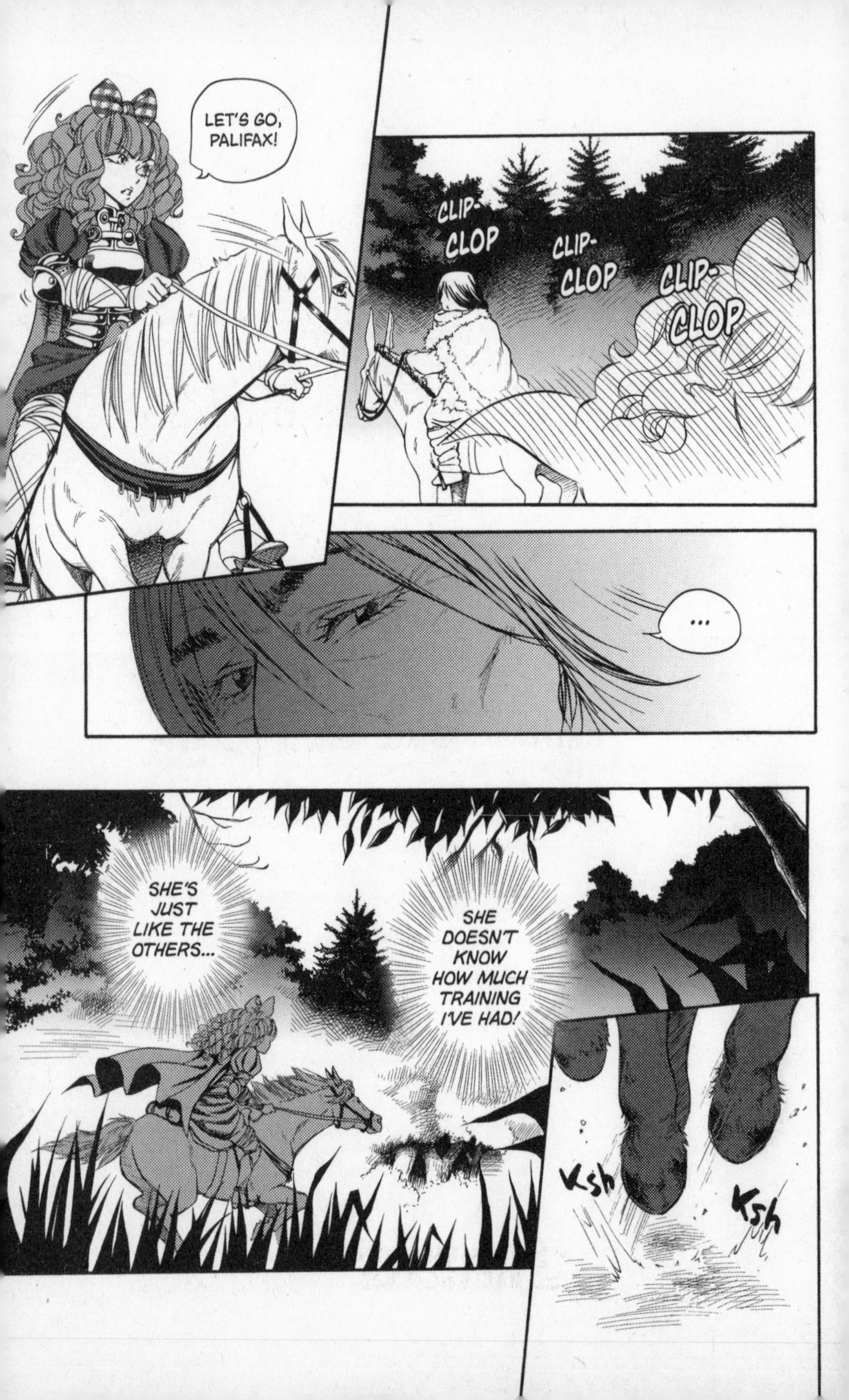
LET'S GO, PALIFAX!
CLIP-CLOP
CLIP-CLOP
CLIP-CLOP
...
SHE'S JUST LIKE THE OTHERS...
SHE DOESN'T KNOW HOW MUCH TRAINING I'VE HAD!
Ksh
Ksh

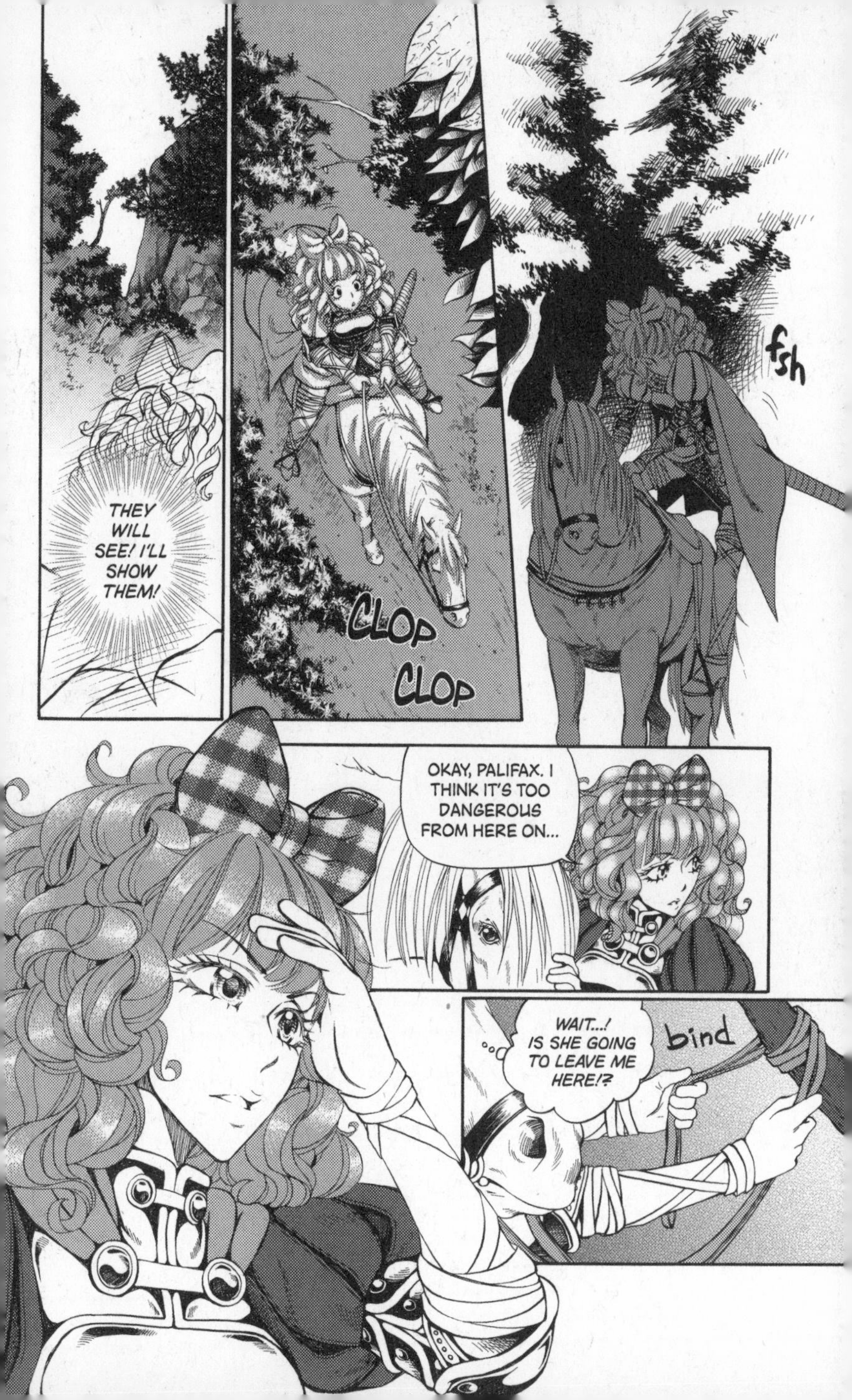

THEY WILL SEE! I'LL SHOW THEM!
CLOP
CLOP
fsh
OKAY, PALIFAX. I THINK IT'S TOO DANGEROUS FROM HERE ON...
WAIT...! IS SHE GOING TO LEAVE ME HERE!?
bind

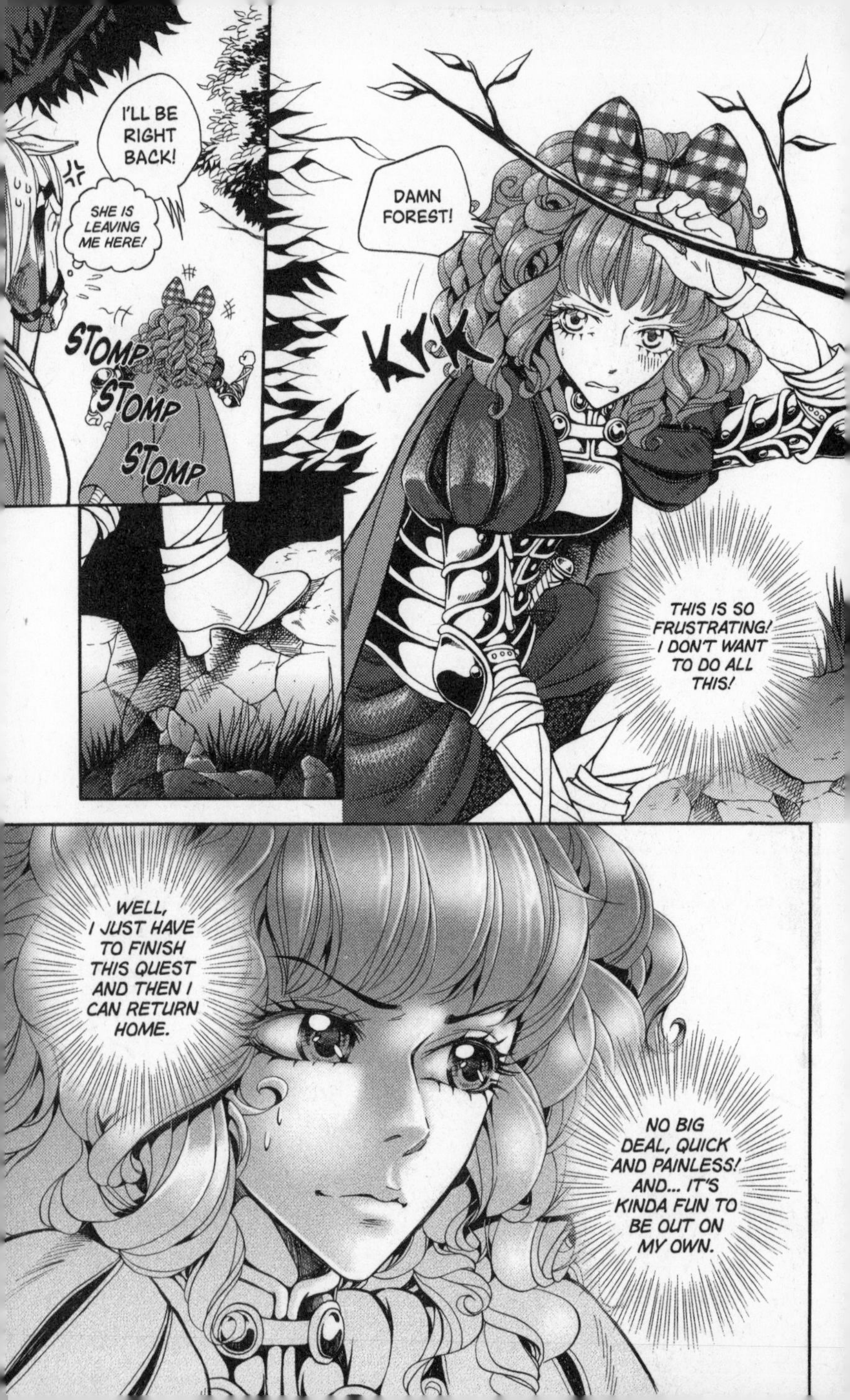
I'LL BE RIGHT BACK!
SHE IS LEAVING ME HERE!
STOMP
STOMP
STOMP
DAMN FOREST!
THIS IS SO FRUSTRATING! I DON'T WANT TO DO ALL THIS!
WELL, I JUST HAVE TO FINISH THIS QUEST AND THEN I CAN RETURN HOME.
NO BIG DEAL, QUICK AND PAINLESS! AND... IT'S KINDA FUN TO BE OUT ON MY OWN.

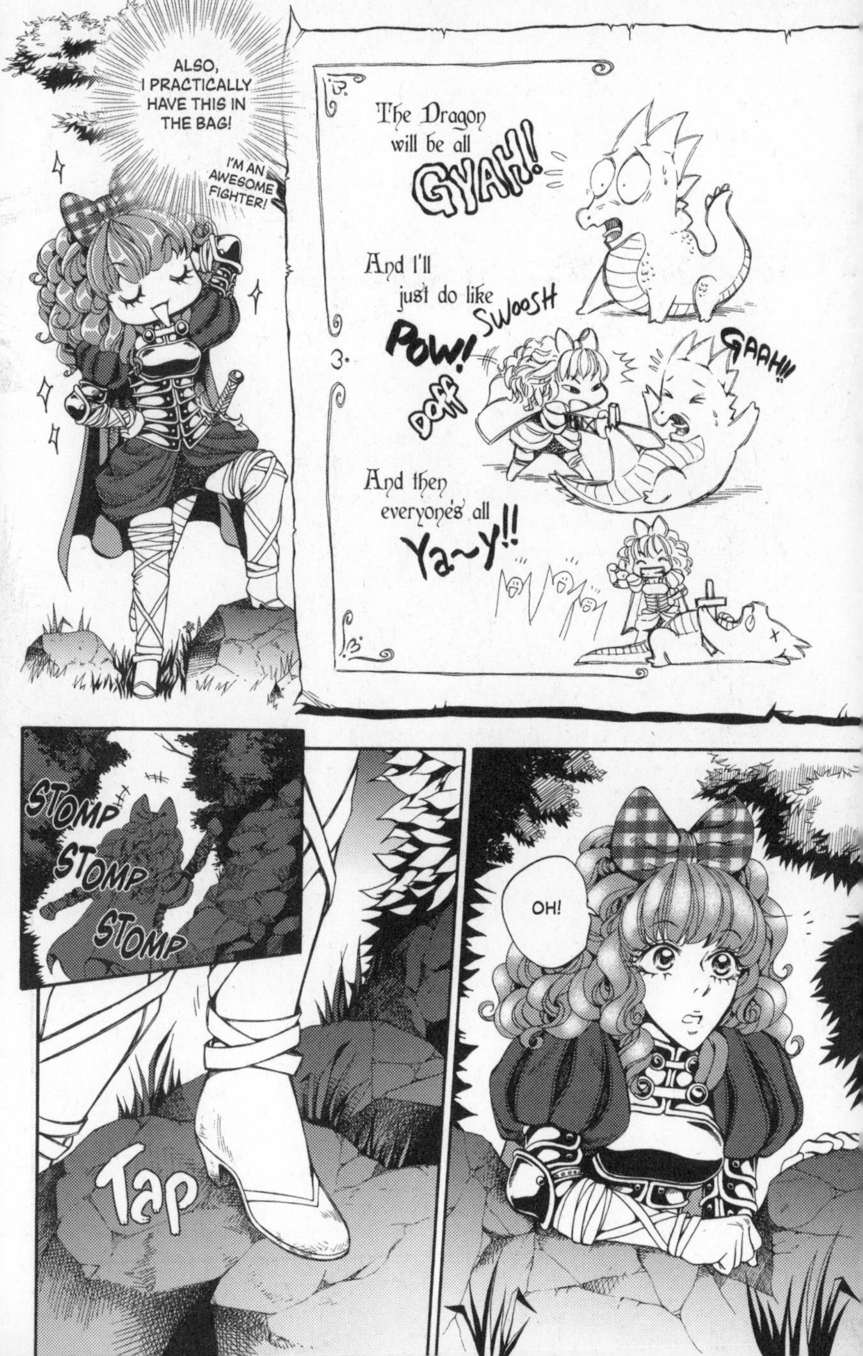
ALSO, I PRACTICALLY HAVE THIS IN THE BAG!
I'M AN AWESOME FIGHTER!
The Dragon will be all
GYAH!!
And I'll just do like
SWOOSH
POW!
DOFF
GAAH!!
And then everyone's all
Ya~y!!
STOMP
STOMP
STOMP
Tap
OH!

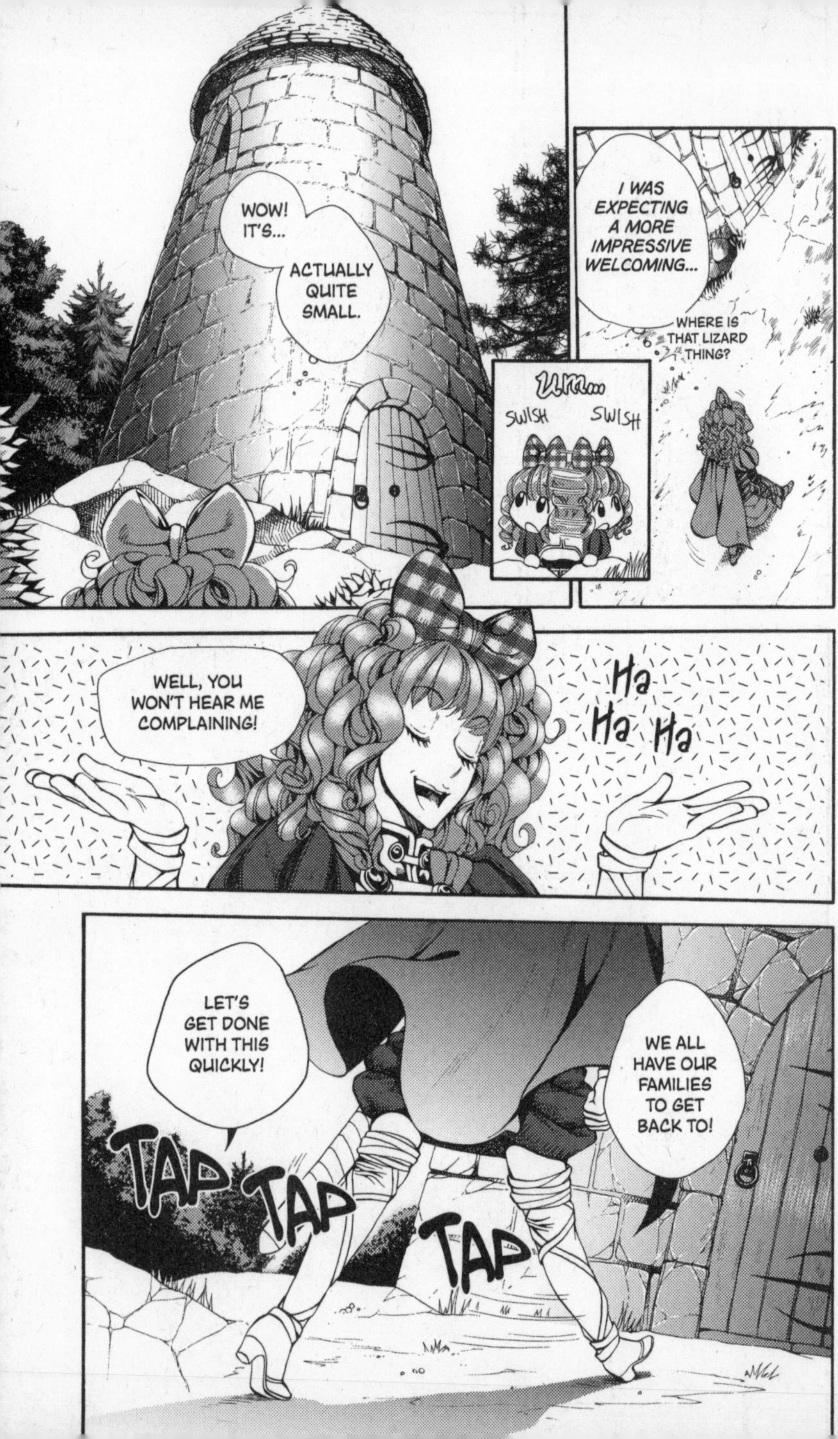
WOW! IT'S...
ACTUALLY QUITE SMALL.
Um...
SWISH
SWISH
I WAS EXPECTING A MORE IMPRESSIVE WELCOMING...
WHERE IS THAT LIZARD THING?
WELL, YOU WON'T HEAR ME COMPLAINING!
Ha Ha Ha
LET'S GET DONE WITH THIS QUICKLY!
WE ALL HAVE OUR FAMILIES TO GET BACK TO!
TAP
TAP
TAP

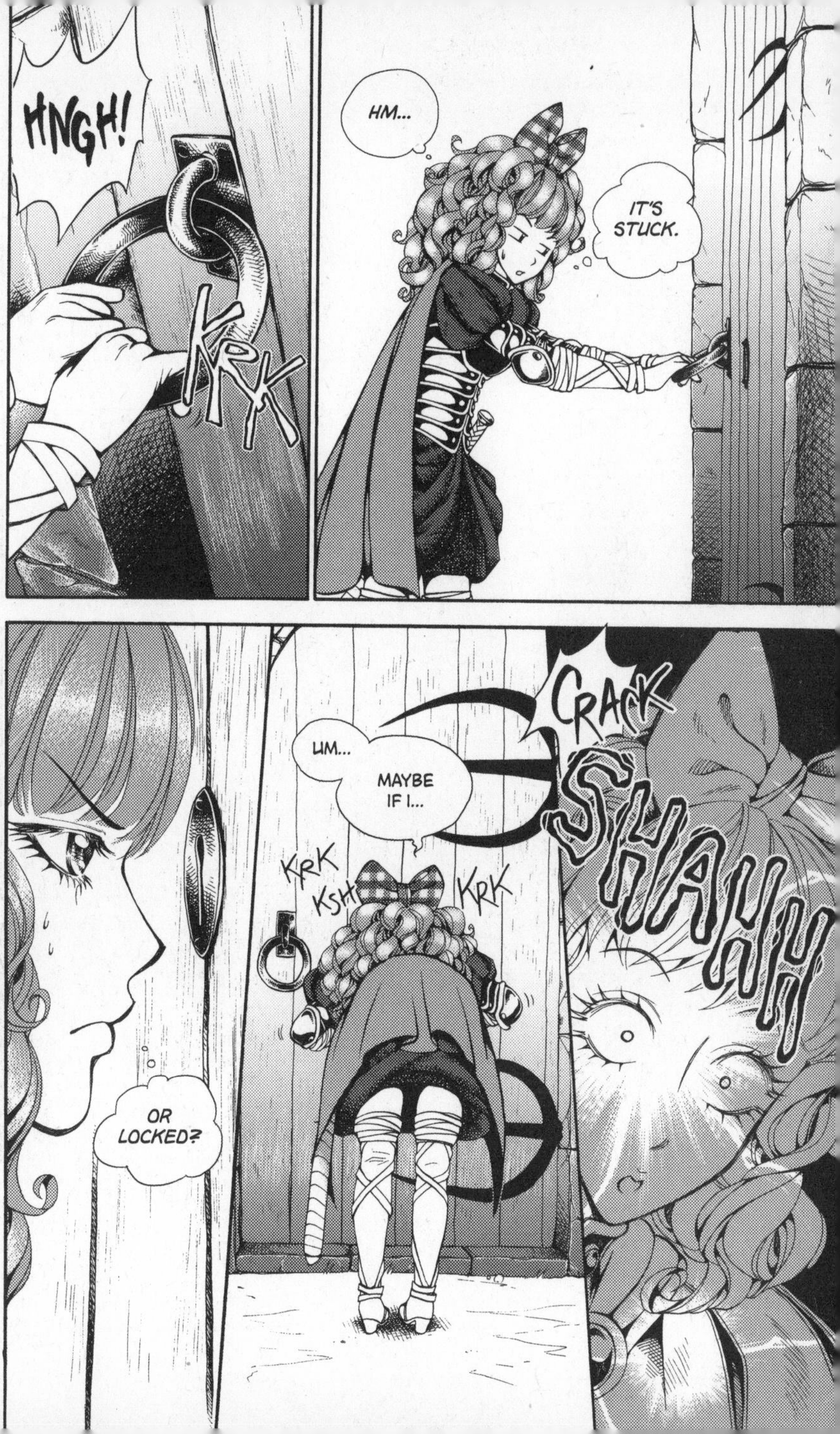
HNGH!
KRK
HM...
IT'S STUCK.
OR LOCKED?
UM...
MAYBE IF I...
KRK
KSH
KRK
CRACK
SHAHH

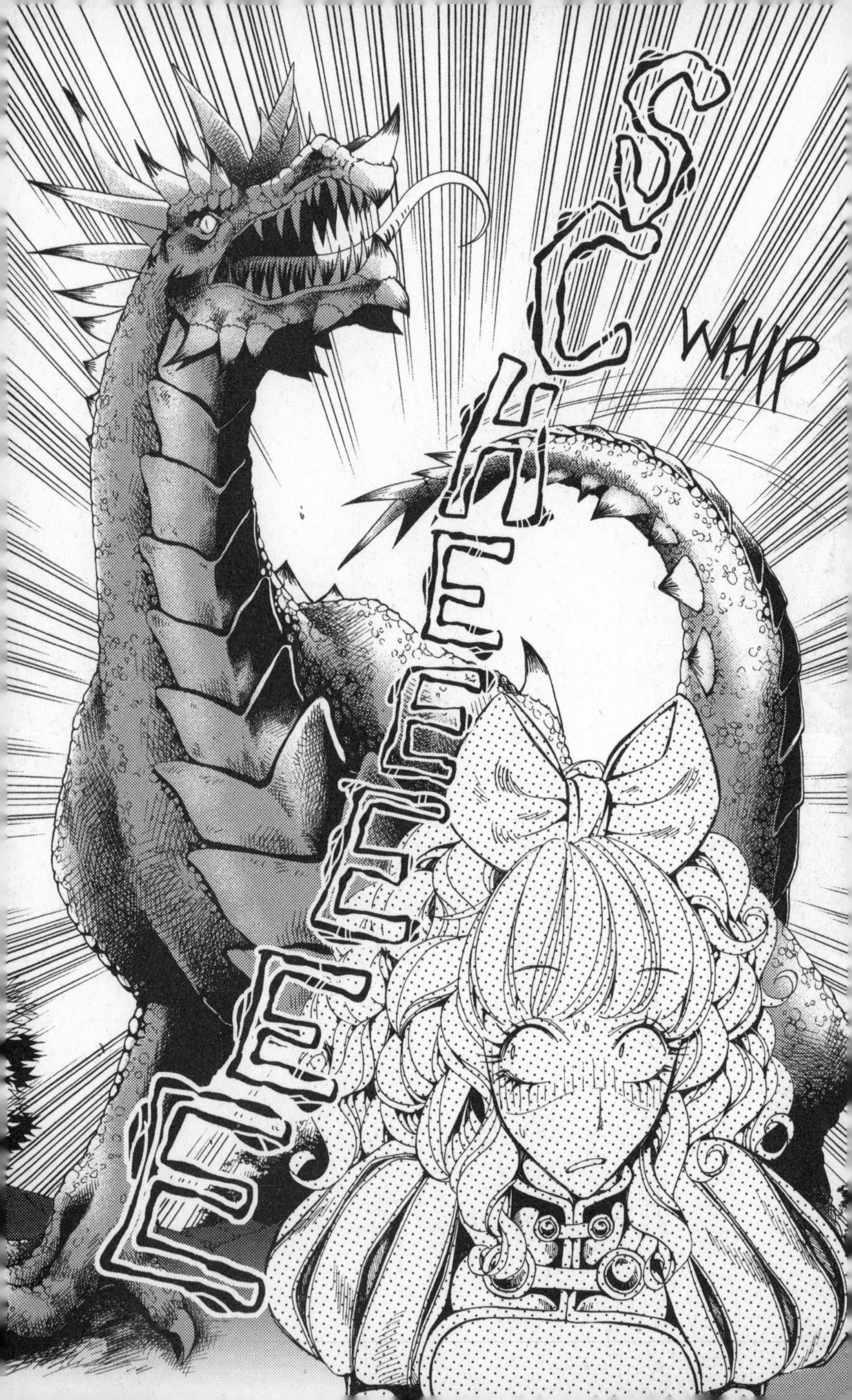
SCHEEEEEE
WHIP

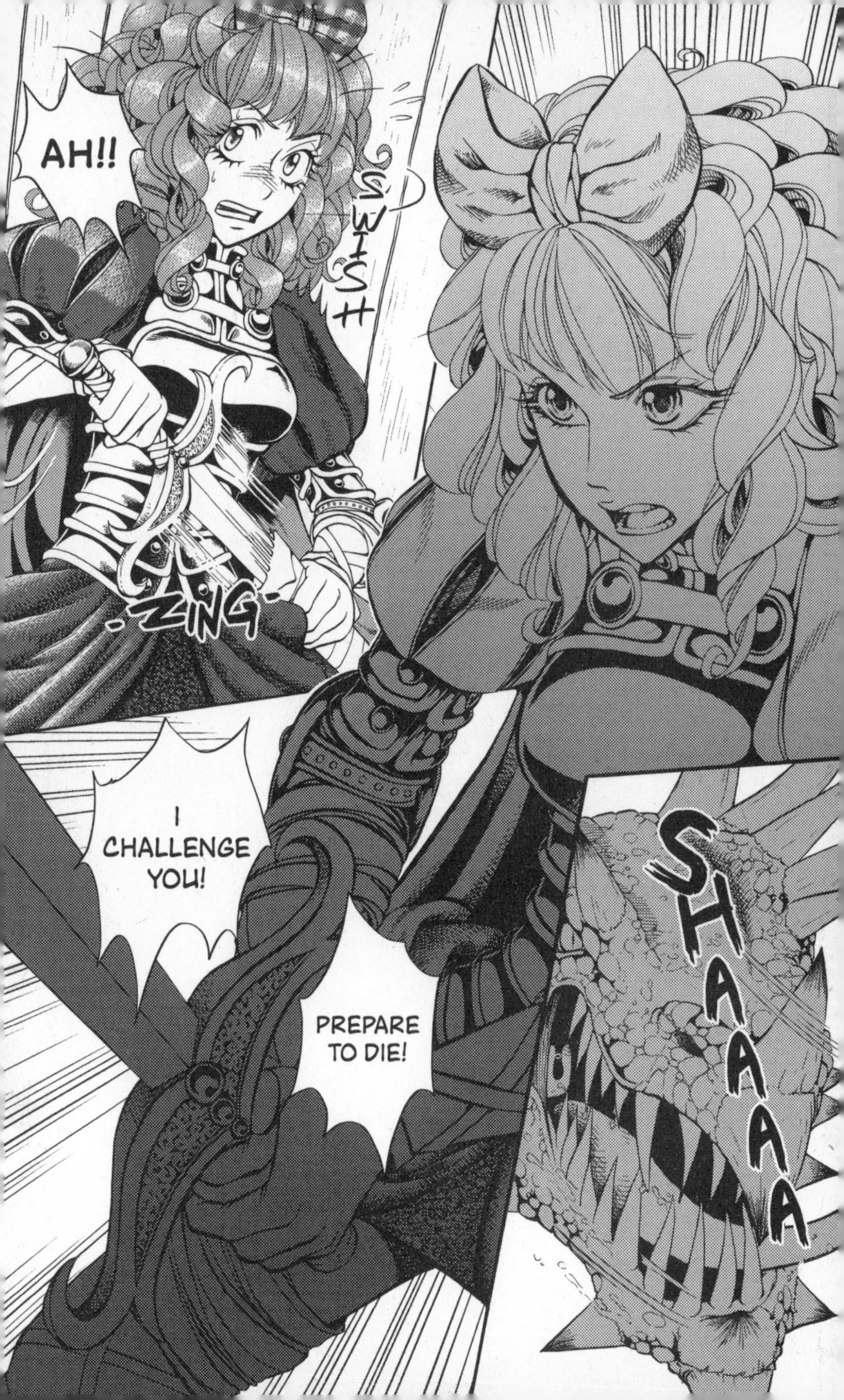
I CHALLENGE YOU!
PREPARE TO DIE!
SHAAAAA
AH!!
SWISH
ZING

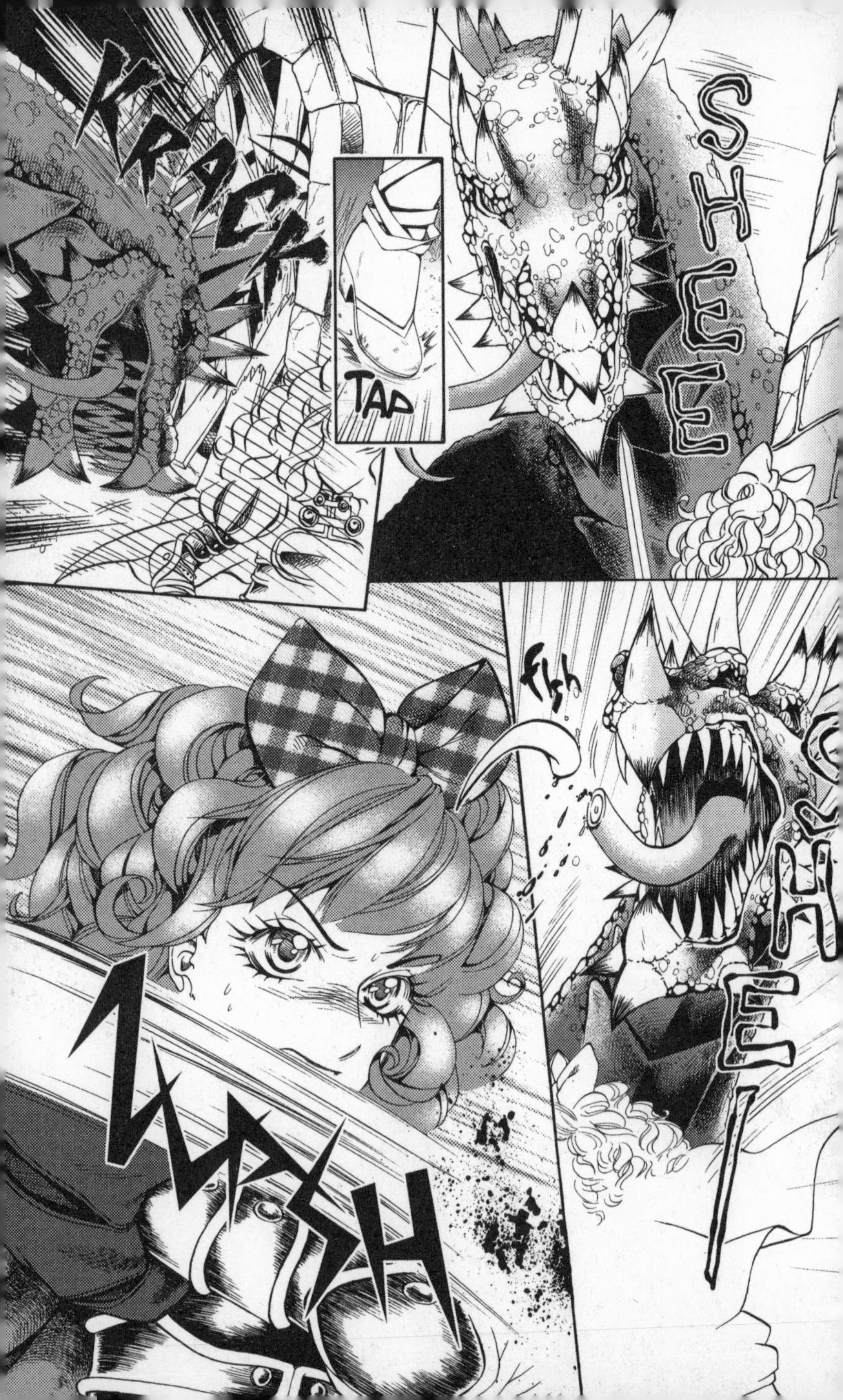
KRACK
TAP
SHEEE
WASH
flsh
SHE!

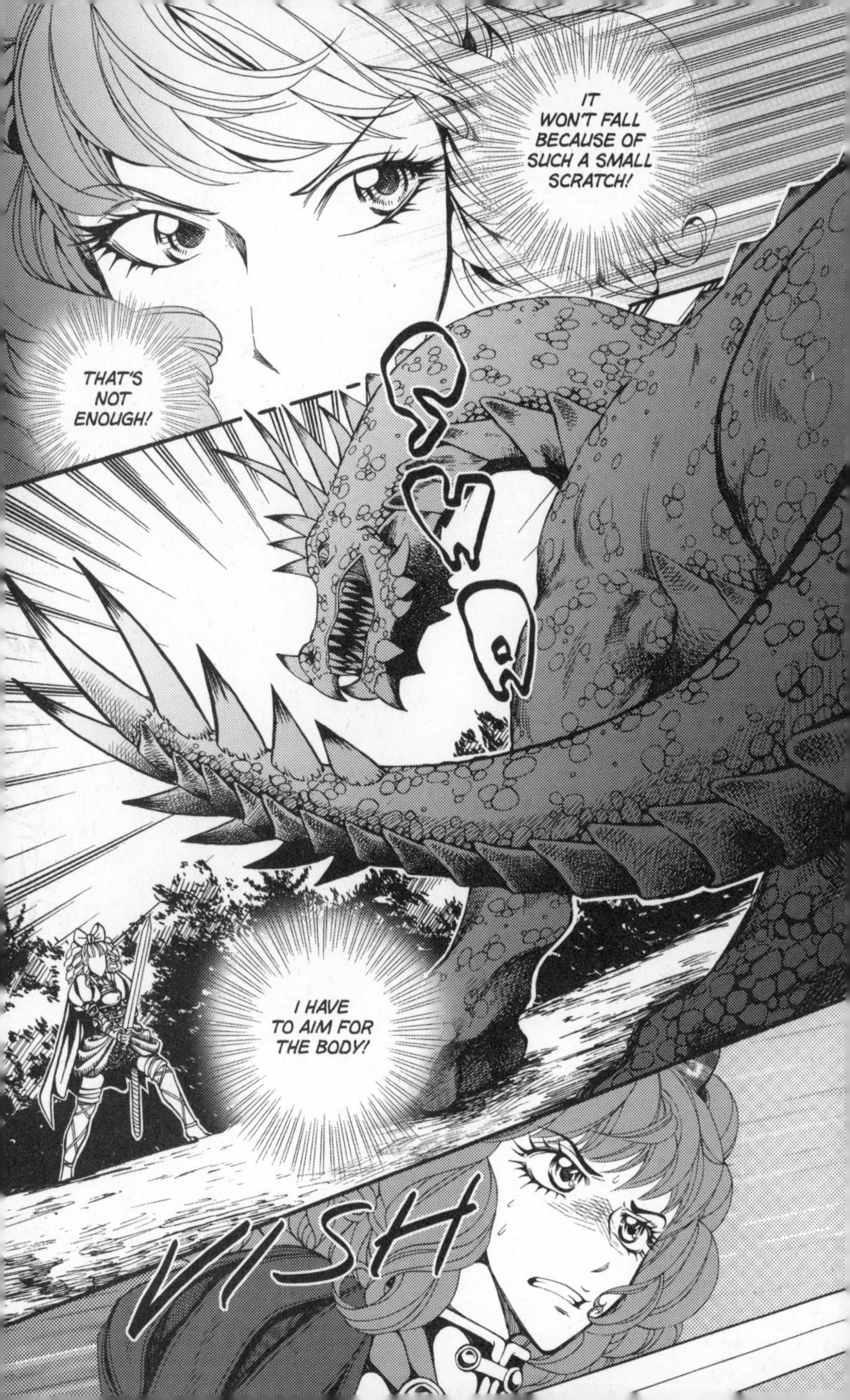
IT WON'T FALL BECAUSE OF SUCH A SMALL SCRATCH!
THAT'S NOT ENOUGH!
I HAVE TO AIM FOR THE BODY!
VISH

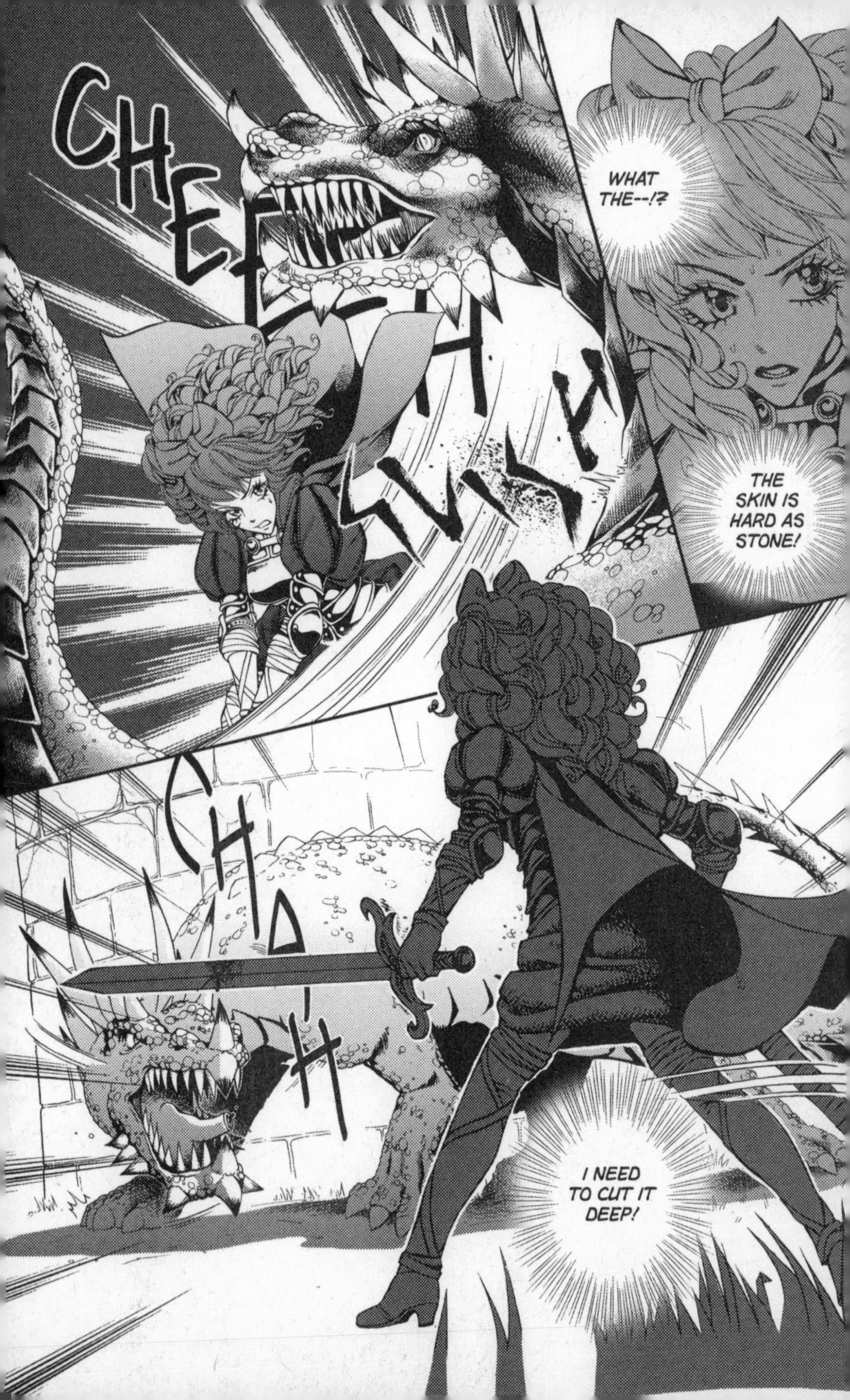
WHAT THE--!?
THE SKIN IS HARD AS STONE!
I NEED TO CUT IT DEEP!

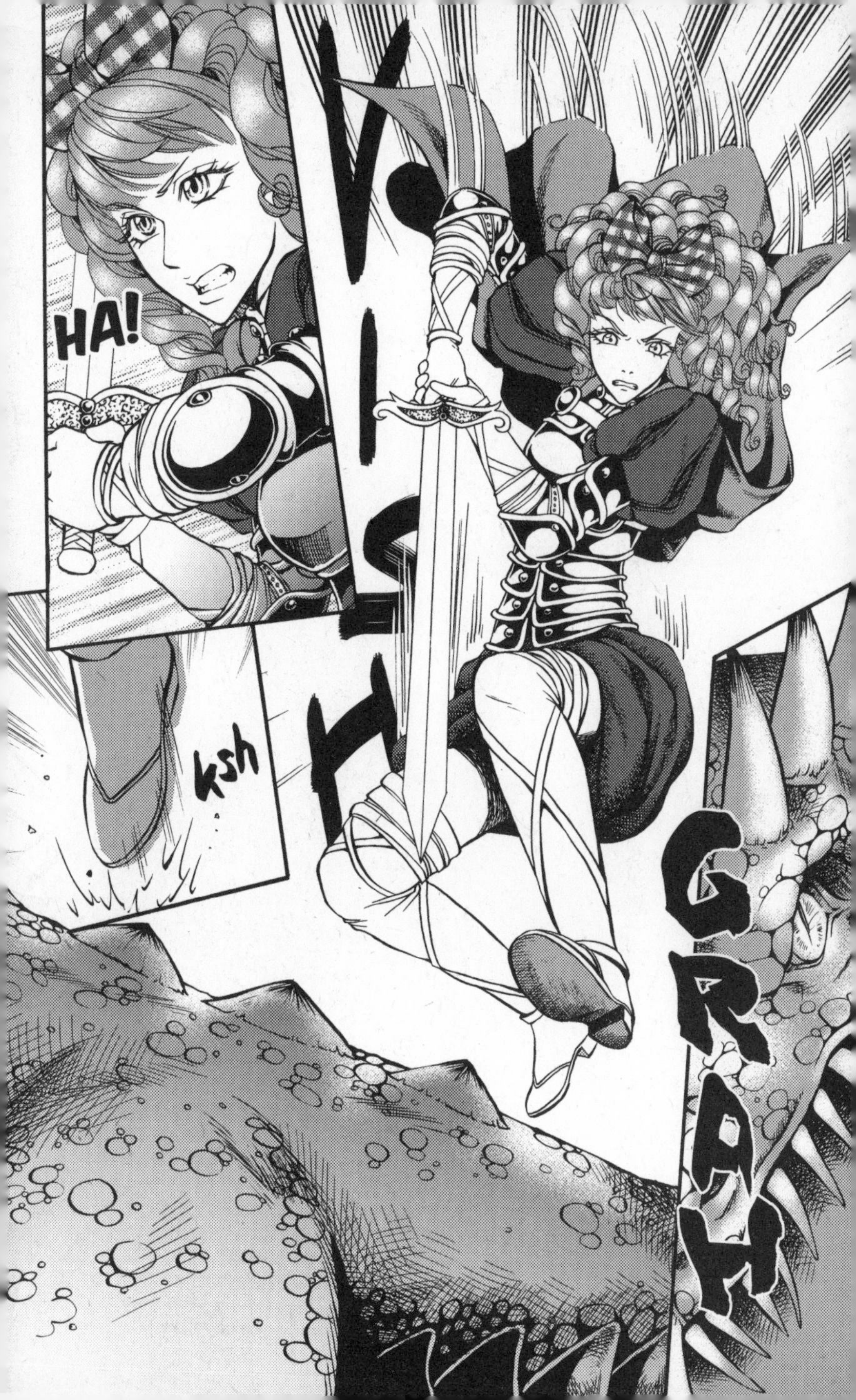

HA!
VISH
ksh
GRAAH

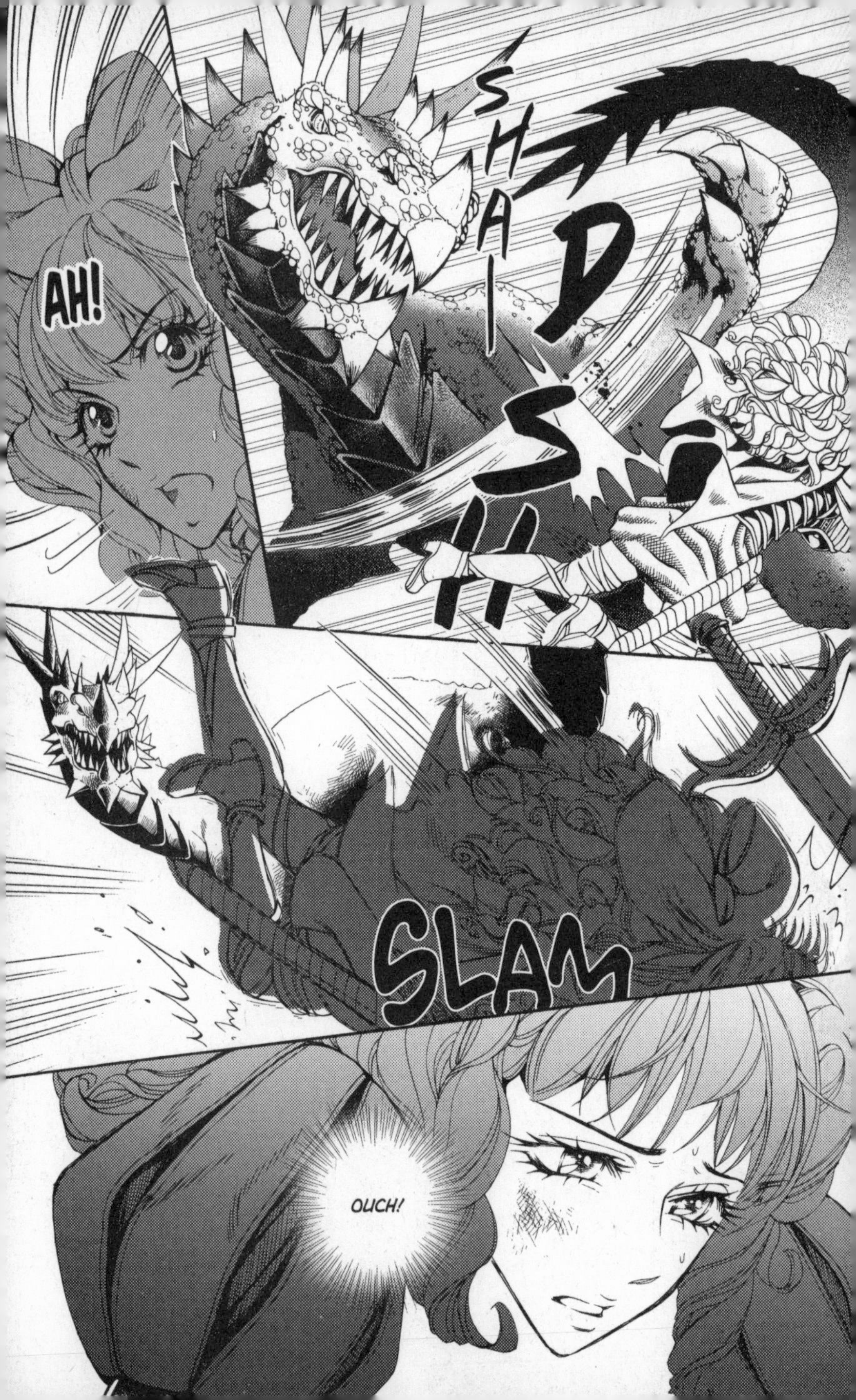
AH!
SHA
DSH
SLAM
OUCH!

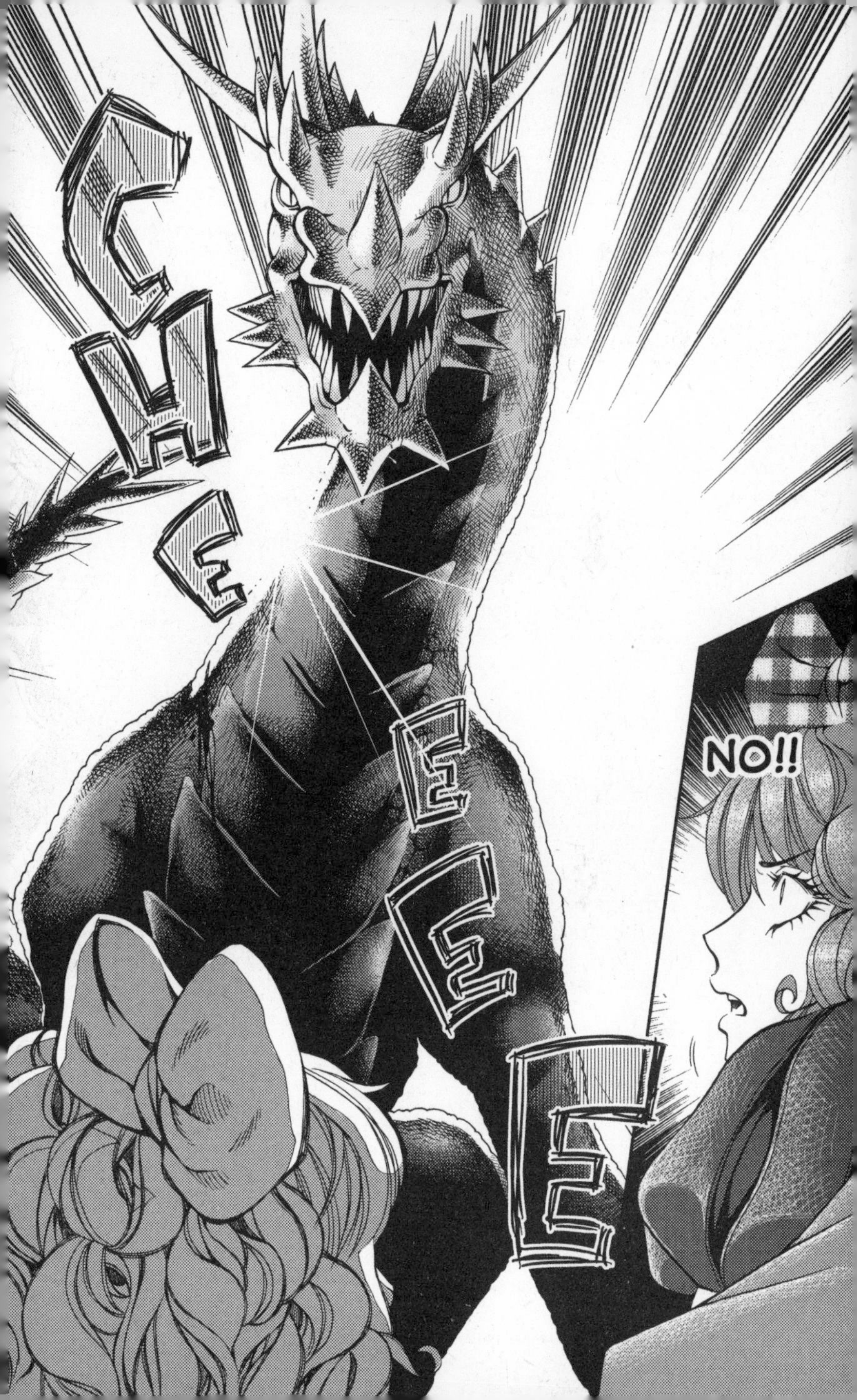
CHEEEE
NO!!

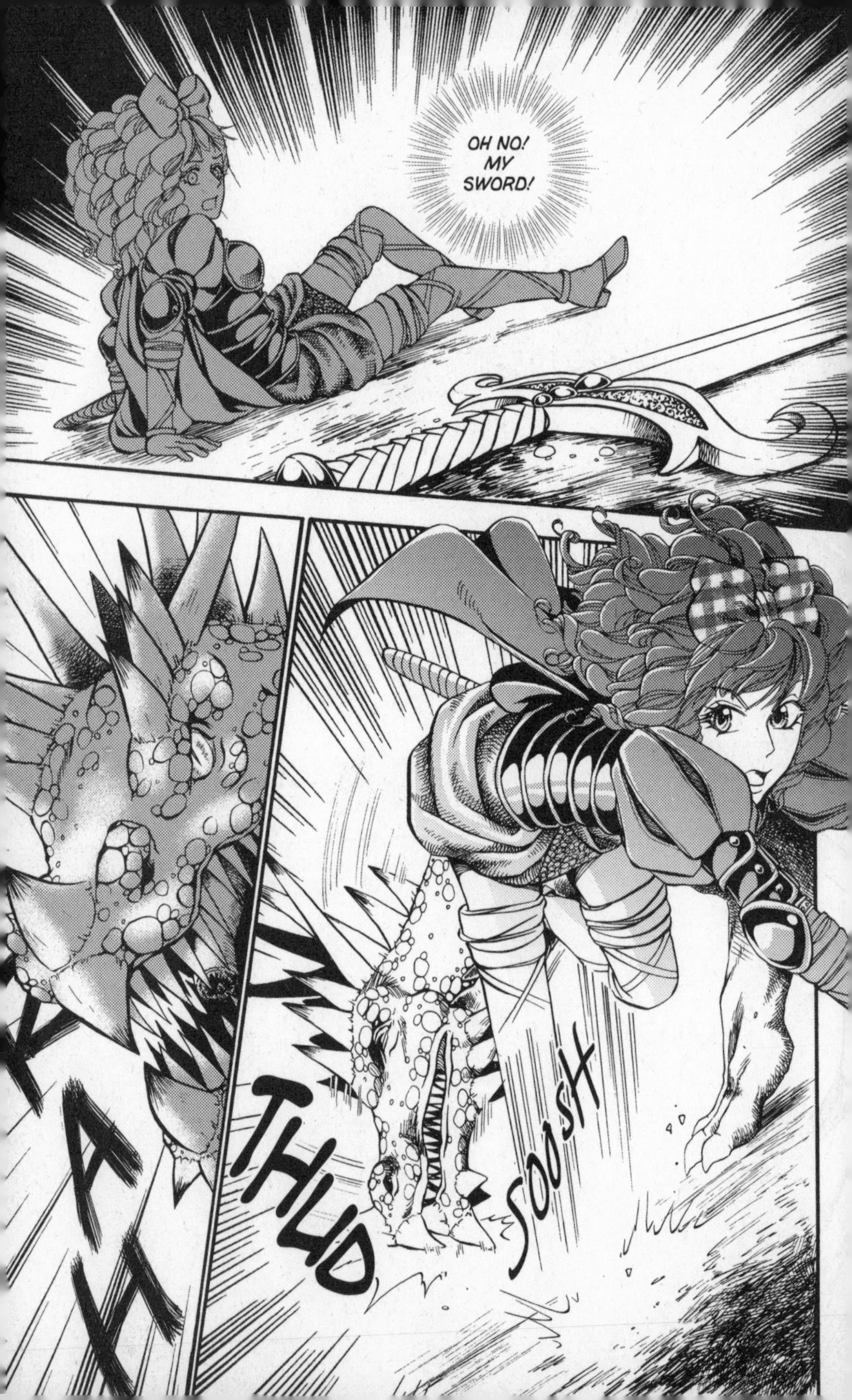

OH NO! MY SWORD!
AAH
THUD
SOOSH

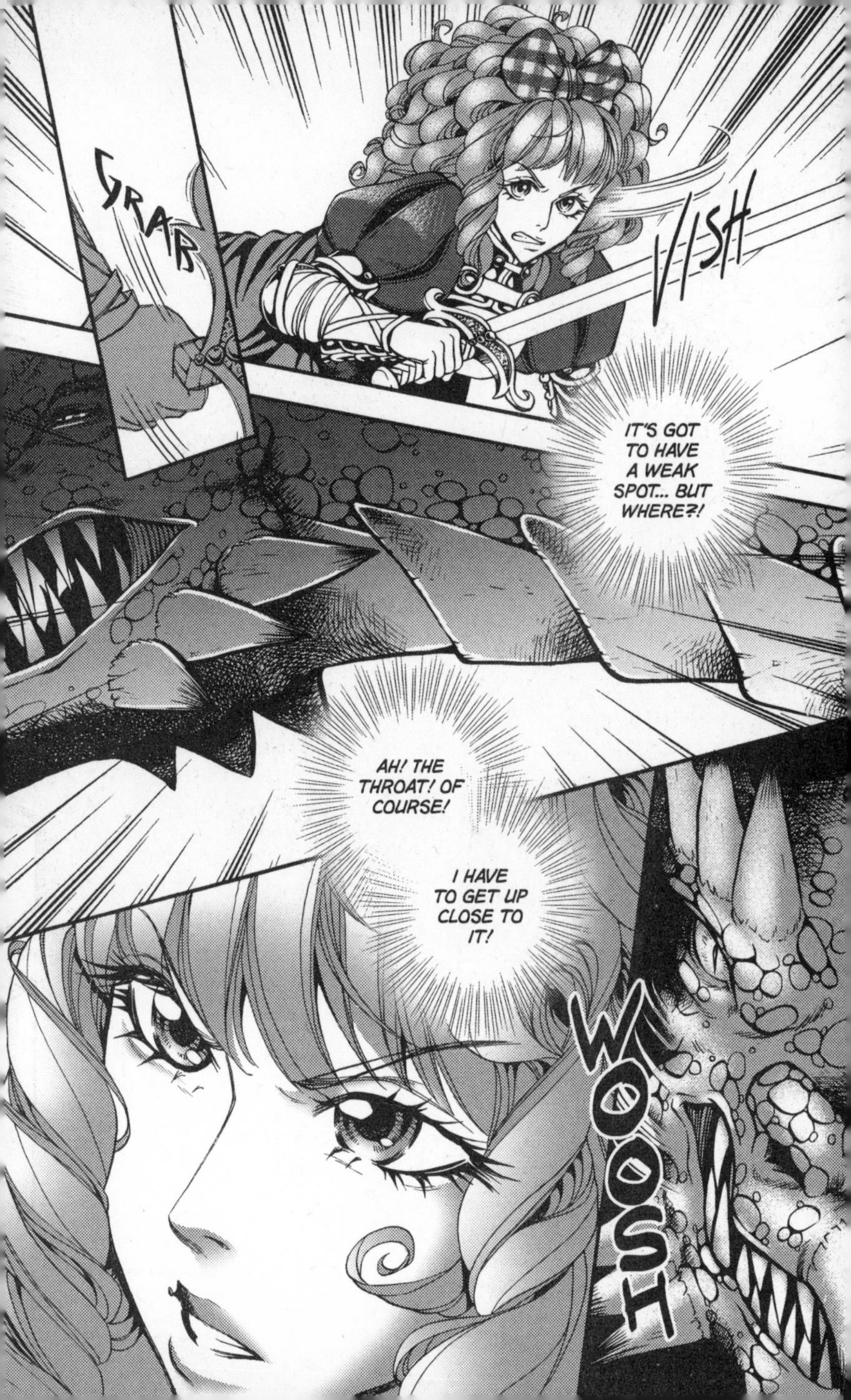
GRAB
VISH
IT'S GOT TO HAVE A WEAK SPOT... BUT WHERE?!
AH! THE THROAT! OF COURSE!
I HAVE TO GET UP CLOSE TO IT!
WOOOSH

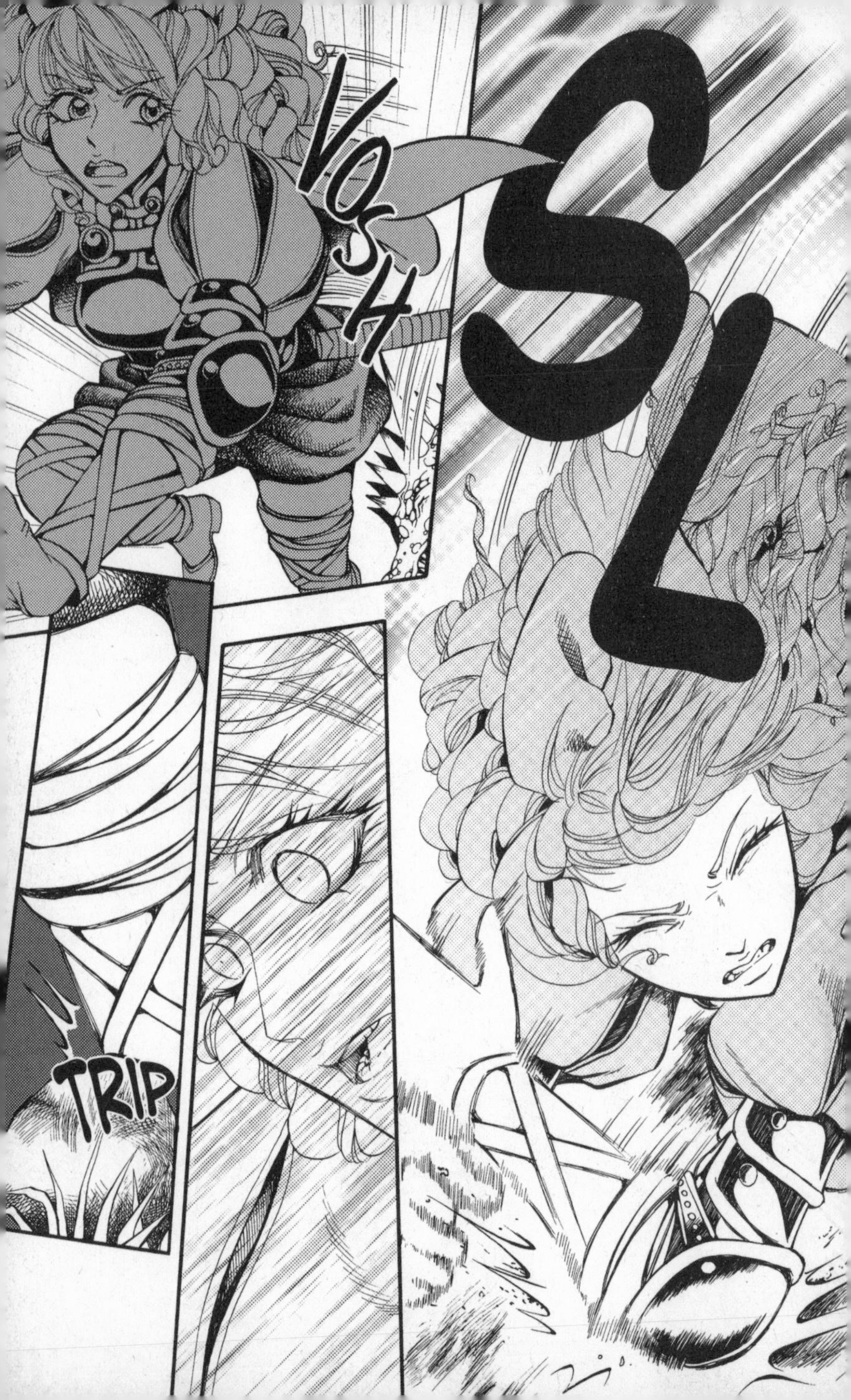
VOSH
SL
TRIP

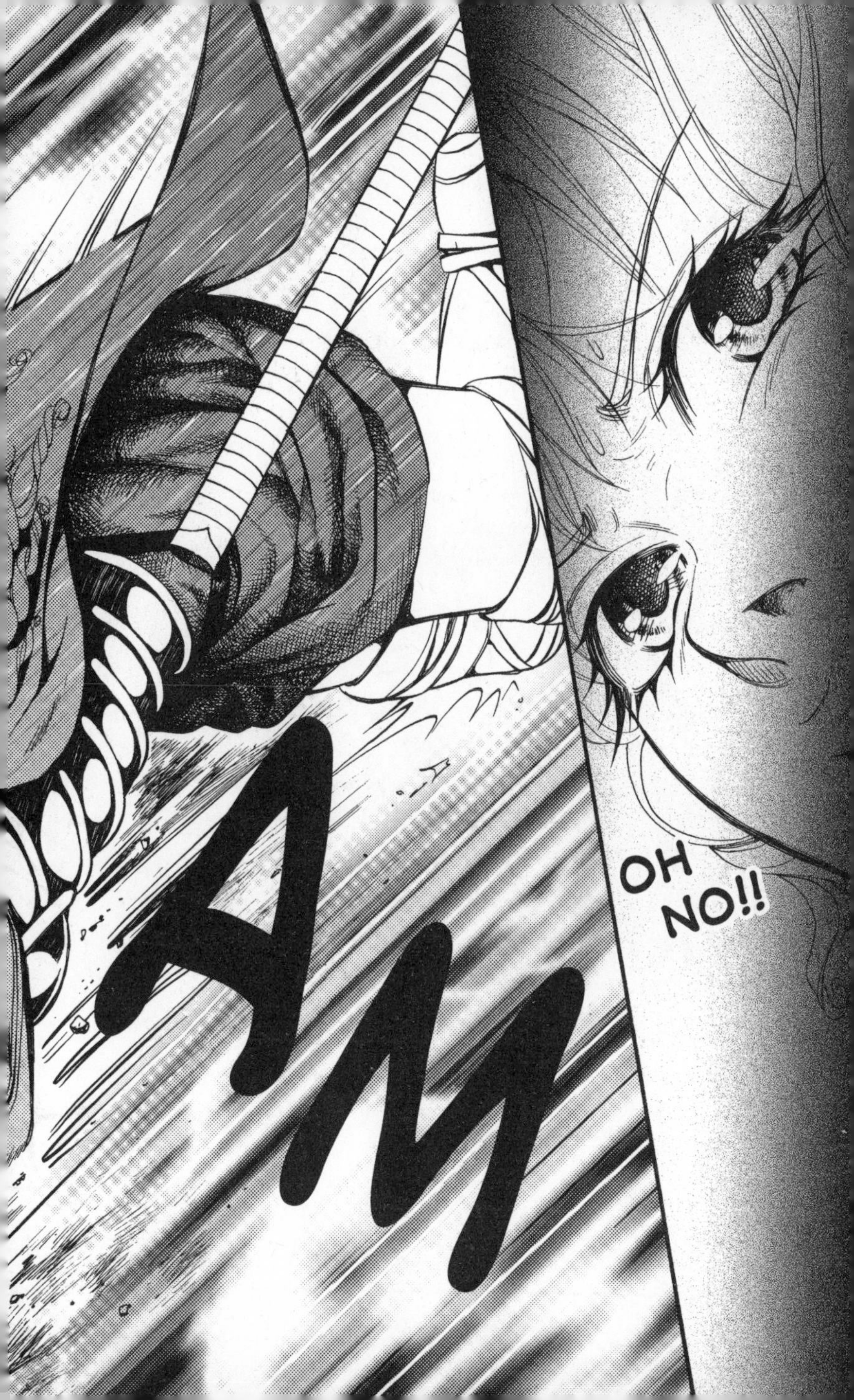
OH NO!!

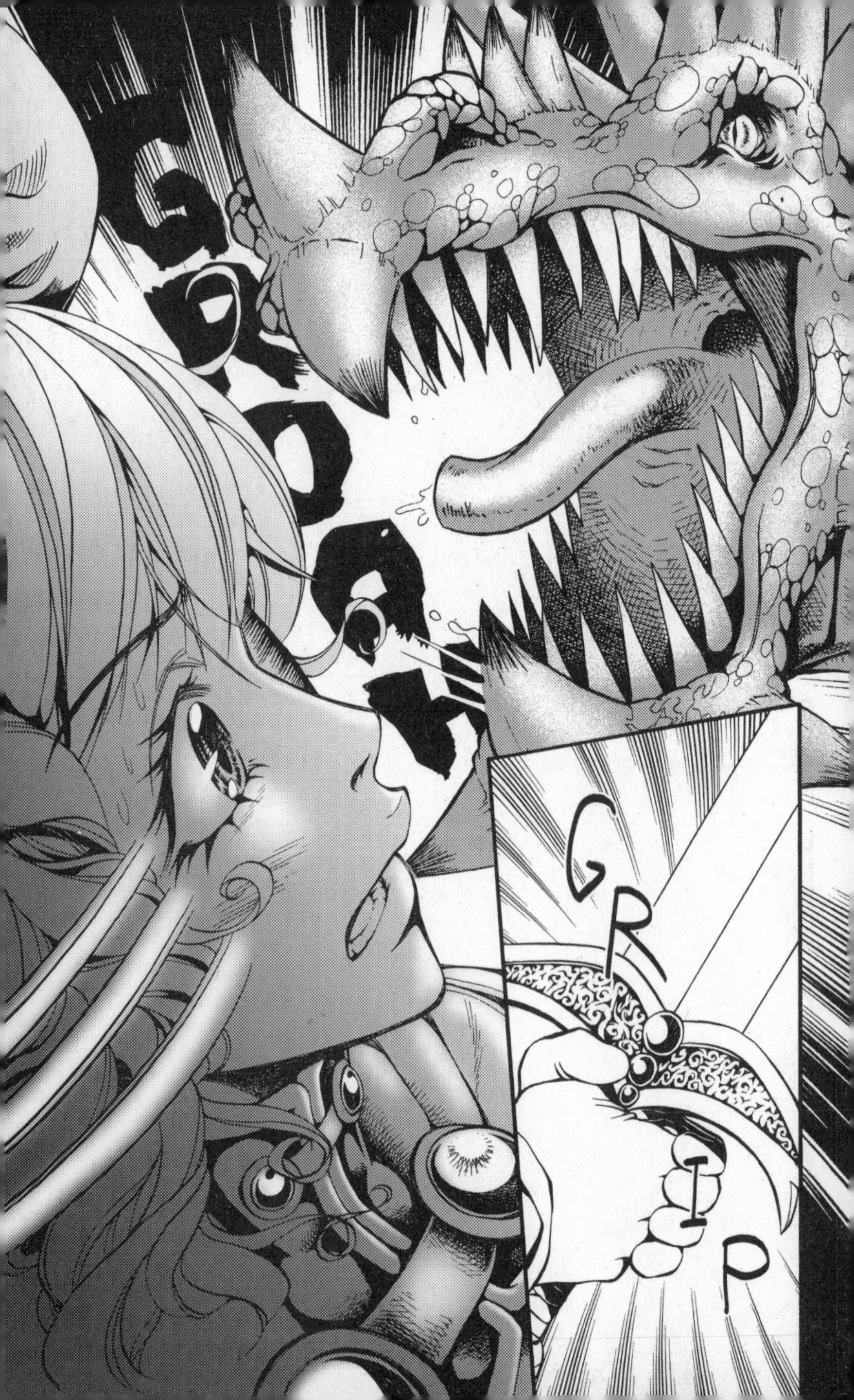
GRIP

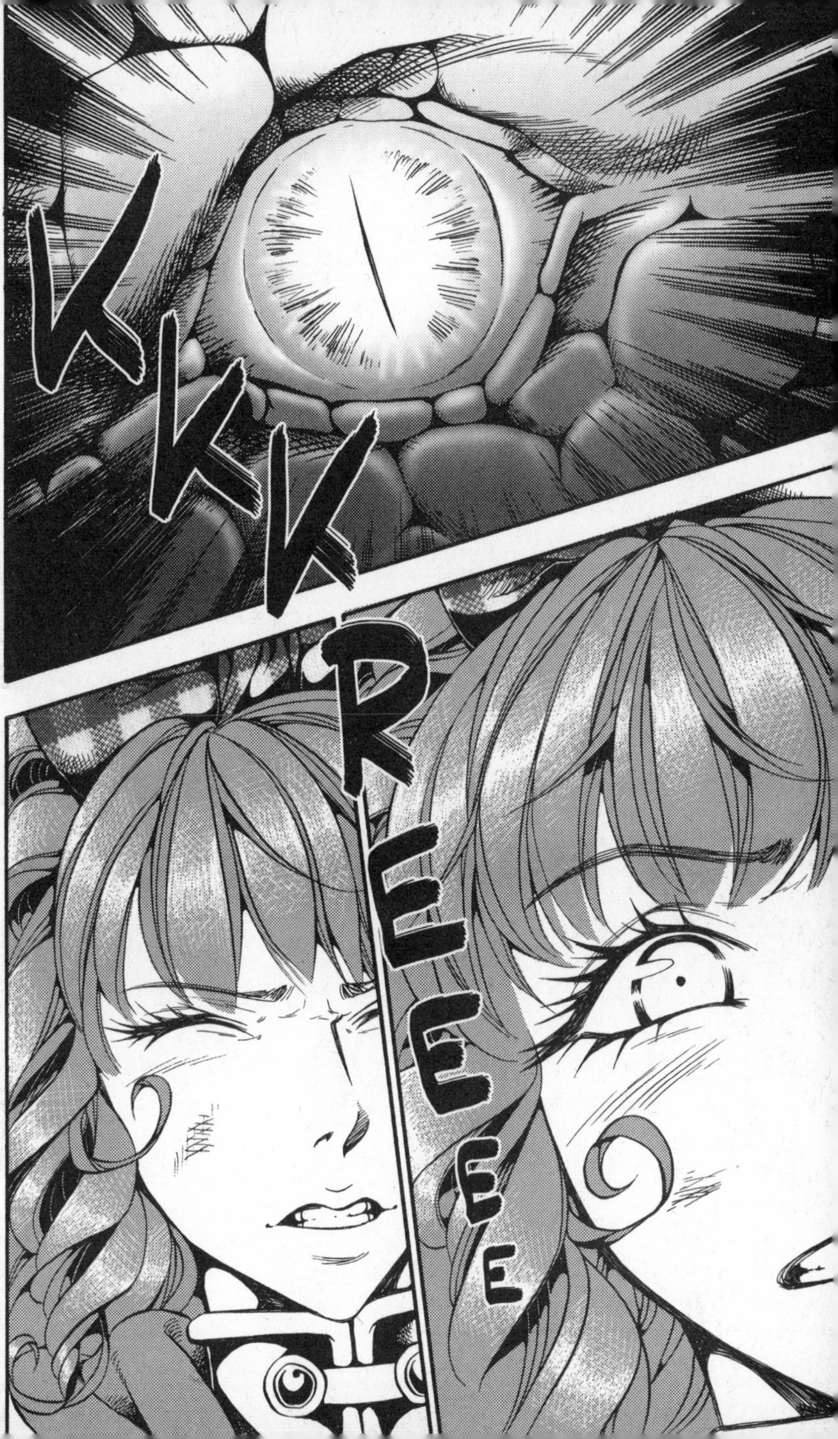
KKKKREEEEEE

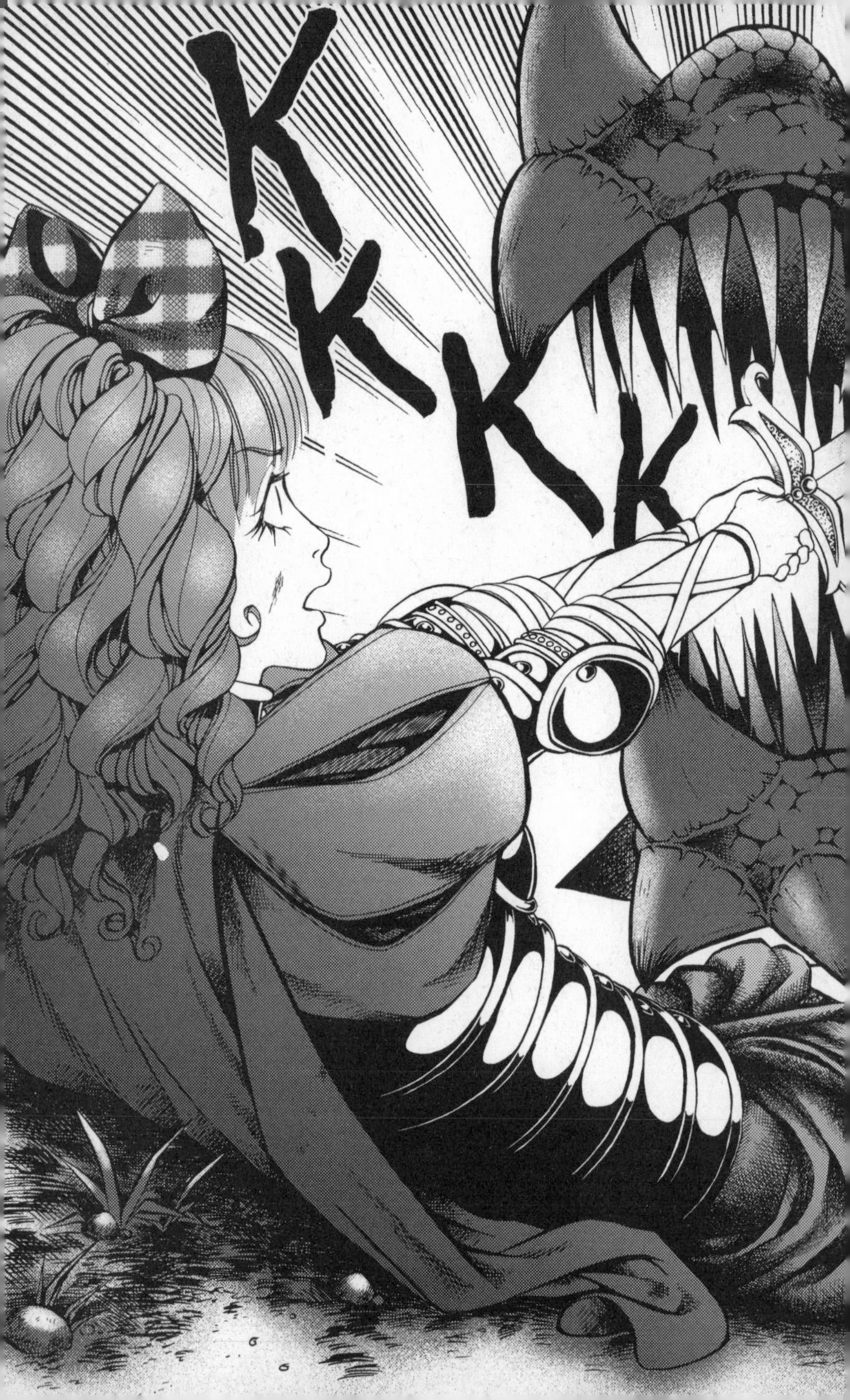
KKKK

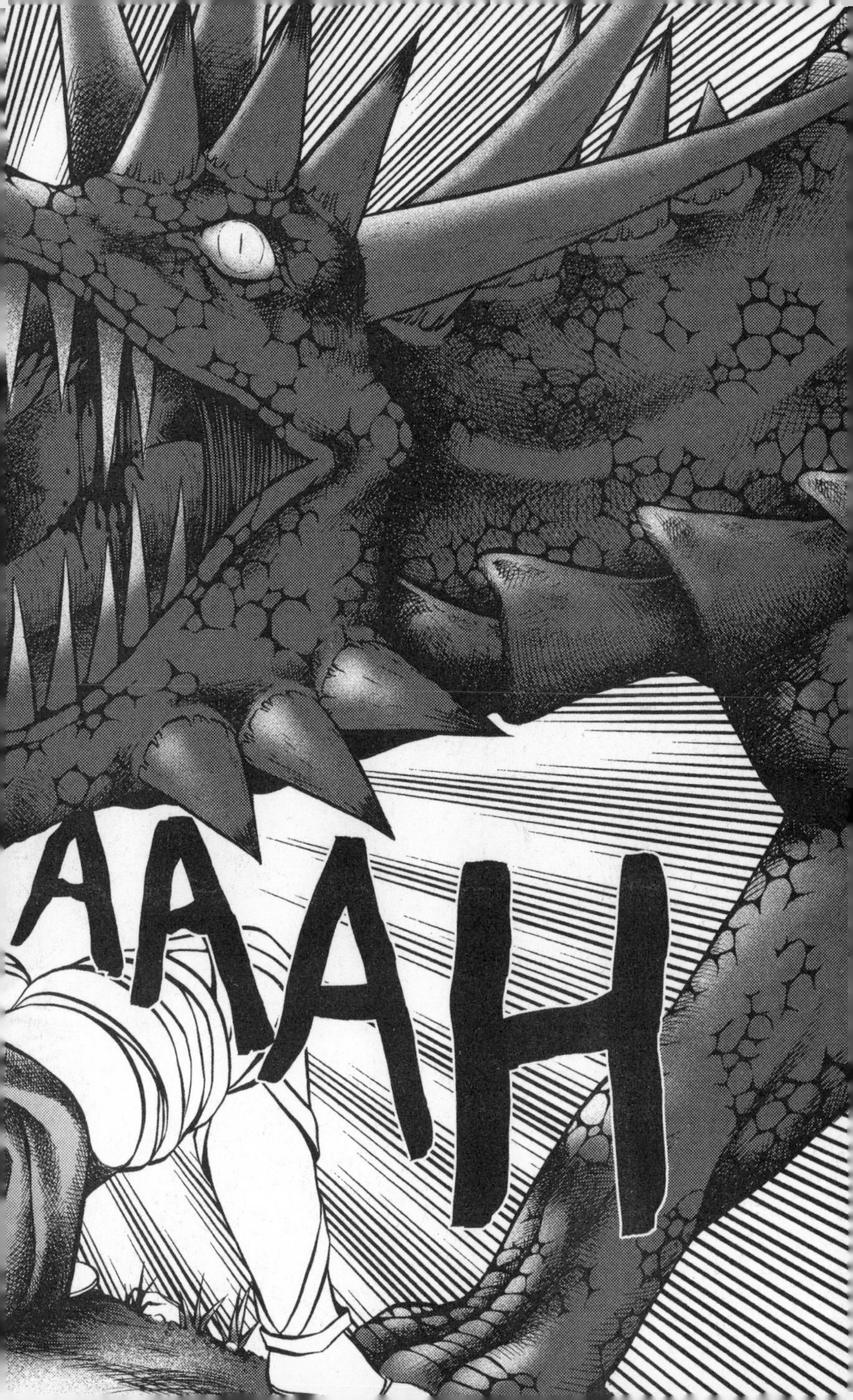
AAAH

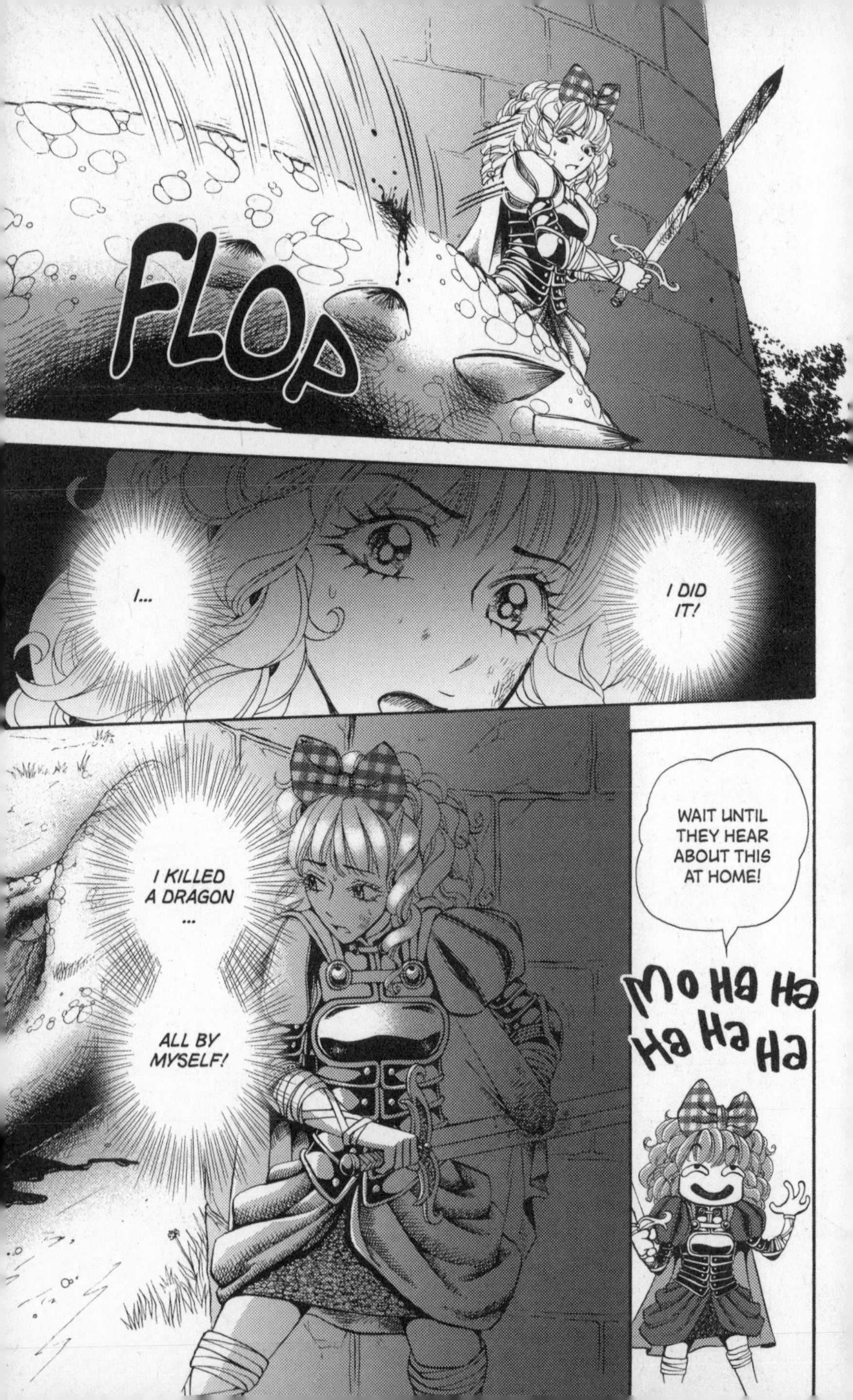
FLOP
I...
I DID IT!
I KILLED A DRAGON ...
ALL BY MYSELF!
WAIT UNTIL THEY HEAR ABOUT THIS AT HOME!
MO HA HA HA HA HA

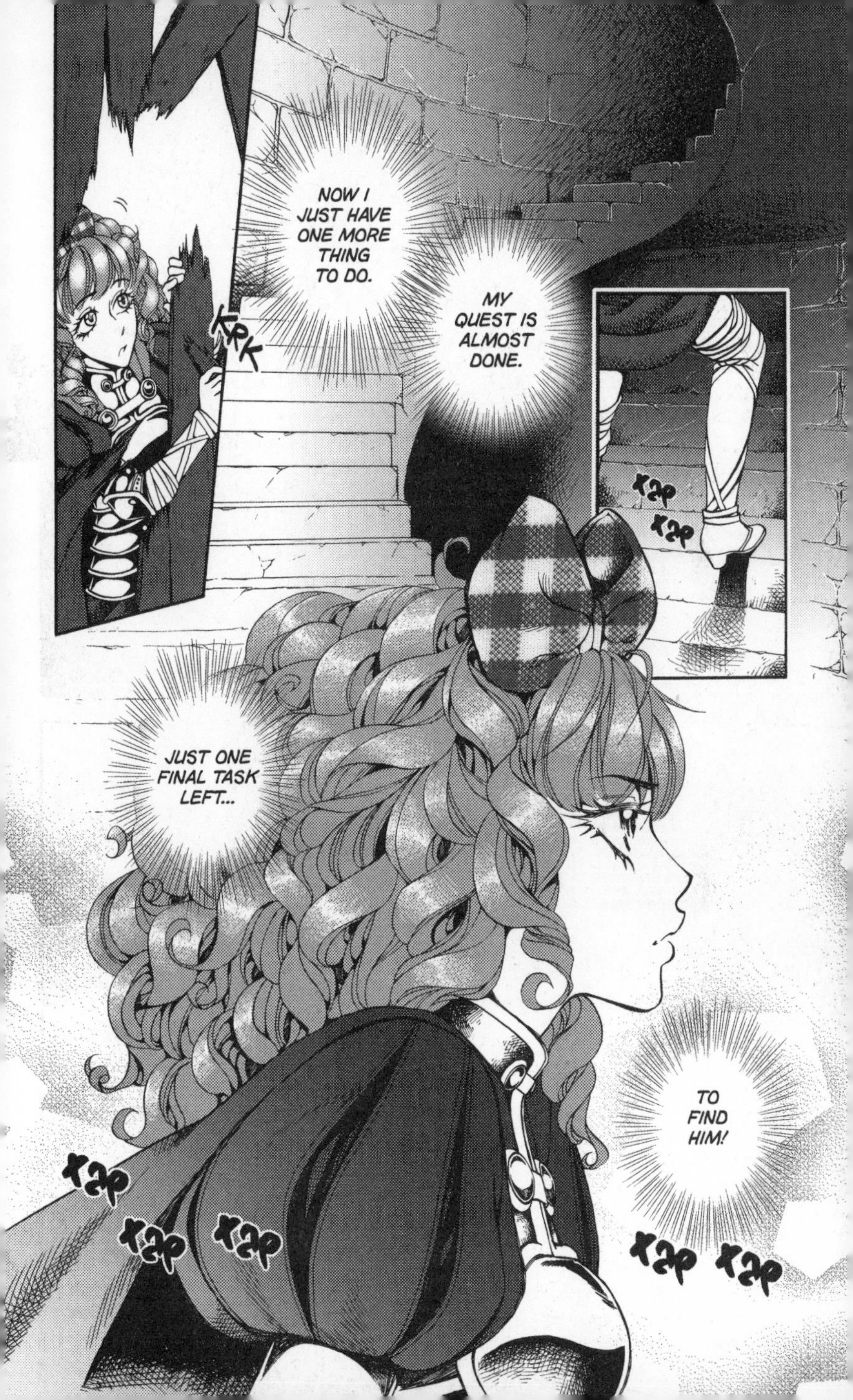
KRK
NOW I JUST HAVE ONE MORE THING TO DO.
MY QUEST IS ALMOST DONE.
TAP
TAP
JUST ONE FINAL TASK LEFT...
TO FIND HIM!
TAP
TAP TAP
TAP TAP

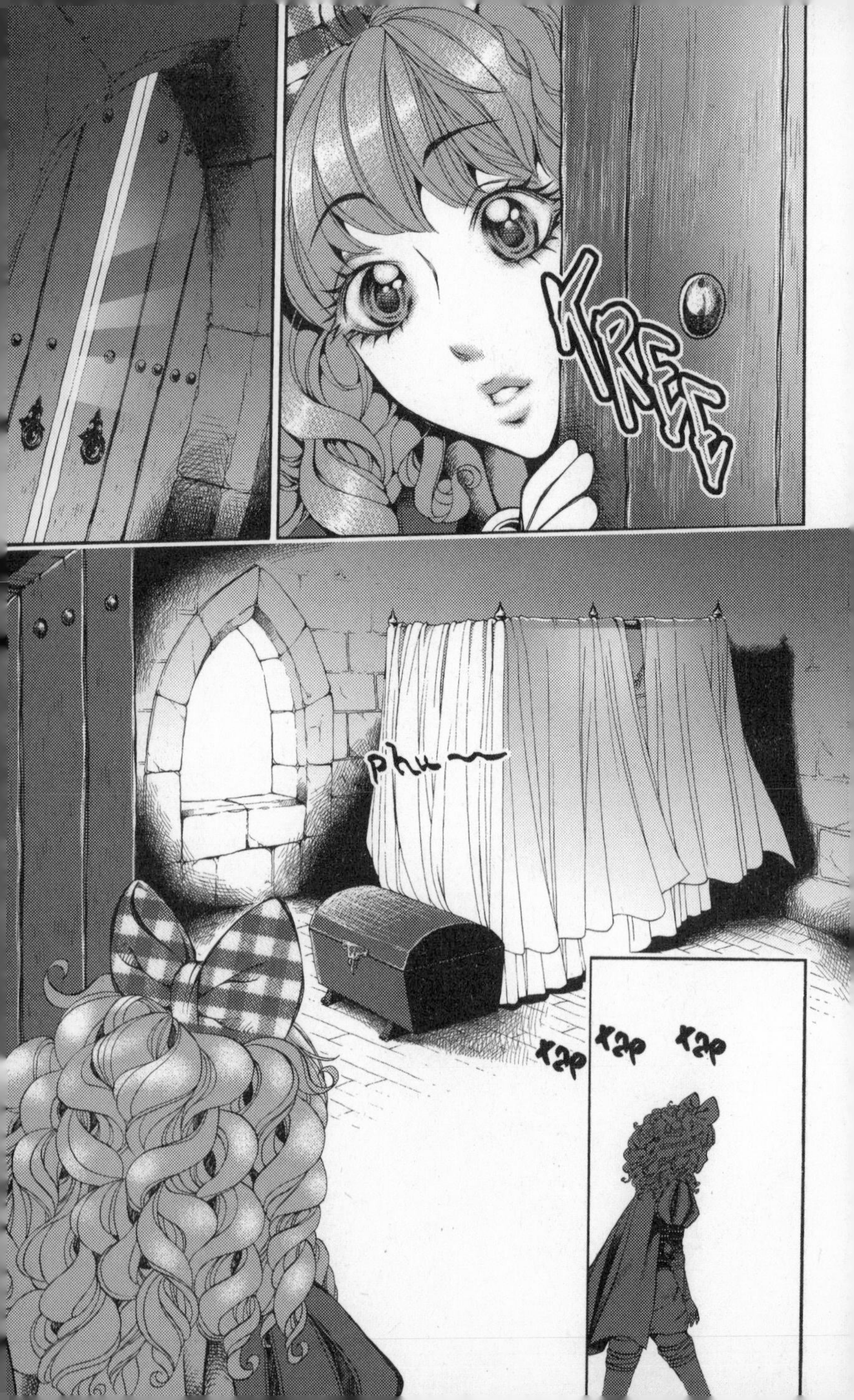
KREEE
phu~~
tap
tap
tap

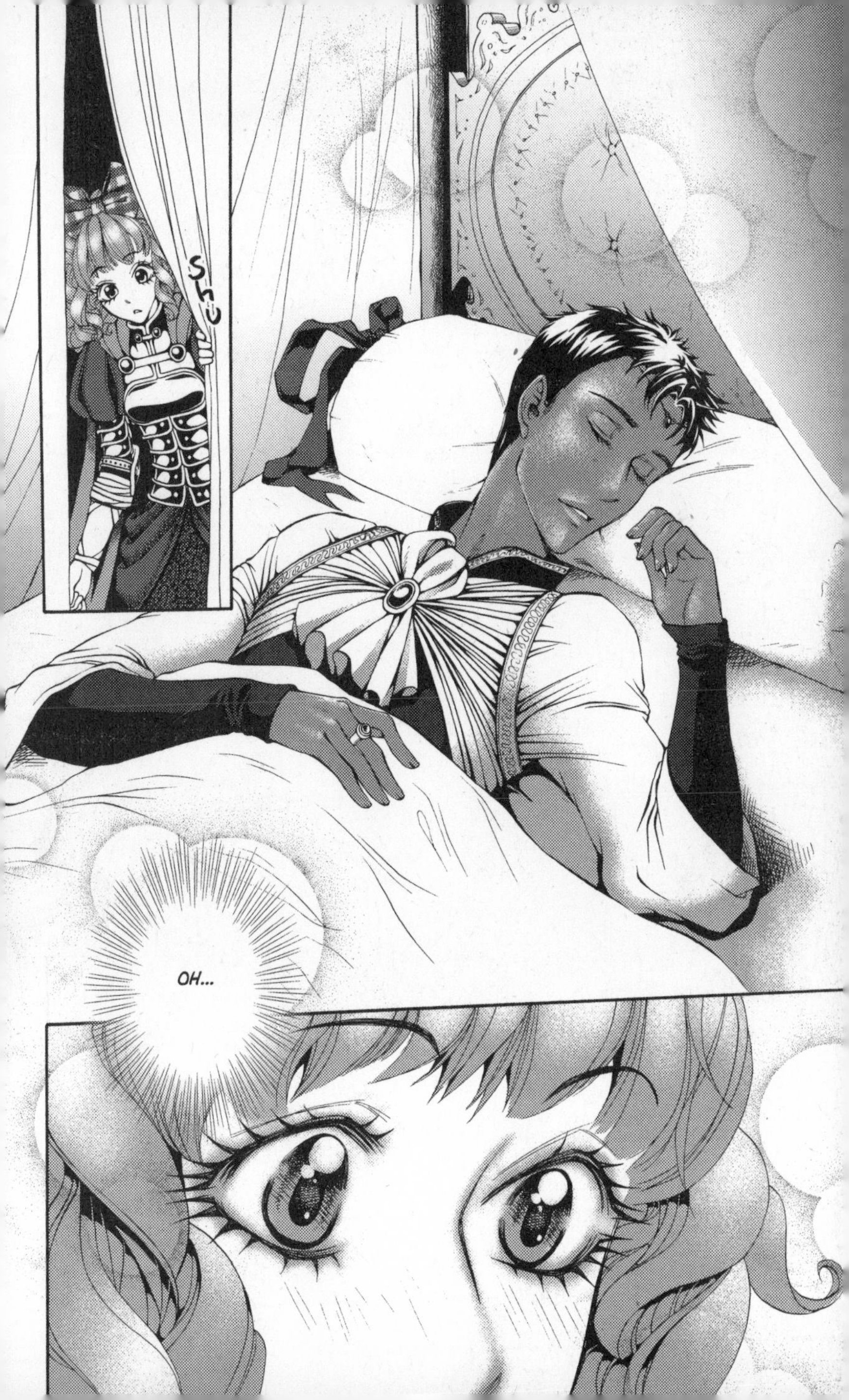
SHU
OH...

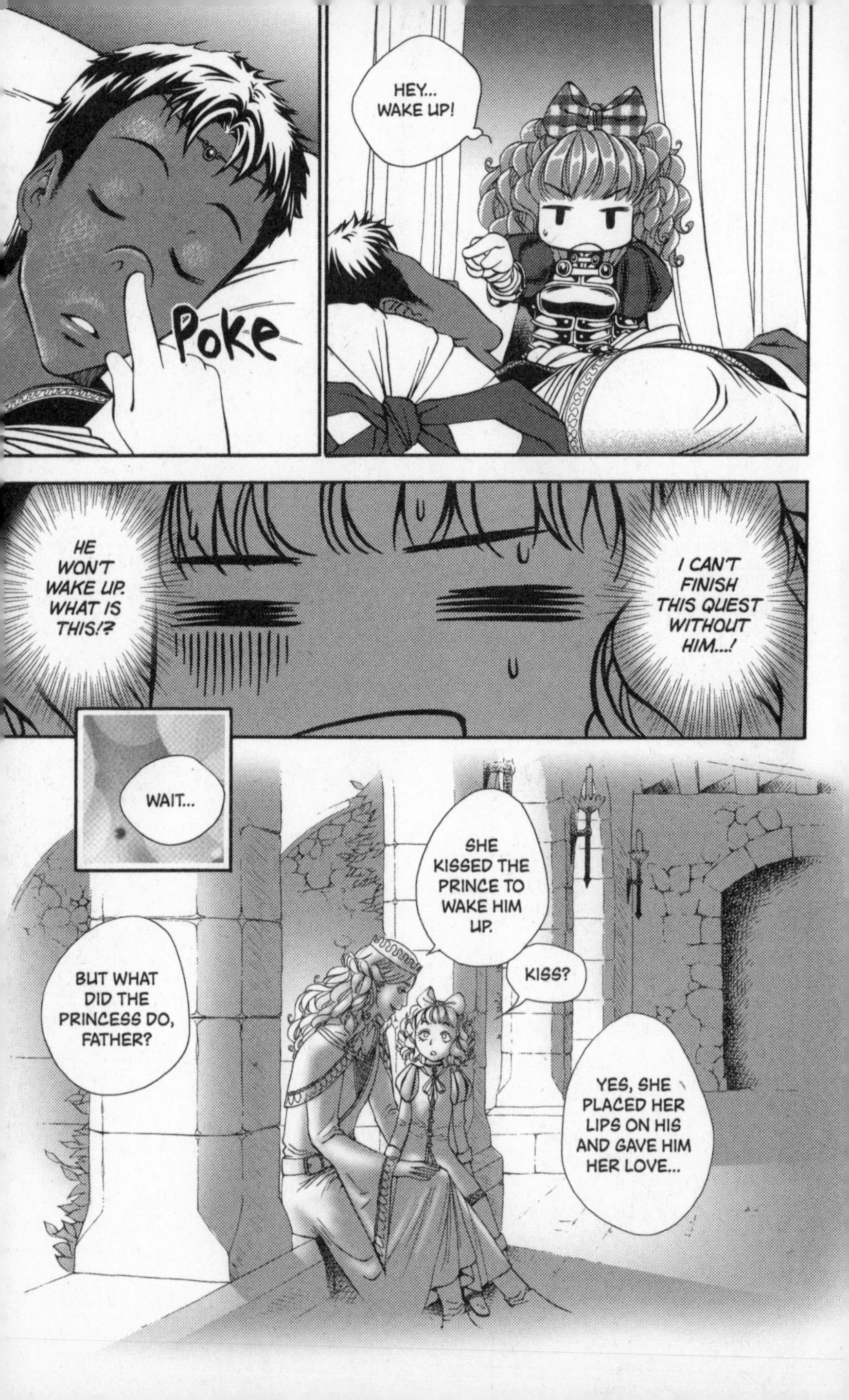
POKE
HEY... WAKE UP!
HE WON'T WAKE UP. WHAT IS THIS!?
I CAN'T FINISH THIS QUEST WITHOUT HIM...!
WAIT...
BUT WHAT DID THE PRINCESS DO, FATHER?
SHE KISSED THE PRINCE TO WAKE HIM UP.
KISS?
YES, SHE PLACED HER LIPS ON HIS AND GAVE HIM HER LOVE...

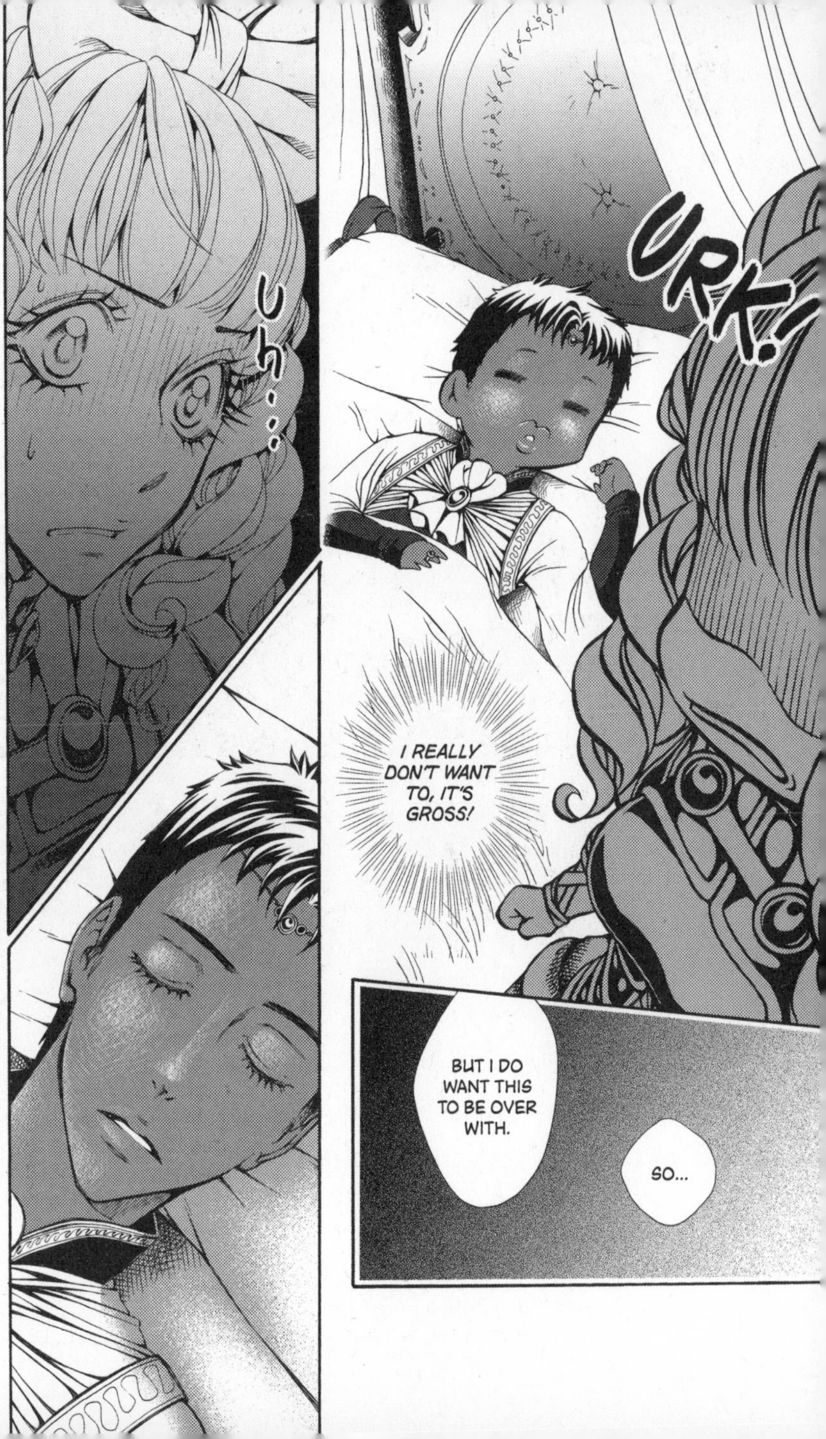
URK!
I REALLY DON'T WANT TO, IT'S GROSS!
BUT I DO WANT THIS TO BE OVER WITH.
SO...

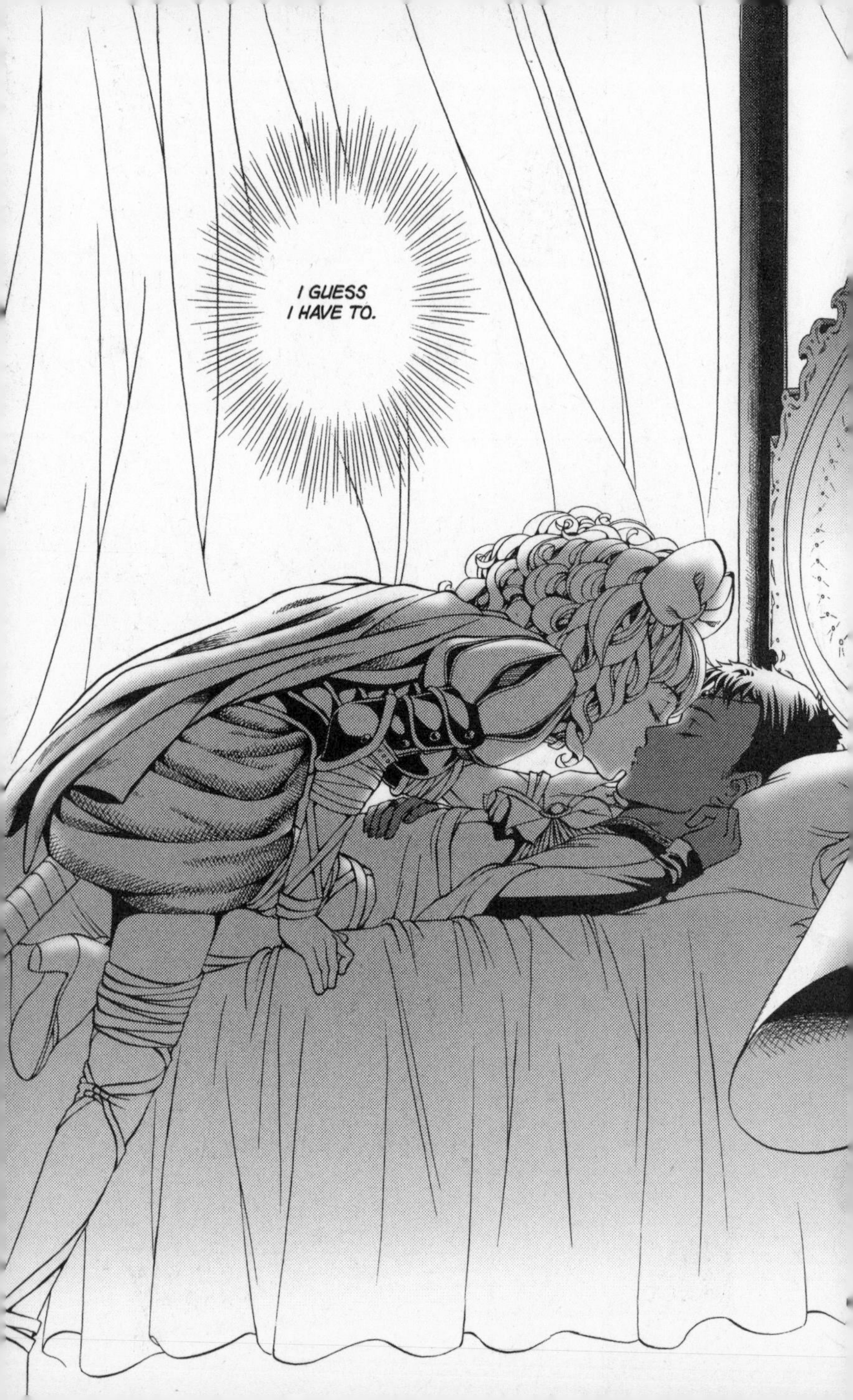
I GUESS
I HAVE TO.

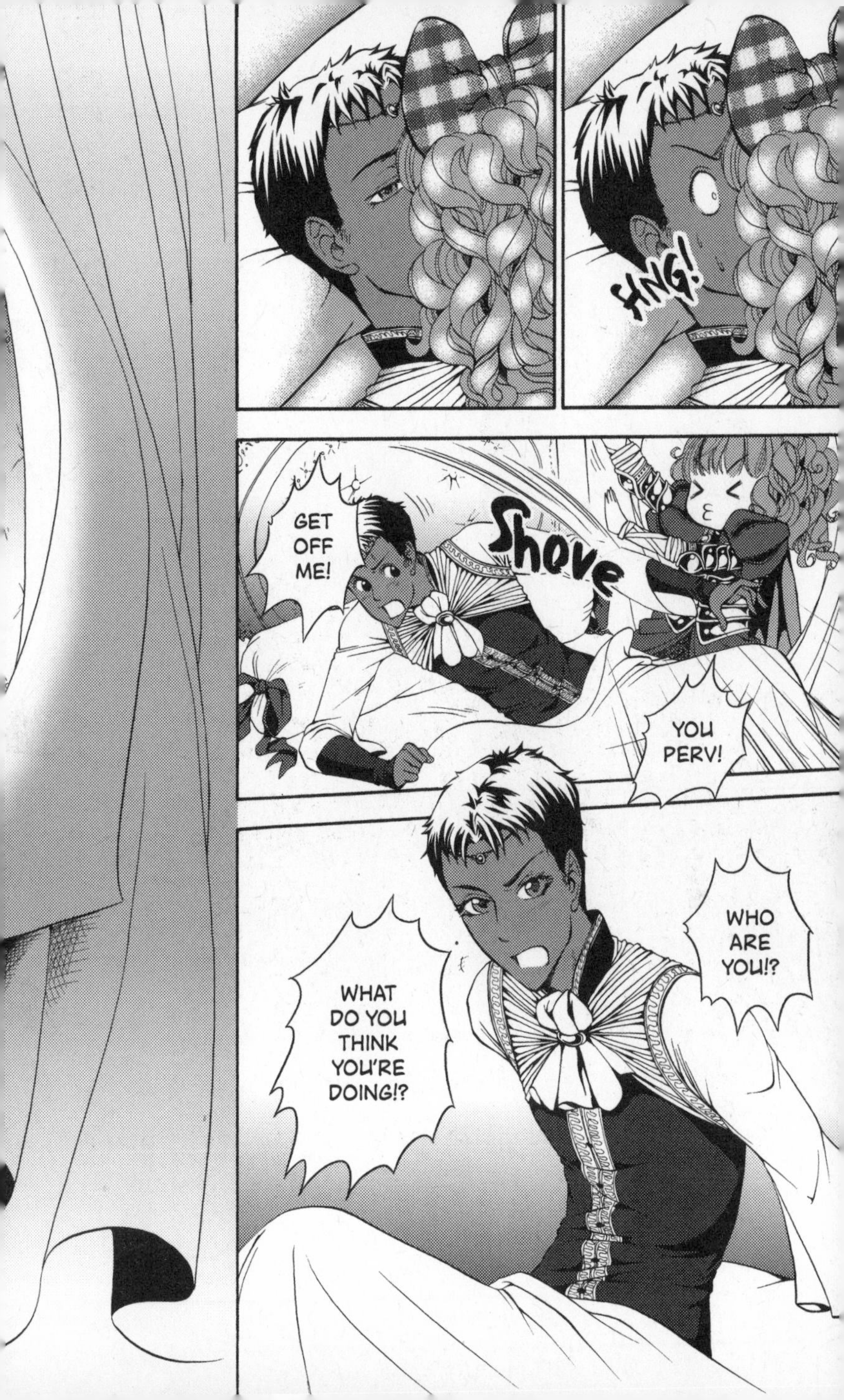
HNG!
GET OFF ME!
Shove
YOU PERV!
WHAT DO YOU THINK YOU'RE DOING!?
WHO ARE YOU!?

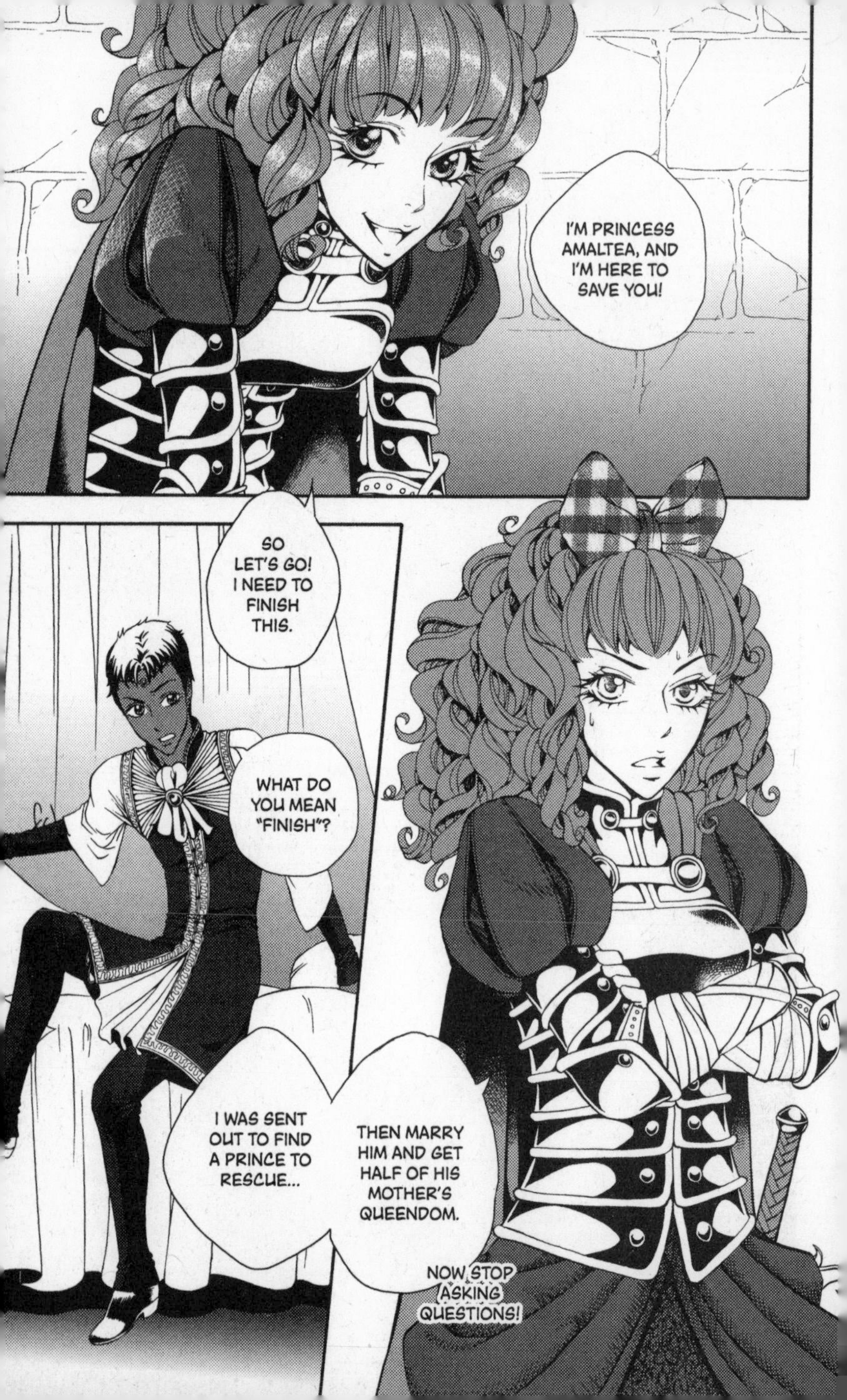
I'M PRINCESS AMALTEA, AND I'M HERE TO SAVE YOU!
SO LET'S GO! I NEED TO FINISH THIS.
WHAT DO YOU MEAN "FINISH"?
I WAS SENT OUT TO FIND A PRINCE TO RESCUE...
THEN MARRY HIM AND GET HALF OF HIS MOTHER'S QUEENDOM.
NOW STOP ASKING QUESTIONS!

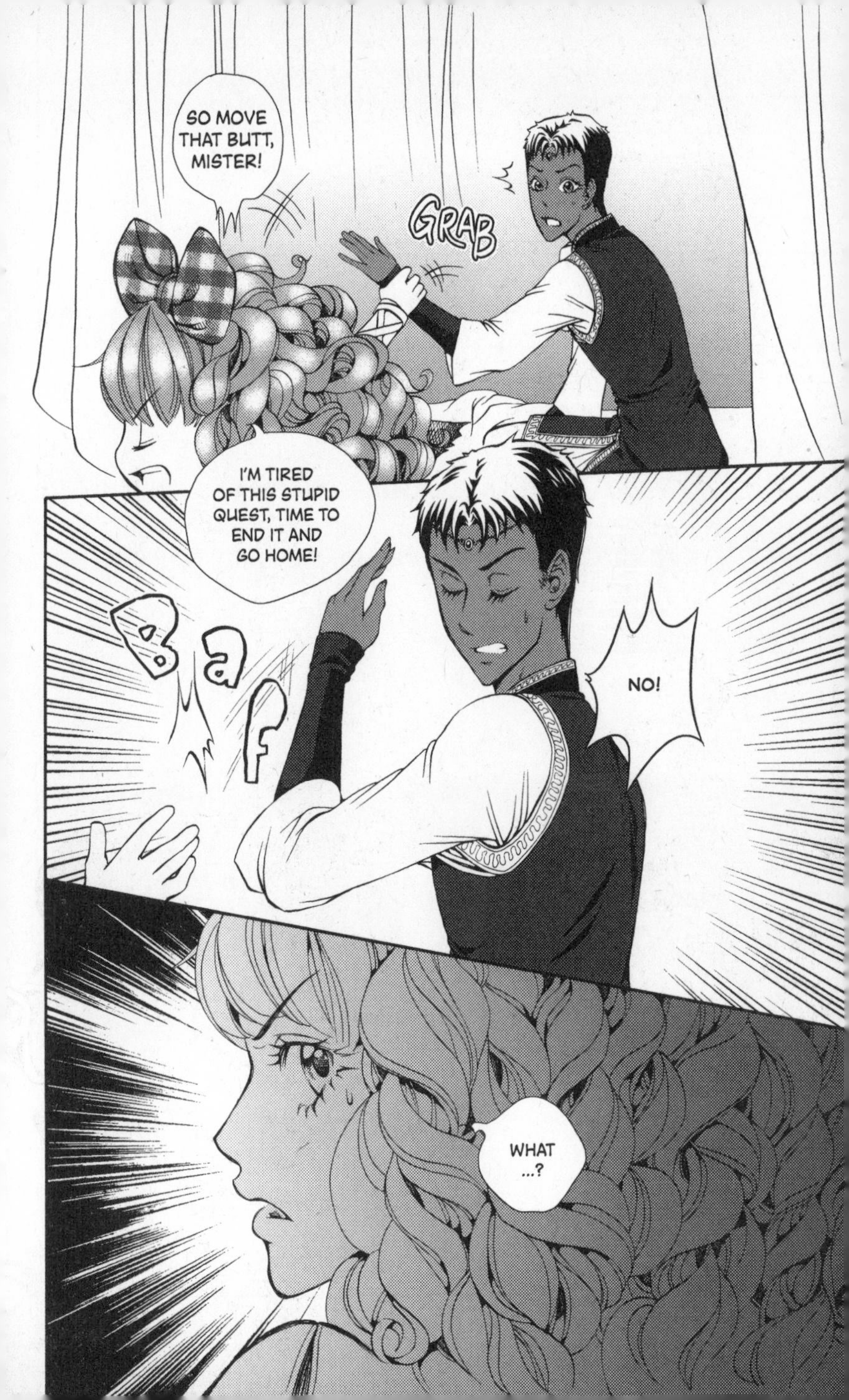
SO MOVE THAT BUTT, MISTER!
GRAB
I'M TIRED OF THIS STUPID QUEST, TIME TO END IT AND GO HOME!
BAF
NO!
WHAT ...?

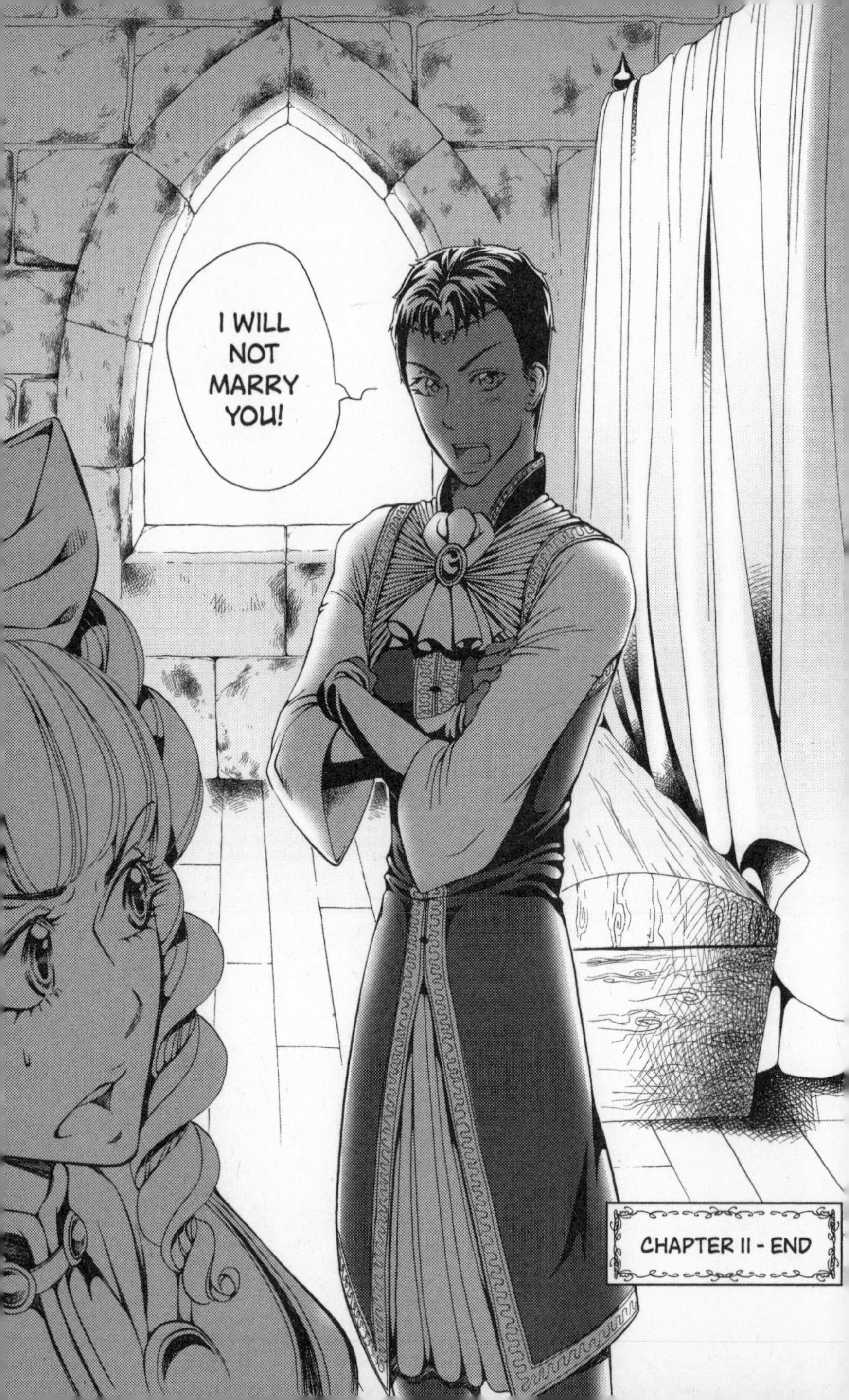
I WILL NOT MARRY YOU!
CHAPTER II - END

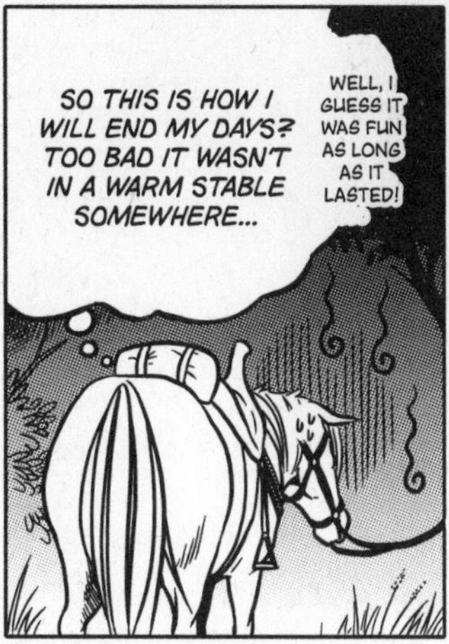
SO THIS IS HOW I WILL END MY DAYS? TOO BAD IT WASN'T IN A WARM STABLE SOMEWHERE...
WELL, I GUESS IT WAS FUN AS LONG AS IT LASTED!

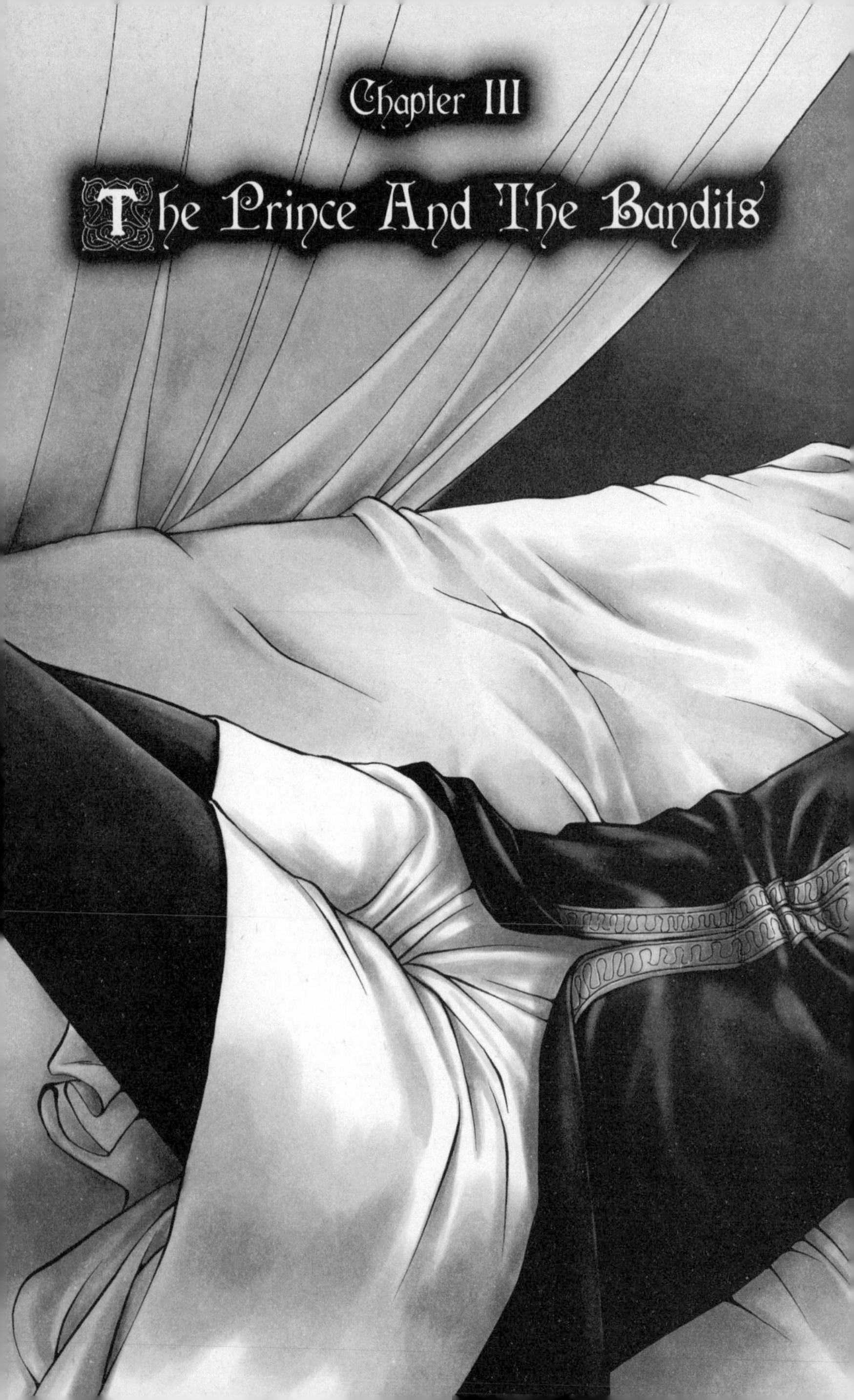
Chapter III
The Prince And The Bandits

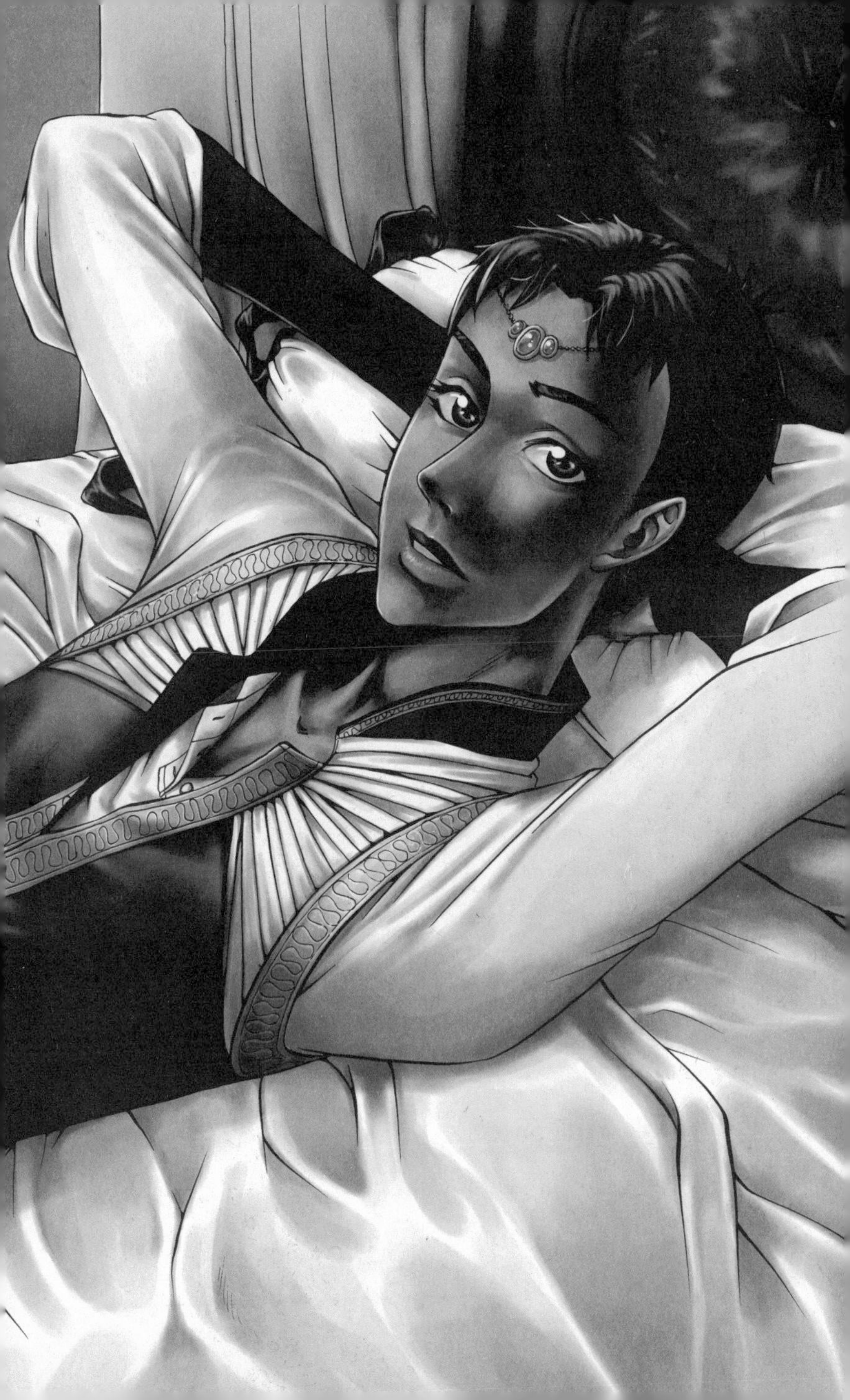

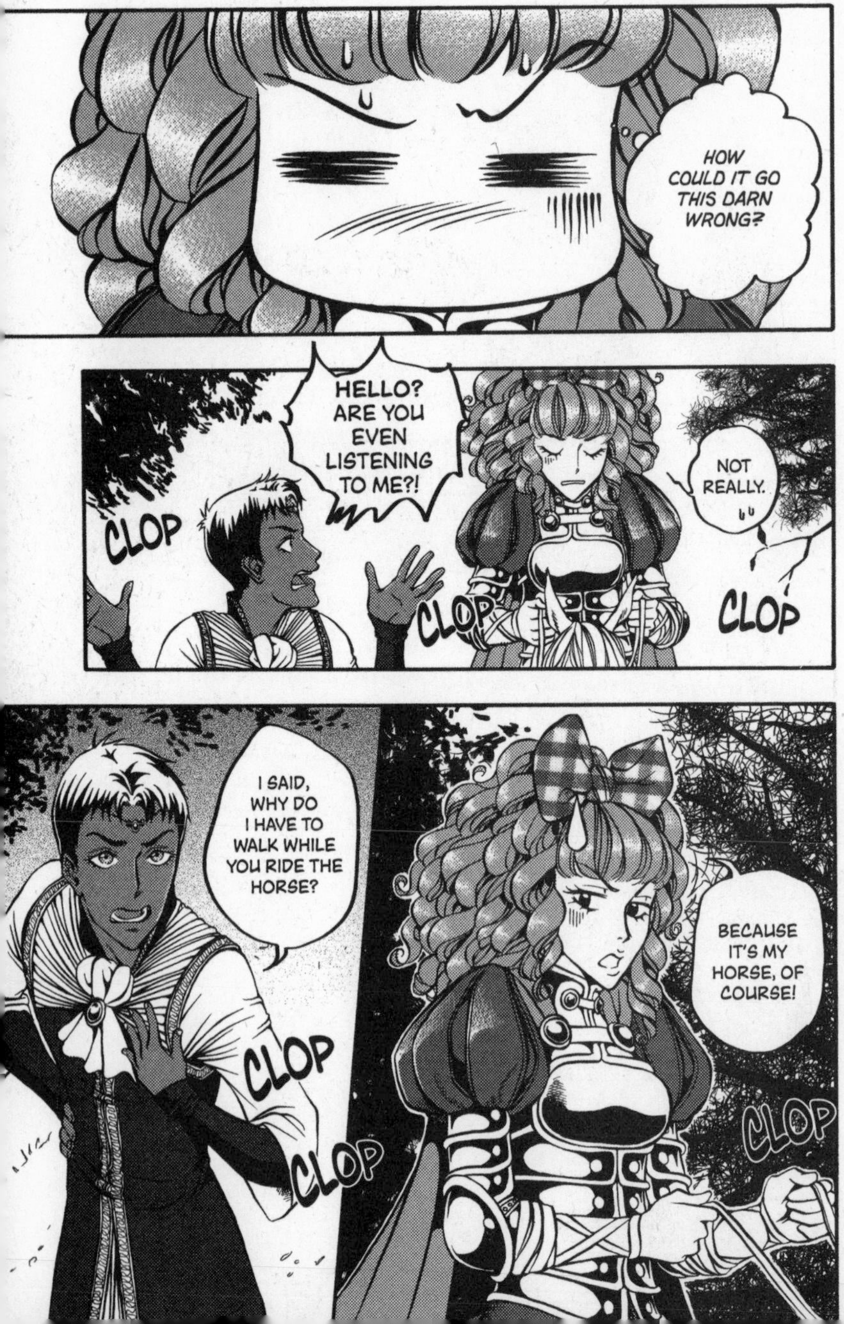
HOW COULD IT GO THIS DARN WRONG?
HELLO? ARE YOU EVEN LISTENING TO ME?!
CLOP
CLOP
NOT REALLY.
CLOP
I SAID, WHY DO I HAVE TO WALK WHILE YOU RIDE THE HORSE?
CLOP
CLOP
BECAUSE IT'S MY HORSE, OF COURSE!
CLOP

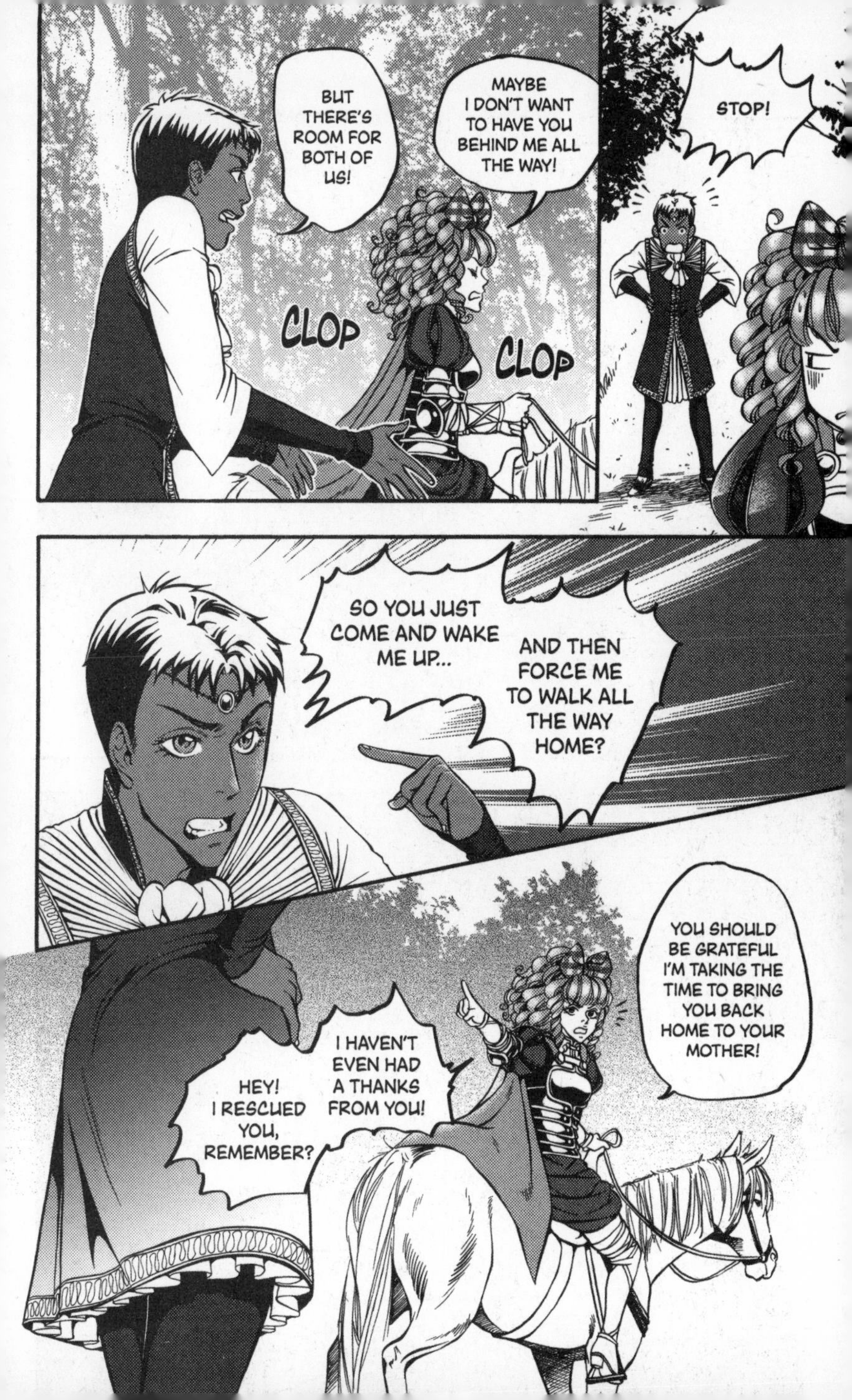
BUT THERE'S ROOM FOR BOTH OF US!
MAYBE I DON'T WANT TO HAVE YOU BEHIND ME ALL THE WAY!
CLOP
CLOP
STOP!
SO YOU JUST COME AND WAKE ME UP...
AND THEN FORCE ME TO WALK ALL THE WAY HOME?
HEY! I RESCUED YOU, REMEMBER?
I HAVEN'T EVEN HAD A THANKS FROM YOU!
YOU SHOULD BE GRATEFUL I'M TAKING THE TIME TO BRING YOU BACK HOME TO YOUR MOTHER!

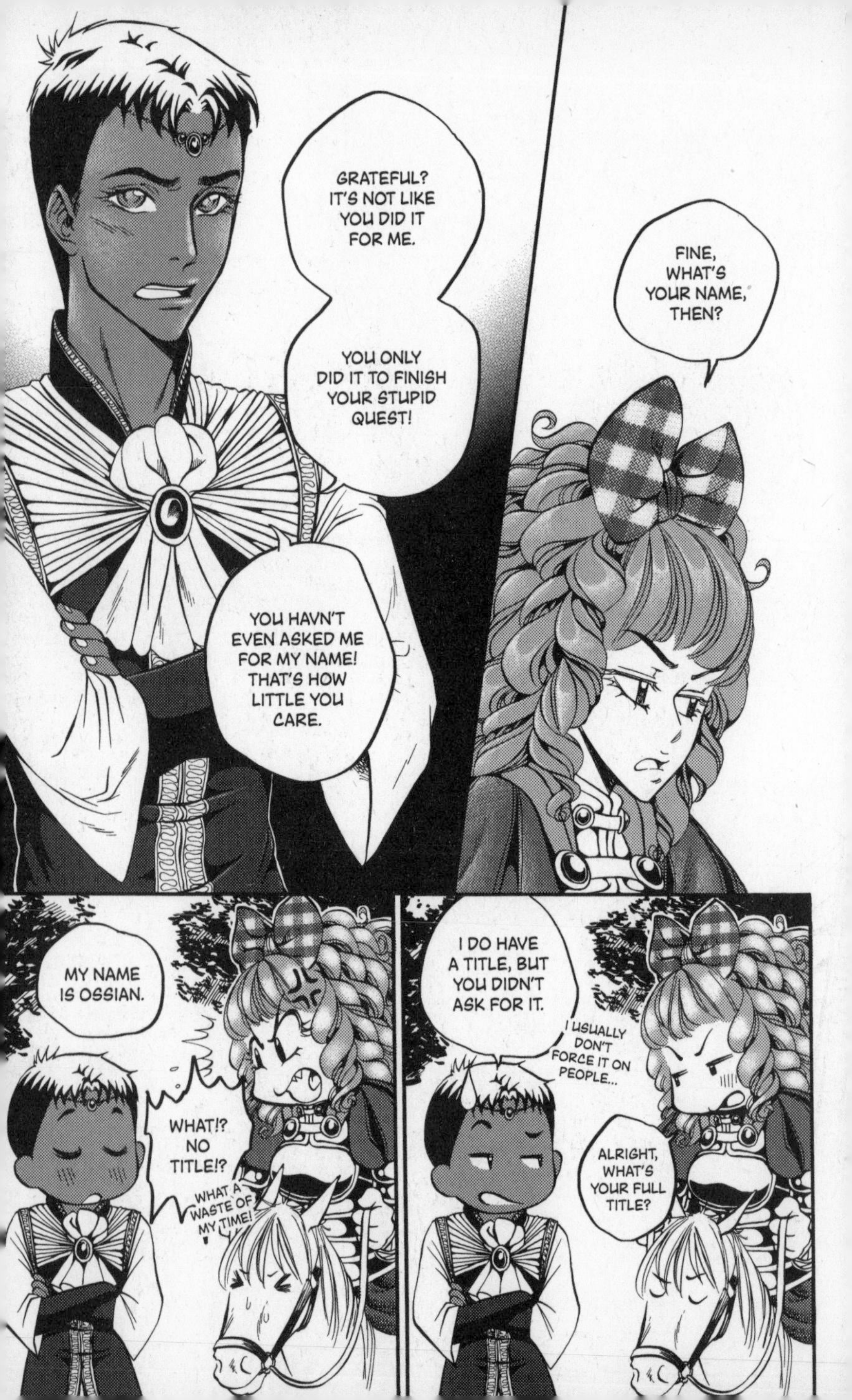
GRATEFUL? IT'S NOT LIKE YOU DID IT FOR ME.
YOU ONLY DID IT TO FINISH YOUR STUPID QUEST!
YOU HAVN'T EVEN ASKED ME FOR MY NAME! THAT'S HOW LITTLE YOU CARE.
FINE, WHAT'S YOUR NAME, THEN?
MY NAME IS OSSIAN.
WHAT!? NO TITLE!?
WHAT A WASTE OF MY TIME!
I DO HAVE A TITLE, BUT YOU DIDN'T ASK FOR IT.
I USUALLY DON'T FORCE IT ON PEOPLE...
ALRIGHT, WHAT'S YOUR FULL TITLE?

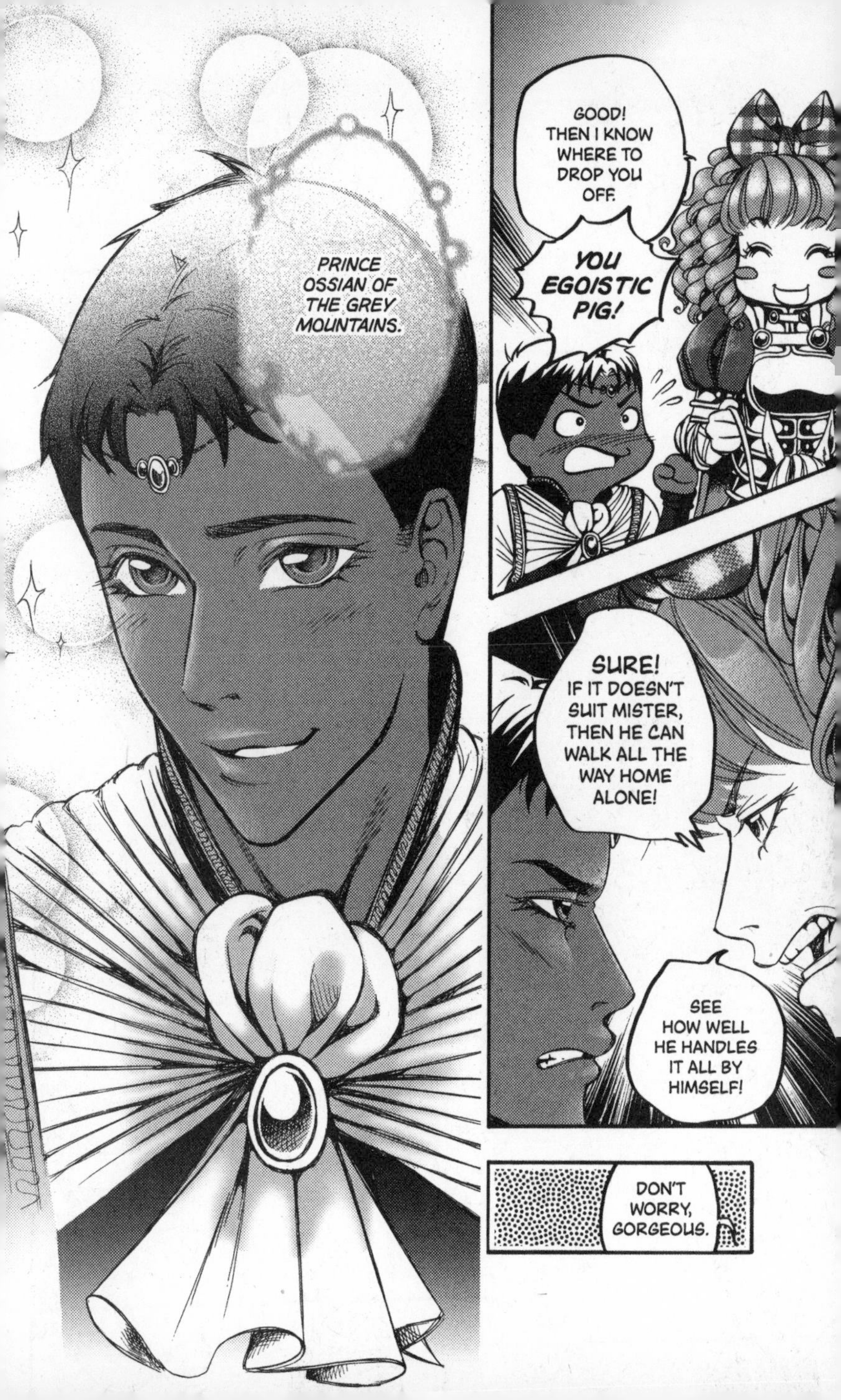
PRINCE OSSIAN OF THE GREY MOUNTAINS.
GOOD! THEN I KNOW WHERE TO DROP YOU OFF.
YOU EGOISTIC PIG!
SURE! IF IT DOESN'T SUIT MISTER, THEN HE CAN WALK ALL THE WAY HOME ALONE!
SEE HOW WELL HE HANDLES IT ALL BY HIMSELF!
DON'T WORRY, GORGEOUS.

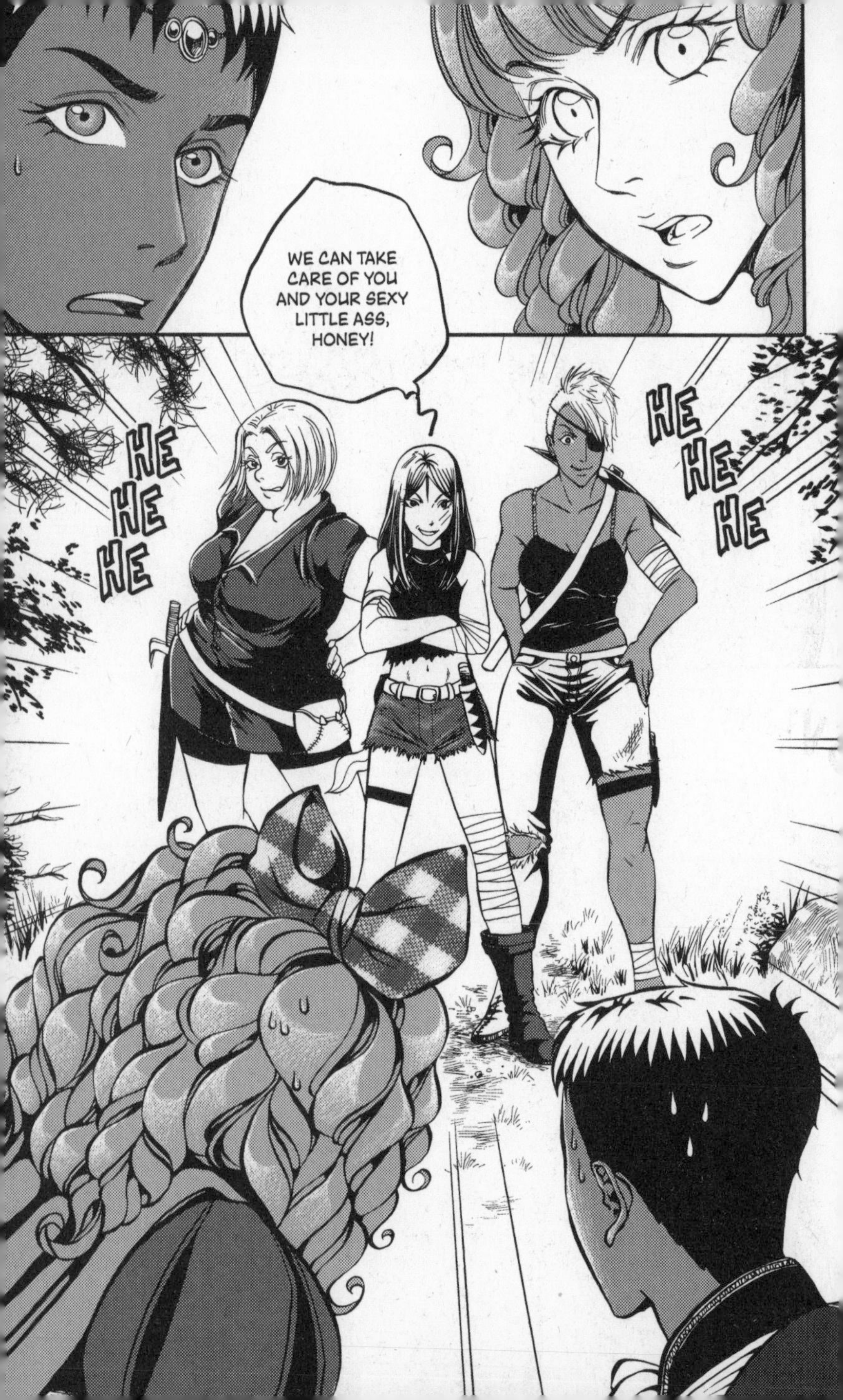
WE CAN TAKE CARE OF YOU AND YOUR SEXY LITTLE ASS, HONEY!
HE HE HE HE
HE HE HE

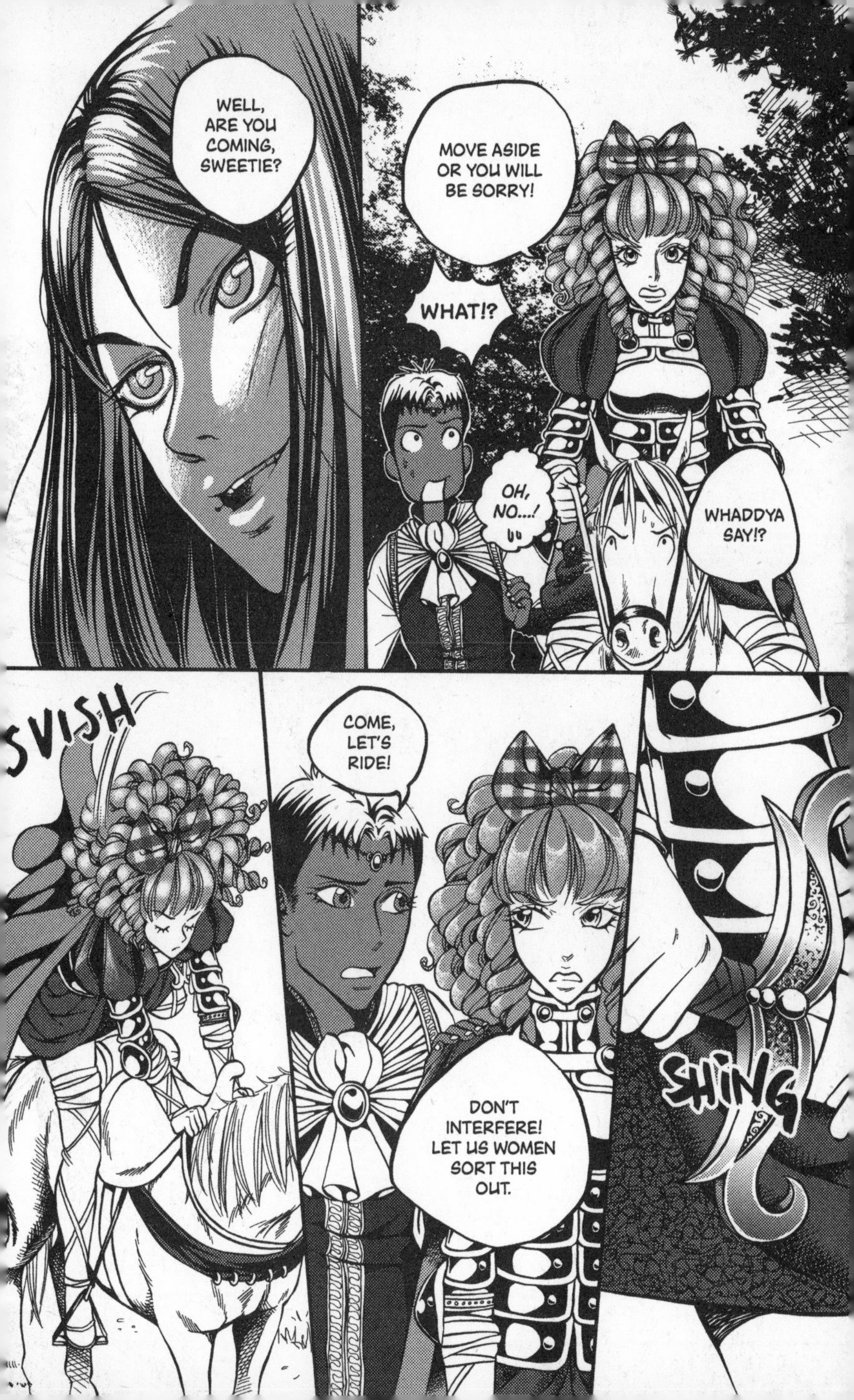
WELL, ARE YOU COMING, SWEETIE?
MOVE ASIDE OR YOU WILL BE SORRY!
WHAT!?
OH, NO...!
WHADDYA SAY!?
SVISH
COME, LET'S RIDE!
DON'T INTERFERE! LET US WOMEN SORT THIS OUT.
SHING

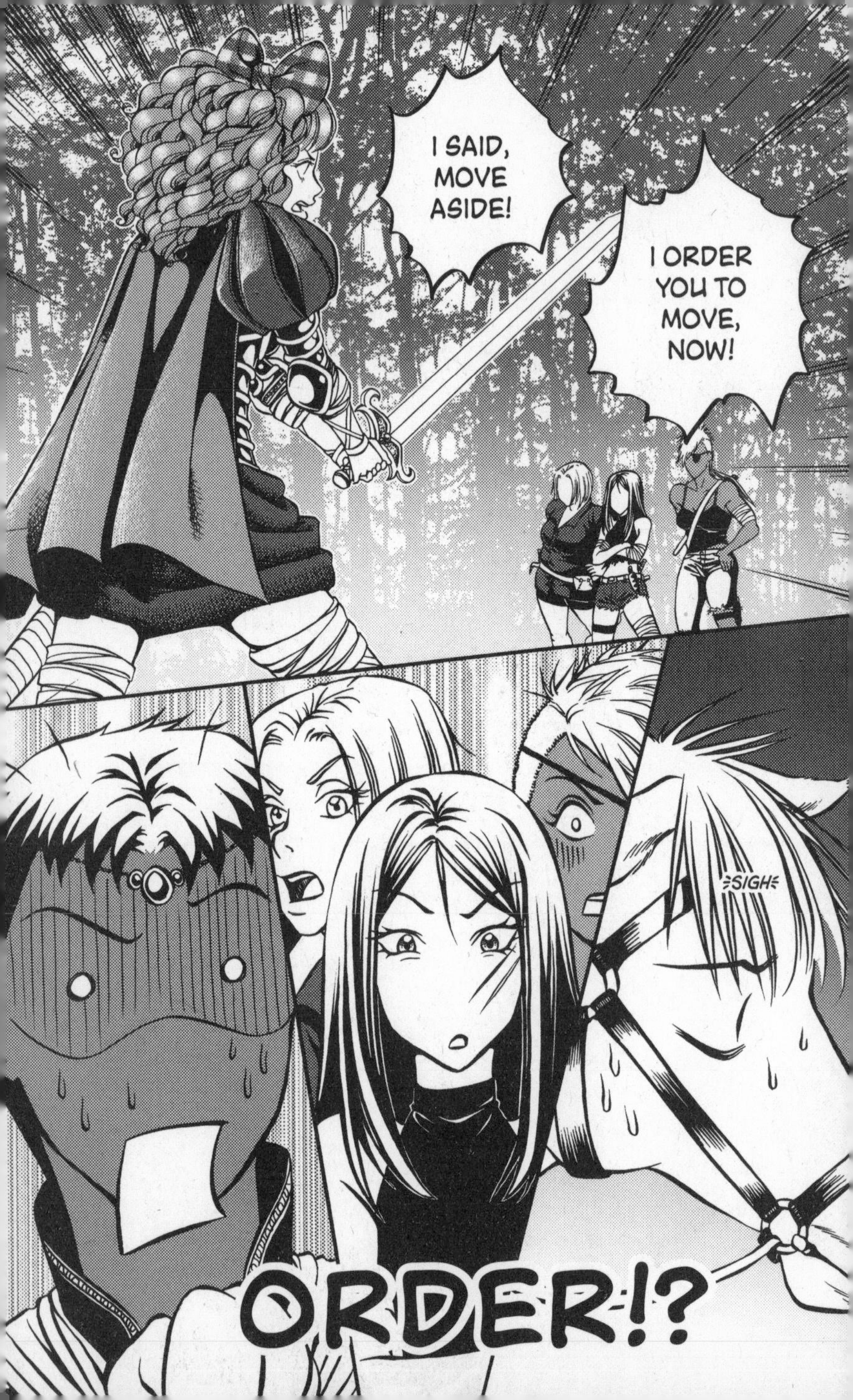
I SAID, MOVE ASIDE!
I ORDER YOU TO MOVE, NOW!
SIGH
ORDER!?

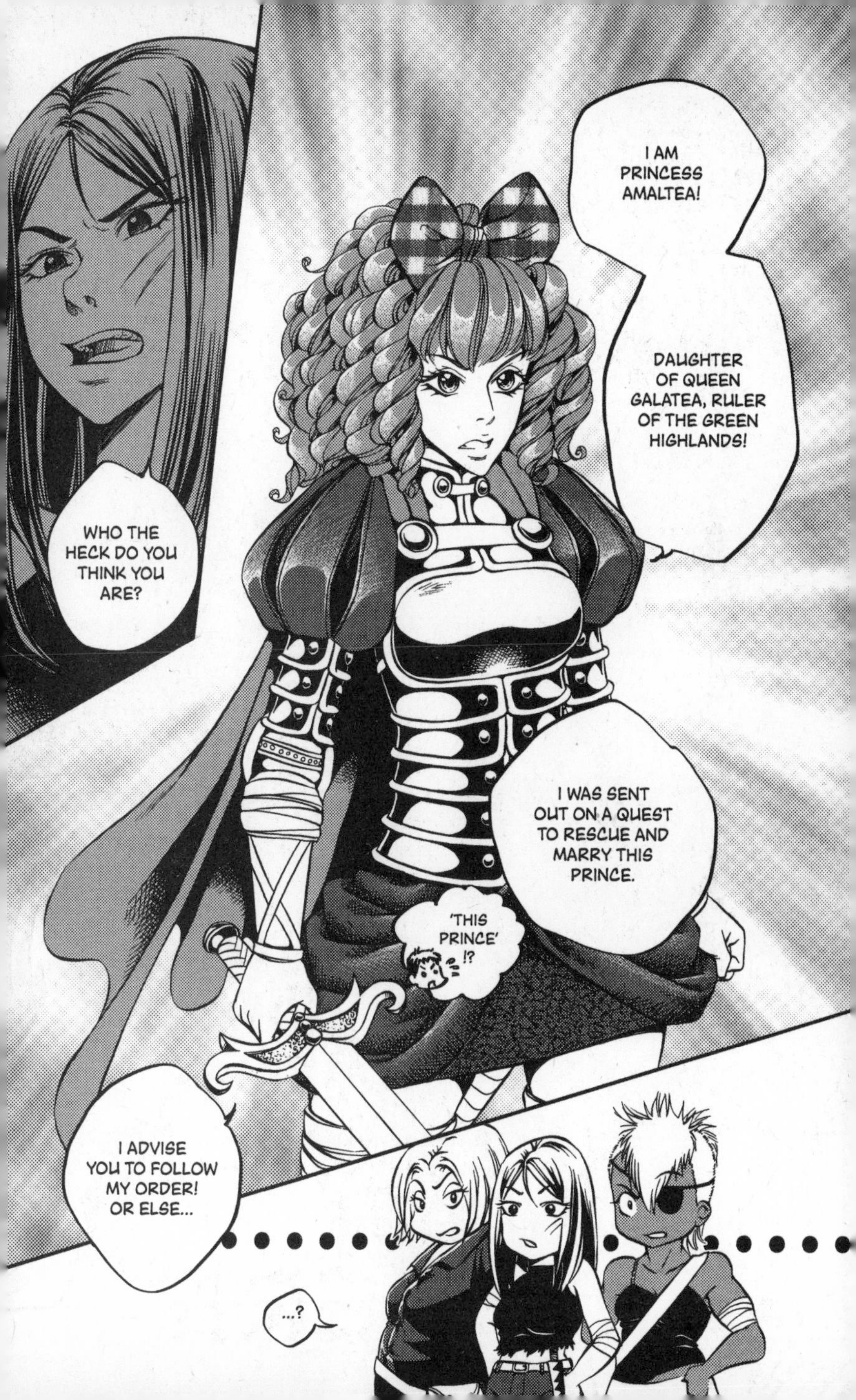
WHO THE HECK DO YOU THINK YOU ARE?
I AM PRINCESS AMALTEA!
DAUGHTER OF QUEEN GALATEA, RULER OF THE GREEN HIGHLANDS!
I WAS SENT OUT ON A QUEST TO RESCUE AND MARRY THIS PRINCE.
'THIS PRINCE' !?
I ADVISE YOU TO FOLLOW MY ORDER! OR ELSE...
...?

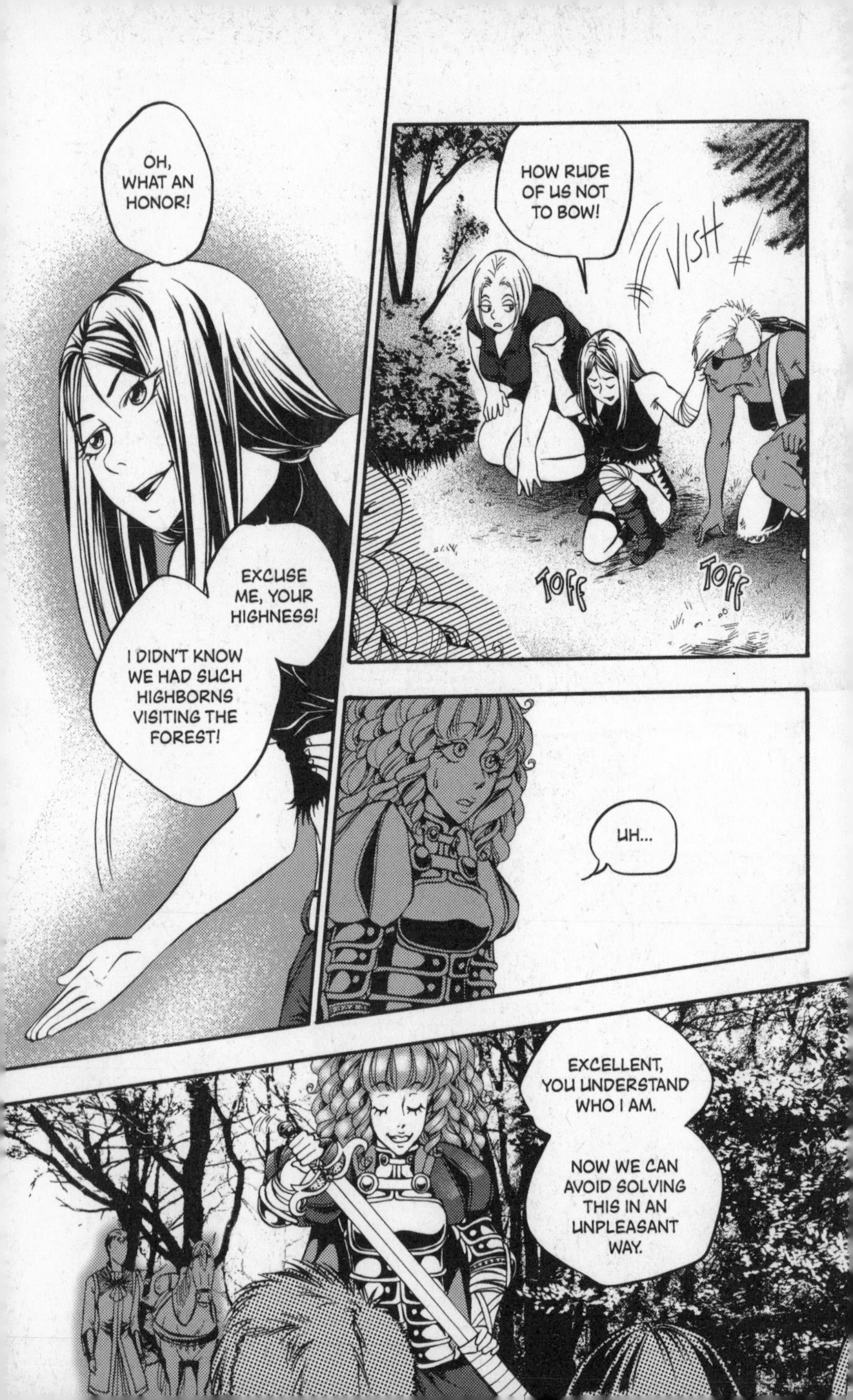
OH, WHAT AN HONOR!
HOW RUDE OF US NOT TO BOW!
VISH
TOFF
TOFF
EXCUSE ME, YOUR HIGHNESS!
I DIDN'T KNOW WE HAD SUCH HIGHBORNS VISITING THE FOREST!
UH...
EXCELLENT, YOU UNDERSTAND WHO I AM.
NOW WE CAN AVOID SOLVING THIS IN AN UNPLEASANT WAY.

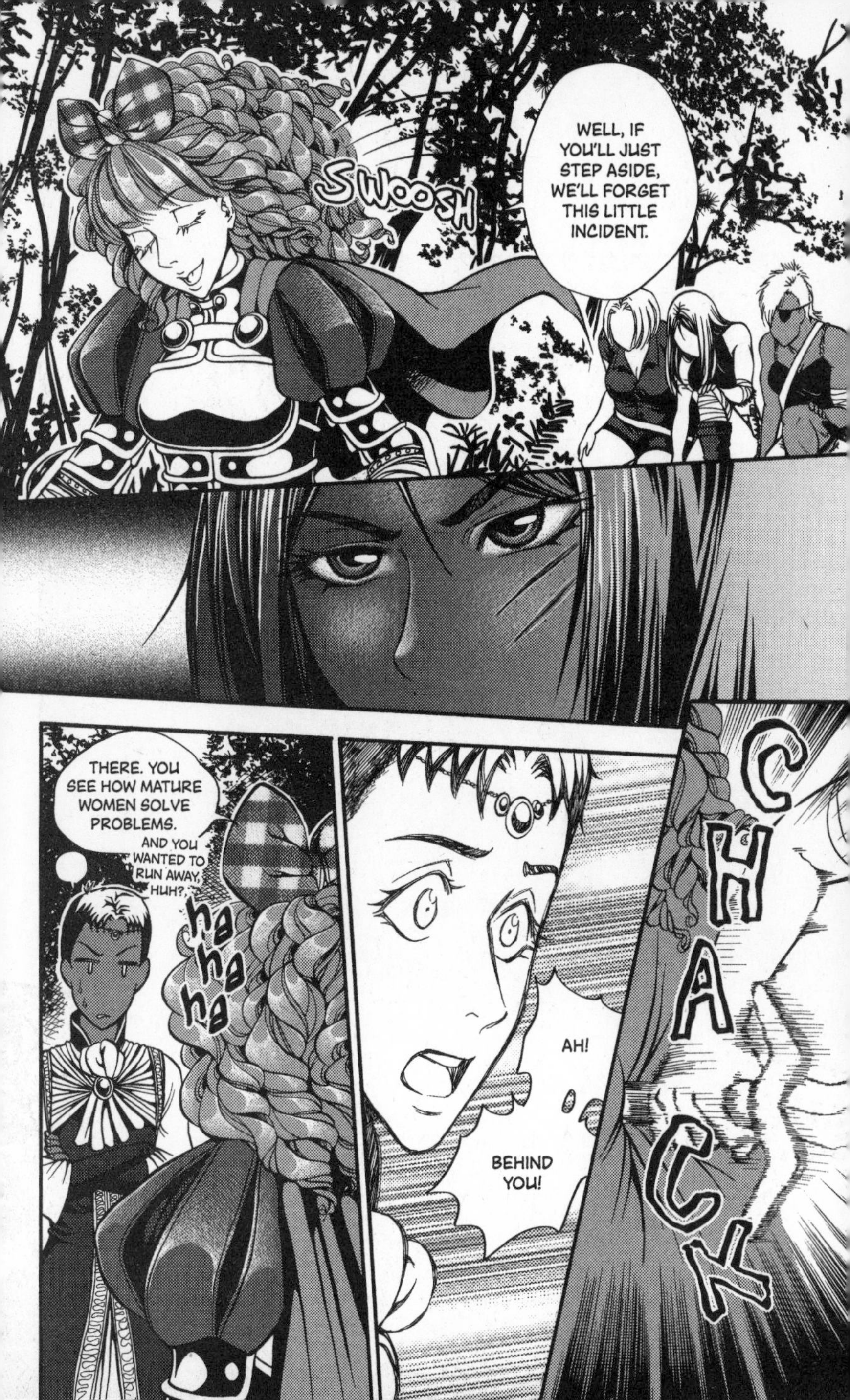
SWOOSH
WELL, IF YOU'LL JUST STEP ASIDE, WE'LL FORGET THIS LITTLE INCIDENT.
THERE. YOU SEE HOW MATURE WOMEN SOLVE PROBLEMS.
AND YOU WANTED TO RUN AWAY, HUH?
hahahaha
AH!
BEHIND YOU!
CHACK

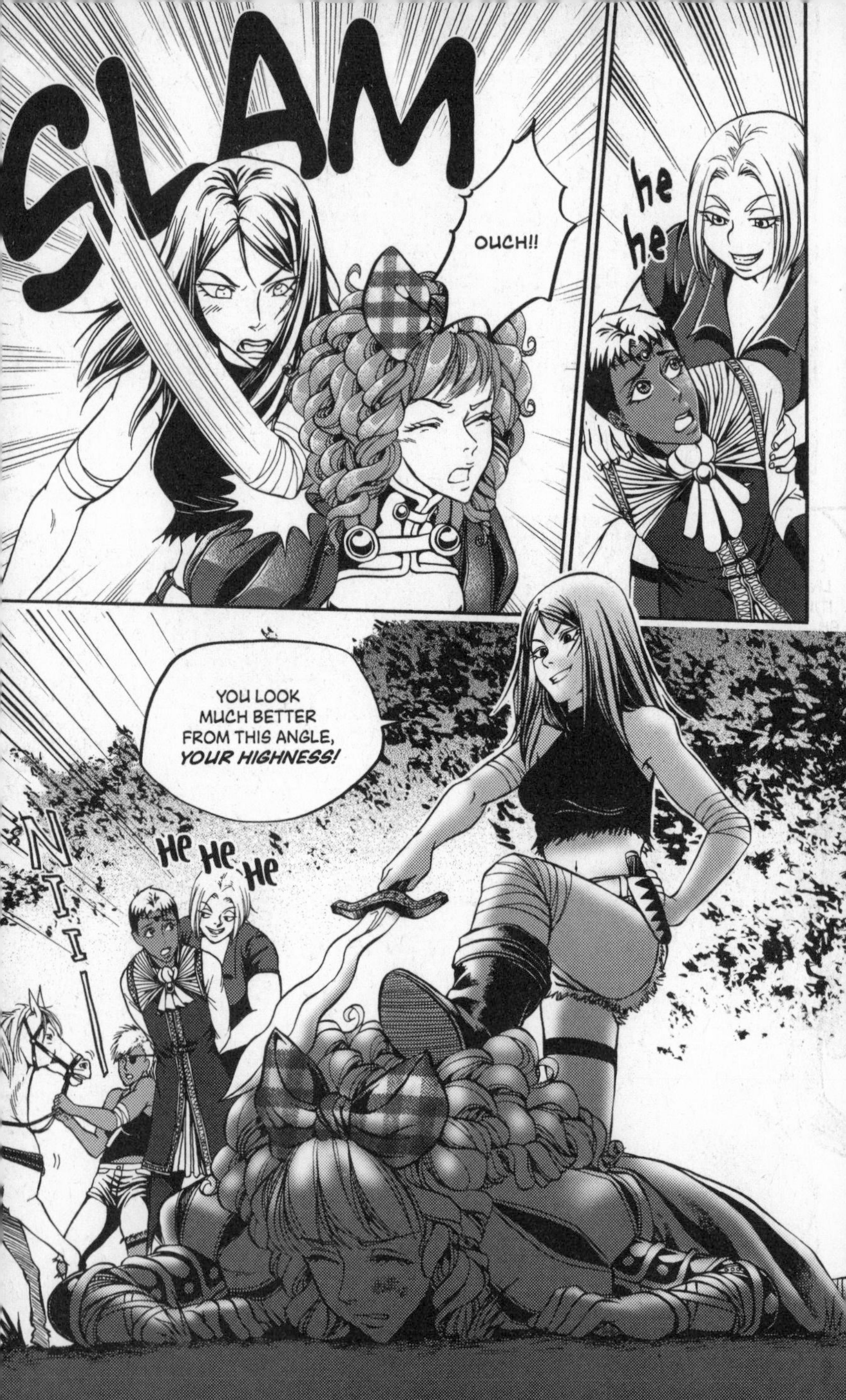
SLAM
OUCH!!
he he
YOU LOOK MUCH BETTER FROM THIS ANGLE, *YOUR HIGHNESS!*
NIII
He He He

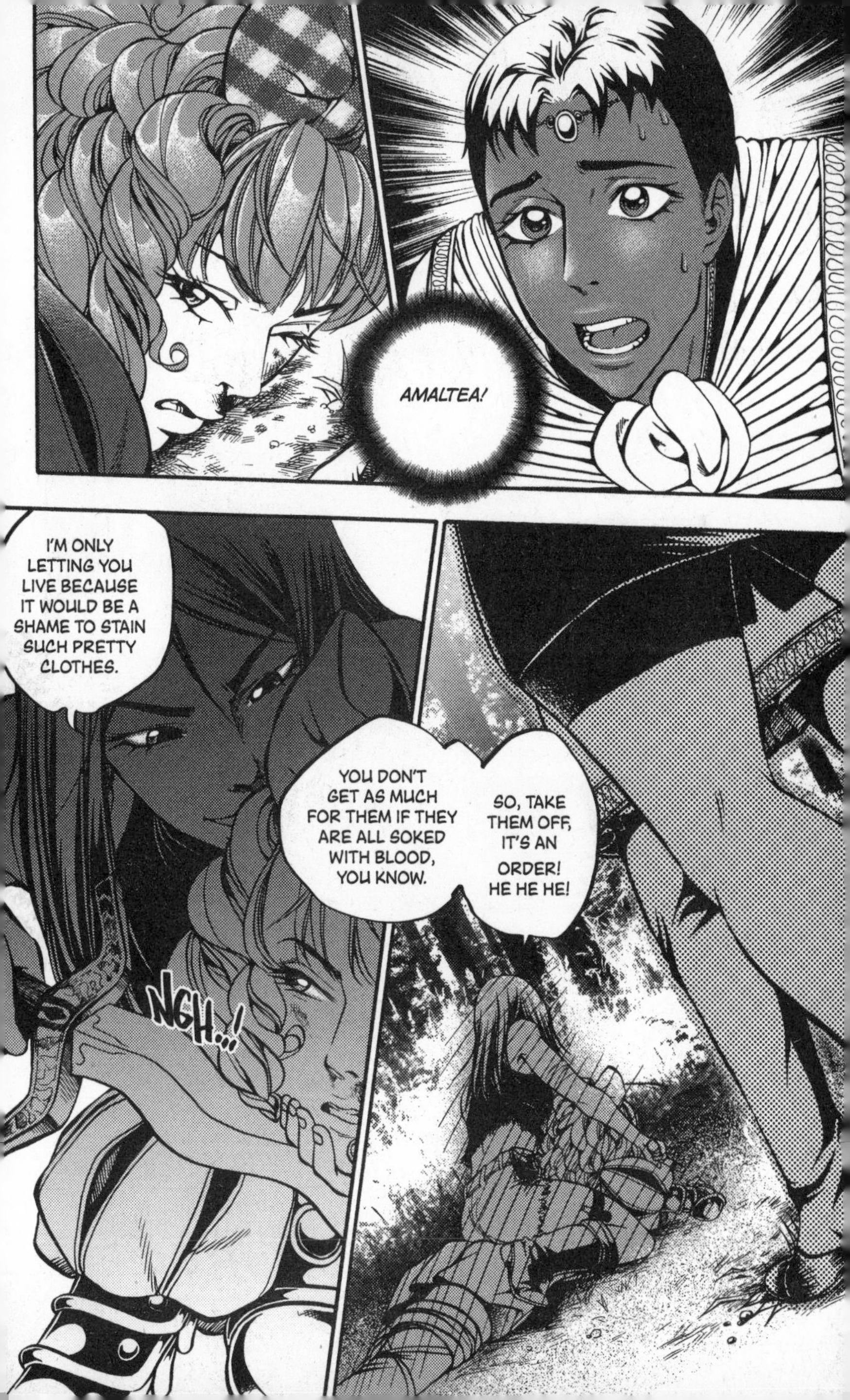
AMALTEA!
I'M ONLY LETTING YOU LIVE BECAUSE IT WOULD BE A SHAME TO STAIN SUCH PRETTY CLOTHES.
NGH...!
YOU DON'T GET AS MUCH FOR THEM IF THEY ARE ALL SOKED WITH BLOOD, YOU KNOW.
SO, TAKE THEM OFF, IT'S AN ORDER! HE HE HE!

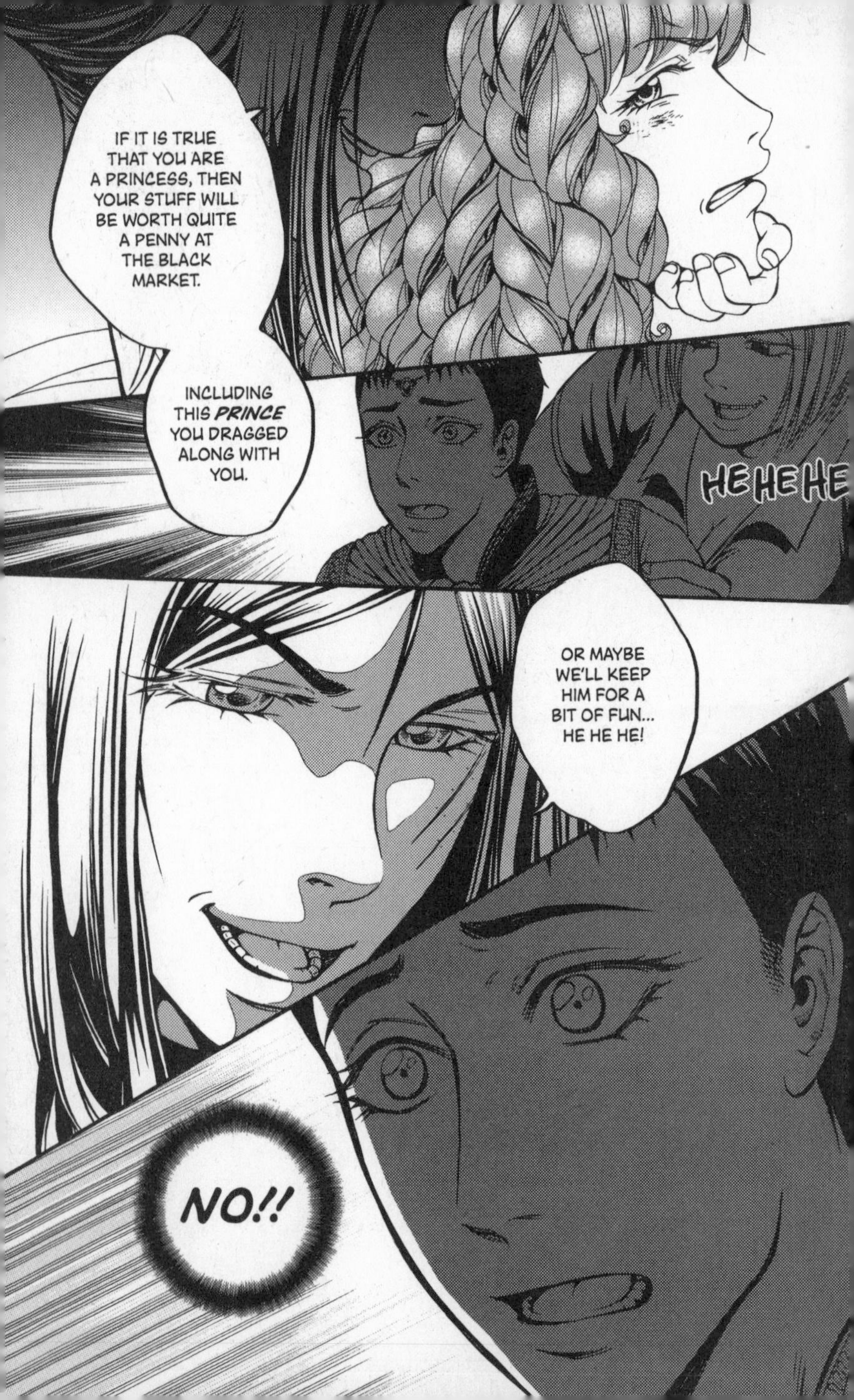
IF IT IS TRUE THAT YOU ARE A PRINCESS, THEN YOUR STUFF WILL BE WORTH QUITE A PENNY AT THE BLACK MARKET.
INCLUDING THIS *PRINCE* YOU DRAGGED ALONG WITH YOU.
HE HE HE
OR MAYBE WE'LL KEEP HIM FOR A BIT OF FUN... HE HE HE!
NO!!

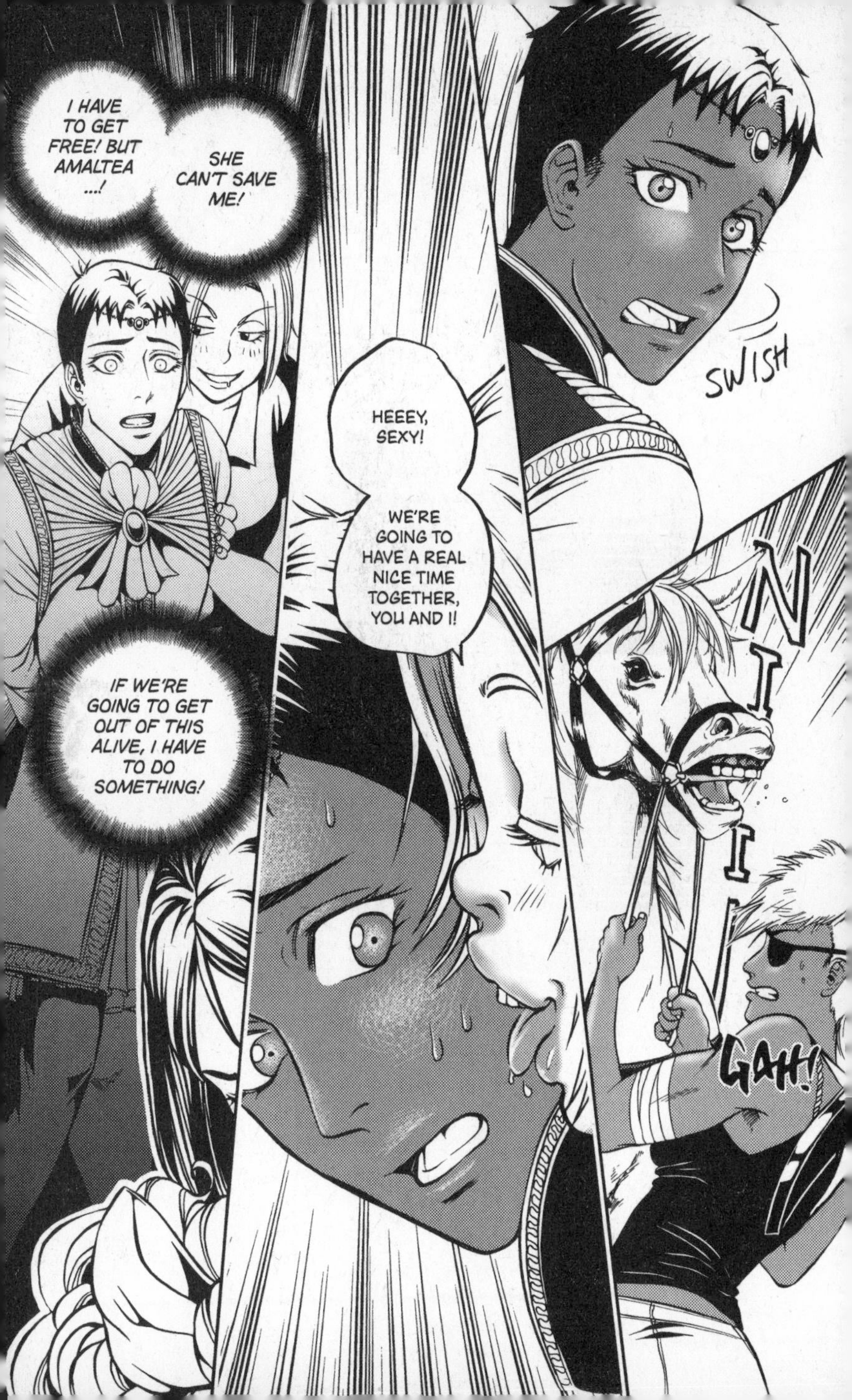
I HAVE TO GET FREE! BUT AMALTEA ...!
SHE CAN'T SAVE ME!
IF WE'RE GOING TO GET OUT OF THIS ALIVE, I HAVE TO DO SOMETHING!
HEEEY, SEXY!
WE'RE GOING TO HAVE A REAL NICE TIME TOGETHER, YOU AND I!
SWISH
NIII
GAH!

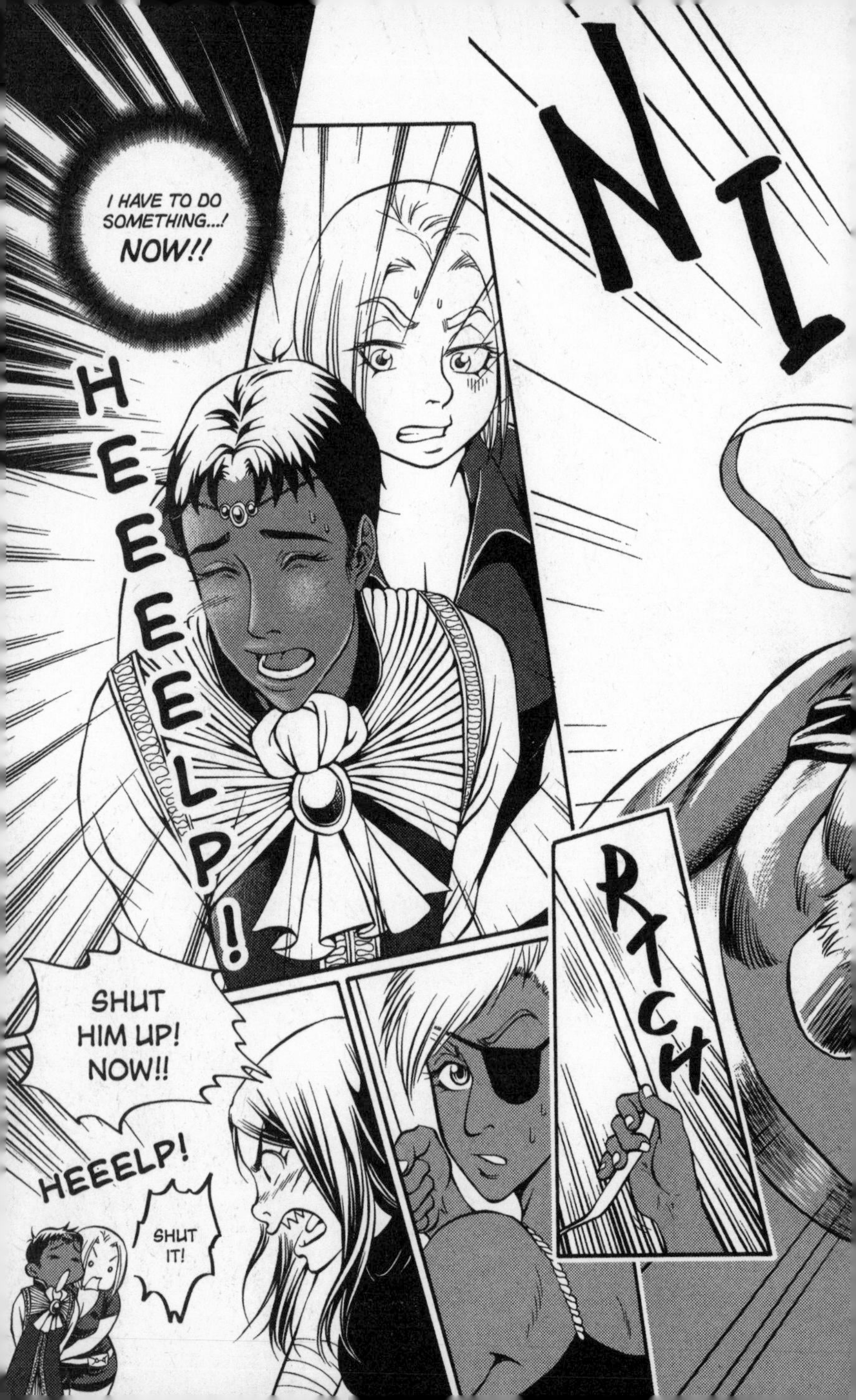
NI
I HAVE TO DO SOMETHING...! NOW!!
HEEEELP!
RTCH
SHUT HIM UP! NOW!!
HEEELP!
SHUT IT!

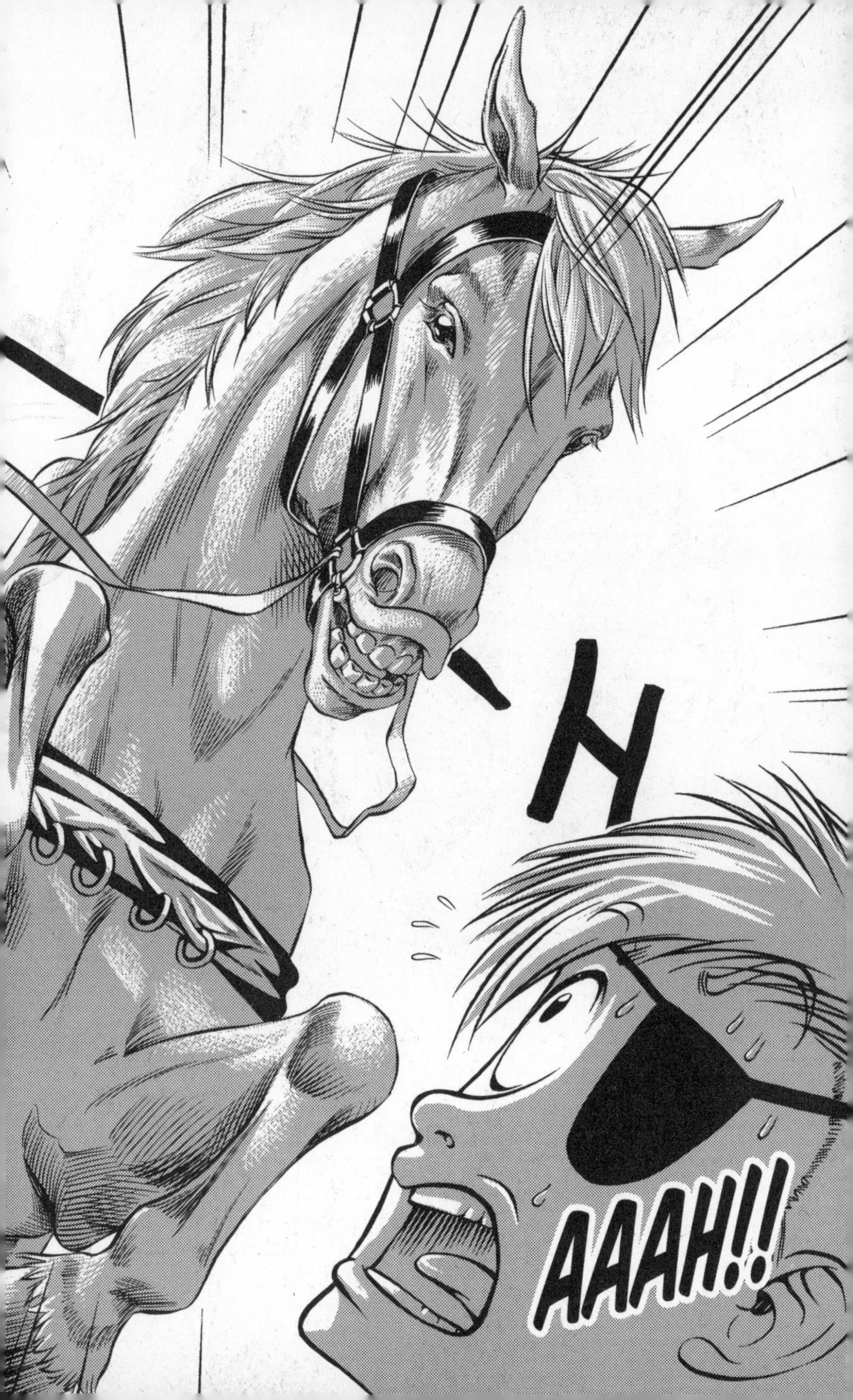
AAAH!!

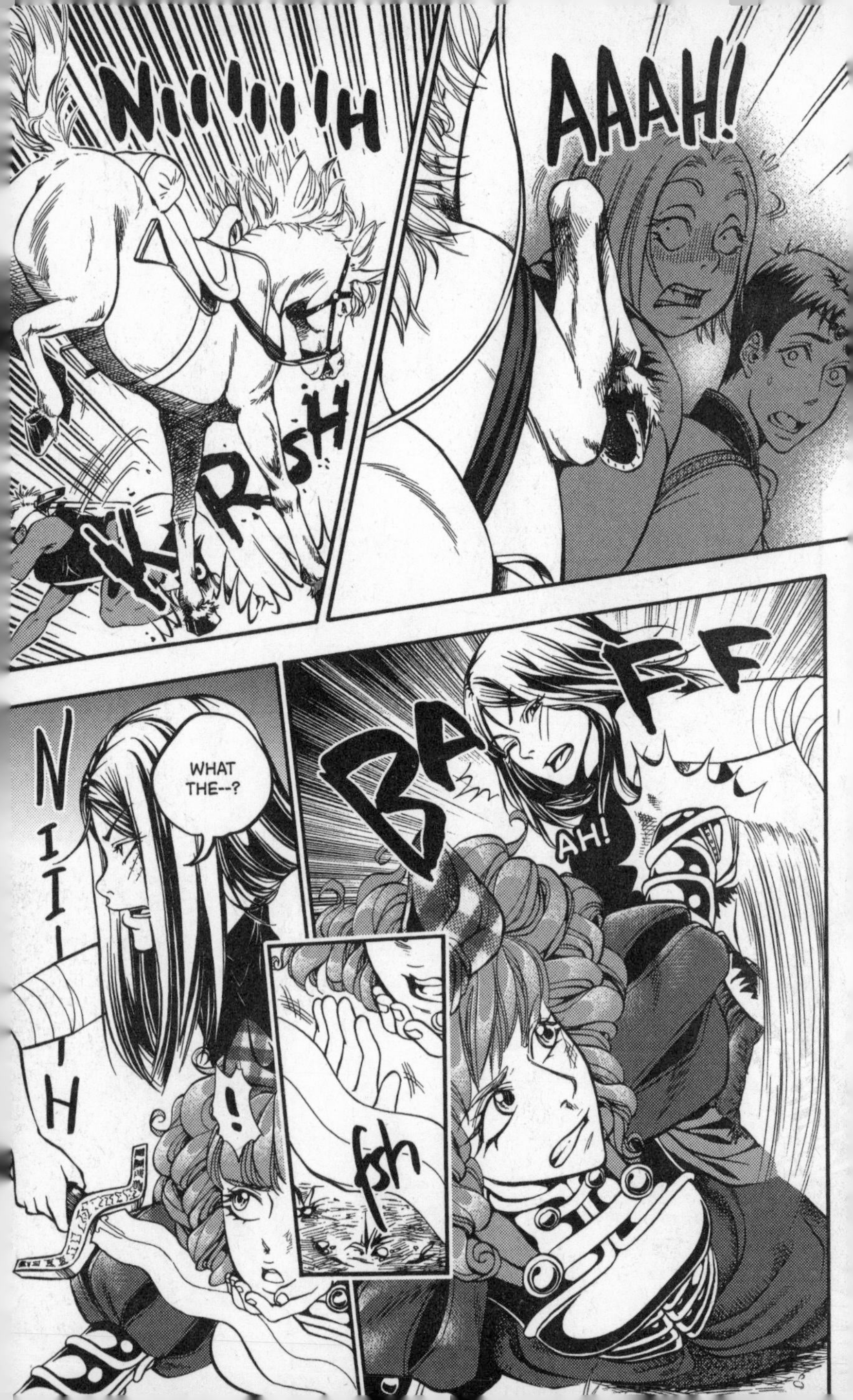
NIIIIIIH
KRSH
AAAH!
NIIIIH
WHAT THE--?
!
BAFF
AH!
fsh

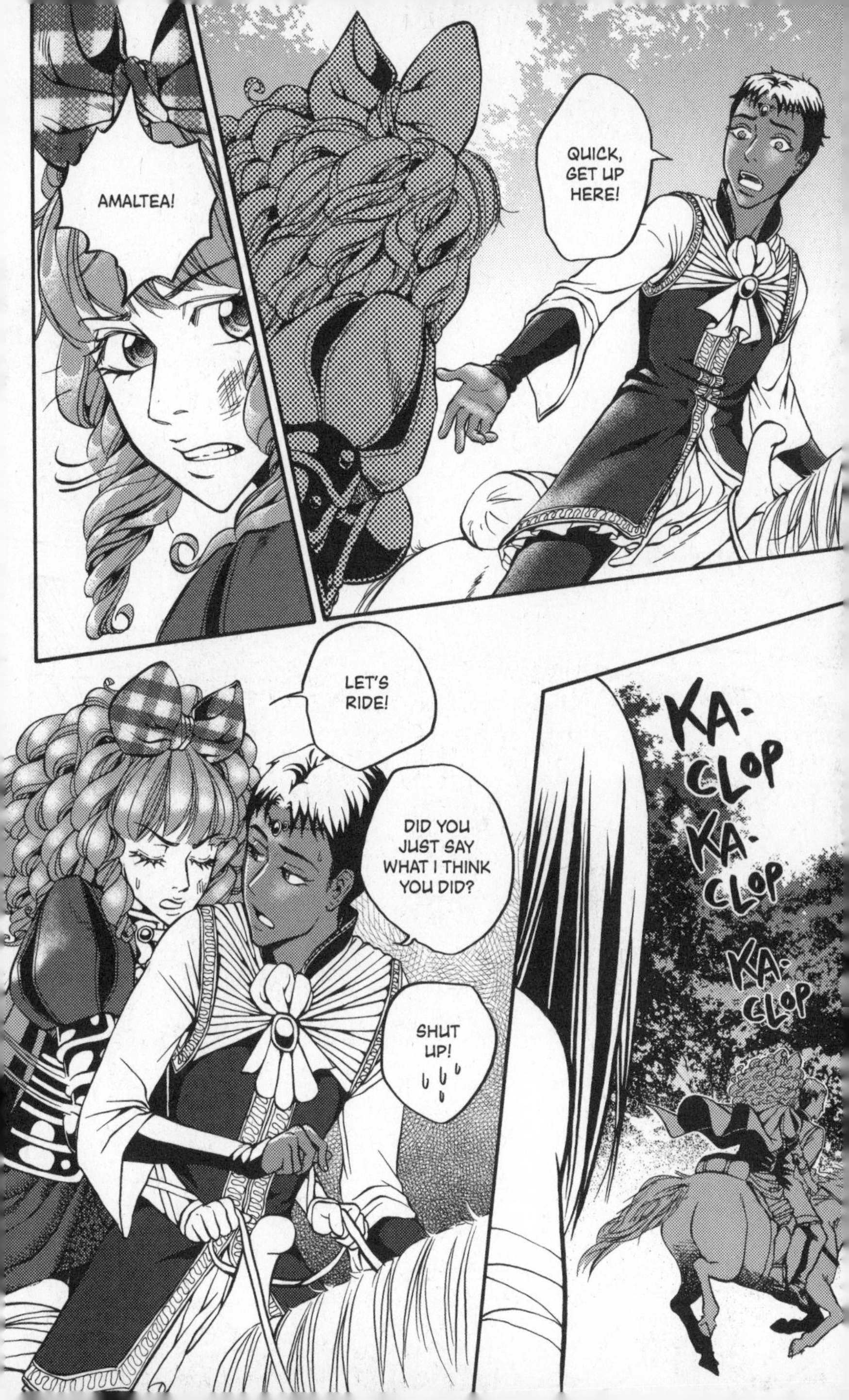
AMALTEA!
QUICK, GET UP HERE!
LET'S RIDE!
DID YOU JUST SAY WHAT I THINK YOU DID?
SHUT UP!
KA-CLOP KA-CLOP KA-CLOP

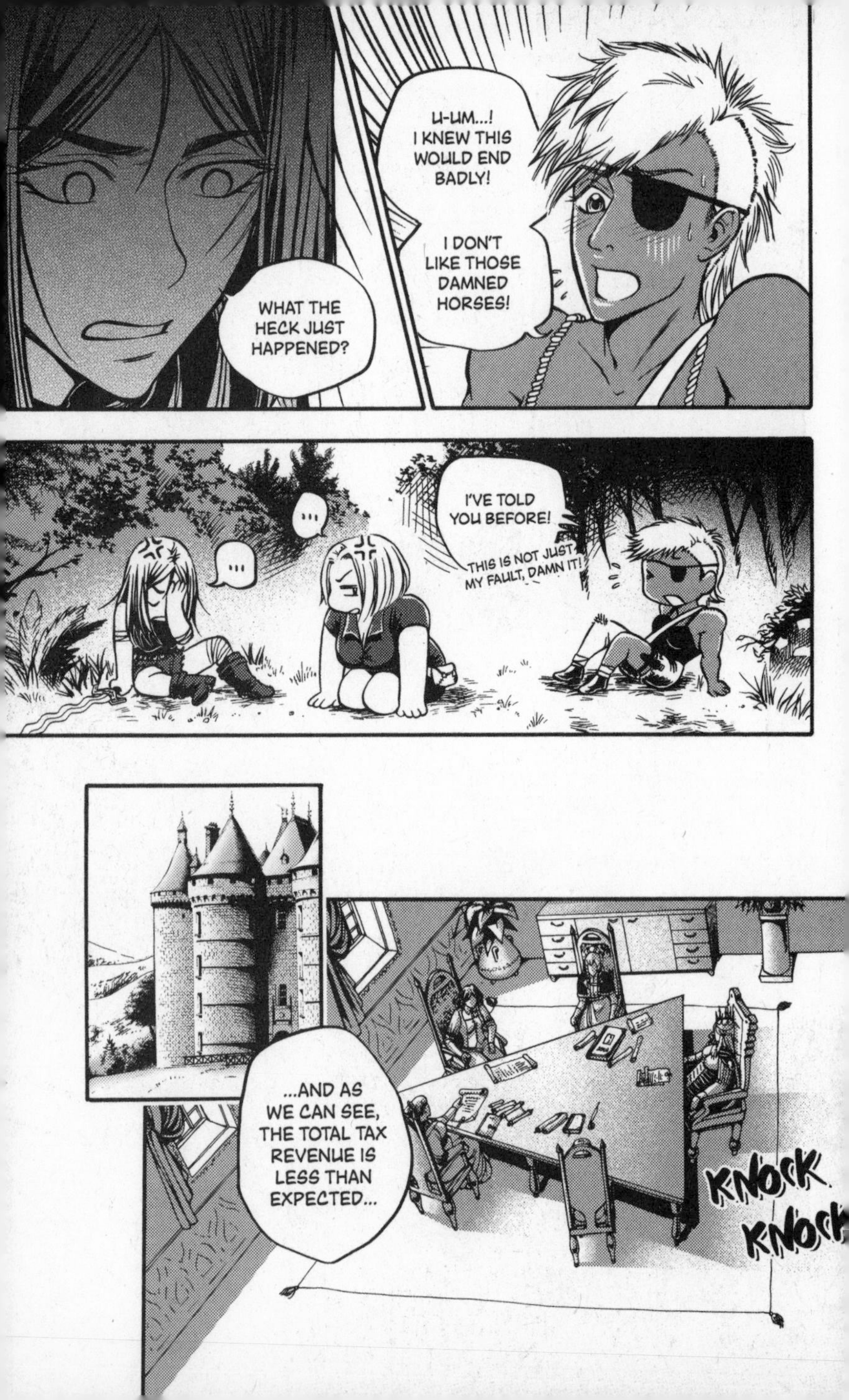
WHAT THE HECK JUST HAPPENED?
U-UM...! I KNEW THIS WOULD END BADLY!
I DON'T LIKE THOSE DAMNED HORSES!
...
...
I'VE TOLD YOU BEFORE!
THIS IS NOT JUST MY FAULT, DAMN IT!
...AND AS WE CAN SEE, THE TOTAL TAX REVENUE IS LESS THAN EXPECTED...
KNOCK
KNOCK

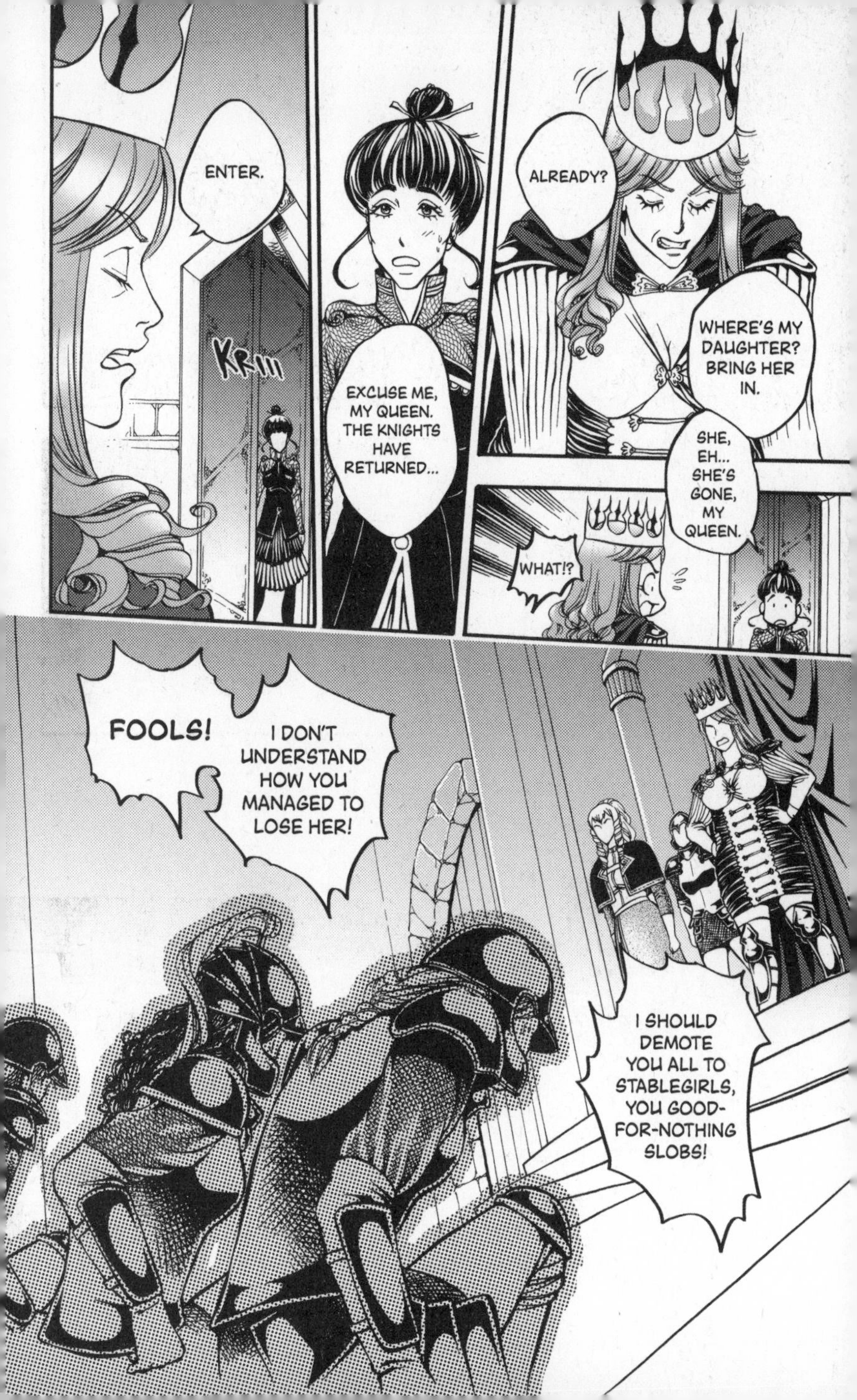
ENTER.
KRIII
EXCUSE ME, MY QUEEN. THE KNIGHTS HAVE RETURNED...
ALREADY?
WHERE'S MY DAUGHTER? BRING HER IN.
WHAT!?
SHE, EH... SHE'S GONE, MY QUEEN.
FOOLS!
I DON'T UNDERSTAND HOW YOU MANAGED TO LOSE HER!
I SHOULD DEMOTE YOU ALL TO STABLEGIRLS, YOU GOOD-FOR-NOTHING SLOBS!

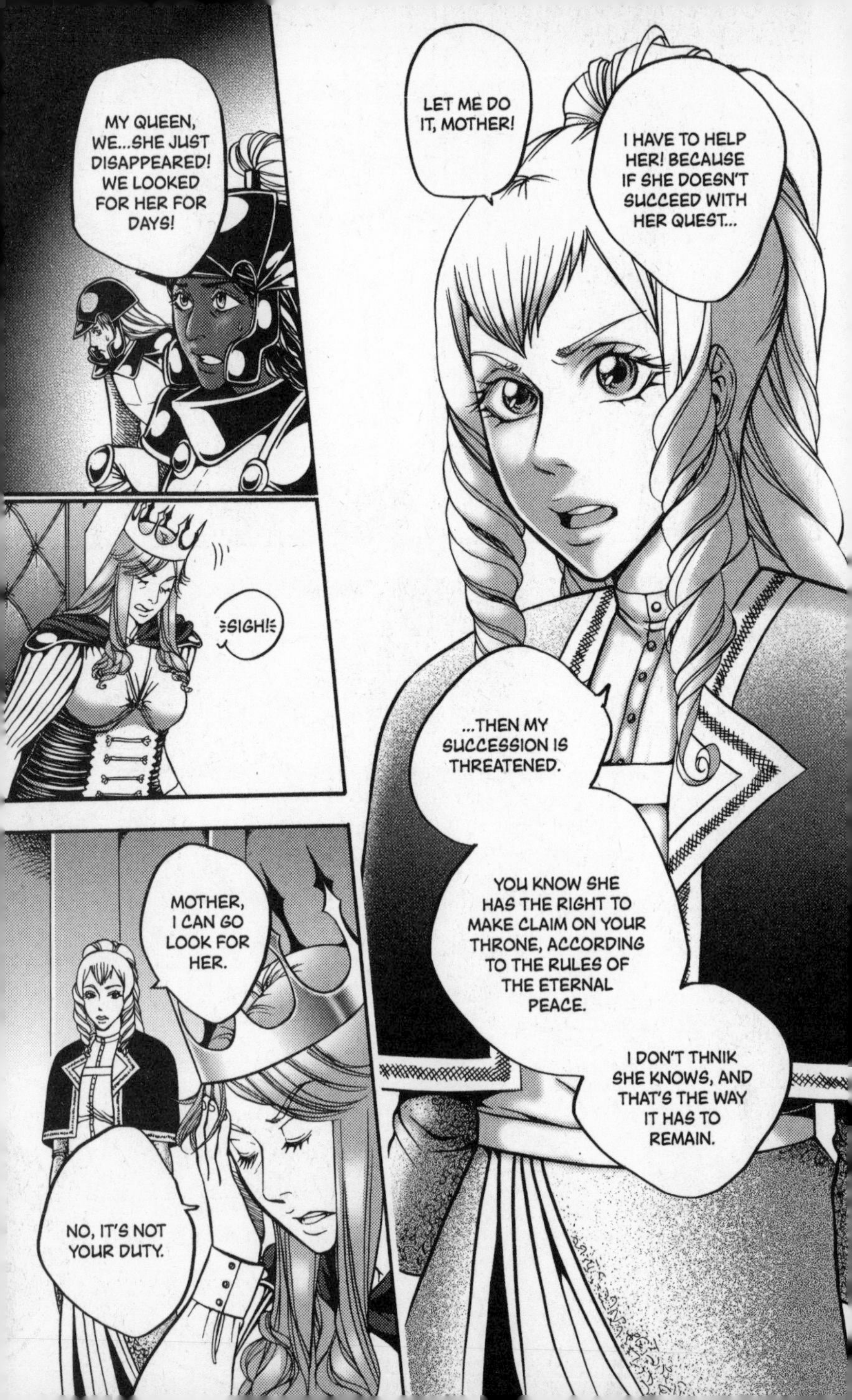
MY QUEEN, WE...SHE JUST DISAPPEARED! WE LOOKED FOR HER FOR DAYS!
SIGH!
MOTHER, I CAN GO LOOK FOR HER.
NO, IT'S NOT YOUR DUTY.
LET ME DO IT, MOTHER!
I HAVE TO HELP HER! BECAUSE IF SHE DOESN'T SUCCEED WITH HER QUEST...
...THEN MY SUCCESSION IS THREATENED.
YOU KNOW SHE HAS THE RIGHT TO MAKE CLAIM ON YOUR THRONE, ACCORDING TO THE RULES OF THE ETERNAL PEACE.
I DON'T THNIK SHE KNOWS, AND THAT'S THE WAY IT HAS TO REMAIN.

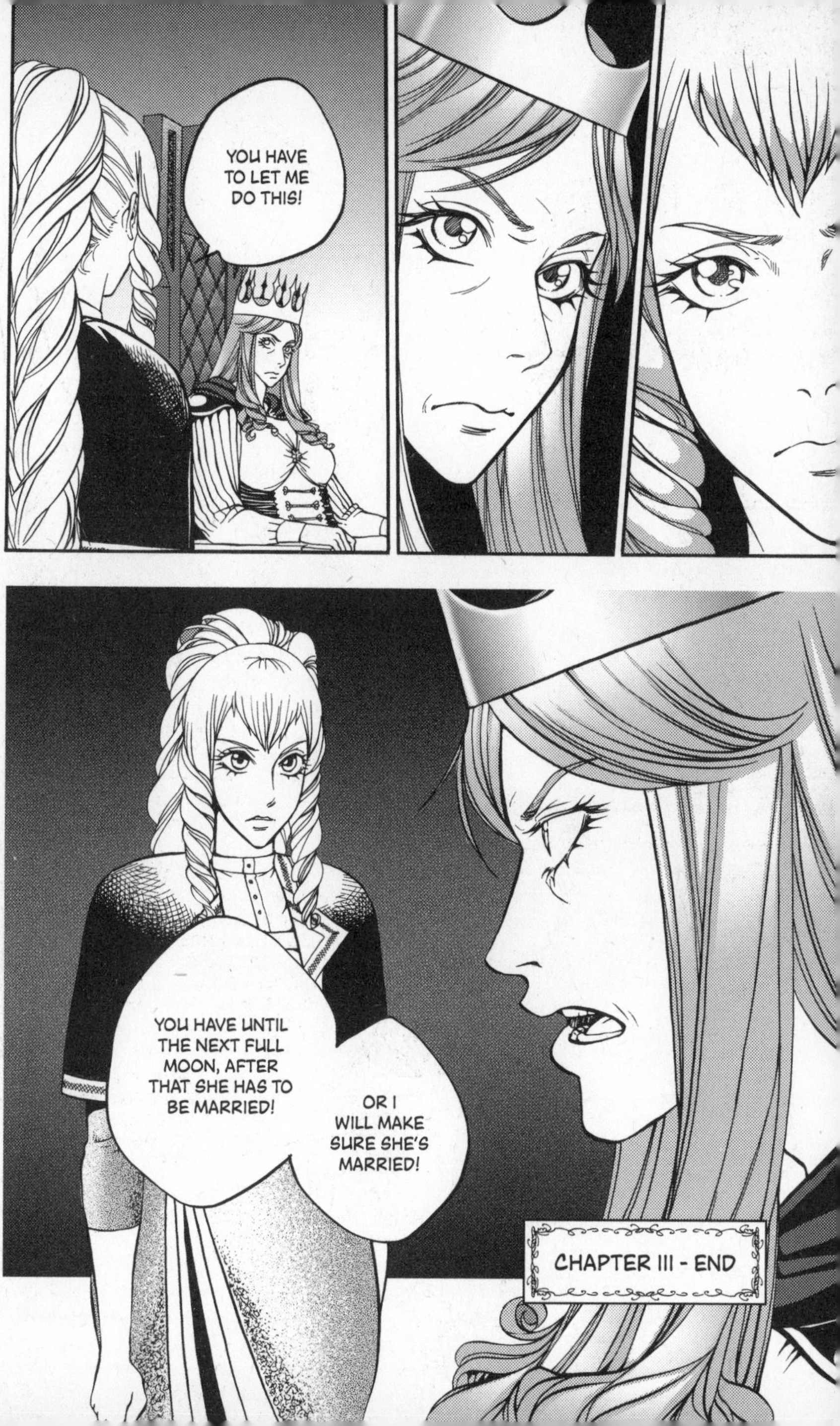
YOU HAVE TO LET ME DO THIS!
YOU HAVE UNTIL THE NEXT FULL MOON, AFTER THAT SHE HAS TO BE MARRIED!
OR I WILL MAKE SURE SHE'S MARRIED!
CHAPTER III - END

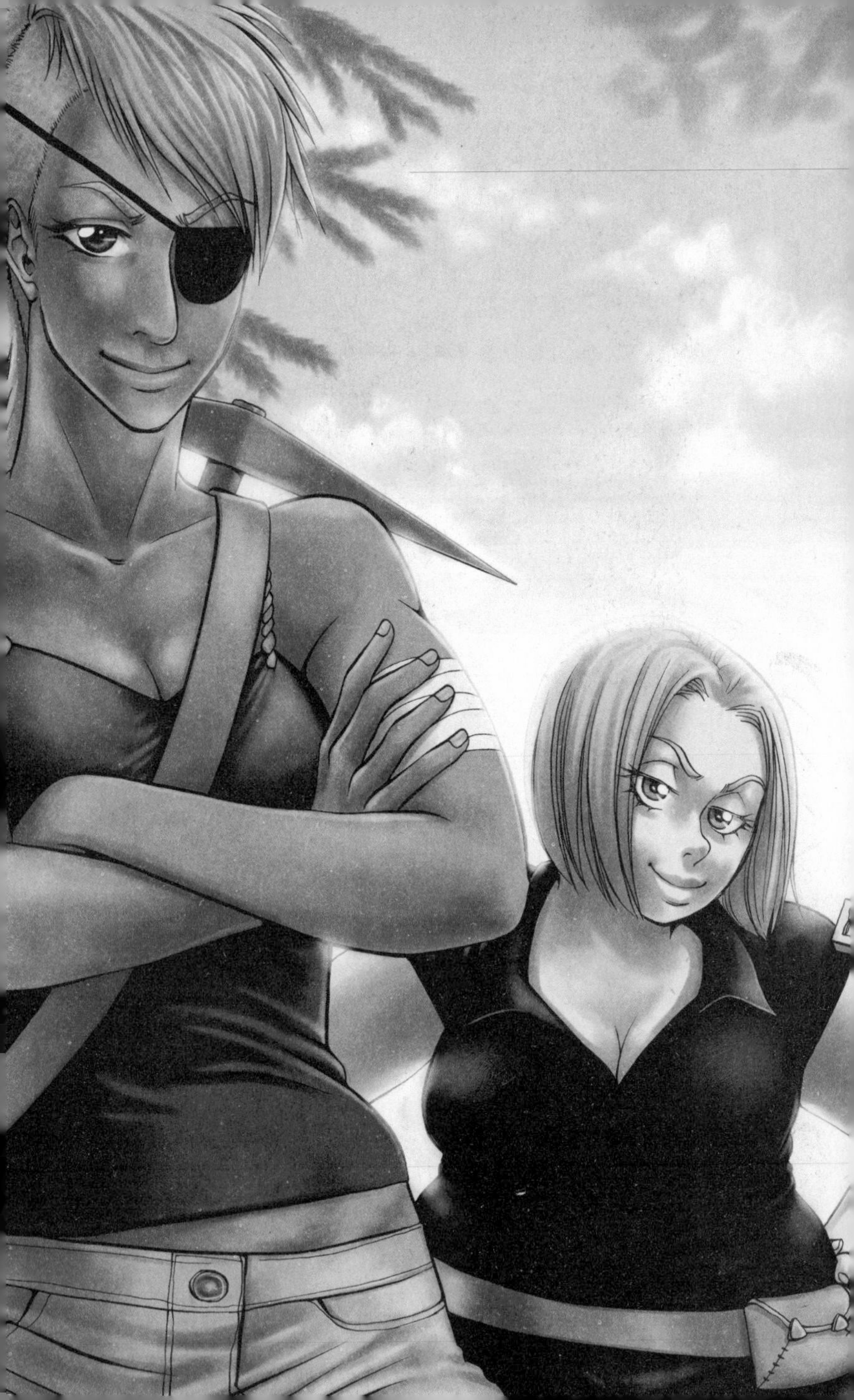

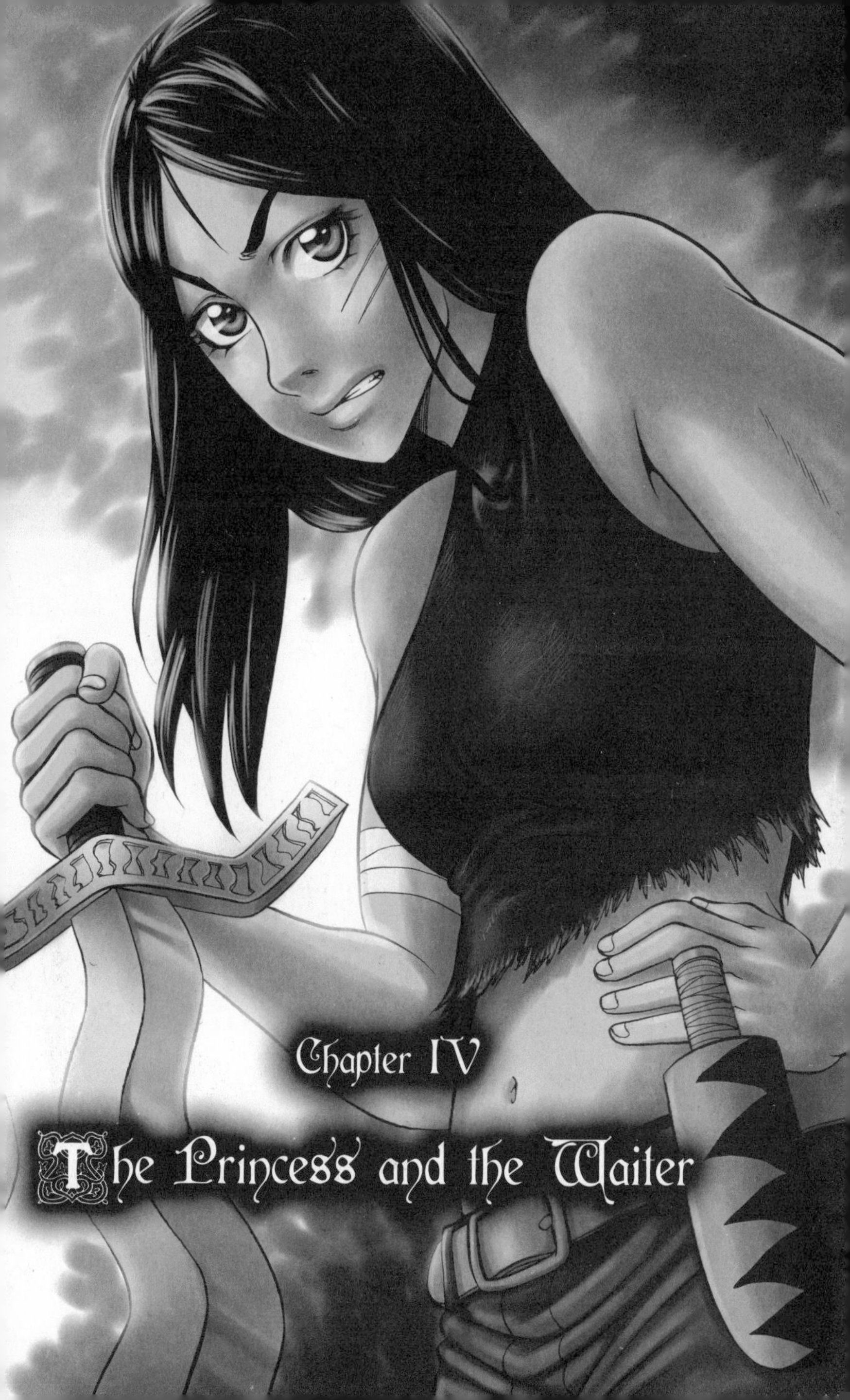
Chapter IV
The Princess and the Waiter

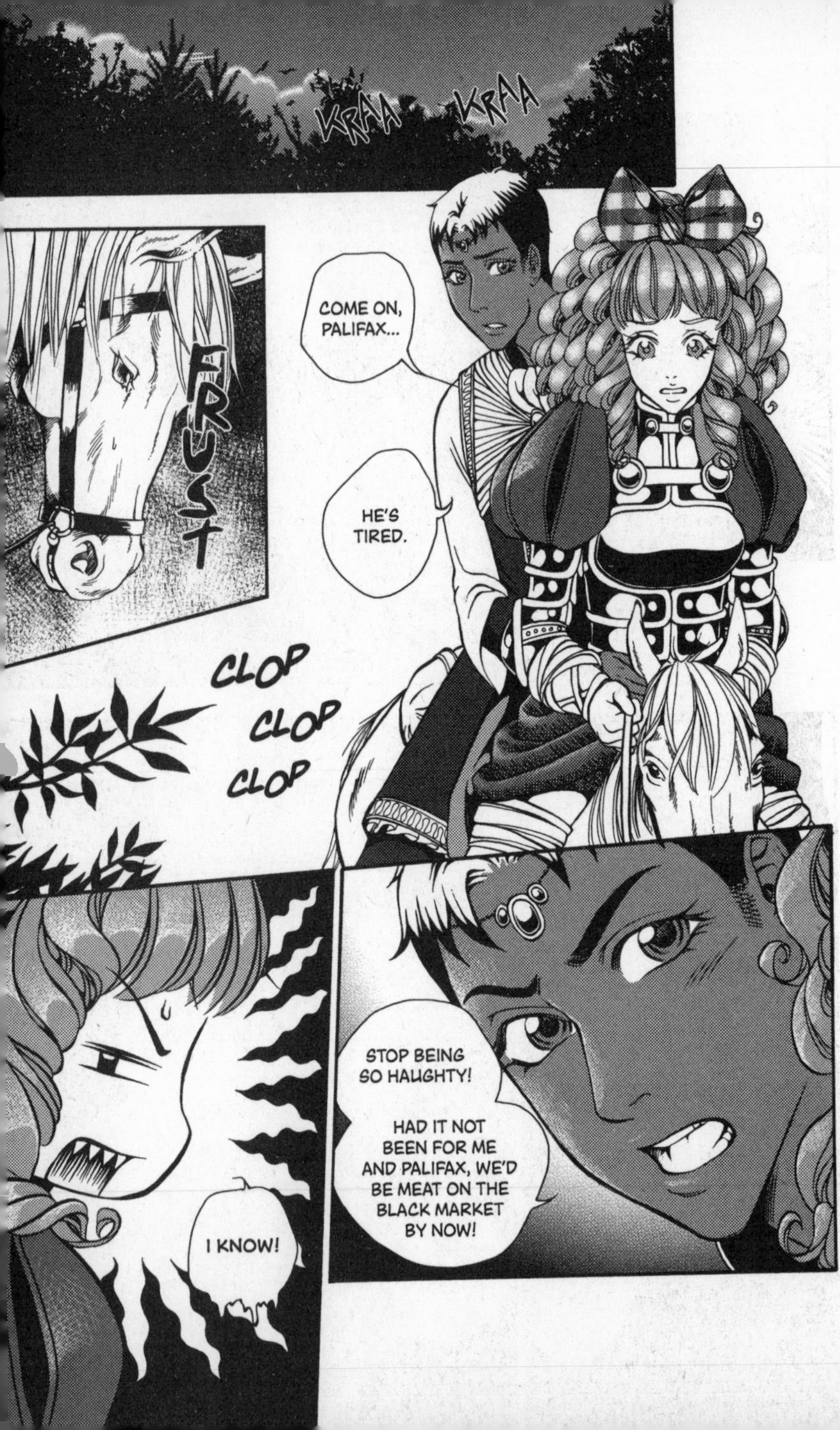
KRAA KRAA
FRUST
COME ON, PALIFAX...
HE'S TIRED.
CLOP CLOP CLOP
I KNOW!
STOP BEING SO HAUGHTY!
HAD IT NOT BEEN FOR ME AND PALIFAX, WE'D BE MEAT ON THE BLACK MARKET BY NOW!

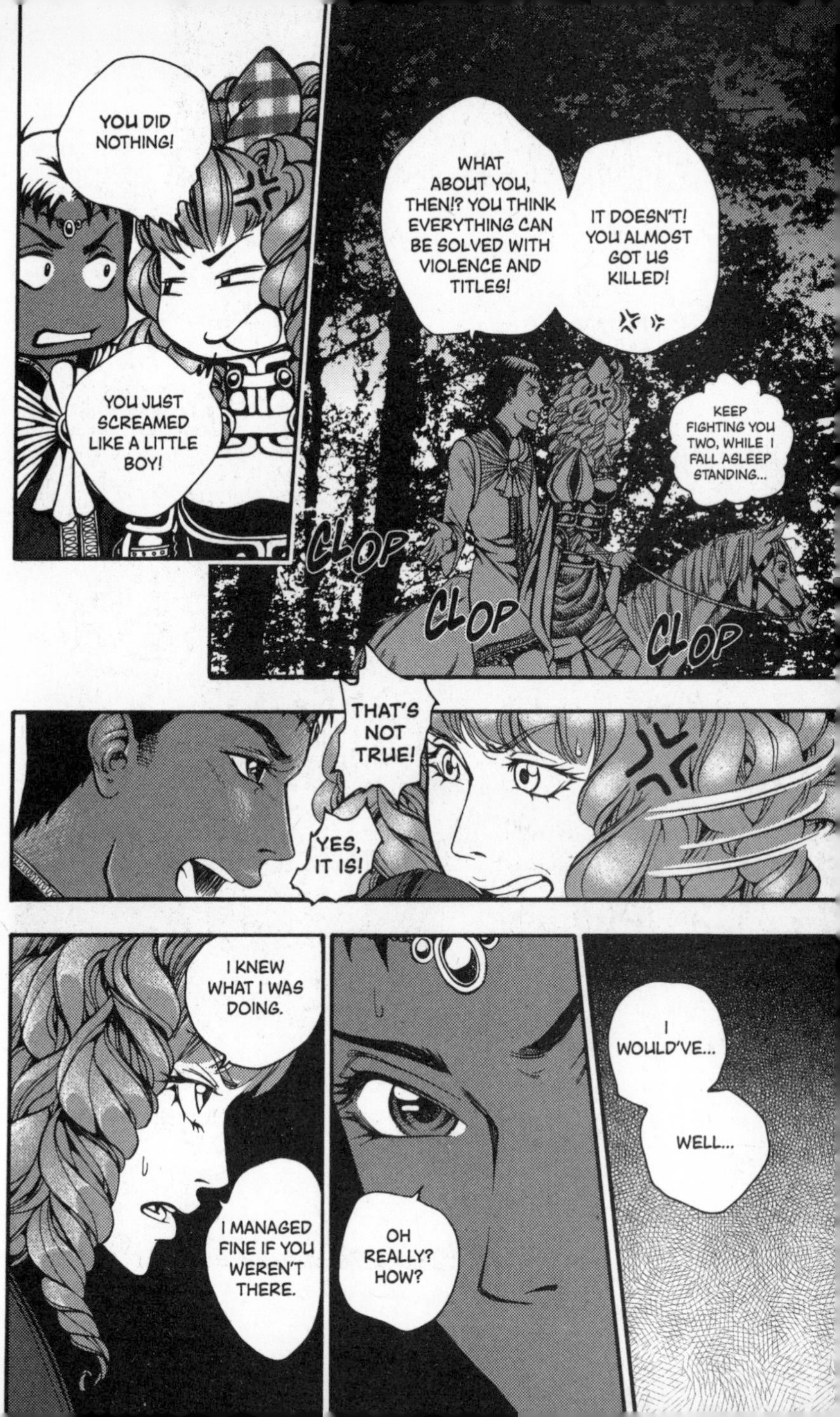
YOU DID NOTHING!
YOU JUST SCREAMED LIKE A LITTLE BOY!
WHAT ABOUT YOU, THEN!? YOU THINK EVERYTHING CAN BE SOLVED WITH VIOLENCE AND TITLES!
IT DOESN'T! YOU ALMOST GOT US KILLED!
KEEP FIGHTING YOU TWO, WHILE I FALL ASLEEP STANDING...
CLOP
CLOP
CLOP
THAT'S NOT TRUE!
YES, IT IS!
I KNEW WHAT I WAS DOING.
I MANAGED FINE IF YOU WEREN'T THERE.
OH REALLY? HOW?
I WOULD'VE...
WELL...

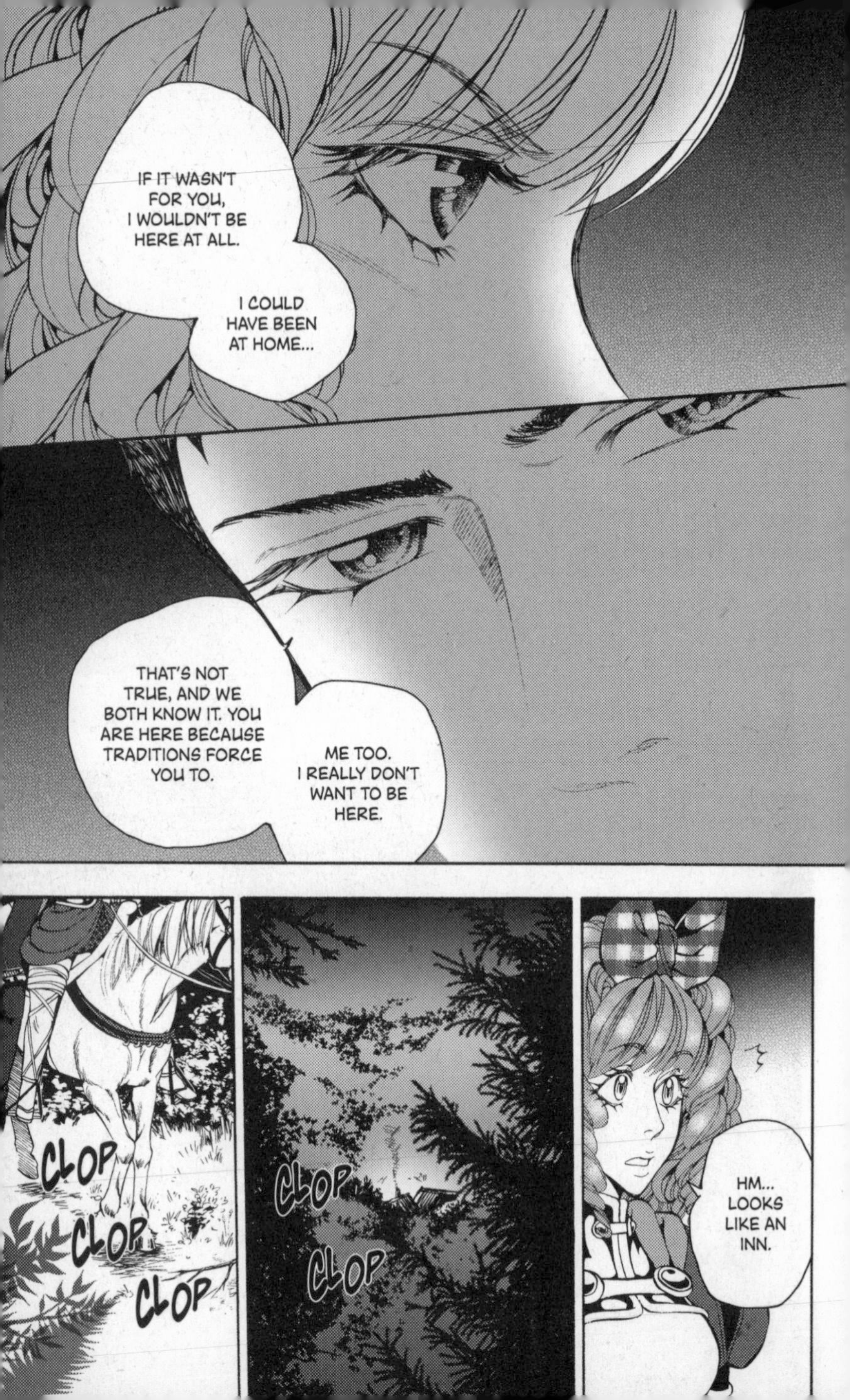

IF IT WASN'T FOR YOU, I WOULDN'T BE HERE AT ALL.
I COULD HAVE BEEN AT HOME...
THAT'S NOT TRUE, AND WE BOTH KNOW IT. YOU ARE HERE BECAUSE TRADITIONS FORCE YOU TO.
ME TOO. I REALLY DON'T WANT TO BE HERE.
CLOP
CLOP
CLOP
CLOP
CLOP
HM... LOOKS LIKE AN INN.

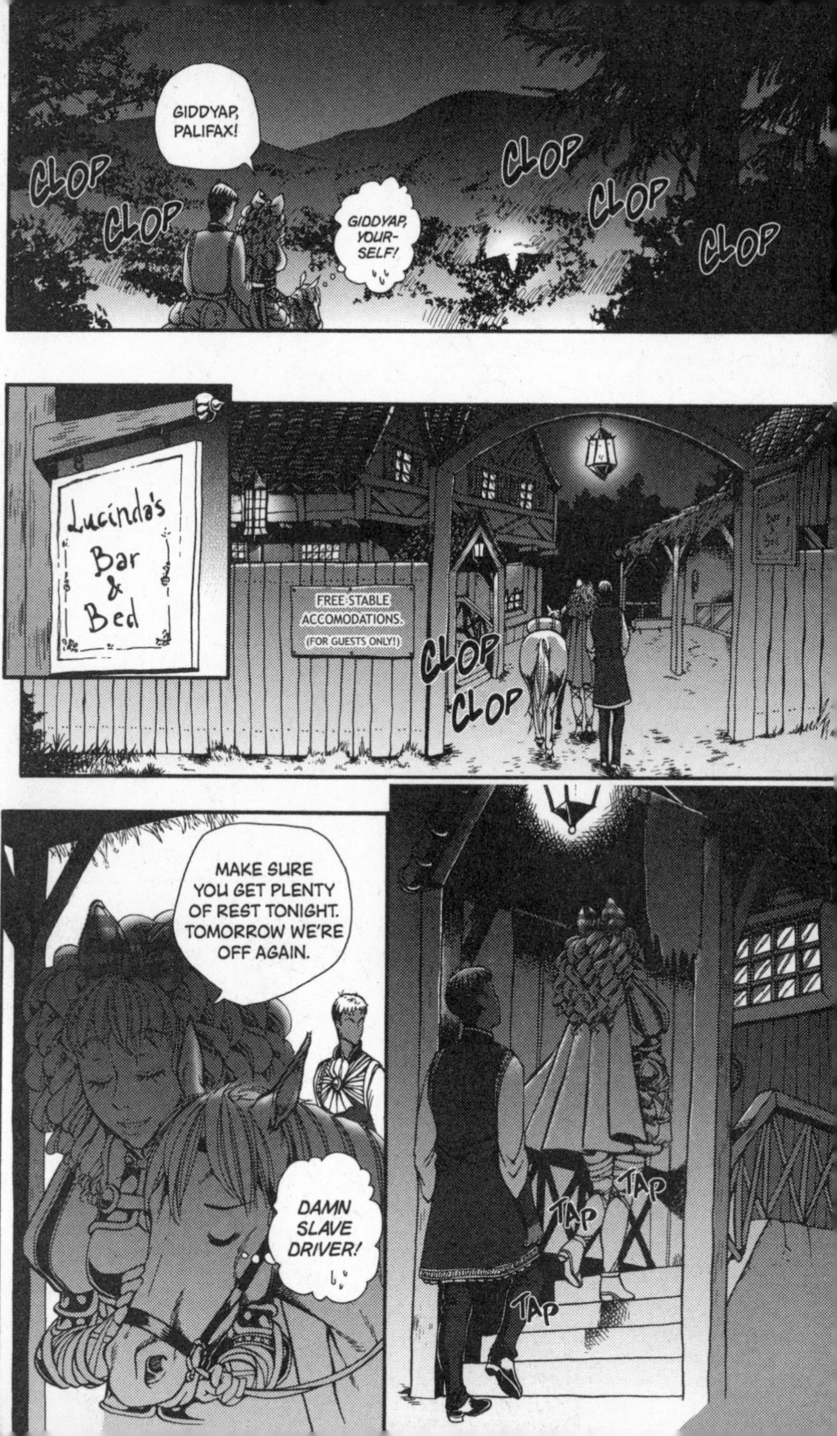

CLOP
CLOP
GIDDYAP, PALIFAX!
GIDDYAP, YOUR-SELF!
CLOP
CLOP
CLOP
Lucinda's Bar & Bed
FREE STABLE ACCOMODATIONS.
(FOR GUESTS ONLY!)
CLOP
CLOP
MAKE SURE YOU GET PLENTY OF REST TONIGHT. TOMORROW WE'RE OFF AGAIN.
DAMN SLAVE DRIVER!
TAP
TAP
TAP

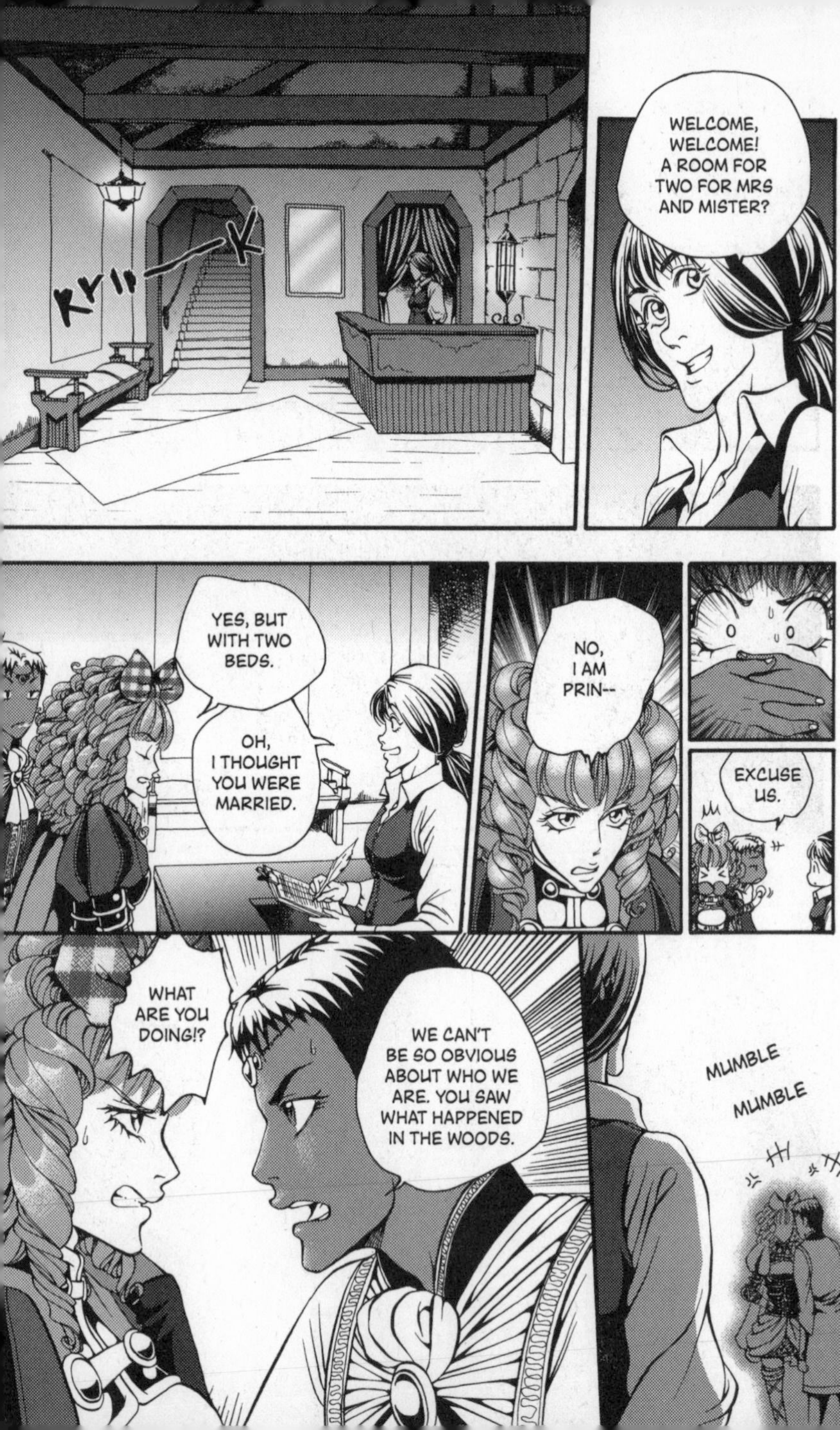
KYIII—K
WELCOME, WELCOME! A ROOM FOR TWO FOR MRS AND MISTER?
YES, BUT WITH TWO BEDS.
OH, I THOUGHT YOU WERE MARRIED.
NO, I AM PRIN--
EXCUSE US.
WHAT ARE YOU DOING!?
WE CAN'T BE SO OBVIOUS ABOUT WHO WE ARE. YOU SAW WHAT HAPPENED IN THE WOODS.
MUMBLE
MUMBLE

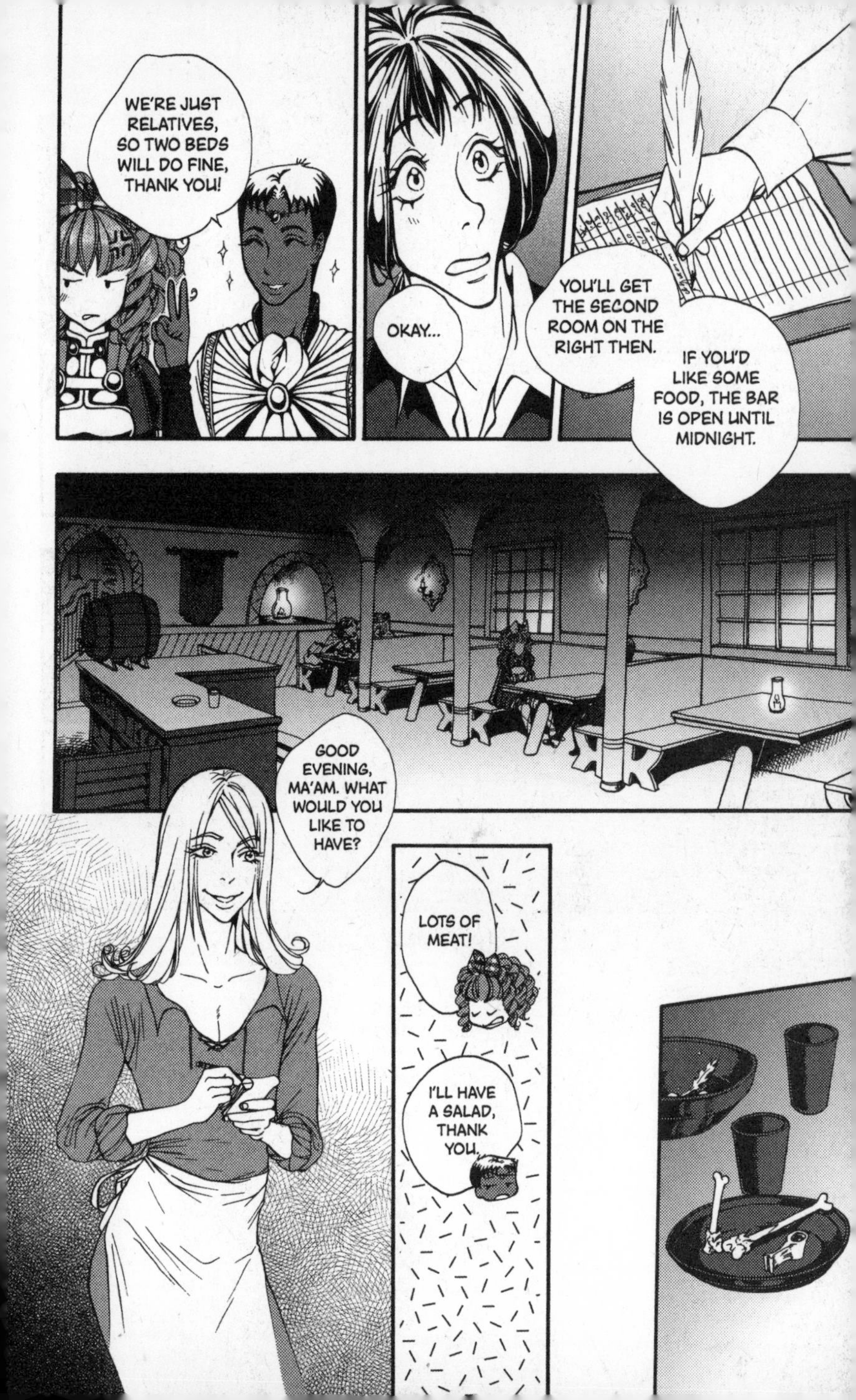
WE'RE JUST RELATIVES, SO TWO BEDS WILL DO FINE, THANK YOU!
OKAY...
YOU'LL GET THE SECOND ROOM ON THE RIGHT THEN.
IF YOU'D LIKE SOME FOOD, THE BAR IS OPEN UNTIL MIDNIGHT.
GOOD EVENING, MA'AM. WHAT WOULD YOU LIKE TO HAVE?
LOTS OF MEAT!
I'LL HAVE A SALAD, THANK YOU.

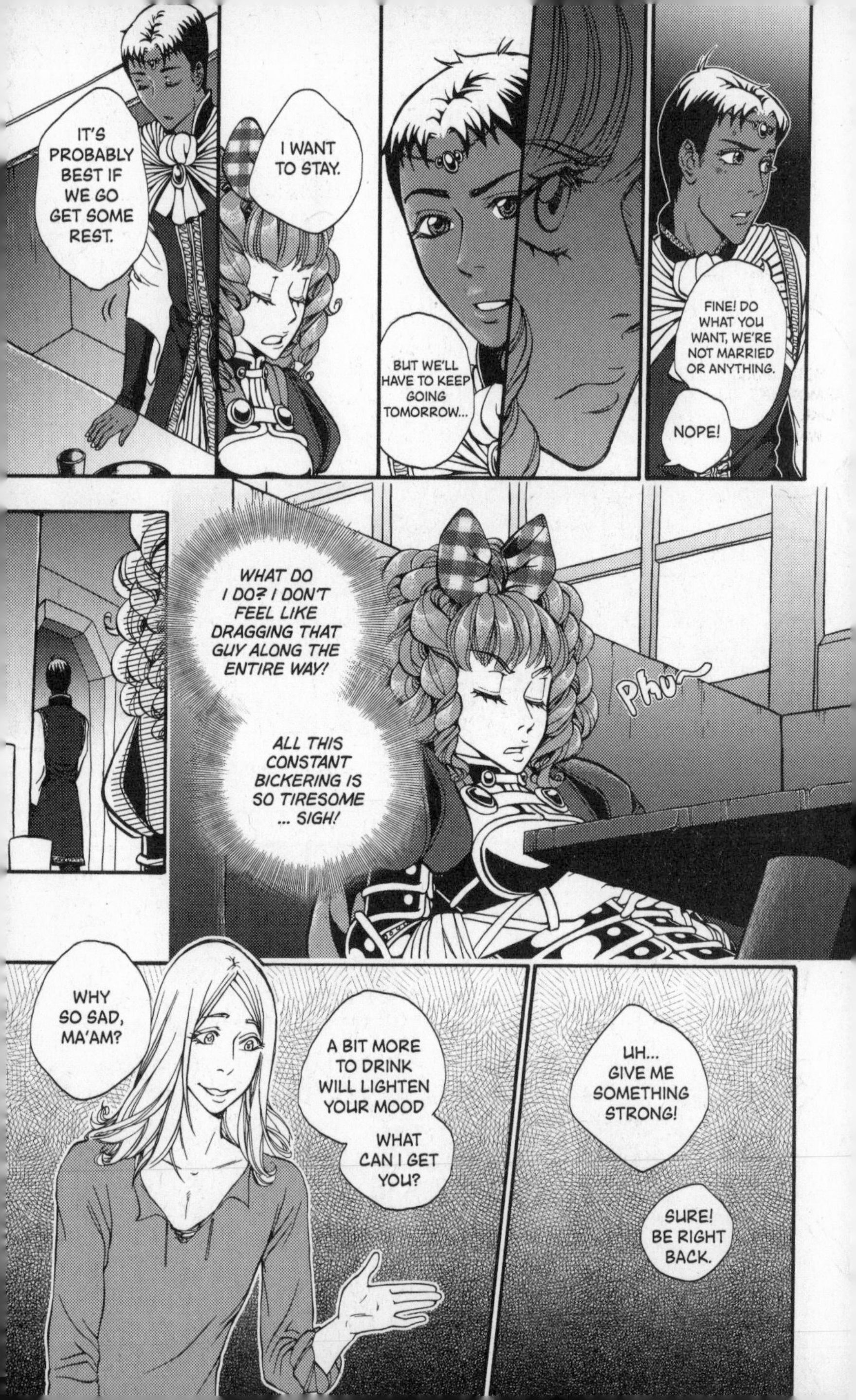
IT'S PROBABLY BEST IF WE GO GET SOME REST.
I WANT TO STAY.
BUT WE'LL HAVE TO KEEP GOING TOMORROW...
FINE! DO WHAT YOU WANT, WE'RE NOT MARRIED OR ANYTHING.
NOPE!
WHAT DO I DO? I DON'T FEEL LIKE DRAGGING THAT GUY ALONG THE ENTIRE WAY!
ALL THIS CONSTANT BICKERING IS SO TIRESOME ... SIGH!
Phu~
WHY SO SAD, MA'AM?
A BIT MORE TO DRINK WILL LIGHTEN YOUR MOOD
WHAT CAN I GET YOU?
UH... GIVE ME SOMETHING STRONG!
SURE! BE RIGHT BACK.

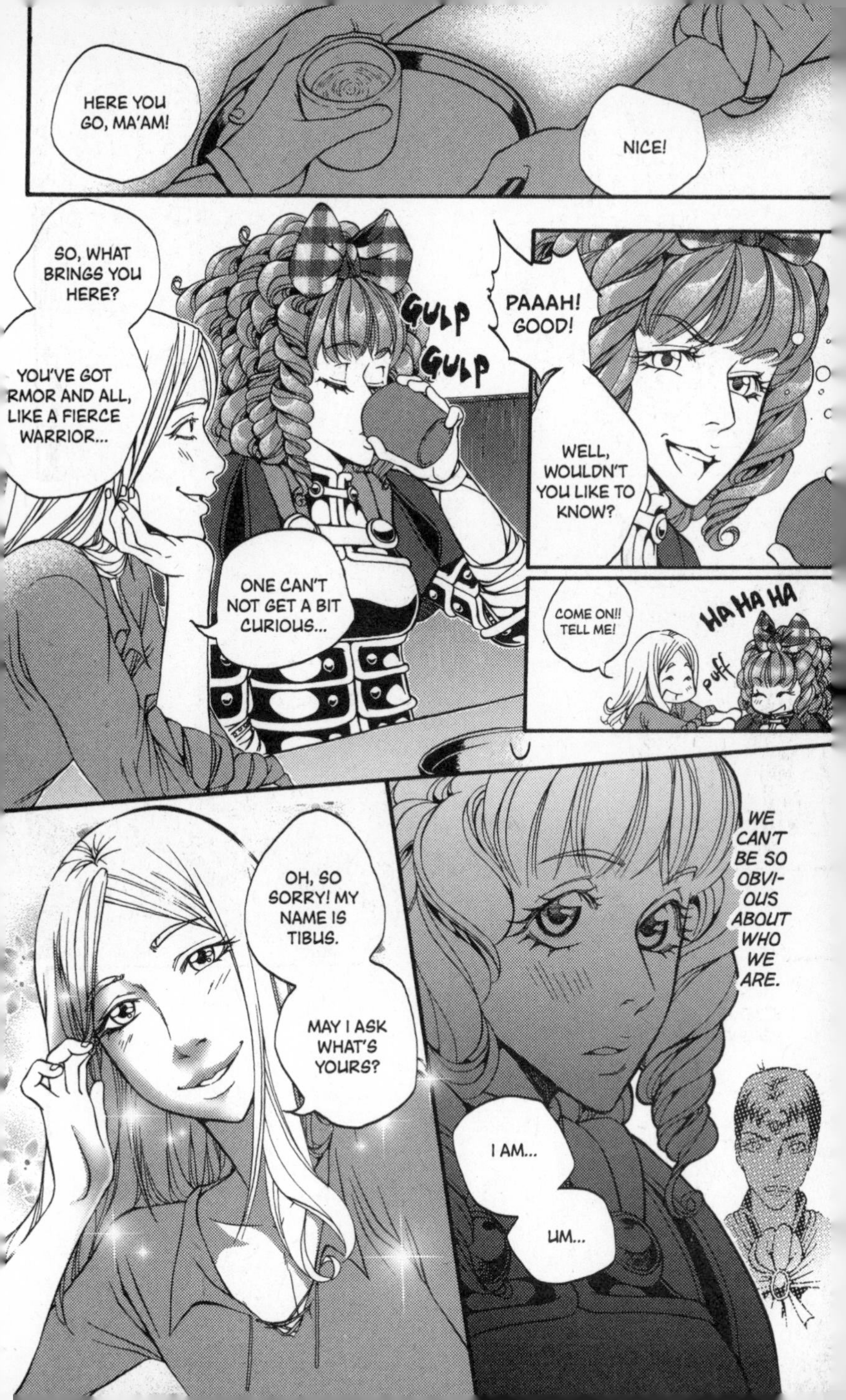
HERE YOU GO, MA'AM!
NICE!
SO, WHAT BRINGS YOU HERE?
YOU'VE GOT RMOR AND ALL, LIKE A FIERCE WARRIOR...
GULP GULP
ONE CAN'T NOT GET A BIT CURIOUS...
PAAAH! GOOD!
WELL, WOULDN'T YOU LIKE TO KNOW?
COME ON!! TELL ME!
HA HA HA
puff
OH, SO SORRY! MY NAME IS TIBUS.
MAY I ASK WHAT'S YOURS?
WE CAN'T BE SO OBVI-OUS ABOUT WHO WE ARE.
I AM...
UM...

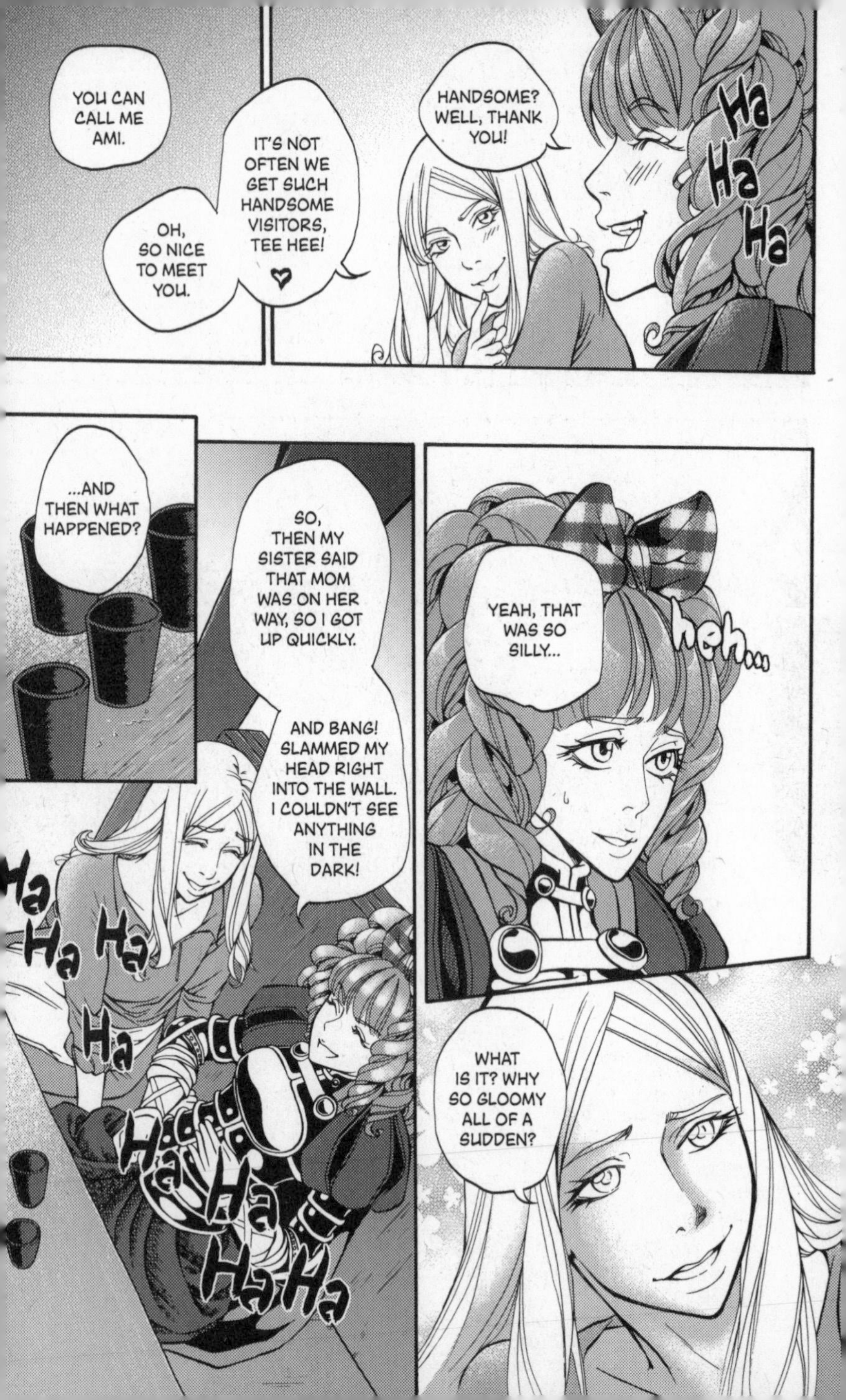
YOU CAN CALL ME AMI.
OH, SO NICE TO MEET YOU.
IT'S NOT OFTEN WE GET SUCH HANDSOME VISITORS, TEE HEE! ♡
HANDSOME? WELL, THANK YOU!
Ha Ha Ha
...AND THEN WHAT HAPPENED?
SO, THEN MY SISTER SAID THAT MOM WAS ON HER WAY, SO I GOT UP QUICKLY.
AND BANG! SLAMMED MY HEAD RIGHT INTO THE WALL. I COULDN'T SEE ANYTHING IN THE DARK!
Ha Ha Ha Ha
Ha Ha Ha Ha Ha
YEAH, THAT WAS SO SILLY...
heh...
WHAT IS IT? WHY SO GLOOMY ALL OF A SUDDEN?

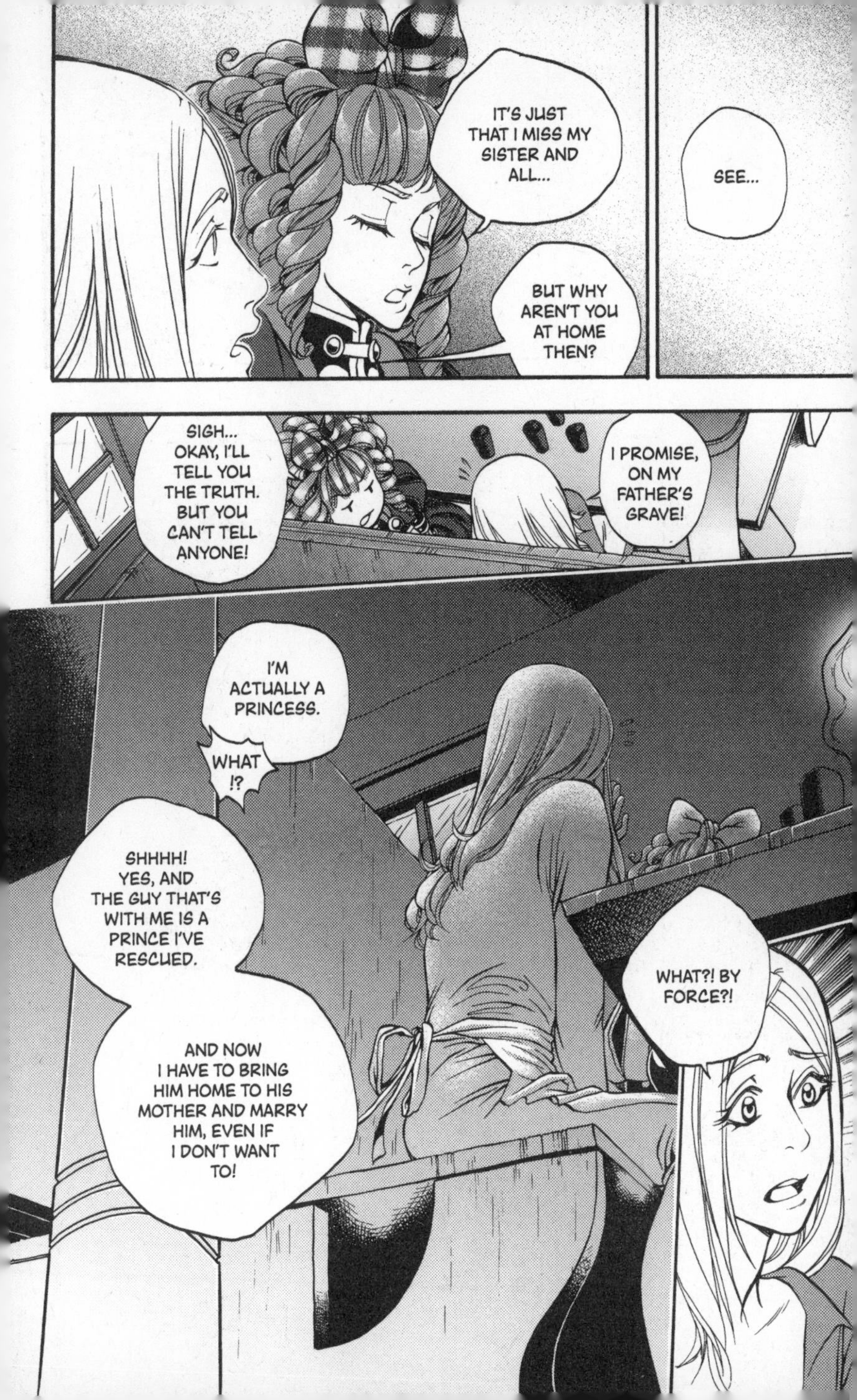
IT'S JUST THAT I MISS MY SISTER AND ALL...
BUT WHY AREN'T YOU AT HOME THEN?
SEE...
SIGH... OKAY, I'LL TELL YOU THE TRUTH. BUT YOU CAN'T TELL ANYONE!
I PROMISE, ON MY FATHER'S GRAVE!
I'M ACTUALLY A PRINCESS.
WHAT !?
SHHHH! YES, AND THE GUY THAT'S WITH ME IS A PRINCE I'VE RESCUED.
AND NOW I HAVE TO BRING HIM HOME TO HIS MOTHER AND MARRY HIM, EVEN IF I DON'T WANT TO!
WHAT?! BY FORCE?!

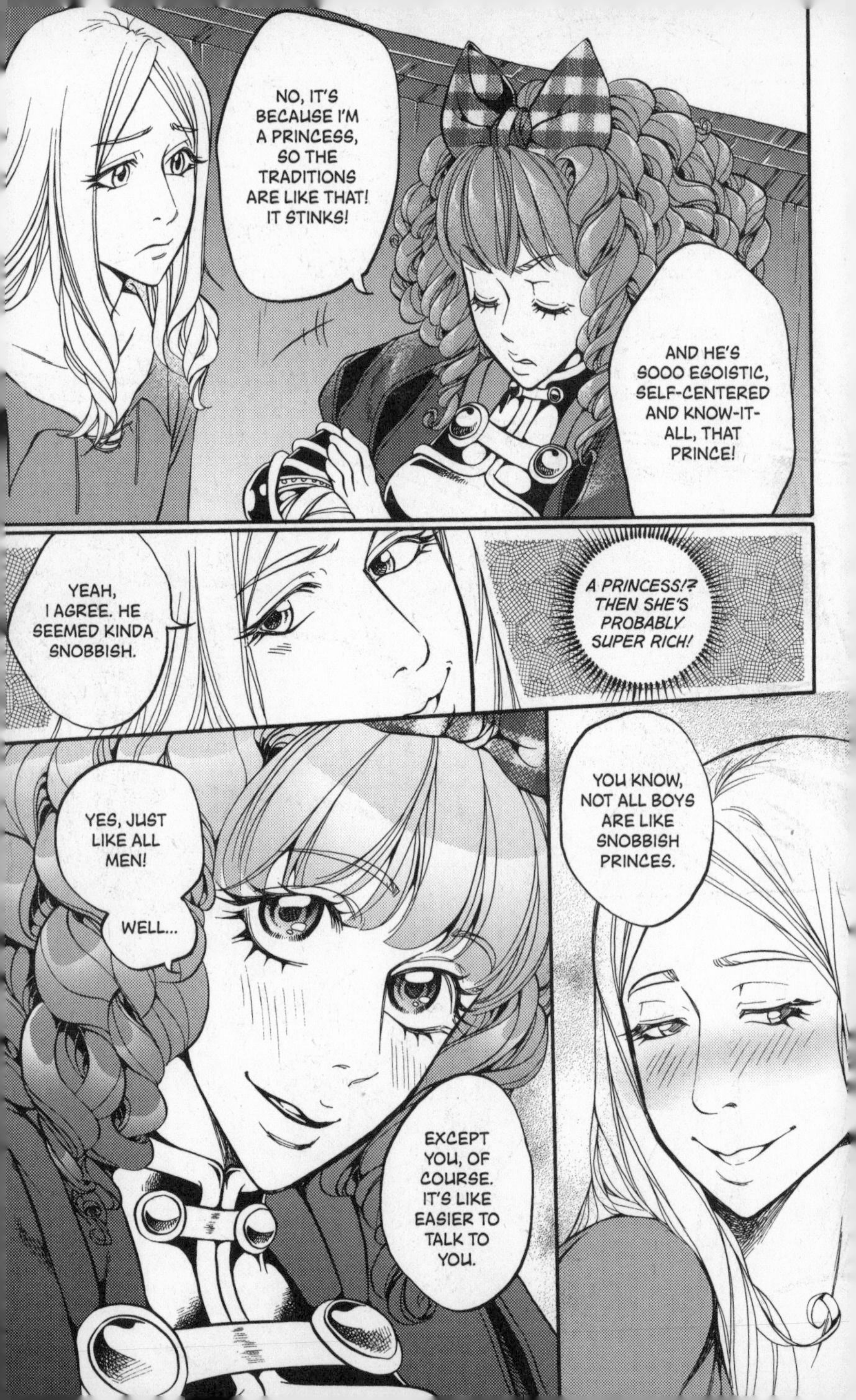
NO, IT'S BECAUSE I'M A PRINCESS, SO THE TRADITIONS ARE LIKE THAT! IT STINKS!
AND HE'S SOOO EGOISTIC, SELF-CENTERED AND KNOW-IT-ALL, THAT PRINCE!
YEAH, I AGREE. HE SEEMED KINDA SNOBBISH.
A PRINCESS!? THEN SHE'S PROBABLY SUPER RICH!
YES, JUST LIKE ALL MEN!
WELL...
EXCEPT YOU, OF COURSE. IT'S LIKE EASIER TO TALK TO YOU.
YOU KNOW, NOT ALL BOYS ARE LIKE SNOBBISH PRINCES.

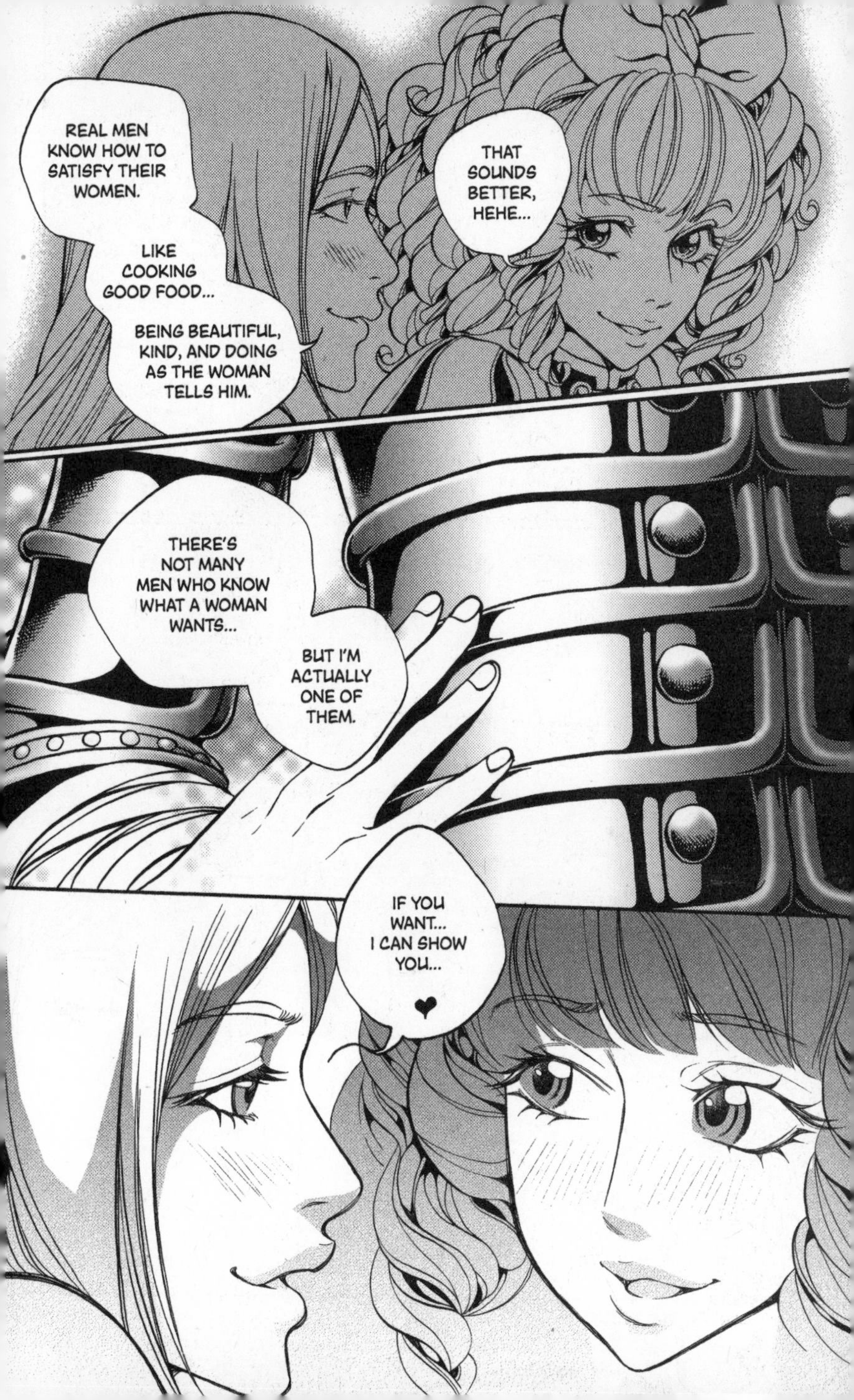
REAL MEN KNOW HOW TO SATISFY THEIR WOMEN.
LIKE COOKING GOOD FOOD...
BEING BEAUTIFUL, KIND, AND DOING AS THE WOMAN TELLS HIM.
THAT SOUNDS BETTER, HEHE...
THERE'S NOT MANY MEN WHO KNOW WHAT A WOMAN WANTS...
BUT I'M ACTUALLY ONE OF THEM.
IF YOU WANT... I CAN SHOW YOU... ♥

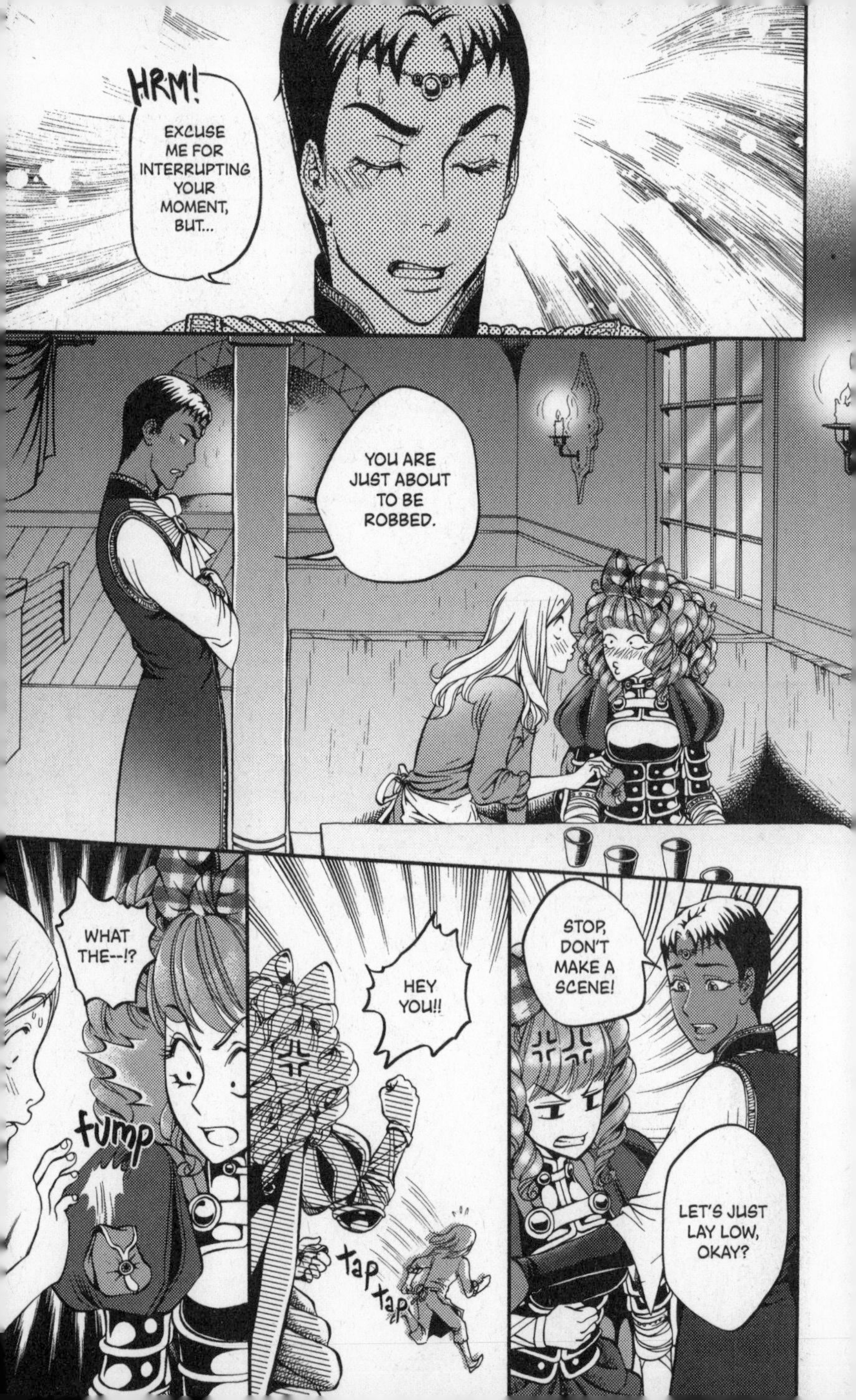
HRM!
EXCUSE ME FOR INTERRUPTING YOUR MOMENT, BUT...
YOU ARE JUST ABOUT TO BE ROBBED.
WHAT THE--!?
fump
HEY YOU!!
tap tap
STOP, DON'T MAKE A SCENE!
LET'S JUST LAY LOW, OKAY?

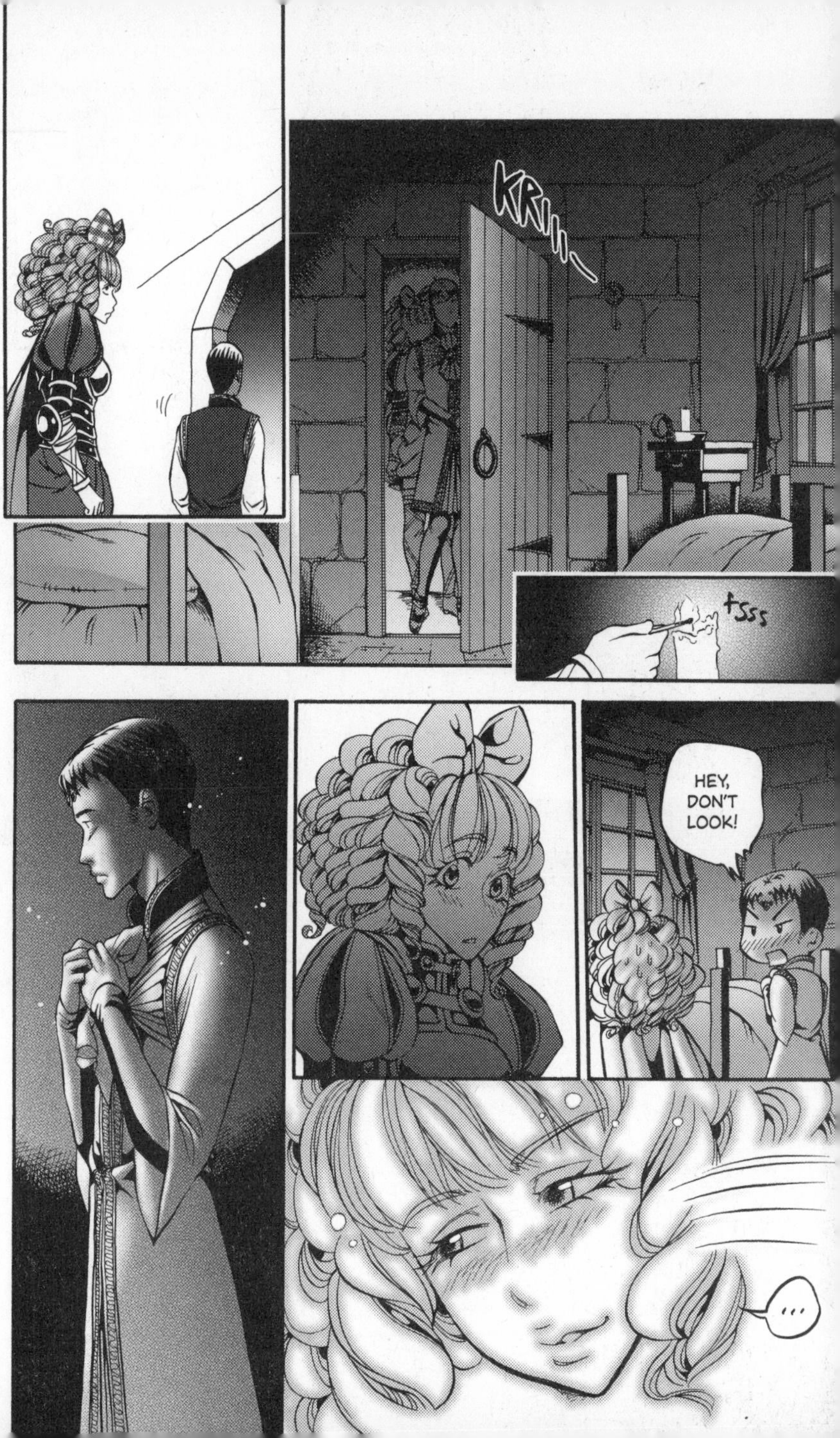
KRIII—
FSSS
HEY, DON'T LOOK!
...

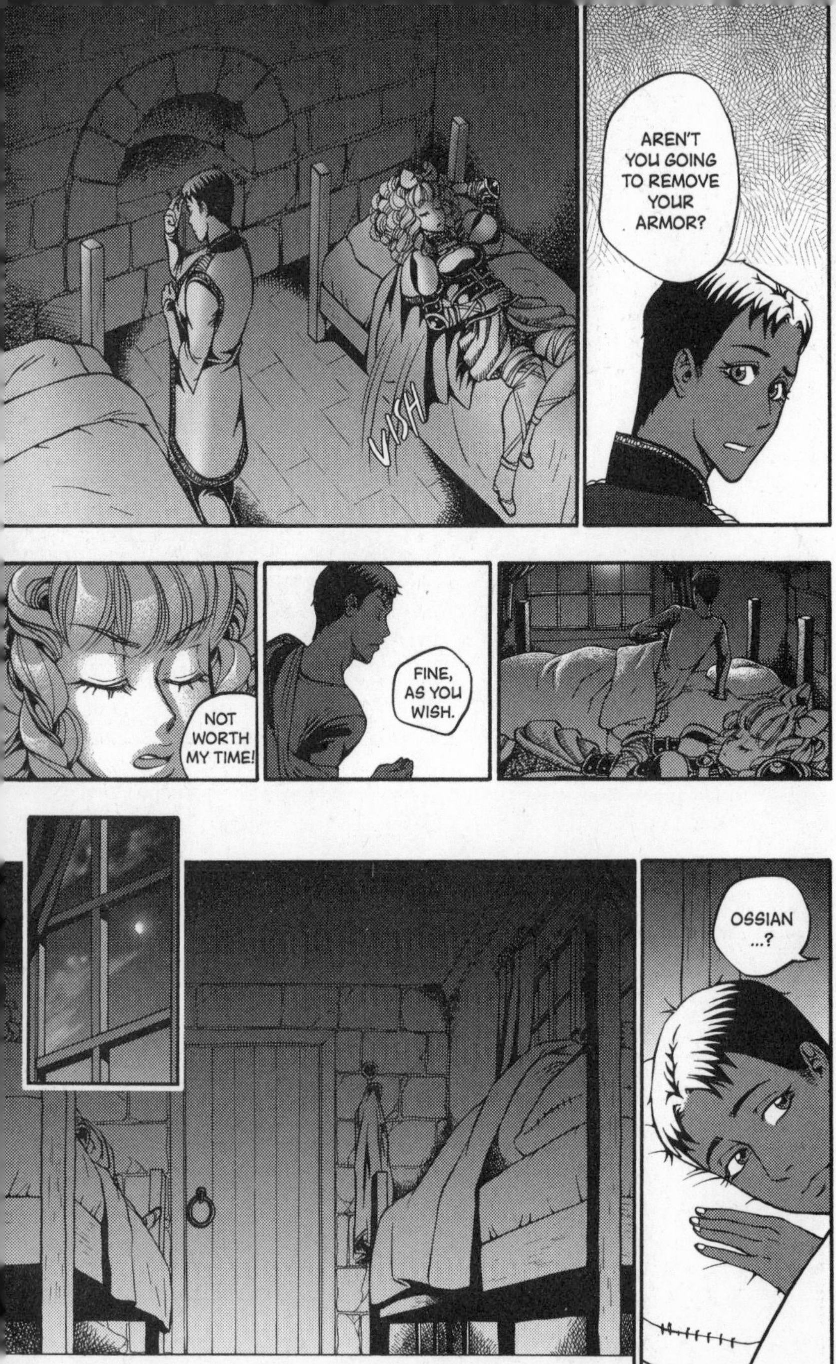
VISH
AREN'T YOU GOING TO REMOVE YOUR ARMOR?
NOT WORTH MY TIME!
FINE, AS YOU WISH.
OSSIAN ...?

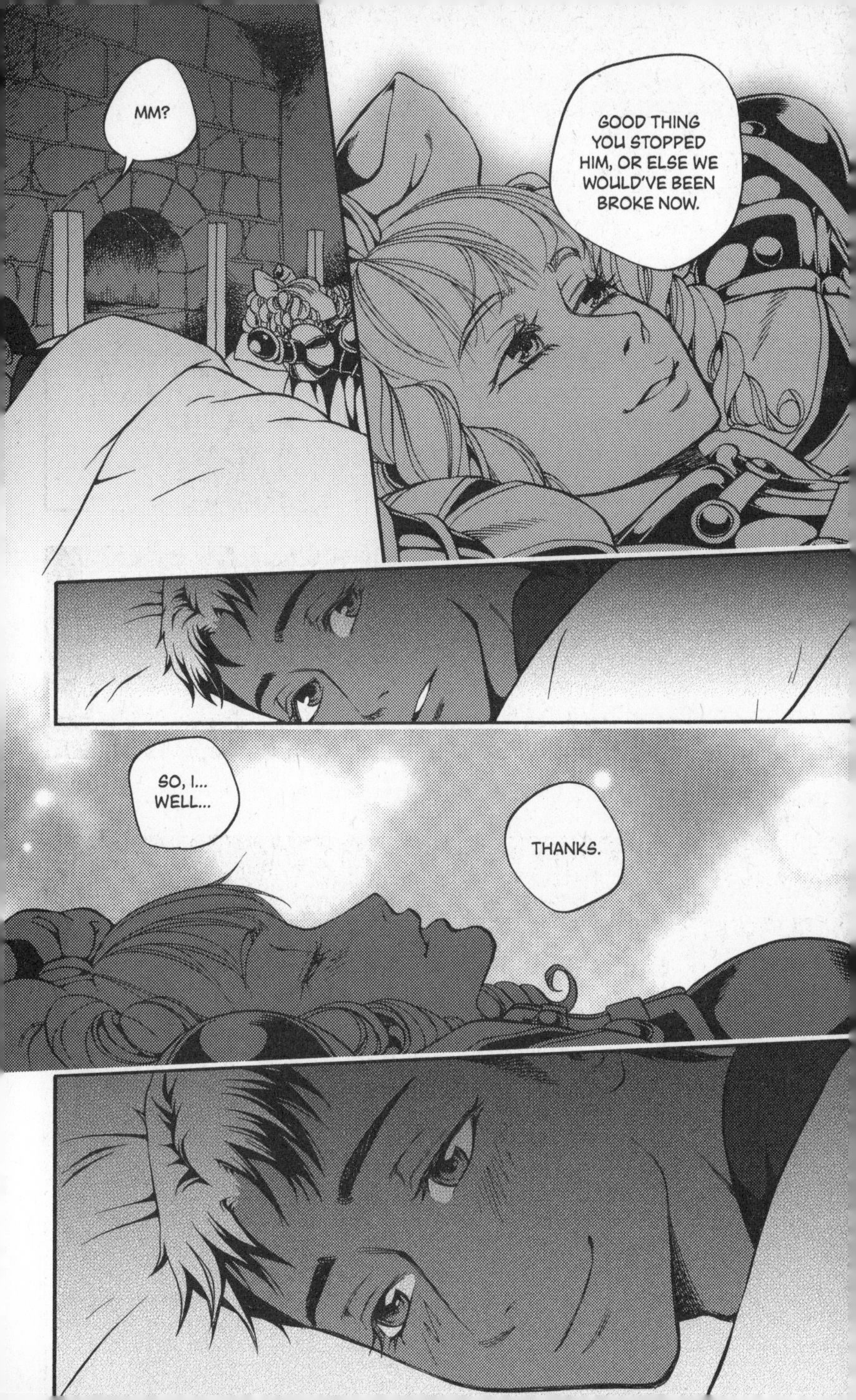
MM?
GOOD THING YOU STOPPED HIM, OR ELSE WE WOULD'VE BEEN BROKE NOW.
SO, I... WELL...
THANKS.

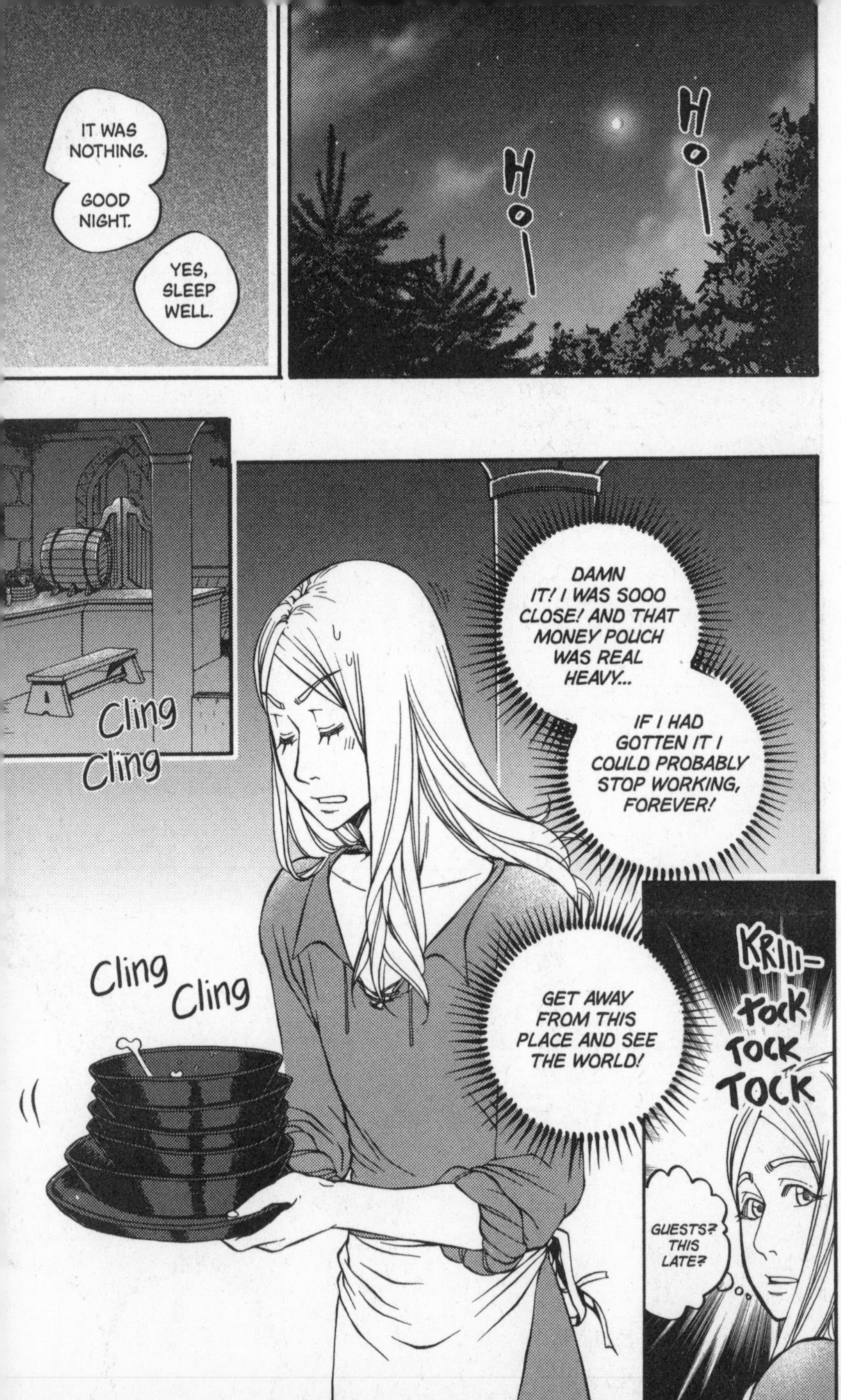
IT WAS NOTHING.
GOOD NIGHT.
YES, SLEEP WELL.
HO-
HO-
Cling Cling
DAMN IT! I WAS SOOO CLOSE! AND THAT MONEY POUCH WAS REAL HEAVY...
IF I HAD GOTTEN IT I COULD PROBABLY STOP WORKING, FOREVER!
Cling Cling
GET AWAY FROM THIS PLACE AND SEE THE WORLD!
KRIII-
TOCK
TOCK
TOCK
GUESTS? THIS LATE?

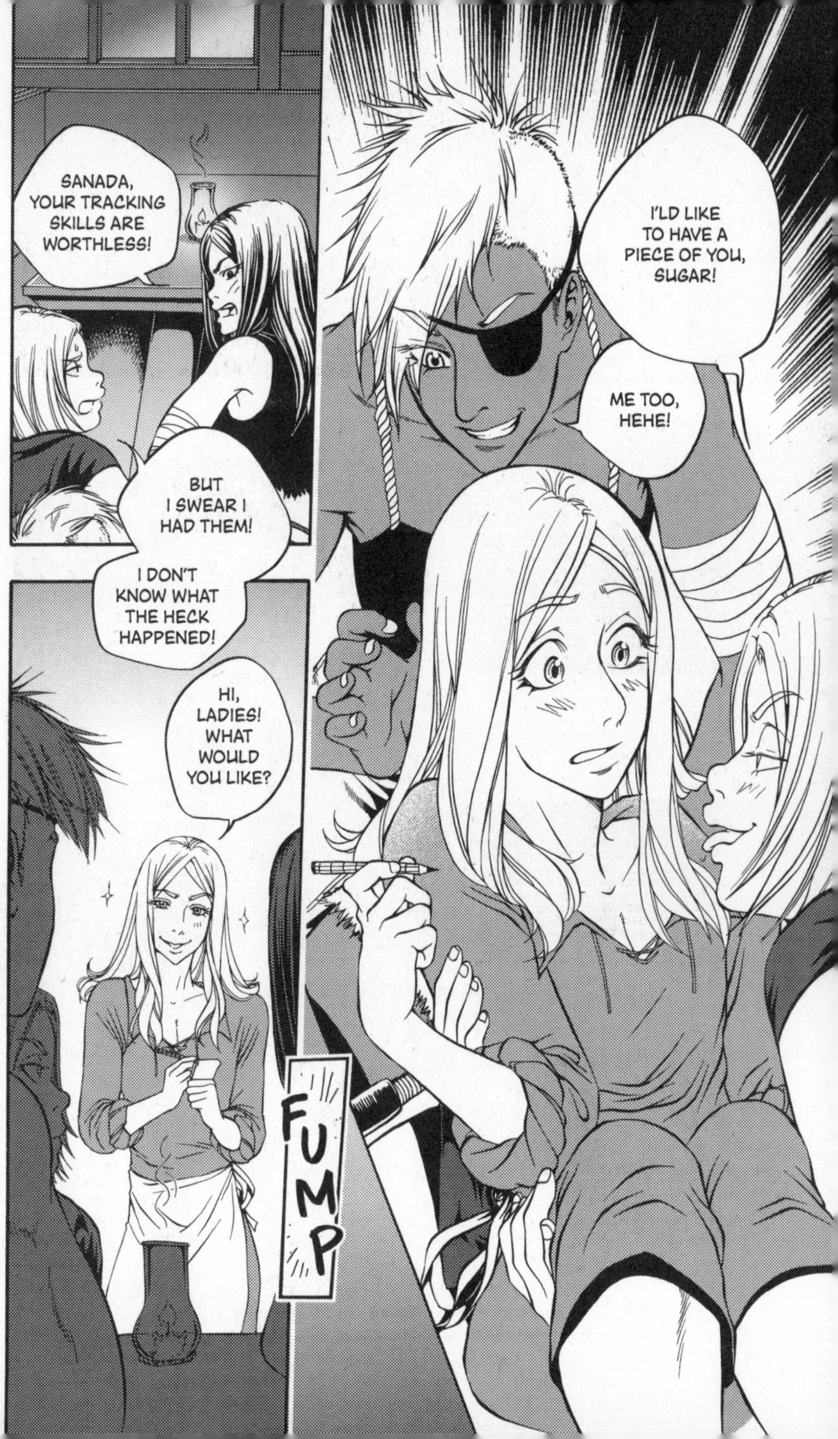
SANADA, YOUR TRACKING SKILLS ARE WORTHLESS!
BUT I SWEAR I HAD THEM!
I DON'T KNOW WHAT THE HECK HAPPENED!
HI, LADIES! WHAT WOULD YOU LIKE?
FUMP
I'LD LIKE TO HAVE A PIECE OF YOU, SUGAR!
ME TOO, HEHE!

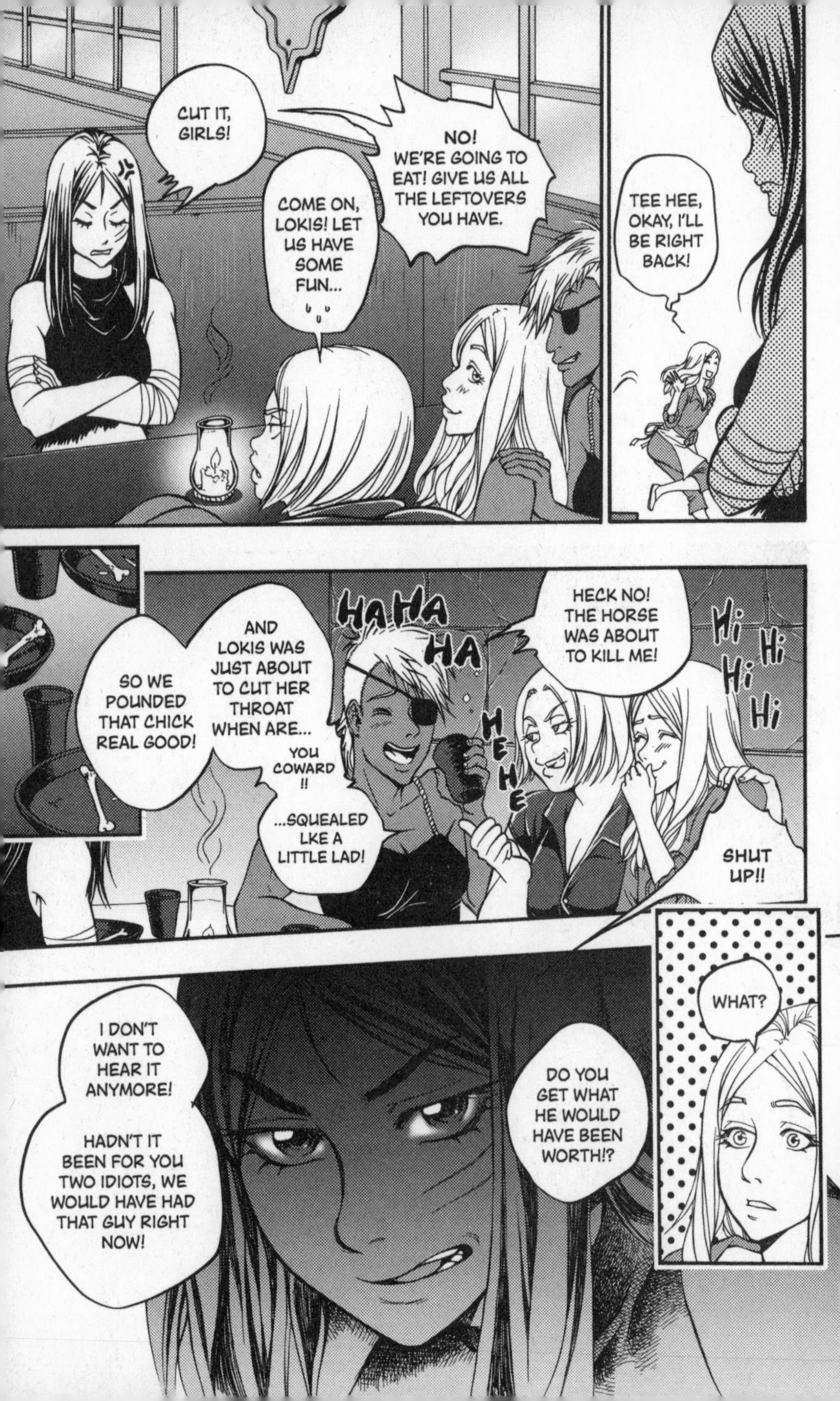
CUT IT, GIRLS!
COME ON, LOKIS! LET US HAVE SOME FUN...
NO! WE'RE GOING TO EAT! GIVE US ALL THE LEFTOVERS YOU HAVE.
TEE HEE, OKAY, I'LL BE RIGHT BACK!
SO WE POUNDED THAT CHICK REAL GOOD!
AND LOKIS WAS JUST ABOUT TO CUT HER THROAT WHEN ARE...
HAHAHA
YOU COWARD !!
...SQUEALED LKE A LITTLE LAD!
HEHEHE
HECK NO! THE HORSE WAS ABOUT TO KILL ME!
Hi Hi Hi Hi
SHUT UP!!
I DON'T WANT TO HEAR IT ANYMORE!
HADN'T IT BEEN FOR YOU TWO IDIOTS, WE WOULD HAVE HAD THAT GUY RIGHT NOW!
DO YOU GET WHAT HE WOULD HAVE BEEN WORTH!?
WHAT?

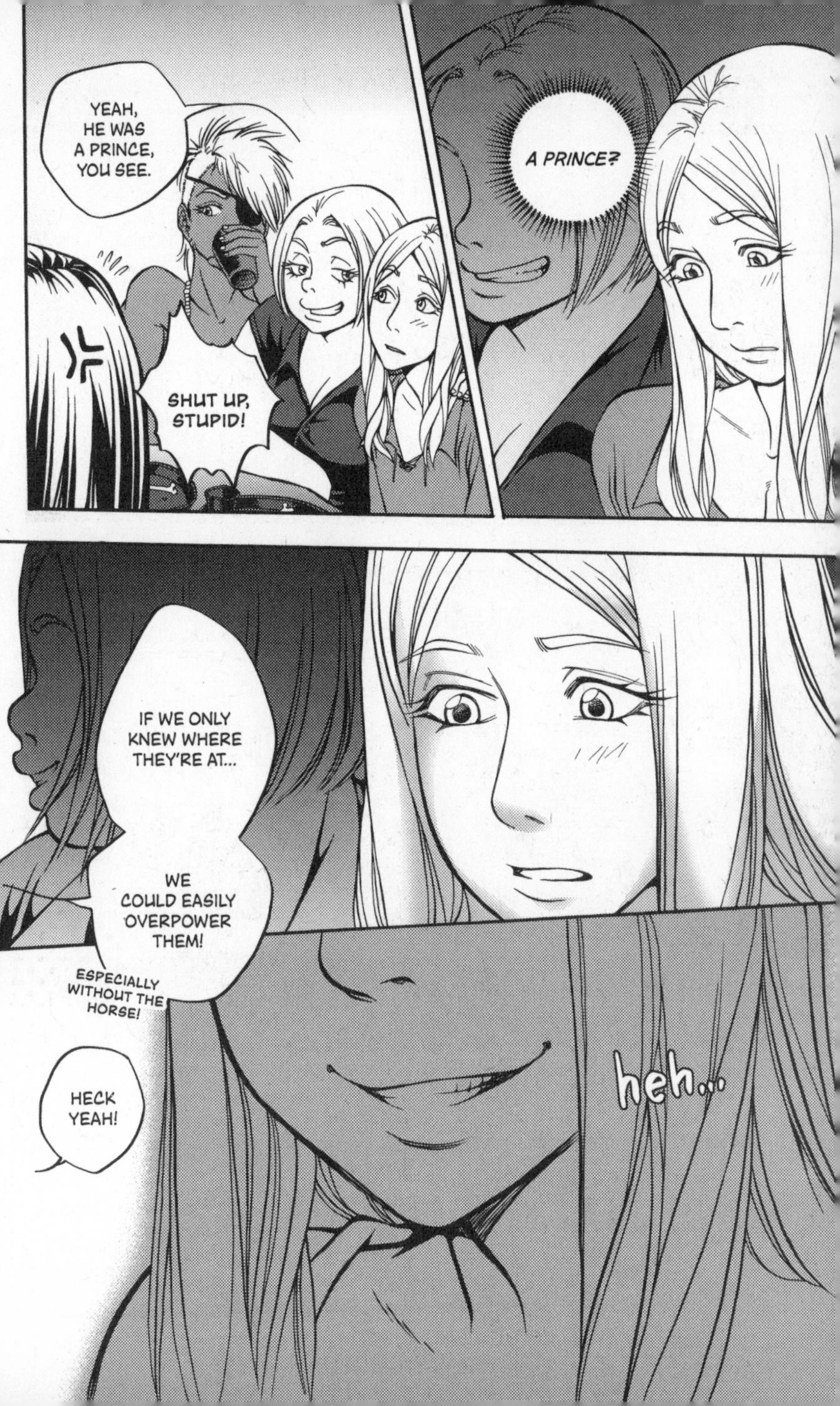

YEAH, HE WAS A PRINCE, YOU SEE.
SHUT UP, STUPID!
A PRINCE?
IF WE ONLY KNEW WHERE THEY'RE AT...
WE COULD EASILY OVERPOWER THEM!
ESPECIALLY WITHOUT THE HORSE!
HECK YEAH!
heh...

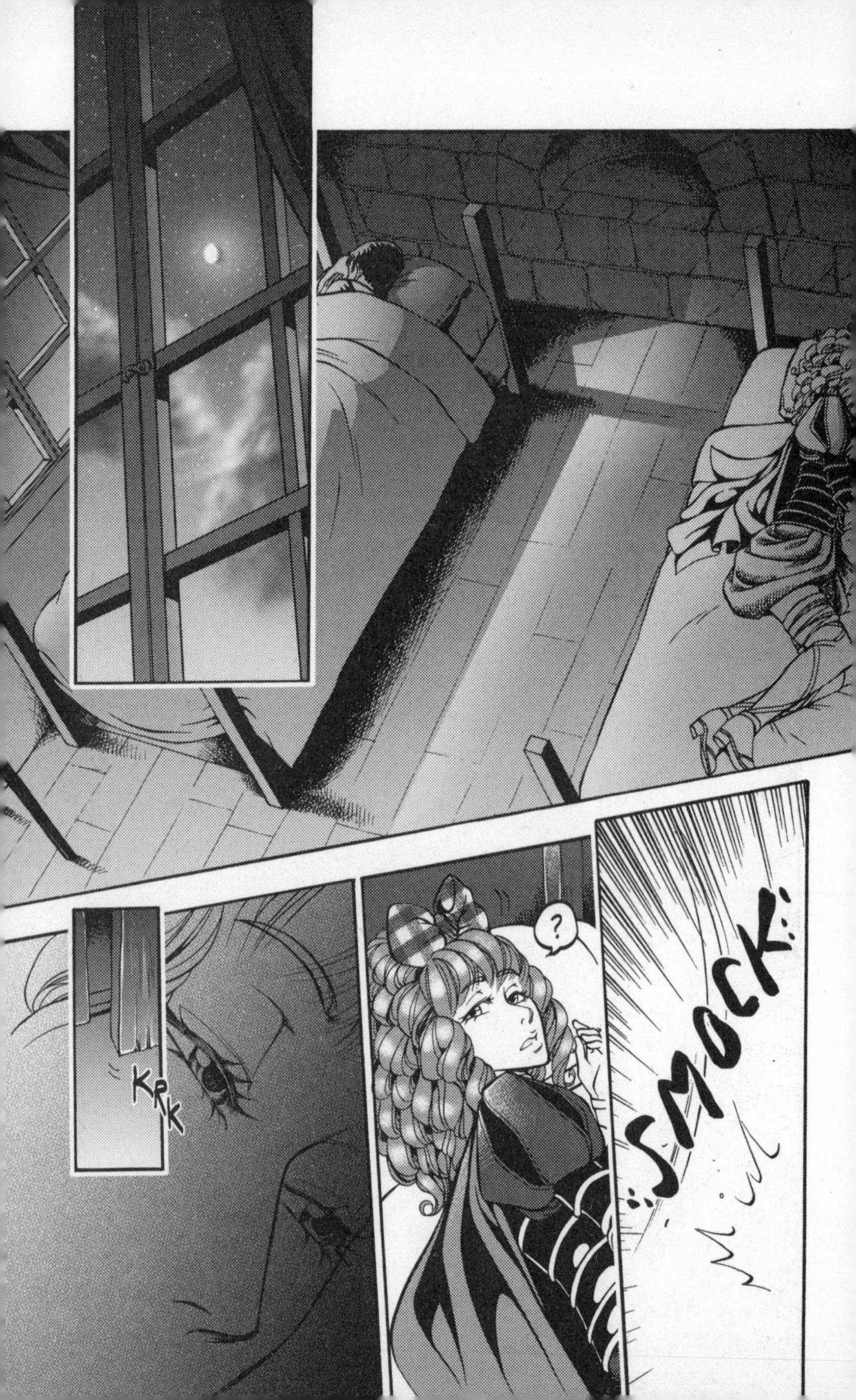
KRK
?
SMOCK

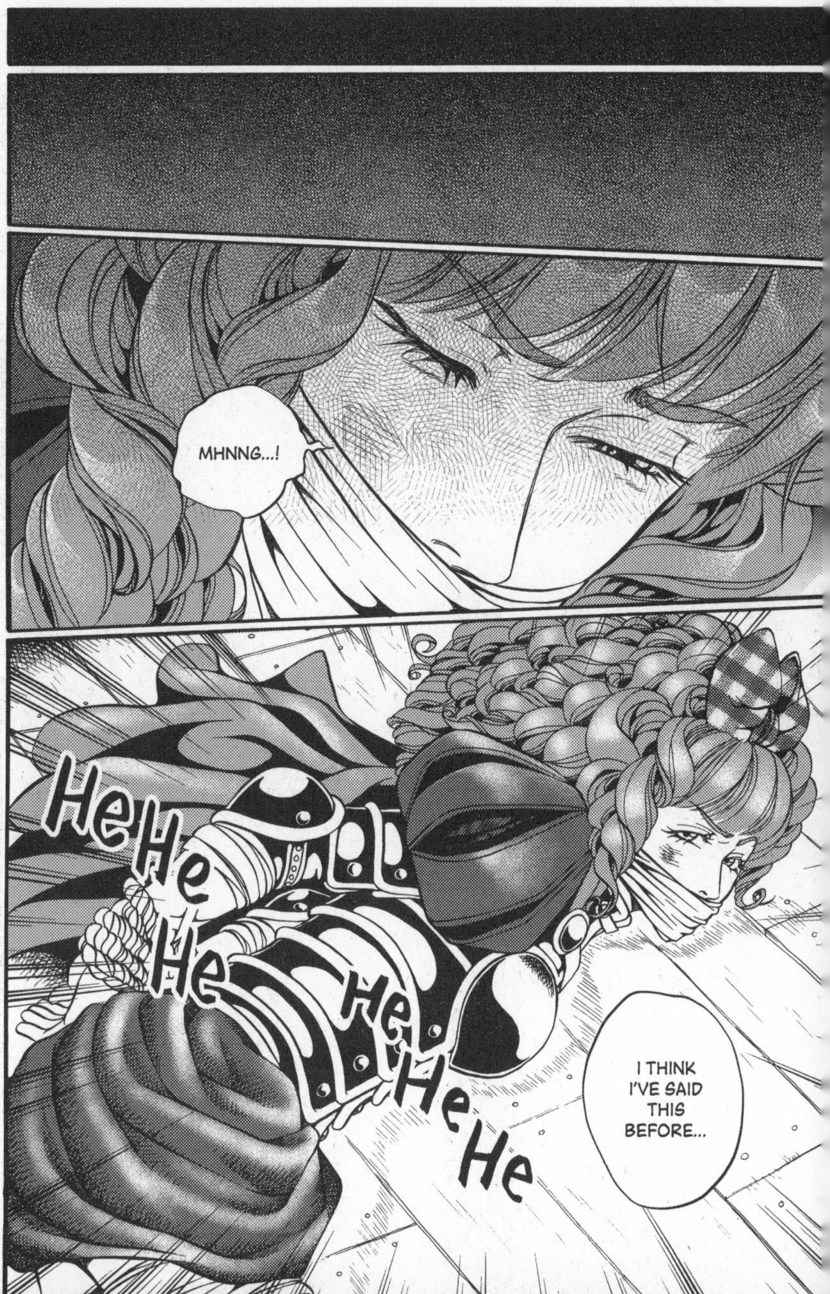
MHNNG...!
He He He He
He He He He
I THINK I'VE SAID THIS BEFORE...

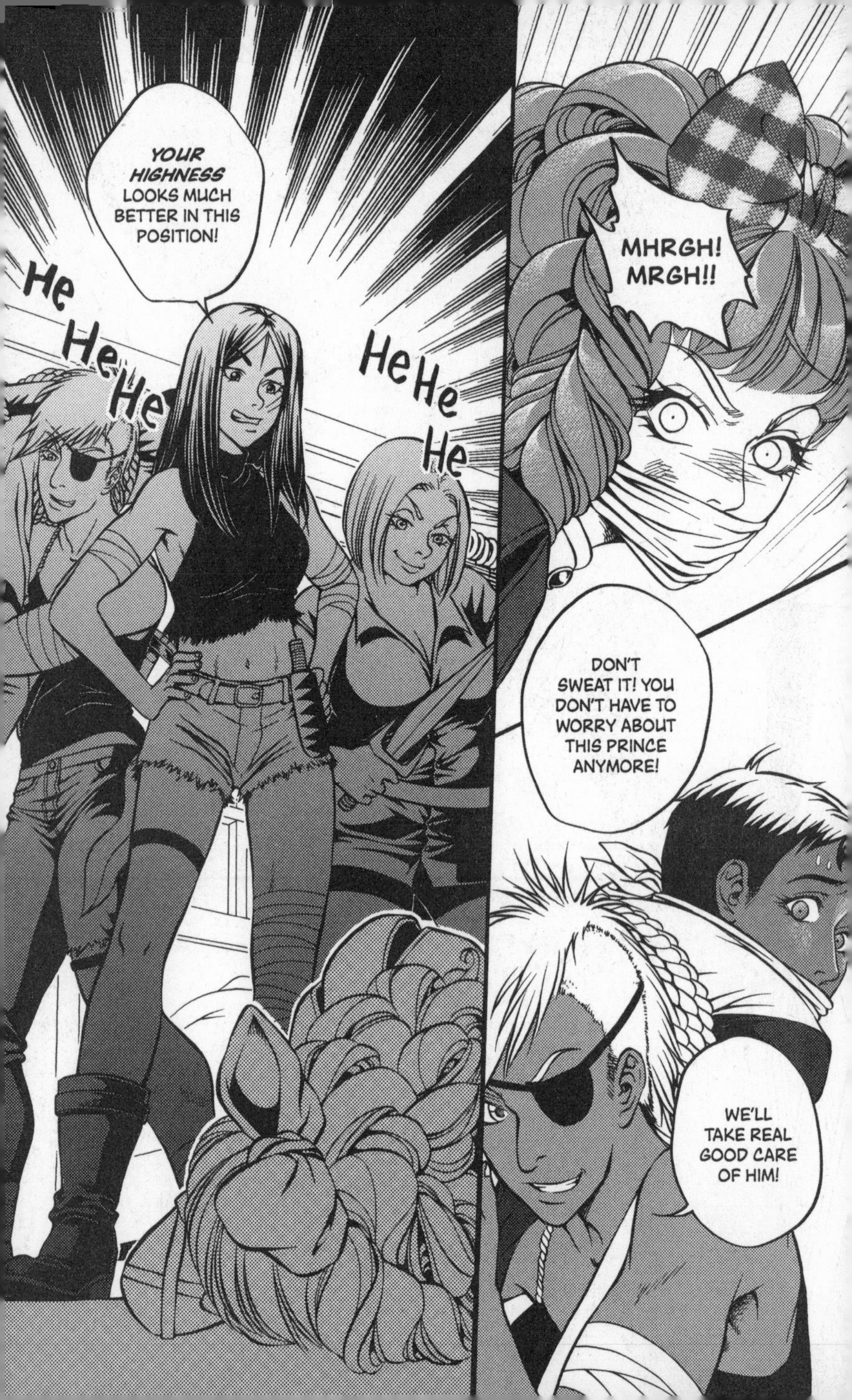
YOUR HIGHNESS LOOKS MUCH BETTER IN THIS POSITION!
He He He He
He He He He
MHRGH! MRGH!!
DON'T SWEAT IT! YOU DON'T HAVE TO WORRY ABOUT THIS PRINCE ANYMORE!
WE'LL TAKE REAL GOOD CARE OF HIM!

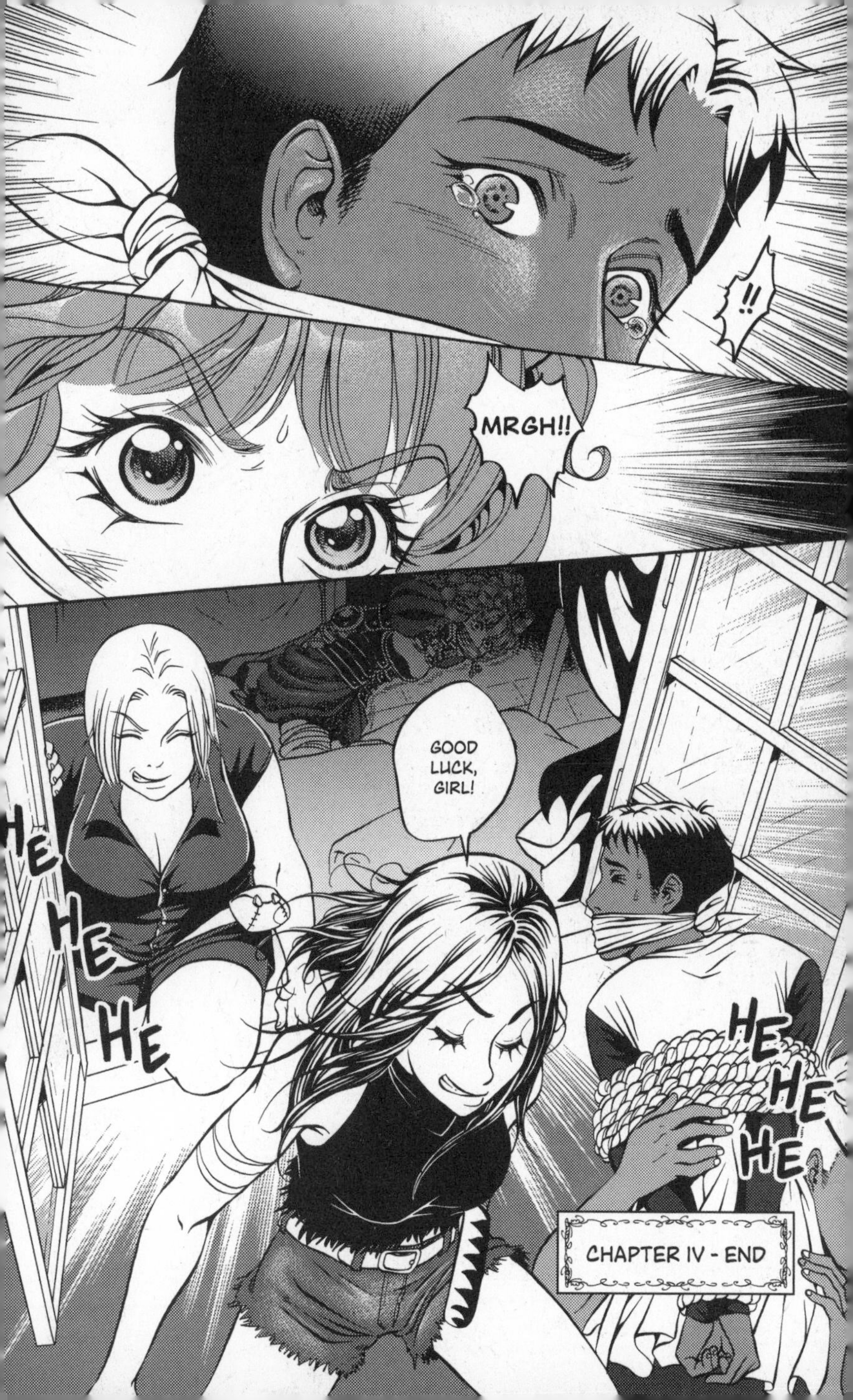
!!
MRGH!!
HE HE HE HE
GOOD LUCK, GIRL!
HE HE HE HE
CHAPTER IV - END

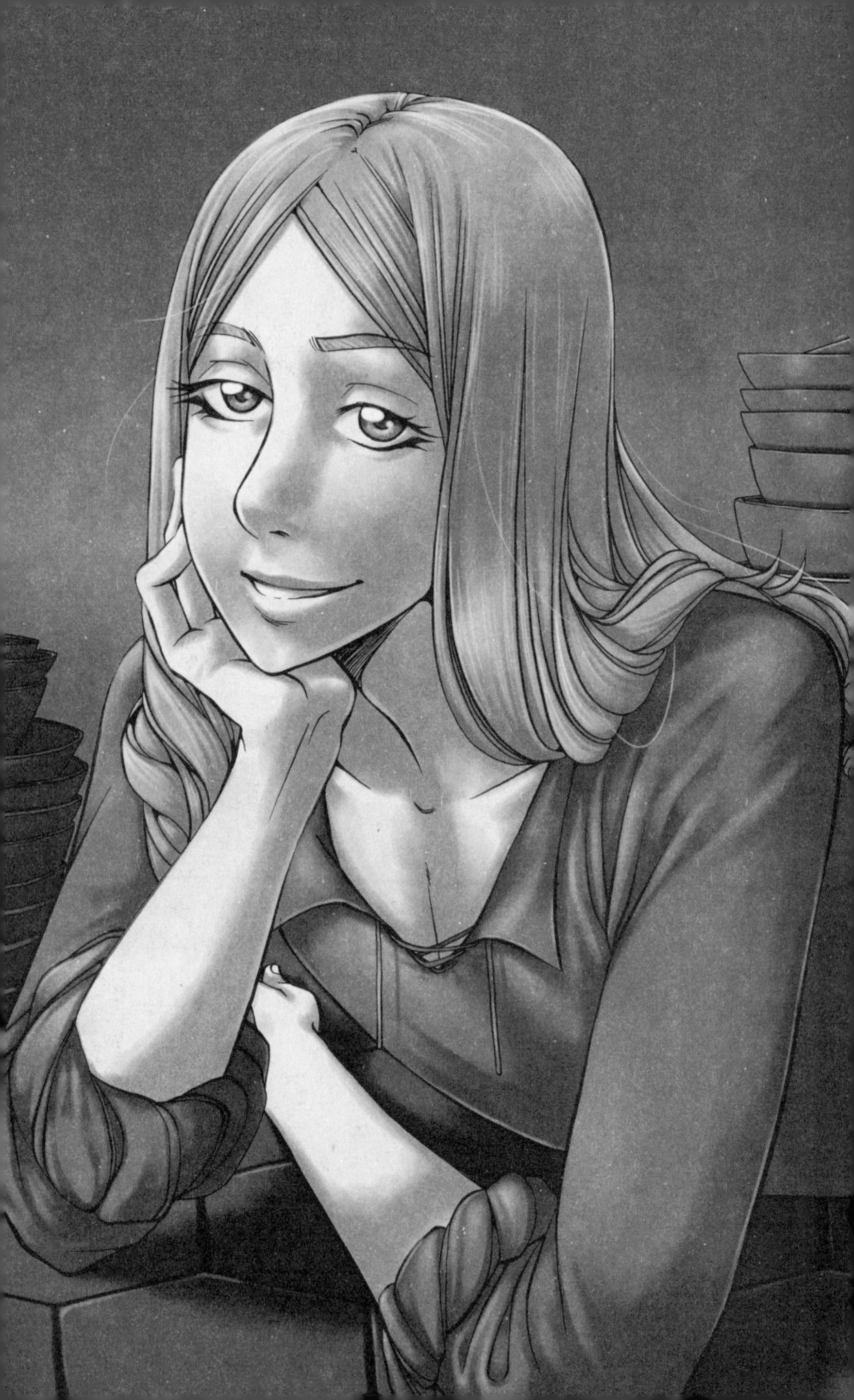

Chapter V

A Prince In Need

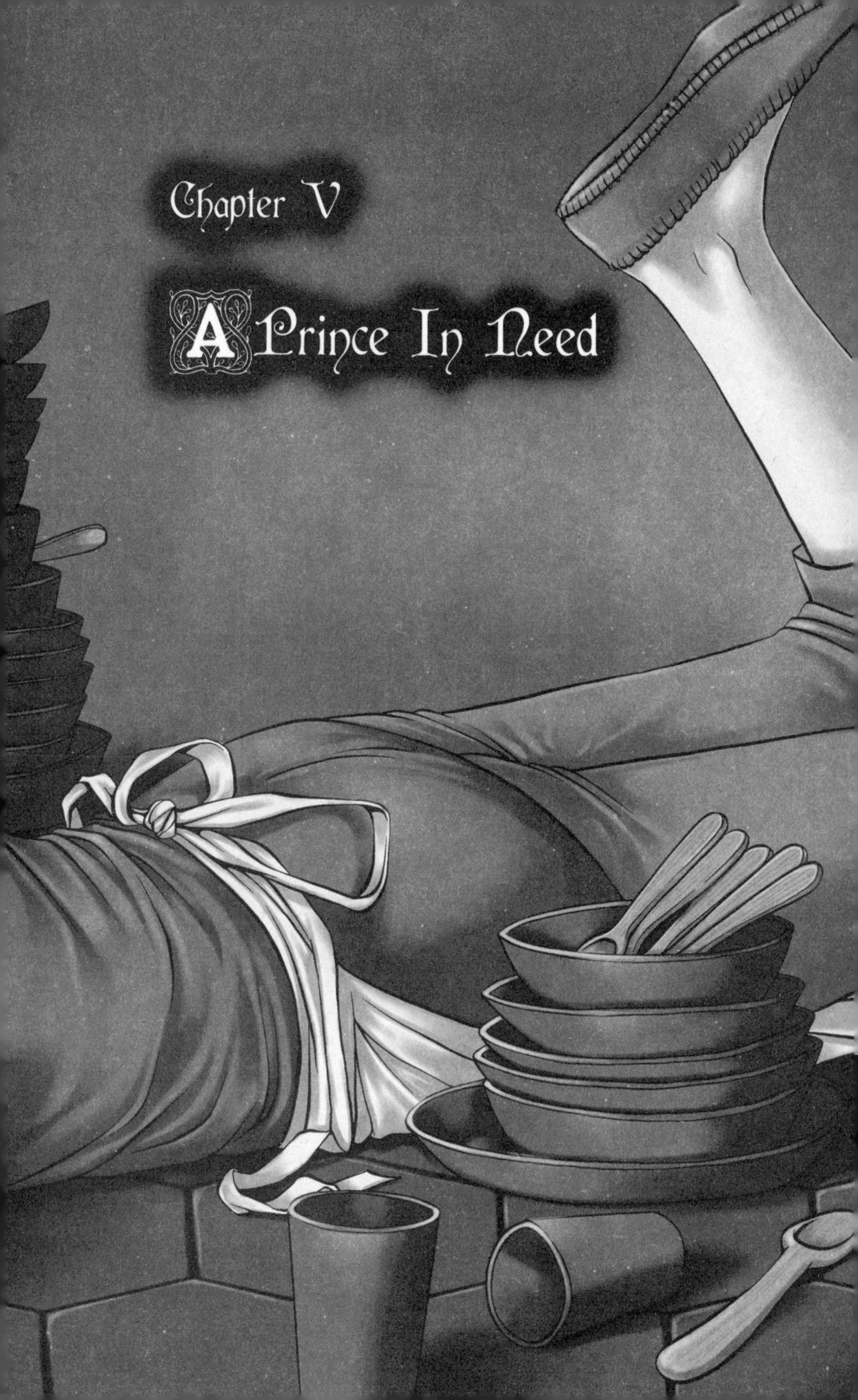

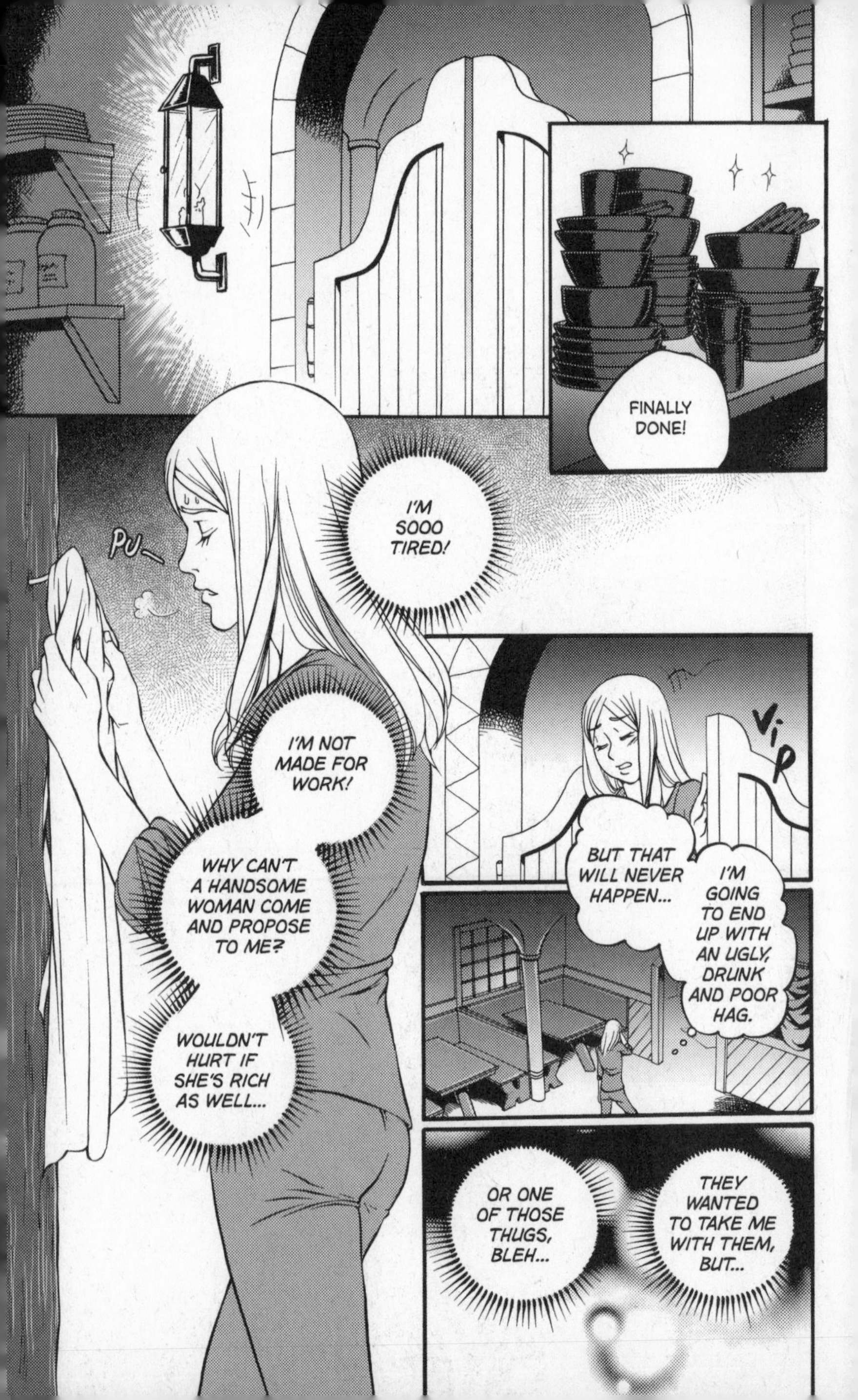
FINALLY DONE!
PU—
I'M SOOO TIRED!
I'M NOT MADE FOR WORK!
WHY CAN'T A HANDSOME WOMAN COME AND PROPOSE TO ME?
WOULDN'T HURT IF SHE'S RICH AS WELL...
VIP
BUT THAT WILL NEVER HAPPEN...
I'M GOING TO END UP WITH AN UGLY, DRUNK AND POOR HAG.
OR ONE OF THOSE THUGS, BLEH...
THEY WANTED TO TAKE ME WITH THEM, BUT...

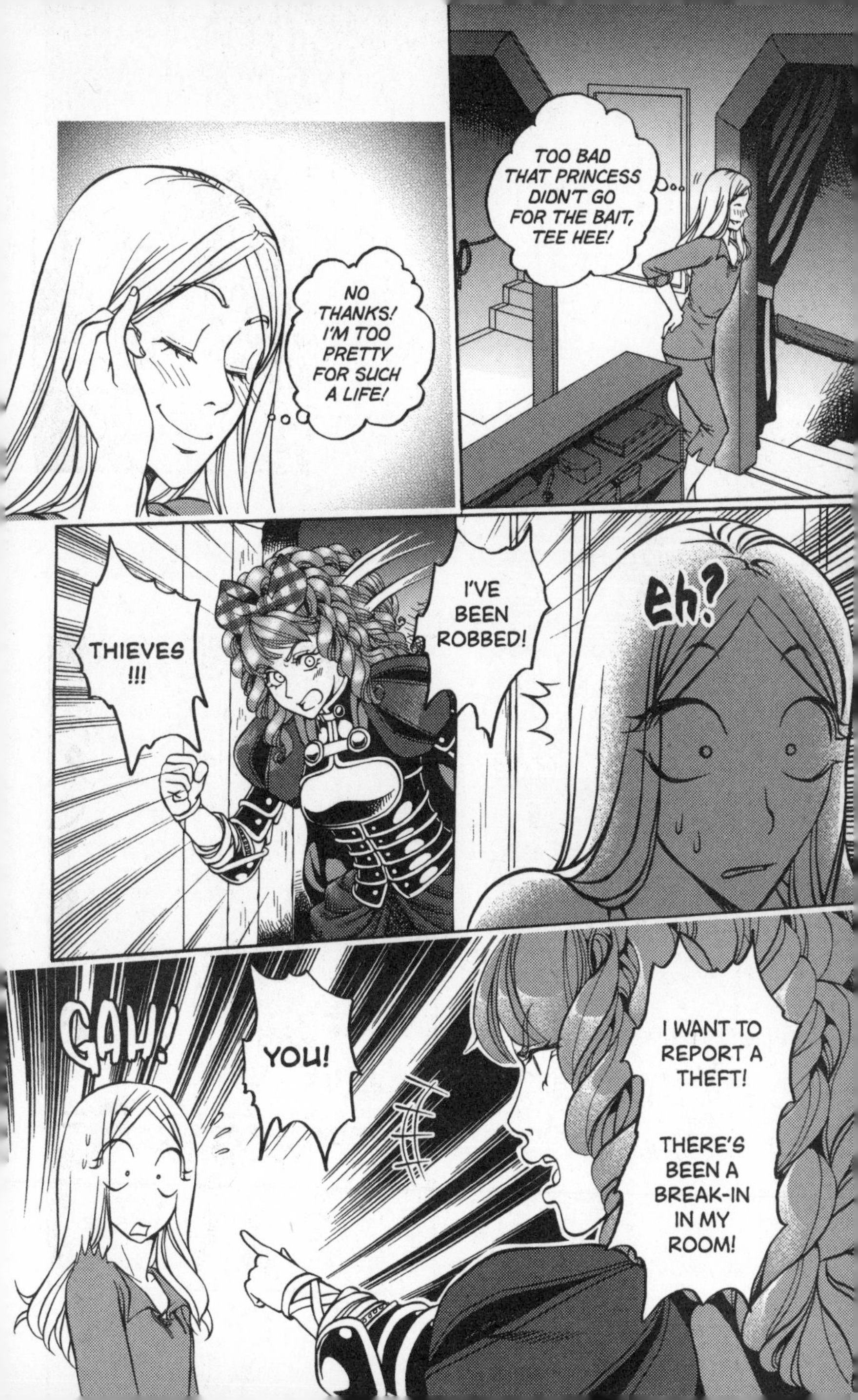
NO THANKS! I'M TOO PRETTY FOR SUCH A LIFE!
TOO BAD THAT PRINCESS DIDN'T GO FOR THE BAIT, TEE HEE!
THIEVES !!!
I'VE BEEN ROBBED!
eh?
GAH!
YOU!
I WANT TO REPORT A THEFT!
THERE'S BEEN A BREAK-IN IN MY ROOM!

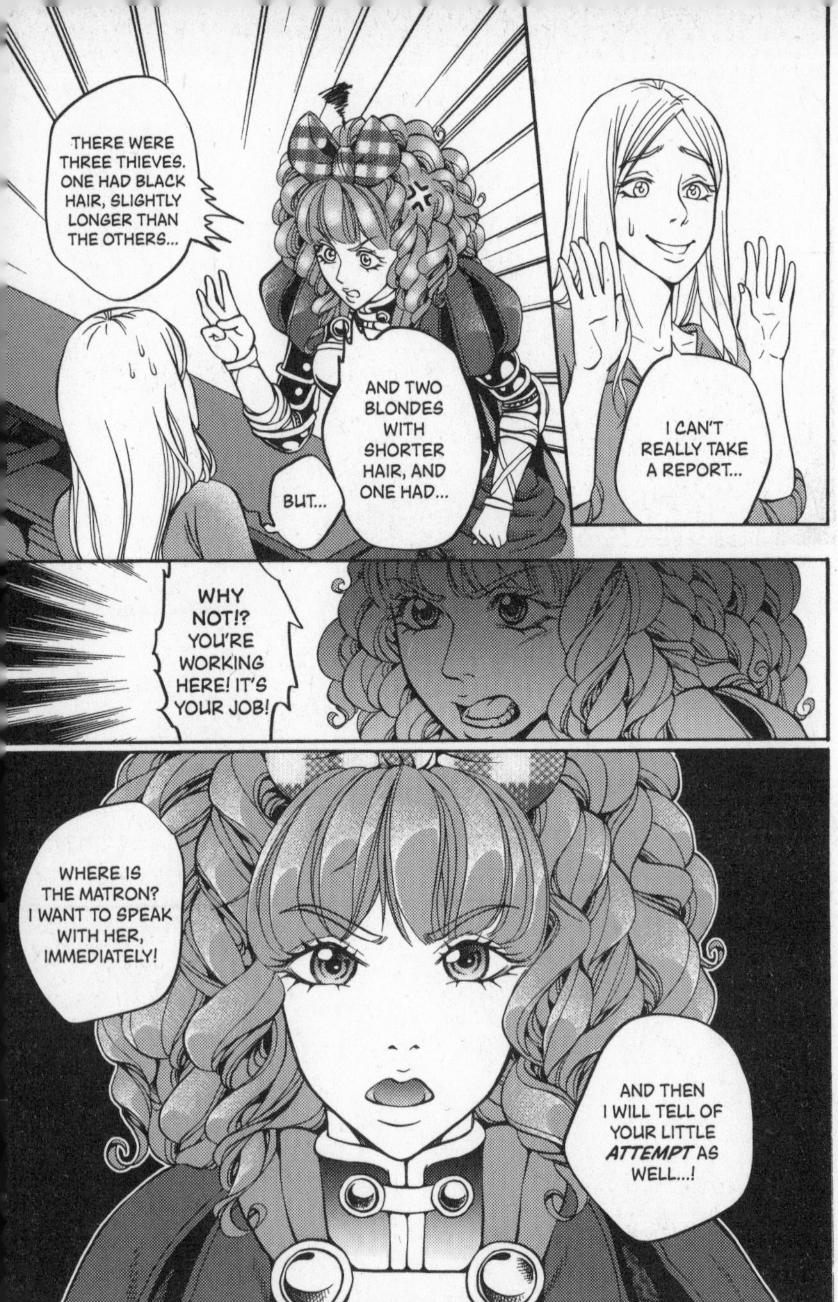

THERE WERE THREE THIEVES. ONE HAD BLACK HAIR, SLIGHTLY LONGER THAN THE OTHERS...
AND TWO BLONDES WITH SHORTER HAIR, AND ONE HAD...
BUT...
I CAN'T REALLY TAKE A REPORT...
WHY NOT!? YOU'RE WORKING HERE! IT'S YOUR JOB!
WHERE IS THE MATRON? I WANT TO SPEAK WITH HER, IMMEDIATELY!
AND THEN I WILL TELL OF YOUR LITTLE *ATTEMPT* AS WELL...!

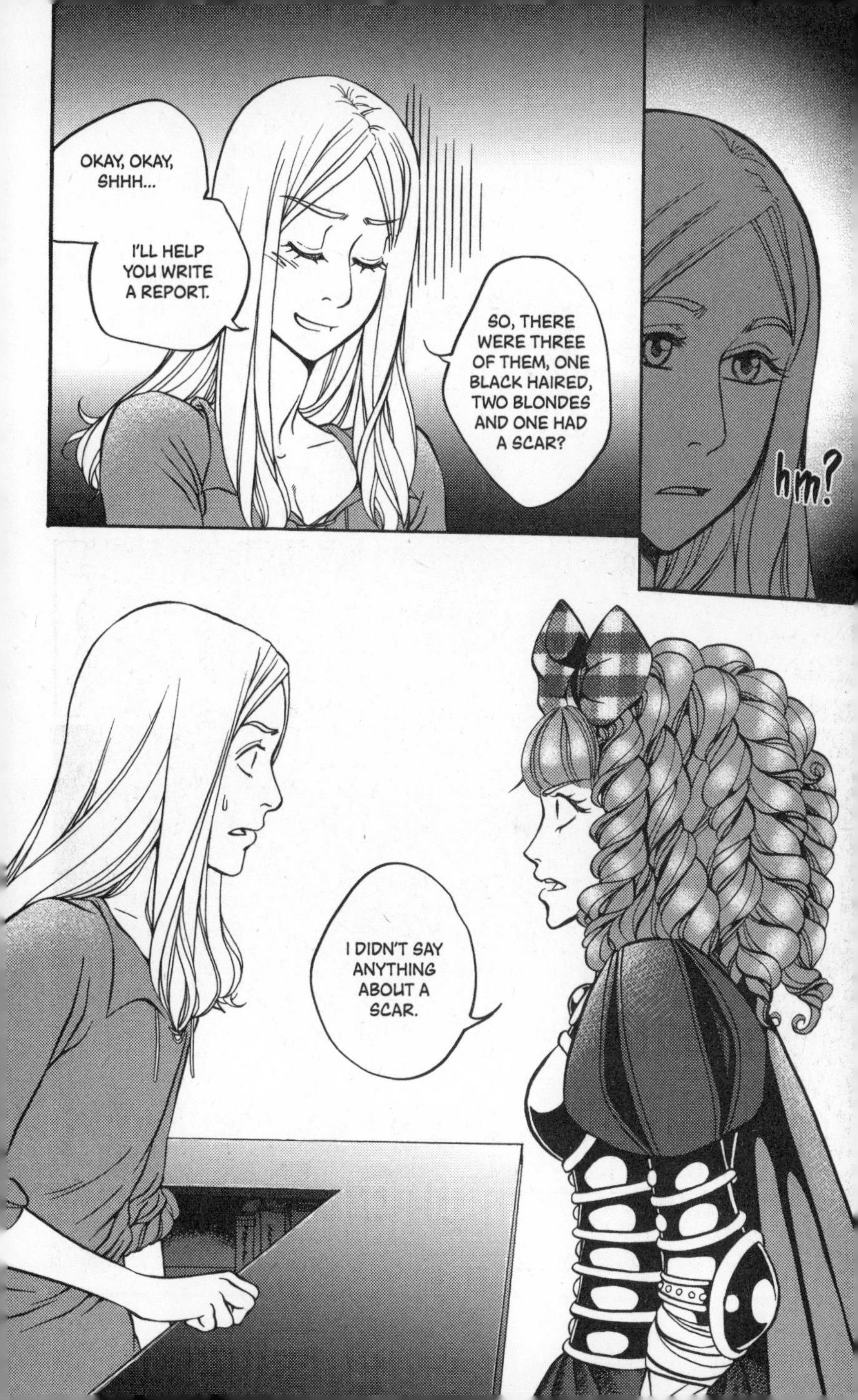
OKAY, OKAY, SHHH...
I'LL HELP YOU WRITE A REPORT.
SO, THERE WERE THREE OF THEM, ONE BLACK HAIRED, TWO BLONDES AND ONE HAD A SCAR?
hm?
I DIDN'T SAY ANYTHING ABOUT A SCAR.

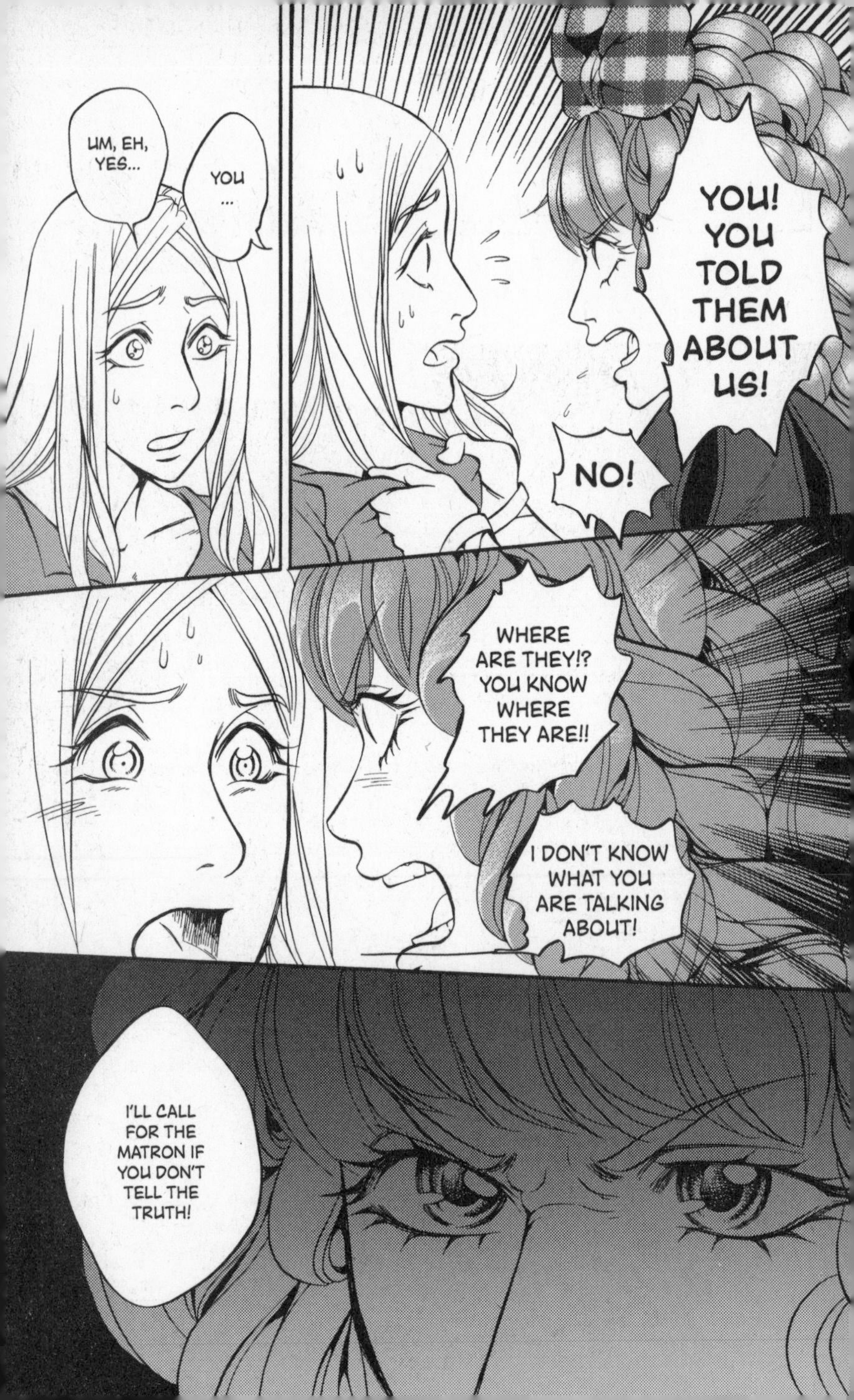
UM, EH, YES...
YOU ...
YOU! YOU TOLD THEM ABOUT US!
NO!
WHERE ARE THEY!? YOU KNOW WHERE THEY ARE!!
I DON'T KNOW WHAT YOU ARE TALKING ABOUT!
I'LL CALL FOR THE MATRON IF YOU DON'T TELL THE TRUTH!

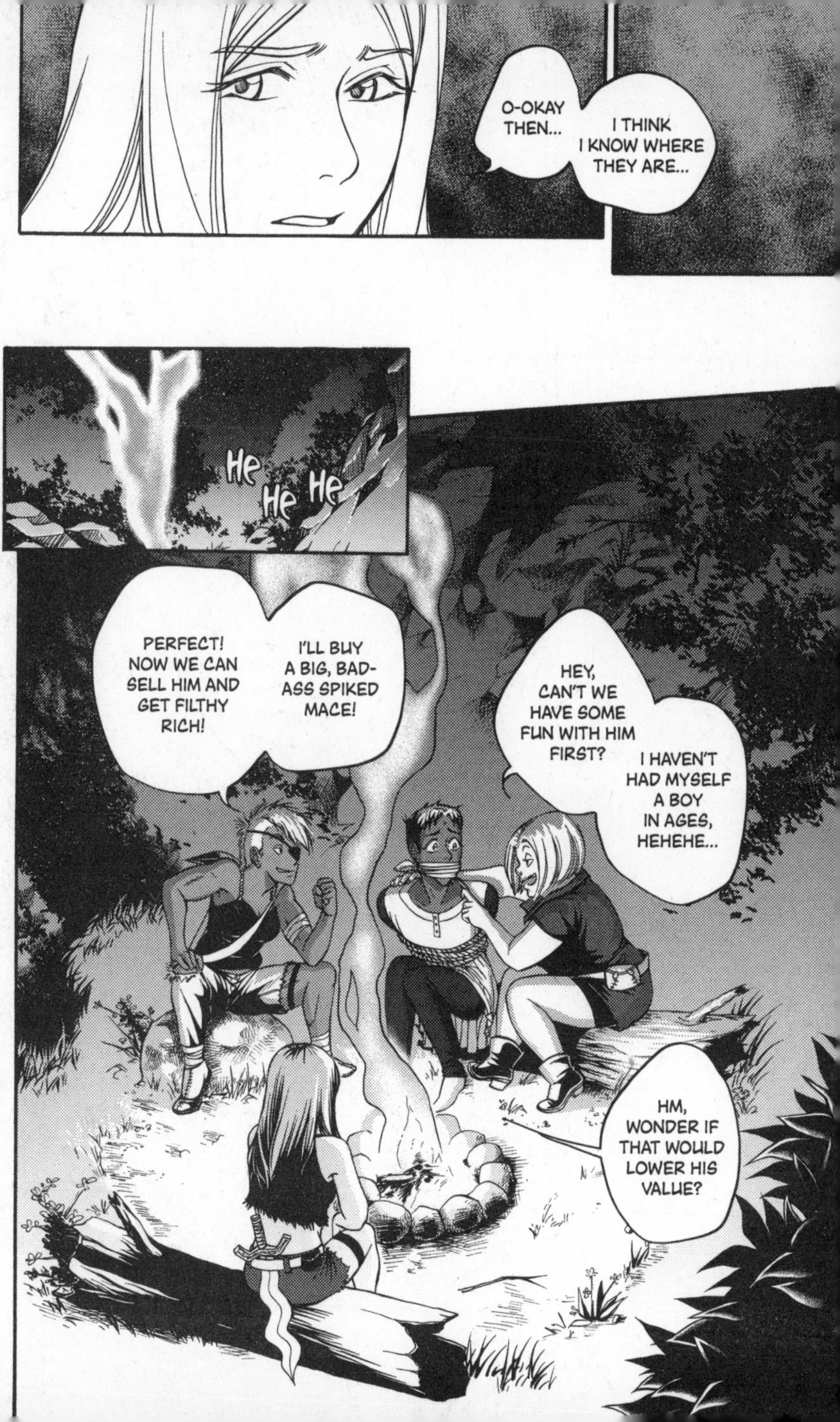
O-OKAY THEN...
I THINK I KNOW WHERE THEY ARE...
He He He
PERFECT! NOW WE CAN SELL HIM AND GET FILTHY RICH!
I'LL BUY A BIG, BAD-ASS SPIKED MACE!
HEY, CAN'T WE HAVE SOME FUN WITH HIM FIRST?
I HAVEN'T HAD MYSELF A BOY IN AGES, HEHEHE...
HM, WONDER IF THAT WOULD LOWER HIS VALUE?

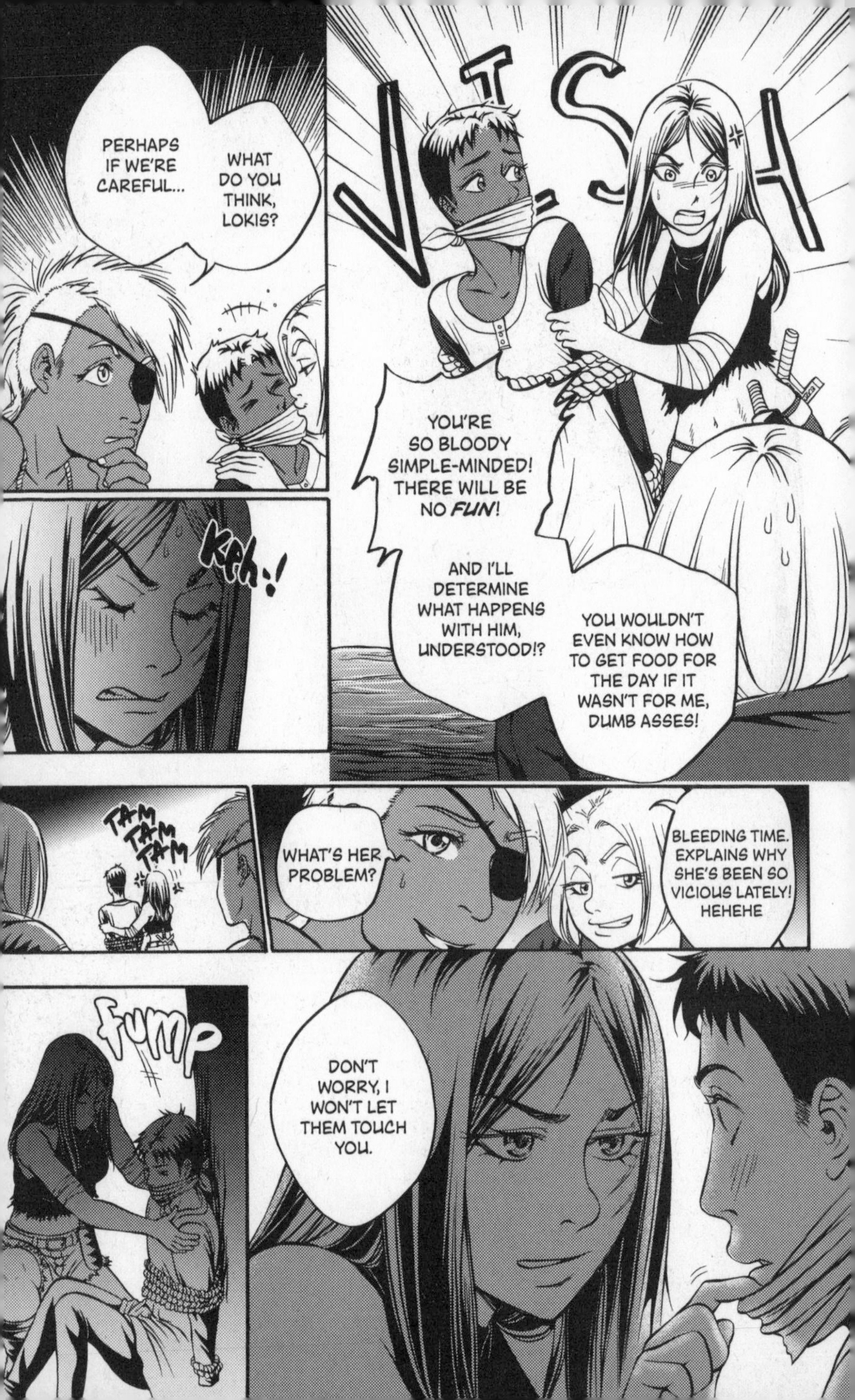
PERHAPS IF WE'RE CAREFUL...
WHAT DO YOU THINK, LOKIS?
Kph!
YOU'RE SO BLOODY SIMPLE-MINDED! THERE WILL BE NO *FUN*!
AND I'LL DETERMINE WHAT HAPPENS WITH HIM, UNDERSTOOD!?
YOU WOULDN'T EVEN KNOW HOW TO GET FOOD FOR THE DAY IF IT WASN'T FOR ME, DUMB ASSES!
TAM TAM TAM
WHAT'S HER PROBLEM?
BLEEDING TIME. EXPLAINS WHY SHE'S BEEN SO VICIOUS LATELY! HEHEHE
FUMP
DON'T WORRY, I WON'T LET THEM TOUCH YOU.

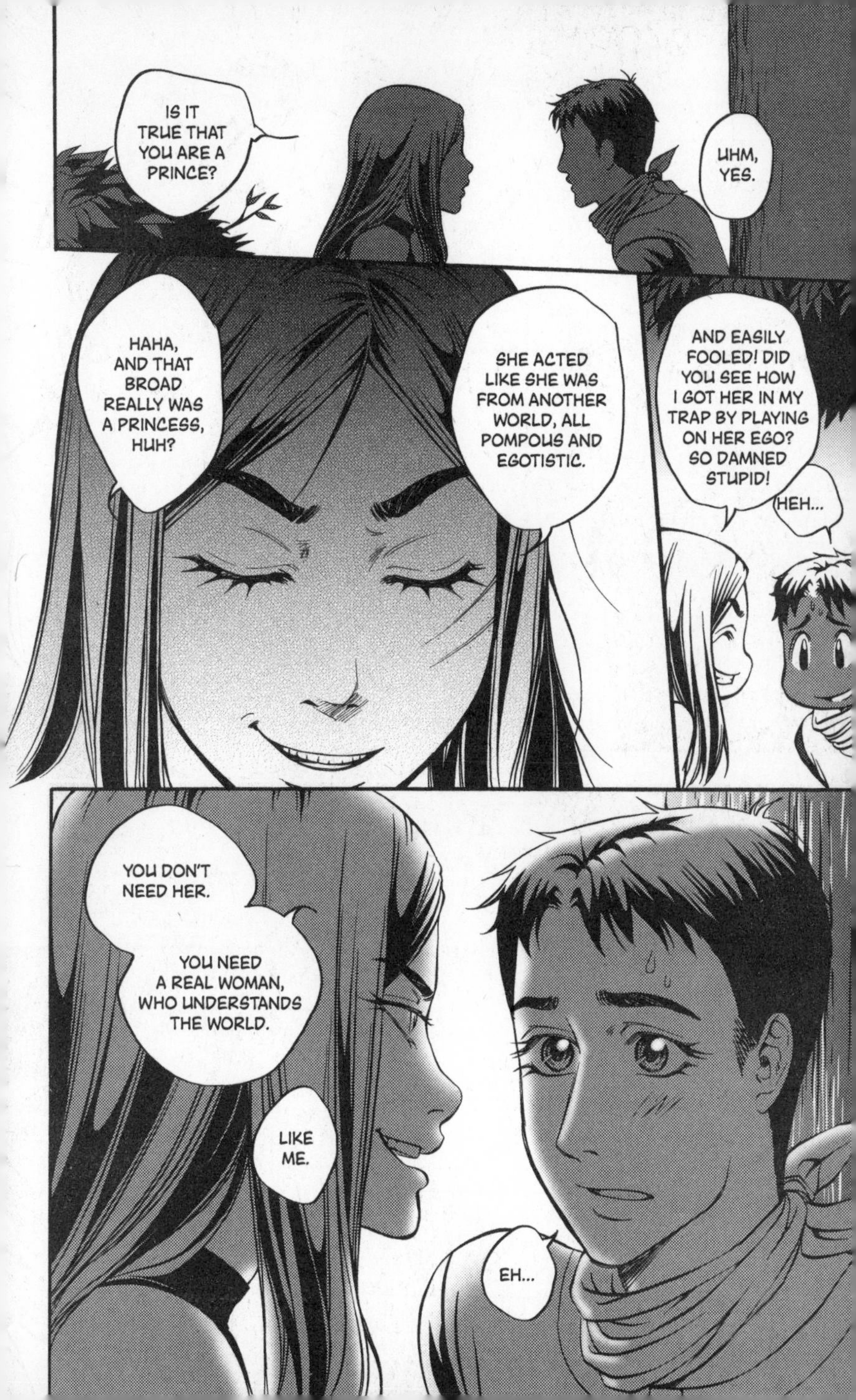
IS IT TRUE THAT YOU ARE A PRINCE?
UHM, YES.
HAHA, AND THAT BROAD REALLY WAS A PRINCESS, HUH?
SHE ACTED LIKE SHE WAS FROM ANOTHER WORLD, ALL POMPOUS AND EGOTISTIC.
AND EASILY FOOLED! DID YOU SEE HOW I GOT HER IN MY TRAP BY PLAYING ON HER EGO? SO DAMNED STUPID!
HEH...
YOU DON'T NEED HER.
YOU NEED A REAL WOMAN, WHO UNDERSTANDS THE WORLD.
LIKE ME.
EH...

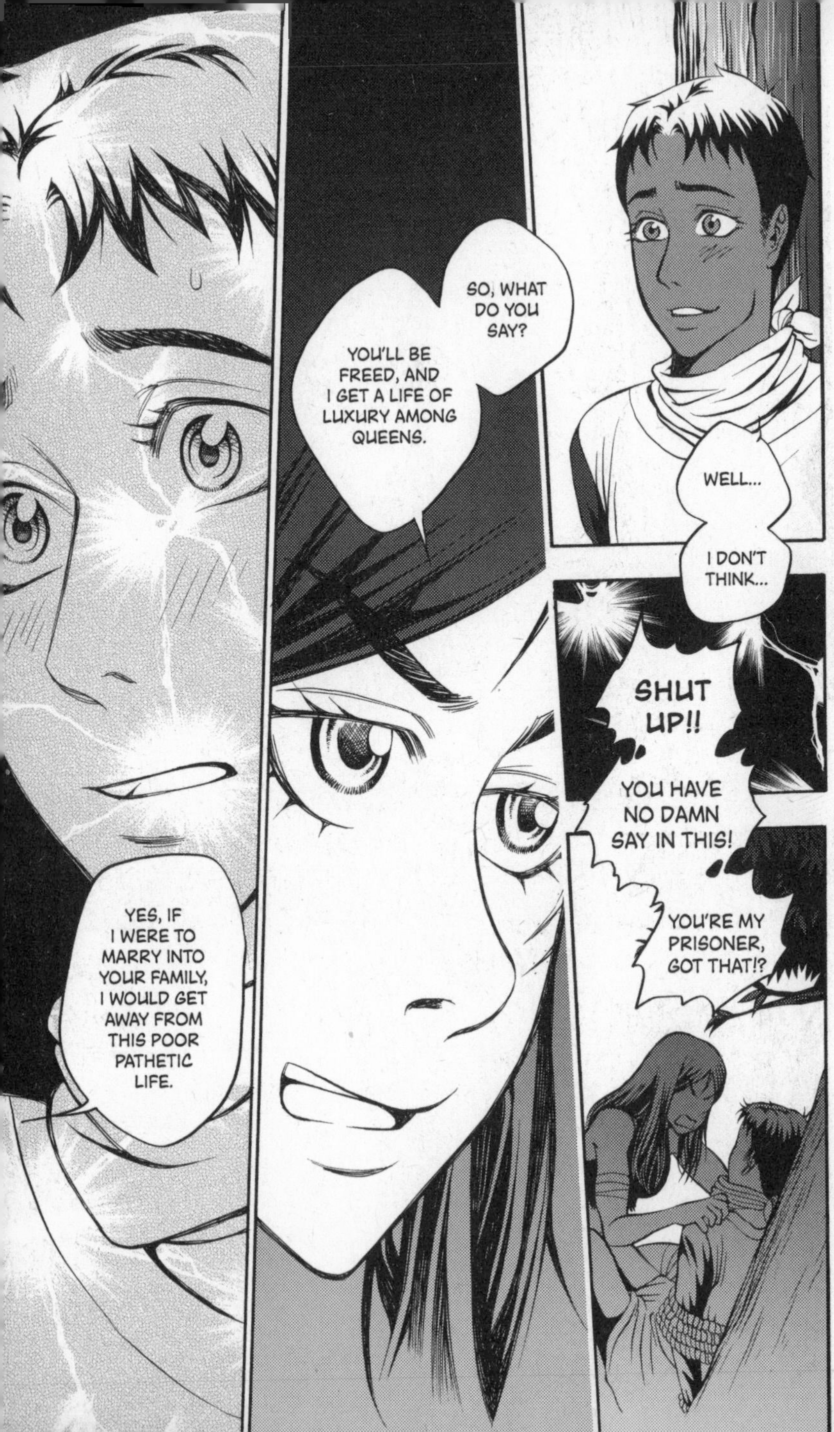
YES, IF I WERE TO MARRY INTO YOUR FAMILY, I WOULD GET AWAY FROM THIS POOR PATHETIC LIFE.
YOU'LL BE FREED, AND I GET A LIFE OF LUXURY AMONG QUEENS.
SO, WHAT DO YOU SAY?
WELL...
I DON'T THINK...
SHUT UP!!
YOU HAVE NO DAMN SAY IN THIS!
YOU'RE MY PRISONER, GOT THAT!?

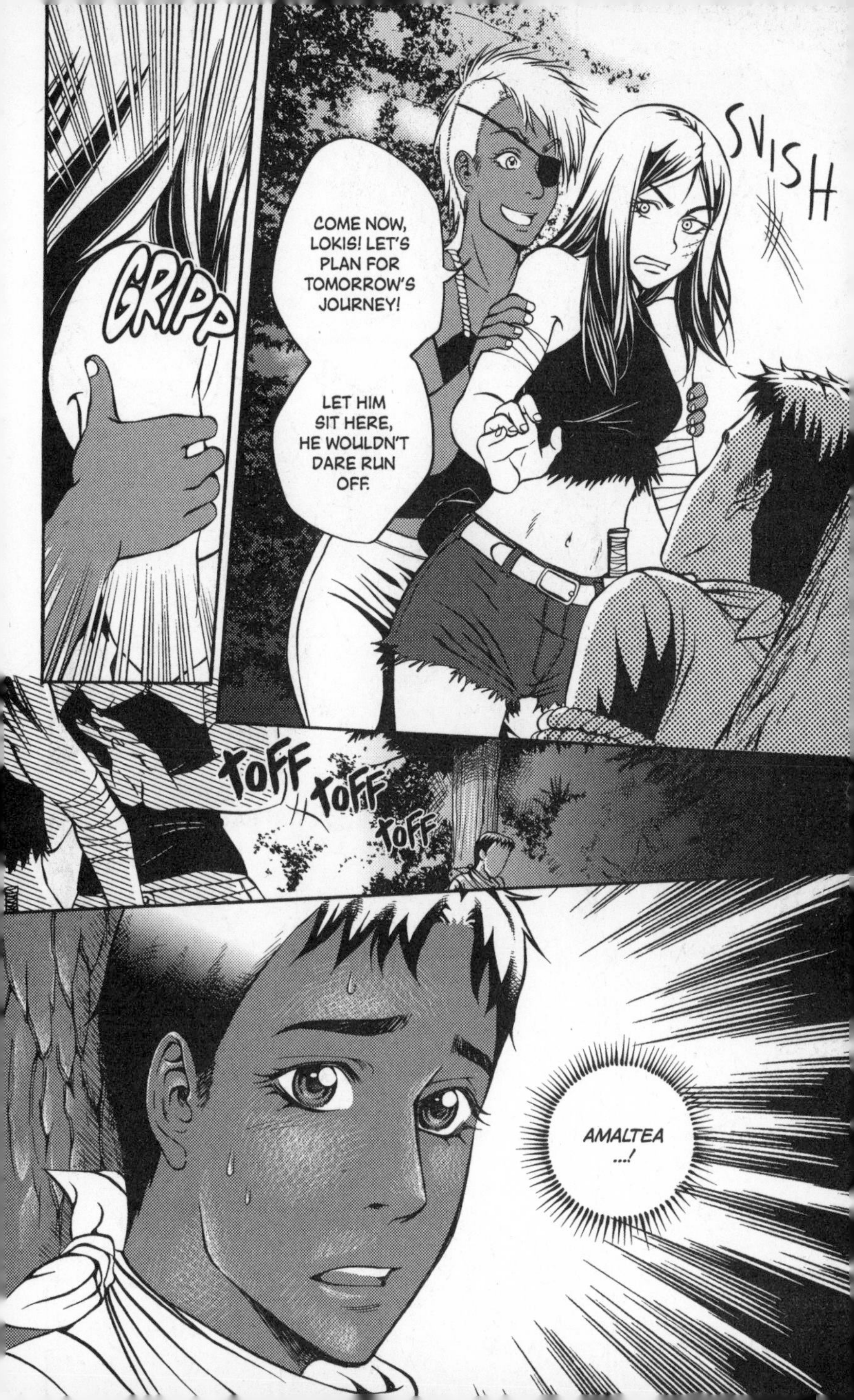
GRIPP
COME NOW, LOKIS! LET'S PLAN FOR TOMORROW'S JOURNEY!
LET HIM SIT HERE, HE WOULDN'T DARE RUN OFF.
SVISH
TOFF
TOFF
TOFF
AMALTEA ...!

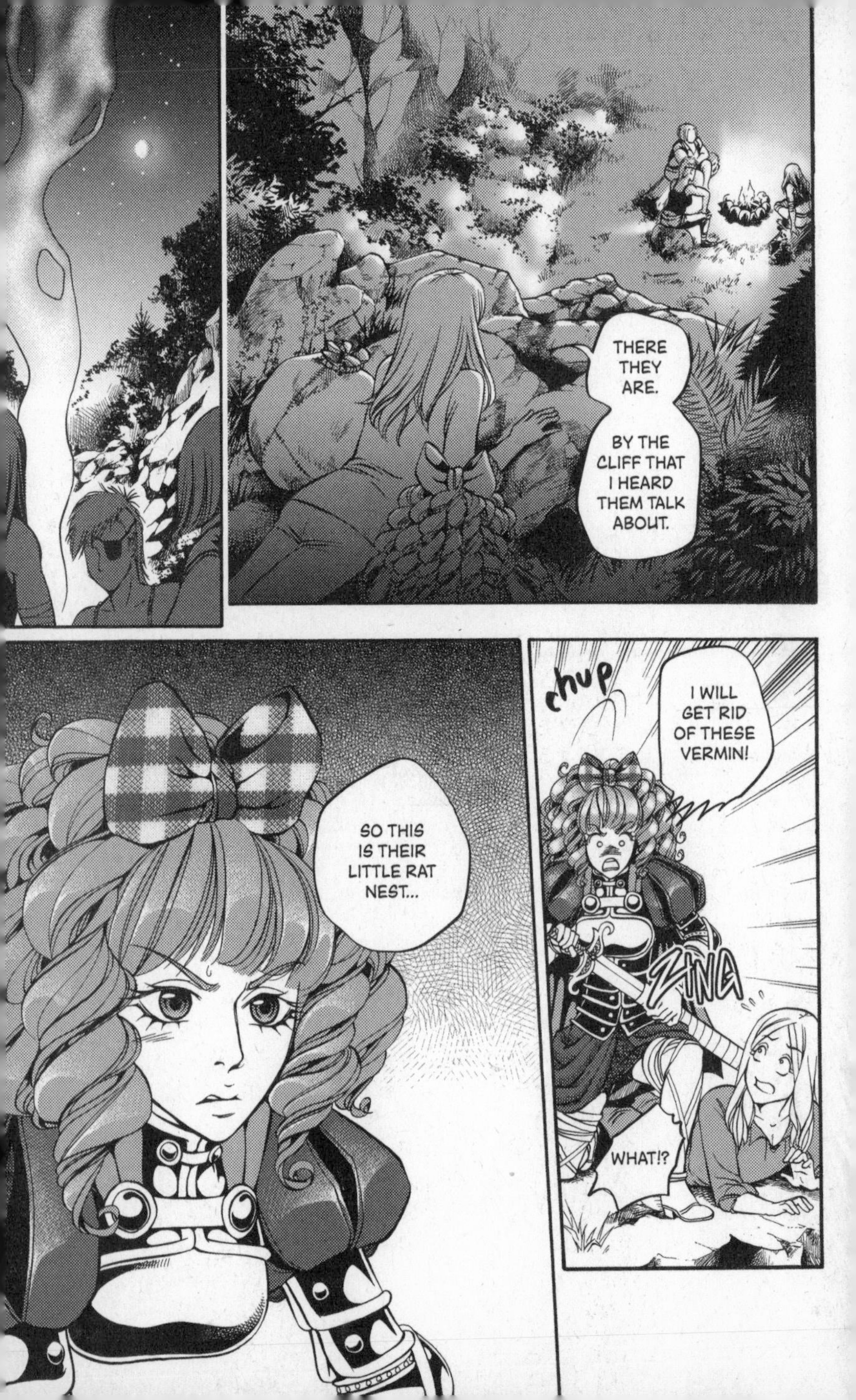
THERE THEY ARE.
BY THE CLIFF THAT I HEARD THEM TALK ABOUT.
SO THIS IS THEIR LITTLE RAT NEST...
chup
I WILL GET RID OF THESE VERMIN!
ZING
WHAT!?

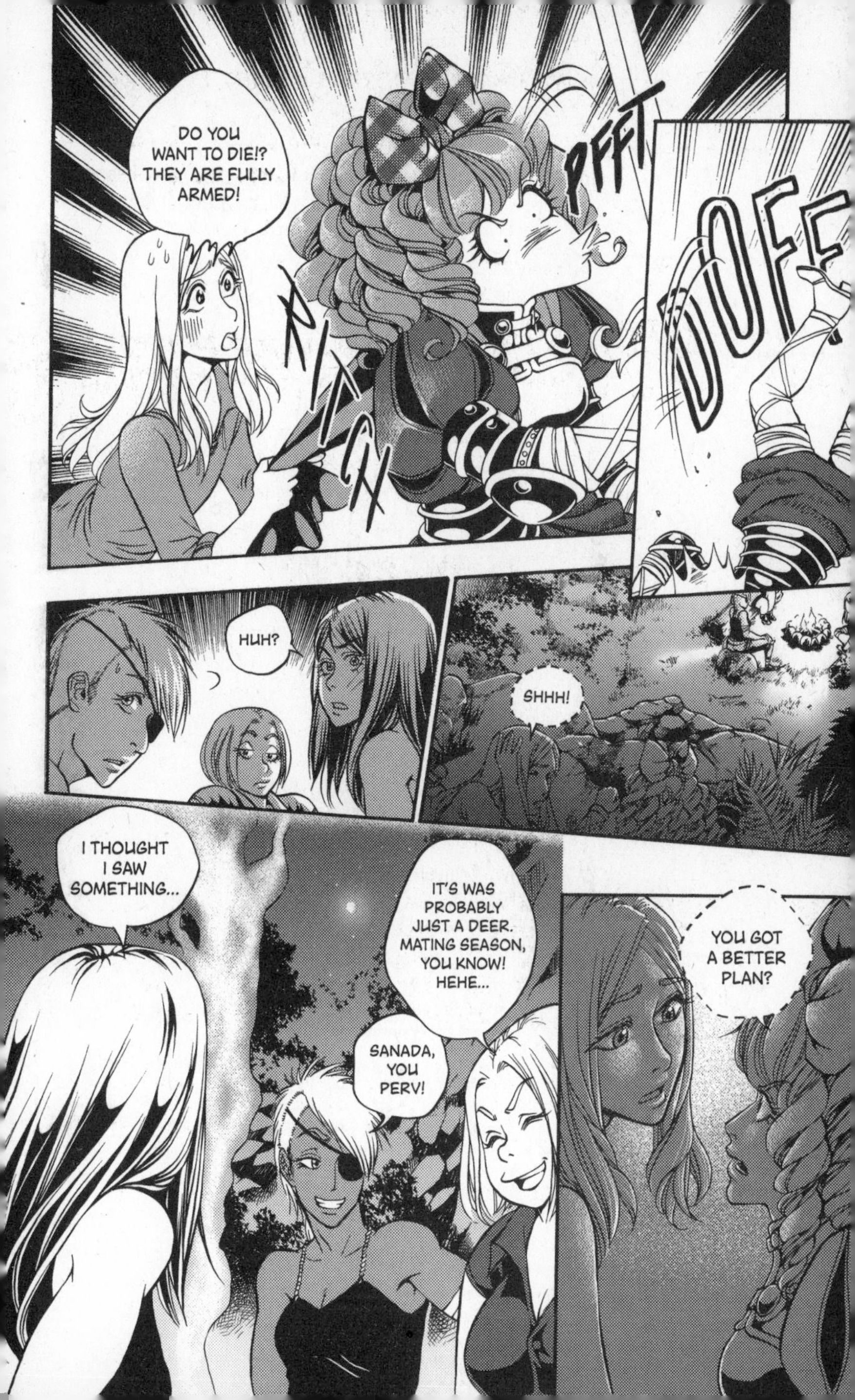
DO YOU WANT TO DIE!? THEY ARE FULLY ARMED!
RITCH
PFFT
DOFF
HUH?
SHHH!
I THOUGHT I SAW SOMETHING...
IT'S WAS PROBABLY JUST A DEER. MATING SEASON, YOU KNOW! HEHE...
SANADA, YOU PERV!
YOU GOT A BETTER PLAN?

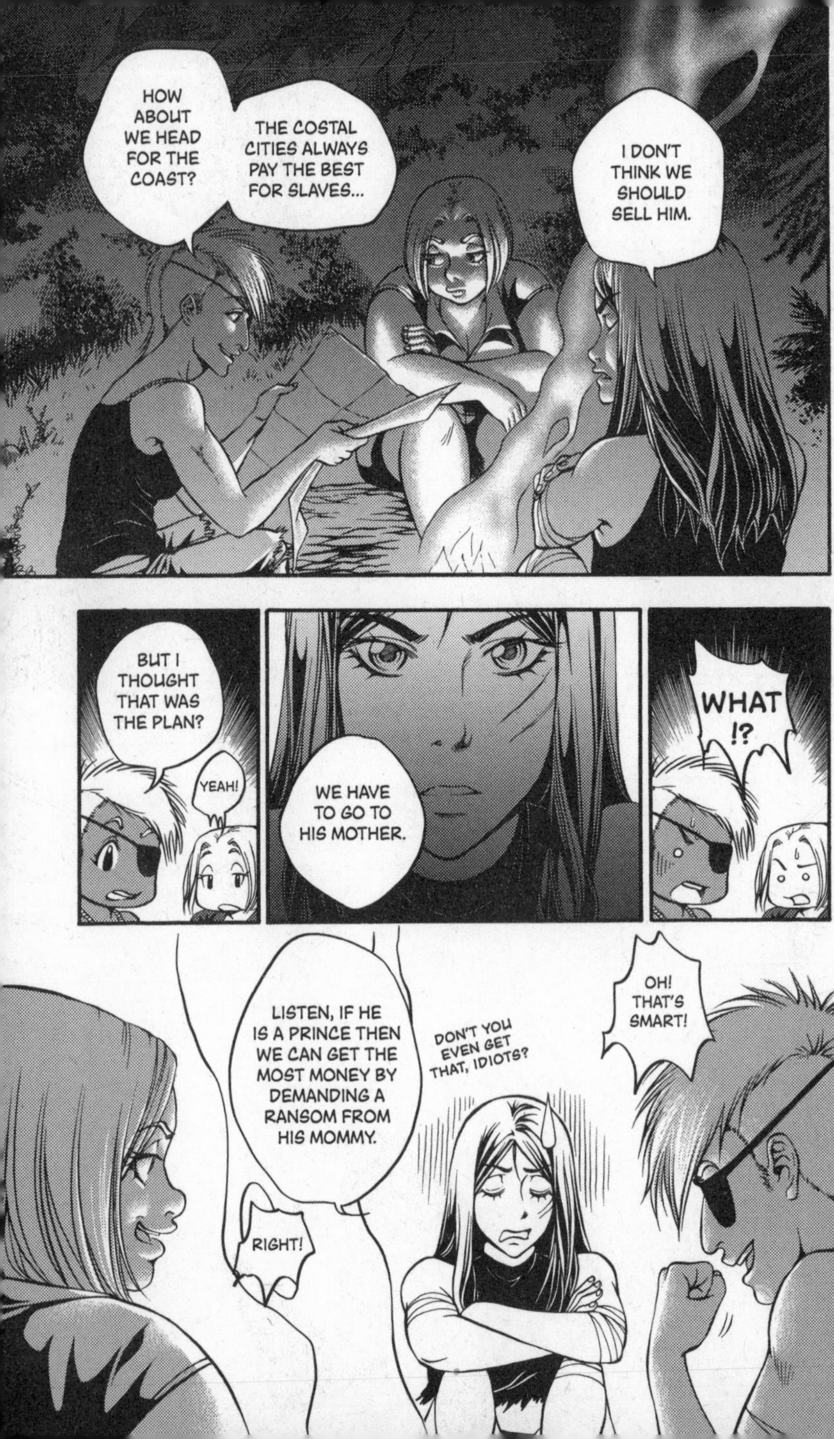
HOW ABOUT WE HEAD FOR THE COAST?
THE COSTAL CITIES ALWAYS PAY THE BEST FOR SLAVES...
I DON'T THINK WE SHOULD SELL HIM.
BUT I THOUGHT THAT WAS THE PLAN?
YEAH!
WE HAVE TO GO TO HIS MOTHER.
WHAT !?
LISTEN, IF HE IS A PRINCE THEN WE CAN GET THE MOST MONEY BY DEMANDING A RANSOM FROM HIS MOMMY.
RIGHT!
DON'T YOU EVEN GET THAT, IDIOTS?
OH! THAT'S SMART!

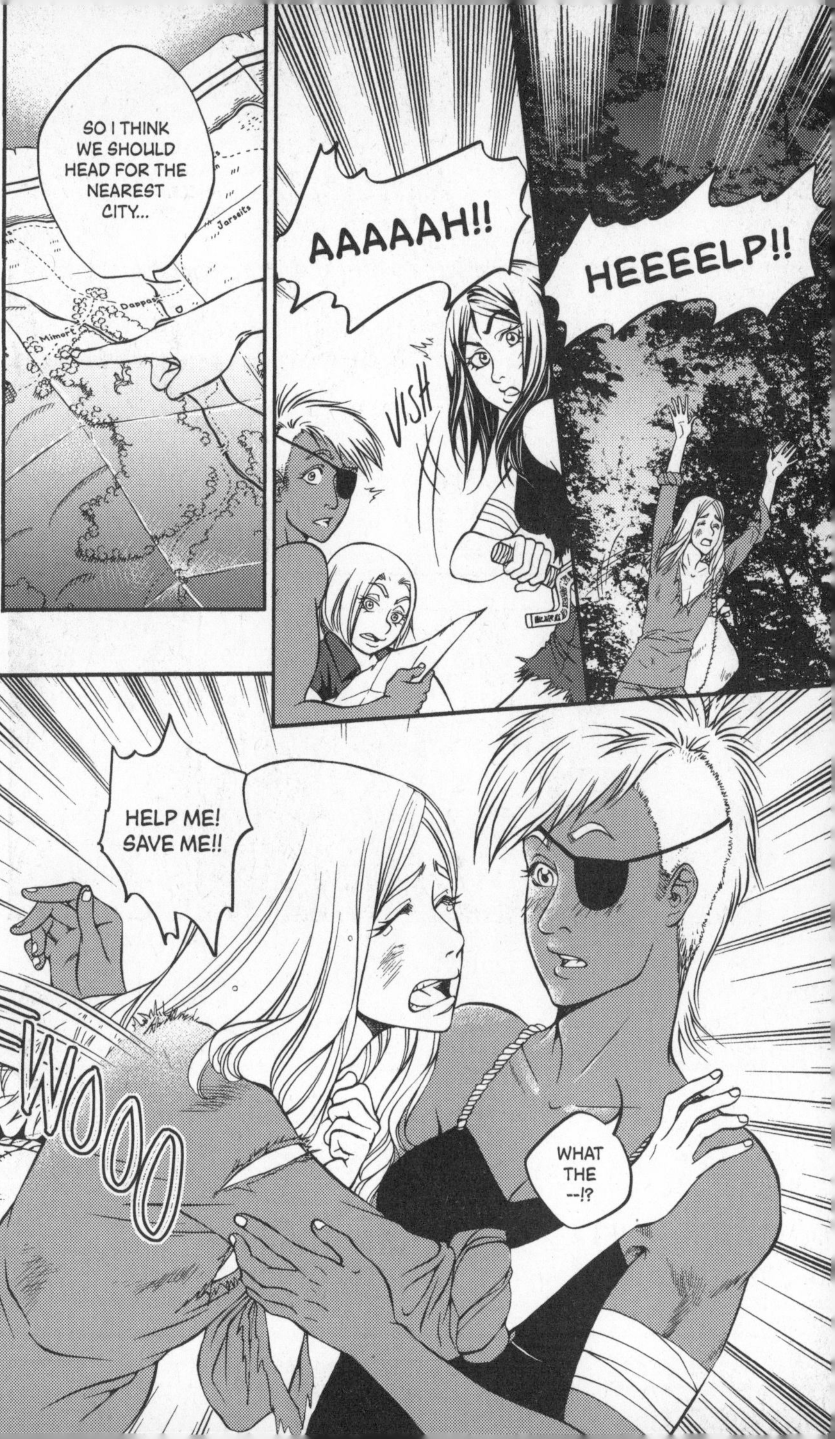
SO I THINK WE SHOULD HEAD FOR THE NEAREST CITY...
AAAAAH!!
VISH
HEEEELP!!
HELP ME! SAVE ME!!
FWOOO
WHAT THE --!?

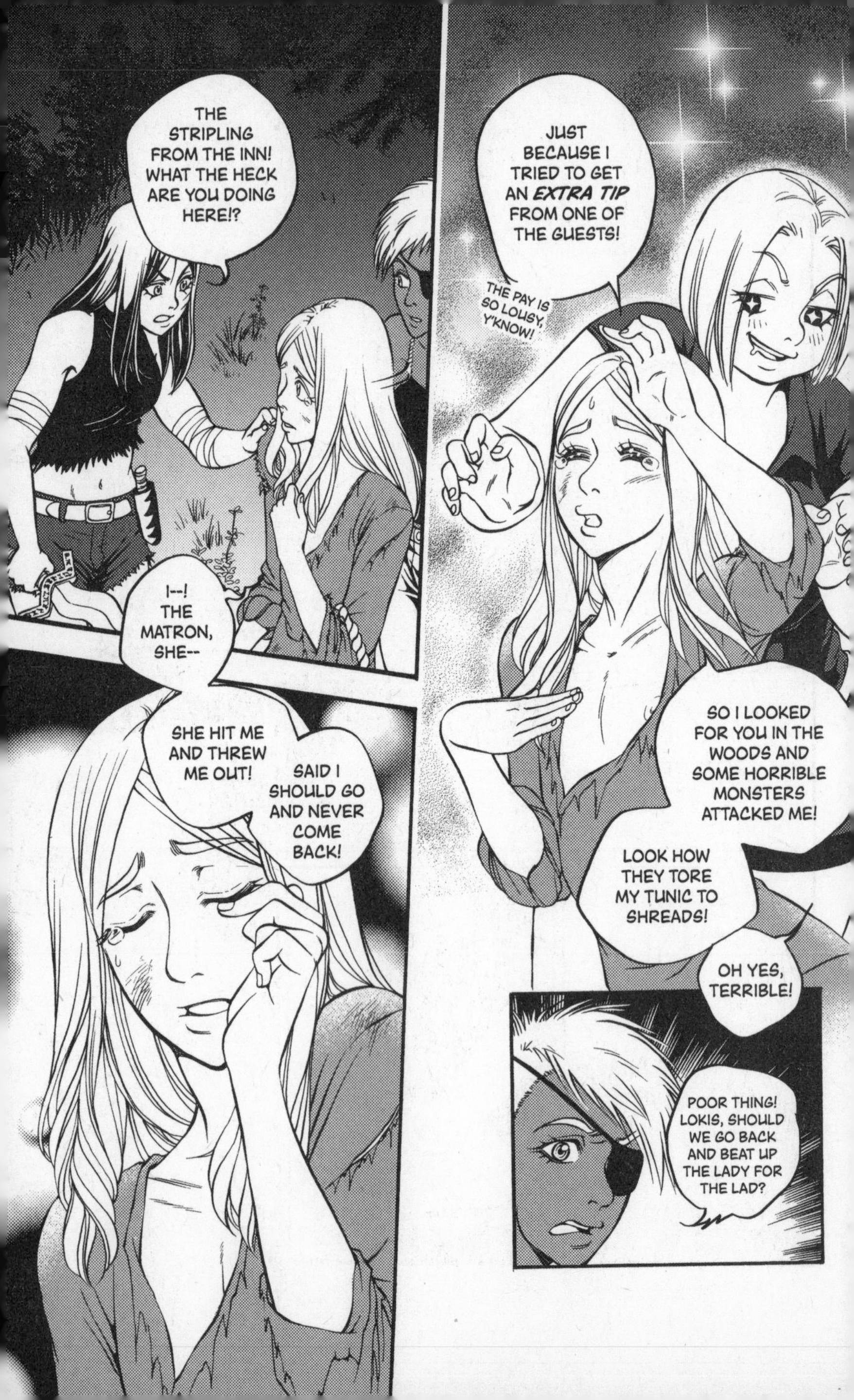
THE STRIPLING FROM THE INN! WHAT THE HECK ARE YOU DOING HERE!?
I--! THE MATRON, SHE--
SHE HIT ME AND THREW ME OUT!
SAID I SHOULD GO AND NEVER COME BACK!
JUST BECAUSE I TRIED TO GET AN ***EXTRA TIP*** FROM ONE OF THE GUESTS!
THE PAY IS SO LOUSY, Y'KNOW!
SO I LOOKED FOR YOU IN THE WOODS AND SOME HORRIBLE MONSTERS ATTACKED ME!
LOOK HOW THEY TORE MY TUNIC TO SHREADS!
OH YES, TERRIBLE!
POOR THING! LOKIS, SHOULD WE GO BACK AND BEAT UP THE LADY FOR THE LAD?

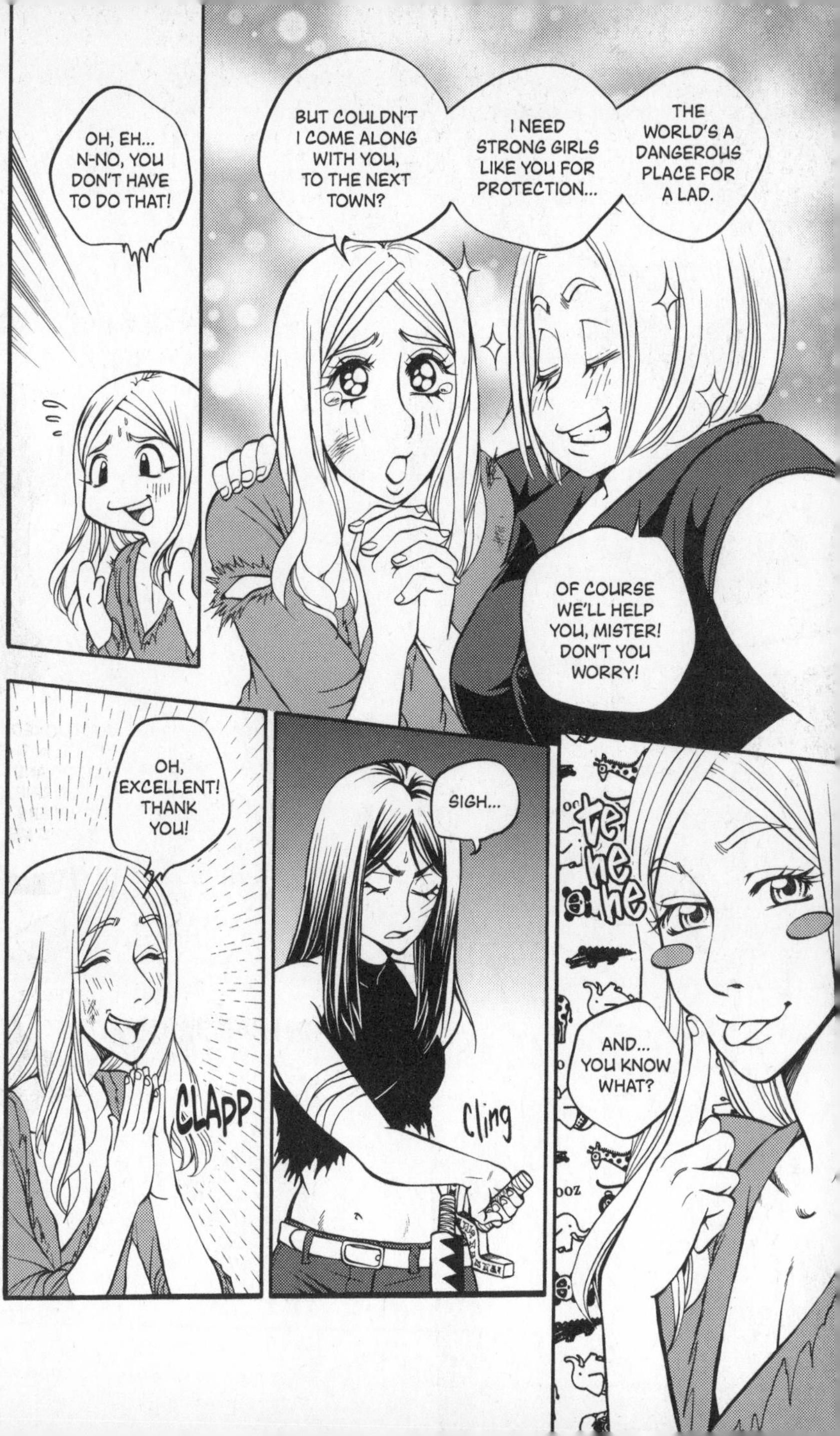
OH, EH... N-NO, YOU DON'T HAVE TO DO THAT!
BUT COULDN'T I COME ALONG WITH YOU, TO THE NEXT TOWN?
I NEED STRONG GIRLS LIKE YOU FOR PROTECTION...
THE WORLD'S A DANGEROUS PLACE FOR A LAD.
OF COURSE WE'LL HELP YOU, MISTER! DON'T YOU WORRY!
OH, EXCELLENT! THANK YOU!
CLAPP
SIGH...
Cling
te he he
AND... YOU KNOW WHAT?

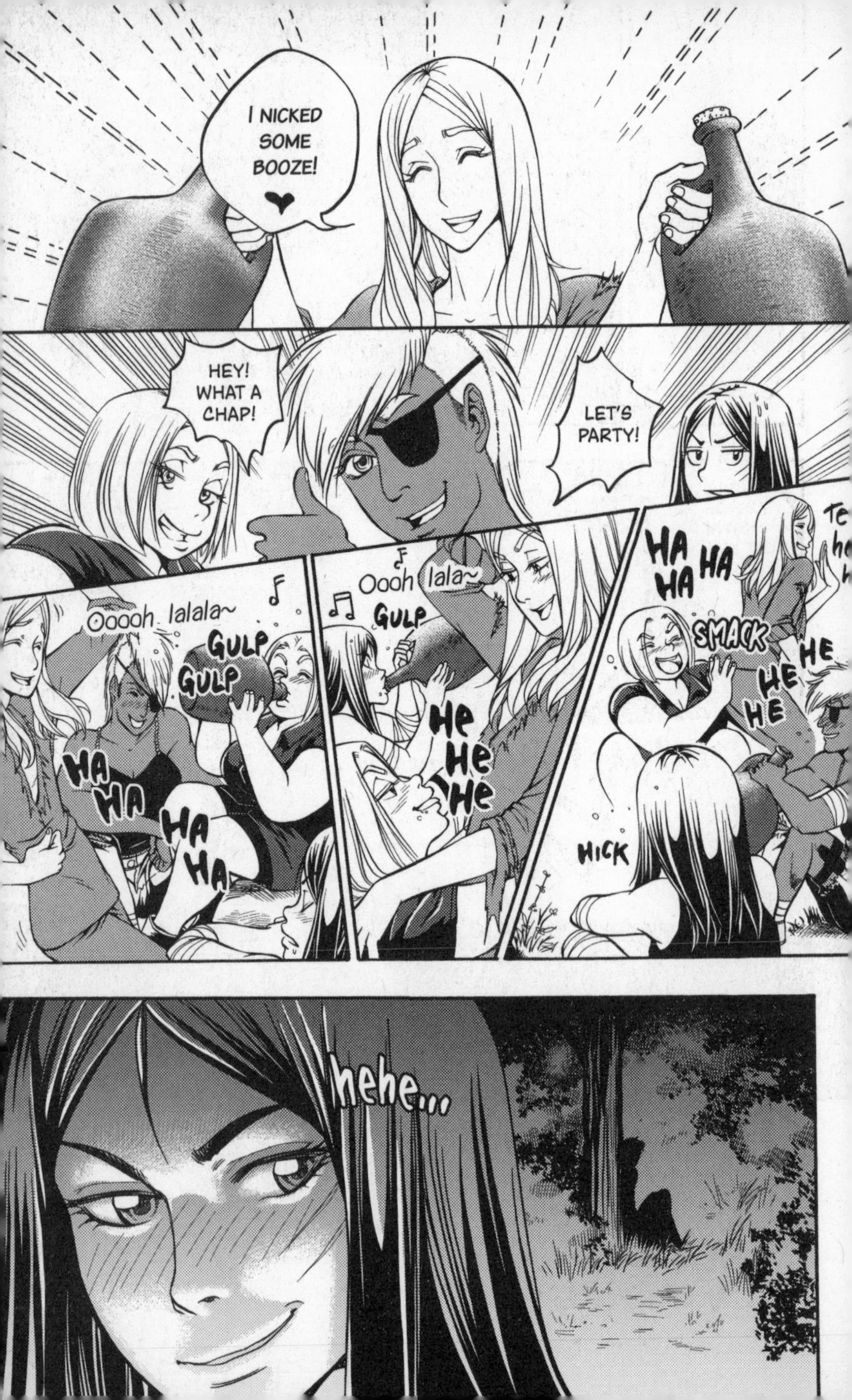
I NICKED SOME BOOZE! ♥
HEY! WHAT A CHAP!
LET'S PARTY!
Ooooh lalala~
GULP
GULP
HA HA
HA HA
Oooh lala~
GULP
He He He
HA HA HA
SMACK
HE HE HE HE
HICK
hehe...

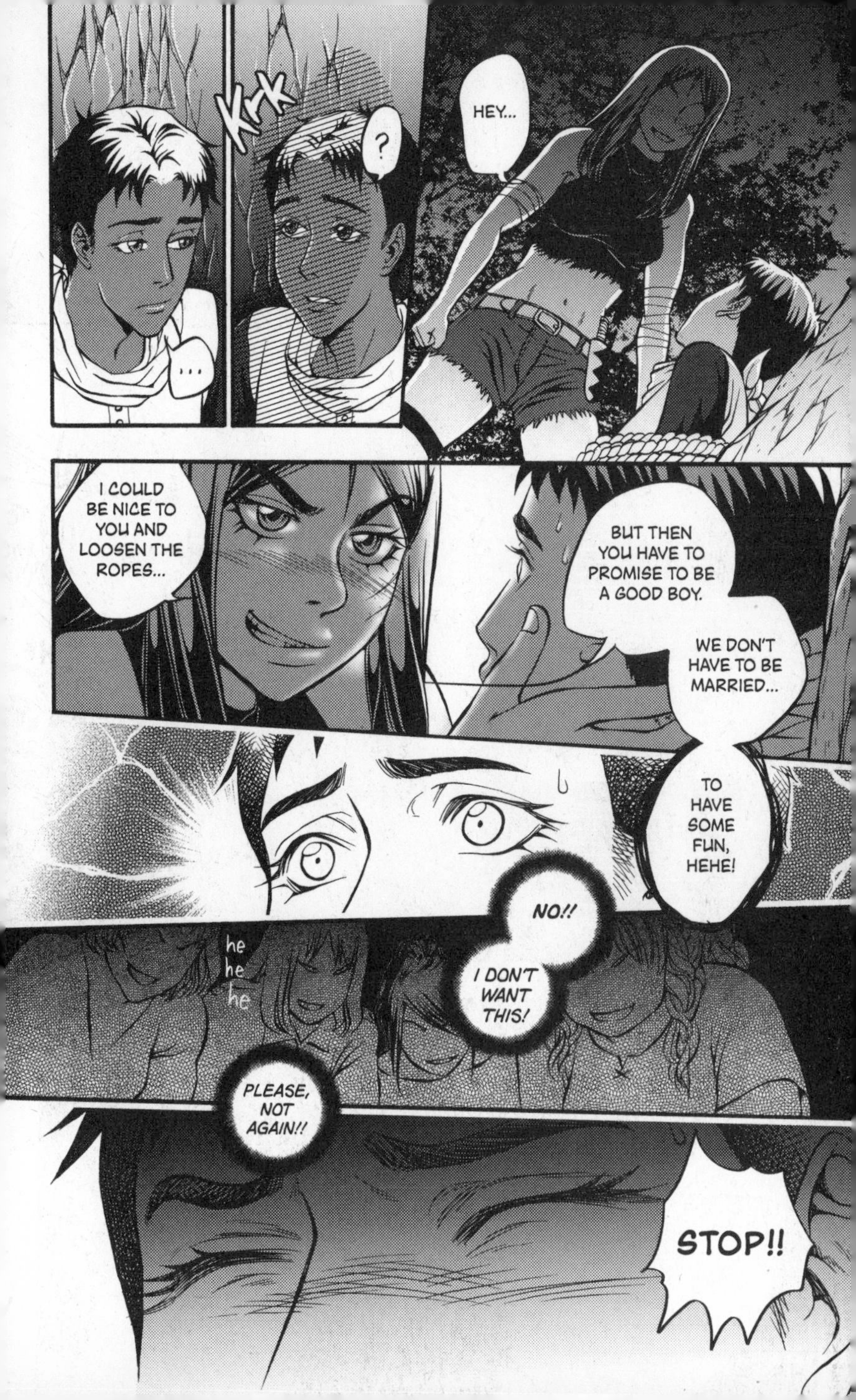
KRK
?
...
HEY...
I COULD BE NICE TO YOU AND LOOSEN THE ROPES...
BUT THEN YOU HAVE TO PROMISE TO BE A GOOD BOY.
WE DON'T HAVE TO BE MARRIED...
TO HAVE SOME FUN, HEHE!
NO!!
he he he
I DON'T WANT THIS!
PLEASE, NOT AGAIN!!
STOP!!

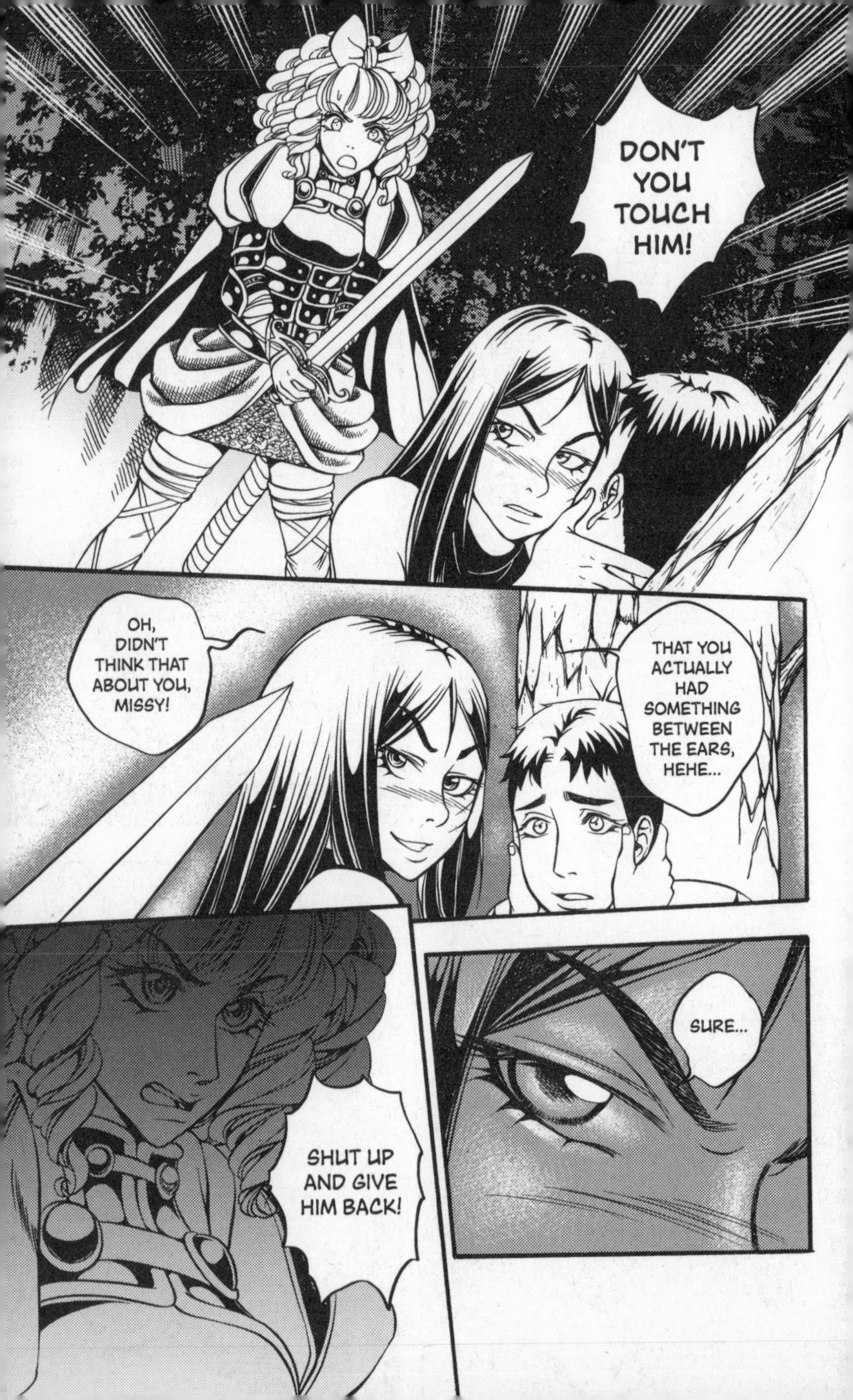
DON'T YOU TOUCH HIM!
OH, DIDN'T THINK THAT ABOUT YOU, MISSY!
THAT YOU ACTUALLY HAD SOMETHING BETWEEN THE EARS, HEHE...
SHUT UP AND GIVE HIM BACK!
SURE...

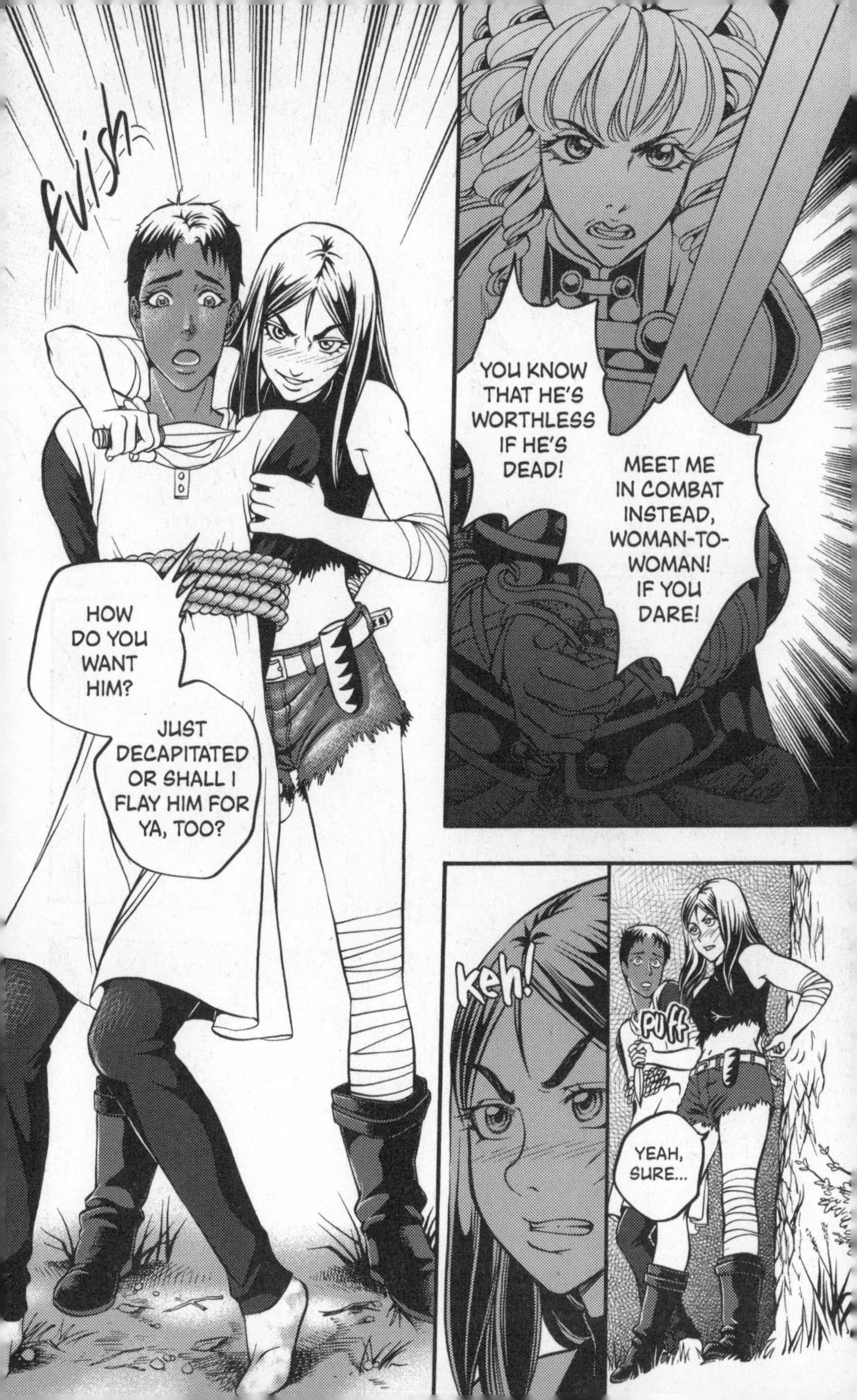
fvish
HOW DO YOU WANT HIM?
JUST DECAPITATED OR SHALL I FLAY HIM FOR YA, TOO?
YOU KNOW THAT HE'S WORTHLESS IF HE'S DEAD!
MEET ME IN COMBAT INSTEAD, WOMAN-TO-WOMAN! IF YOU DARE!
keh!
puff
YEAH, SURE...

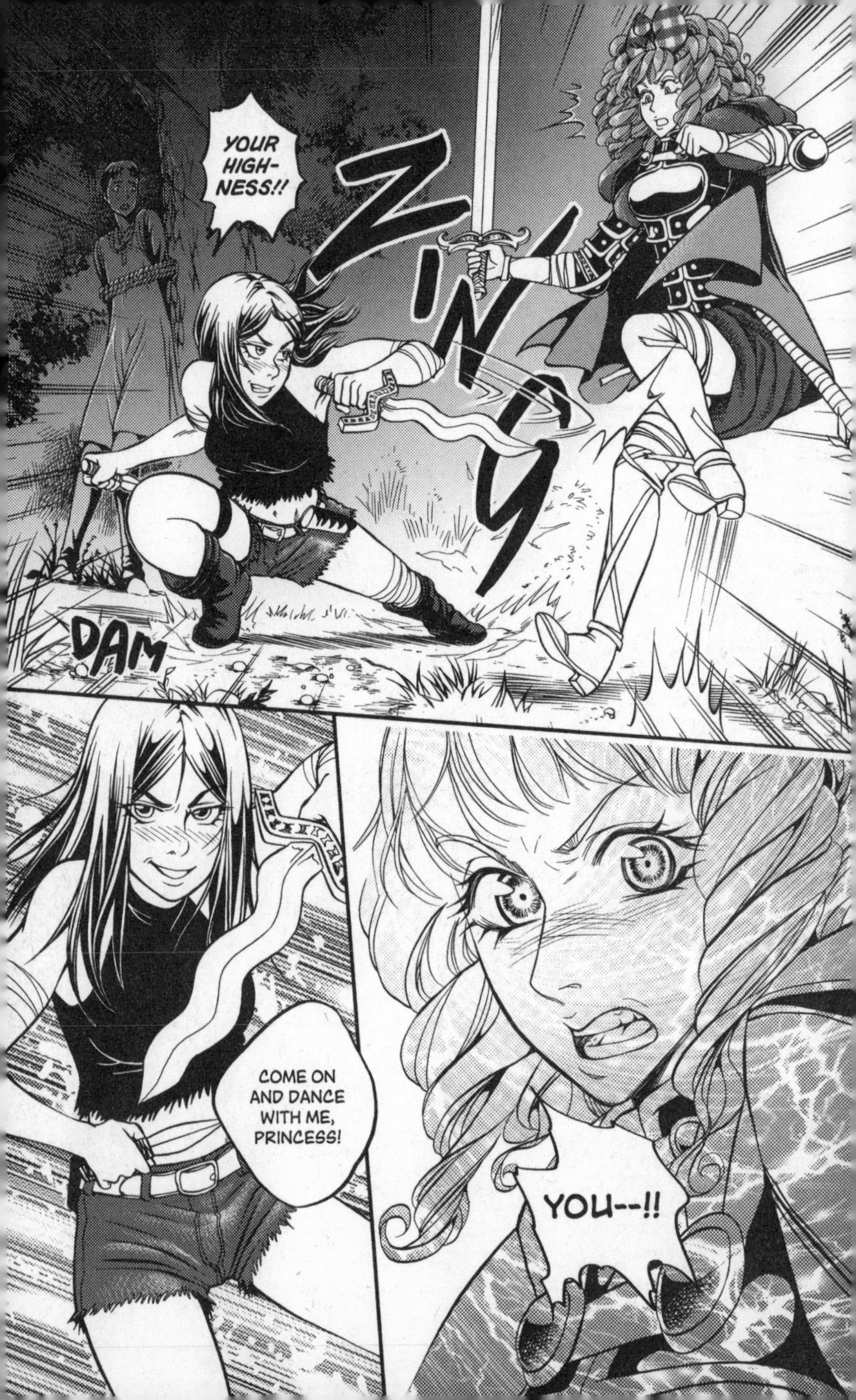
YOUR HIGH-NESS!!
ZINNG
DAM
COME ON AND DANCE WITH ME, PRINCESS!
YOU--!!

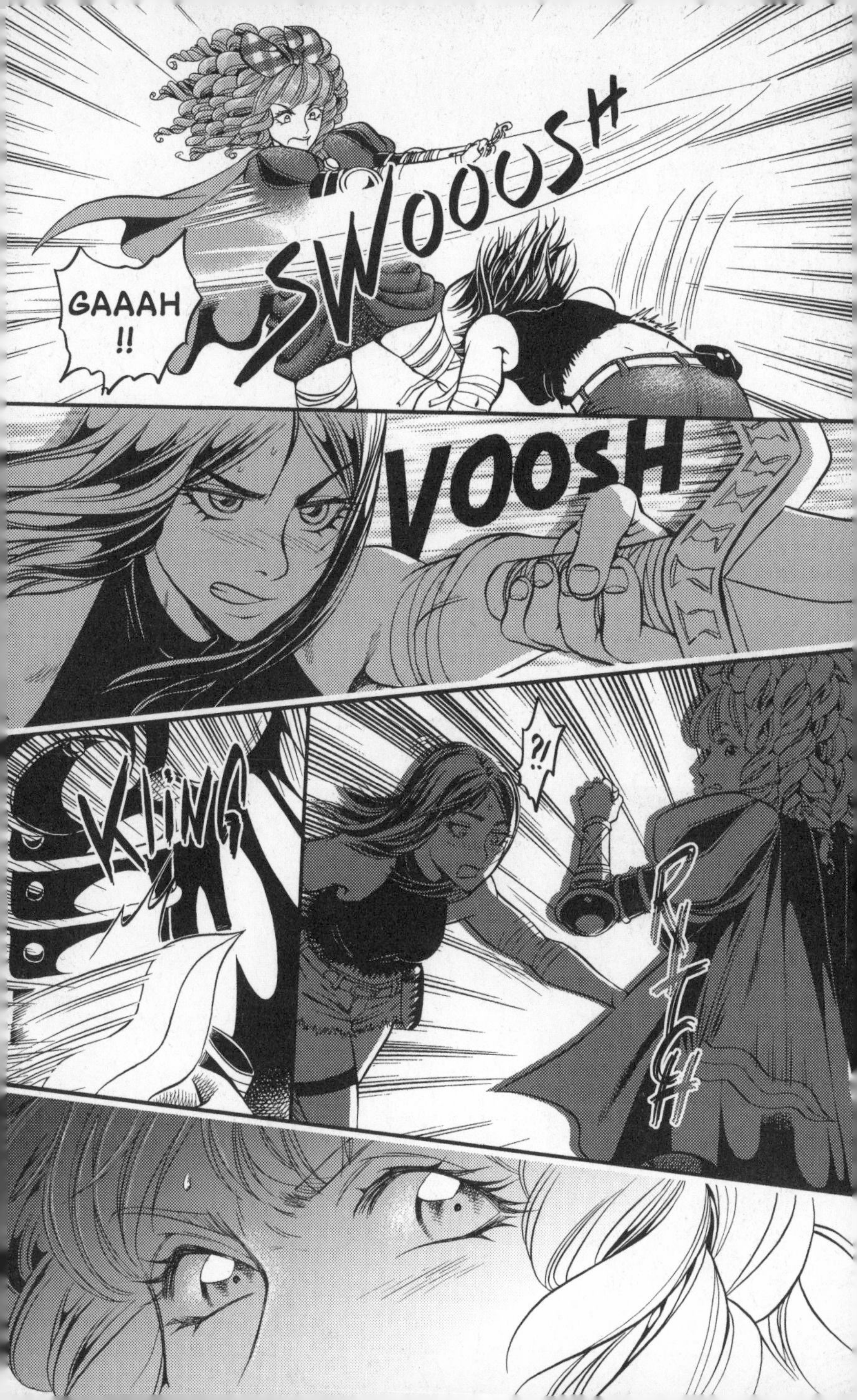
GAAAH !!
SWOOOSH
VOOSH
KLING
?!

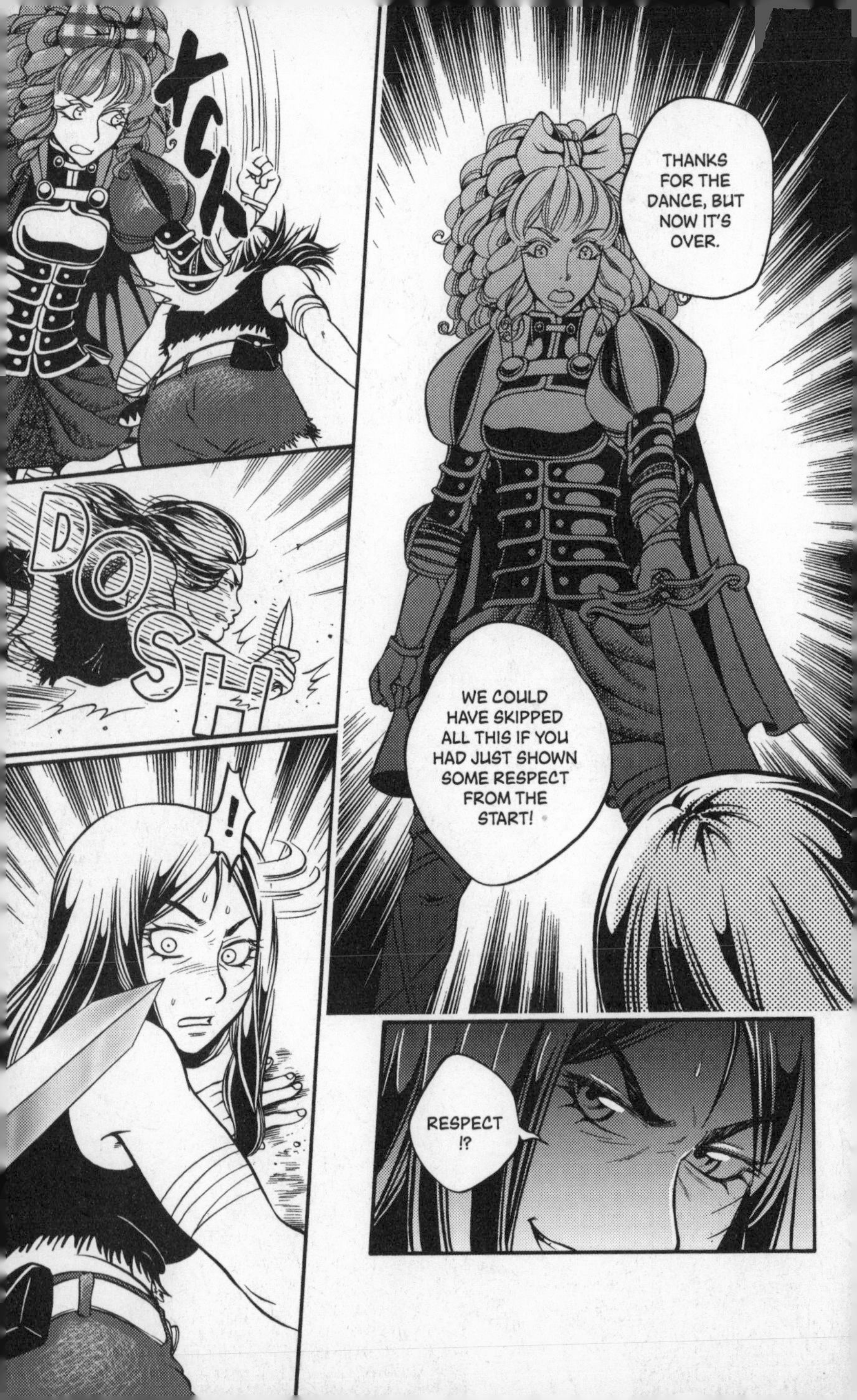
TCH
DOSH
!
THANKS FOR THE DANCE, BUT NOW IT'S OVER.
WE COULD HAVE SKIPPED ALL THIS IF YOU HAD JUST SHOWN SOME RESPECT FROM THE START!
RESPECT !?

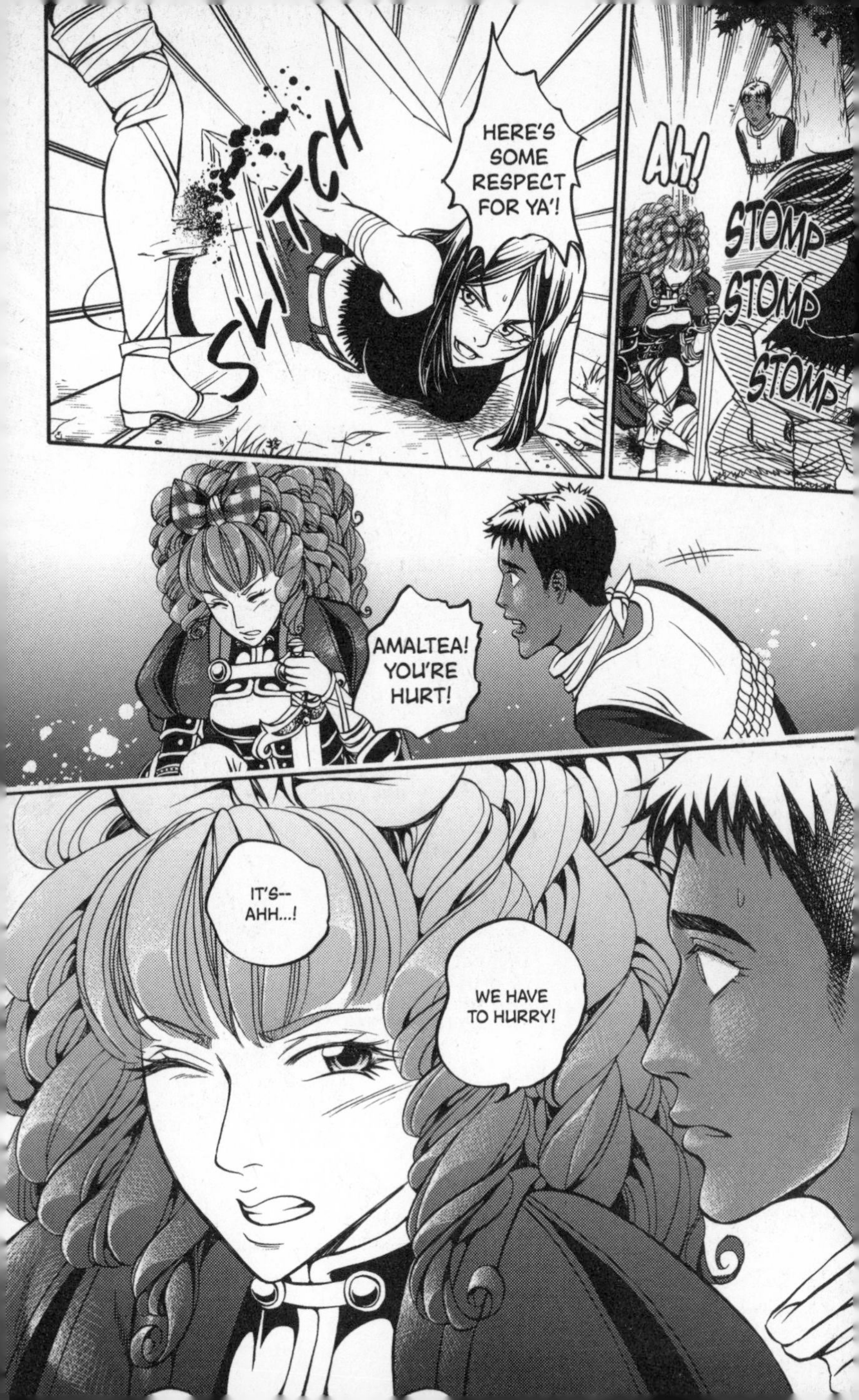
SWITCH
HERE'S SOME RESPECT FOR YA'!
Ah!
STOMP
STOMP
STOMP
AMALTEA! YOU'RE HURT!
IT'S-- AHH...!
WE HAVE TO HURRY!

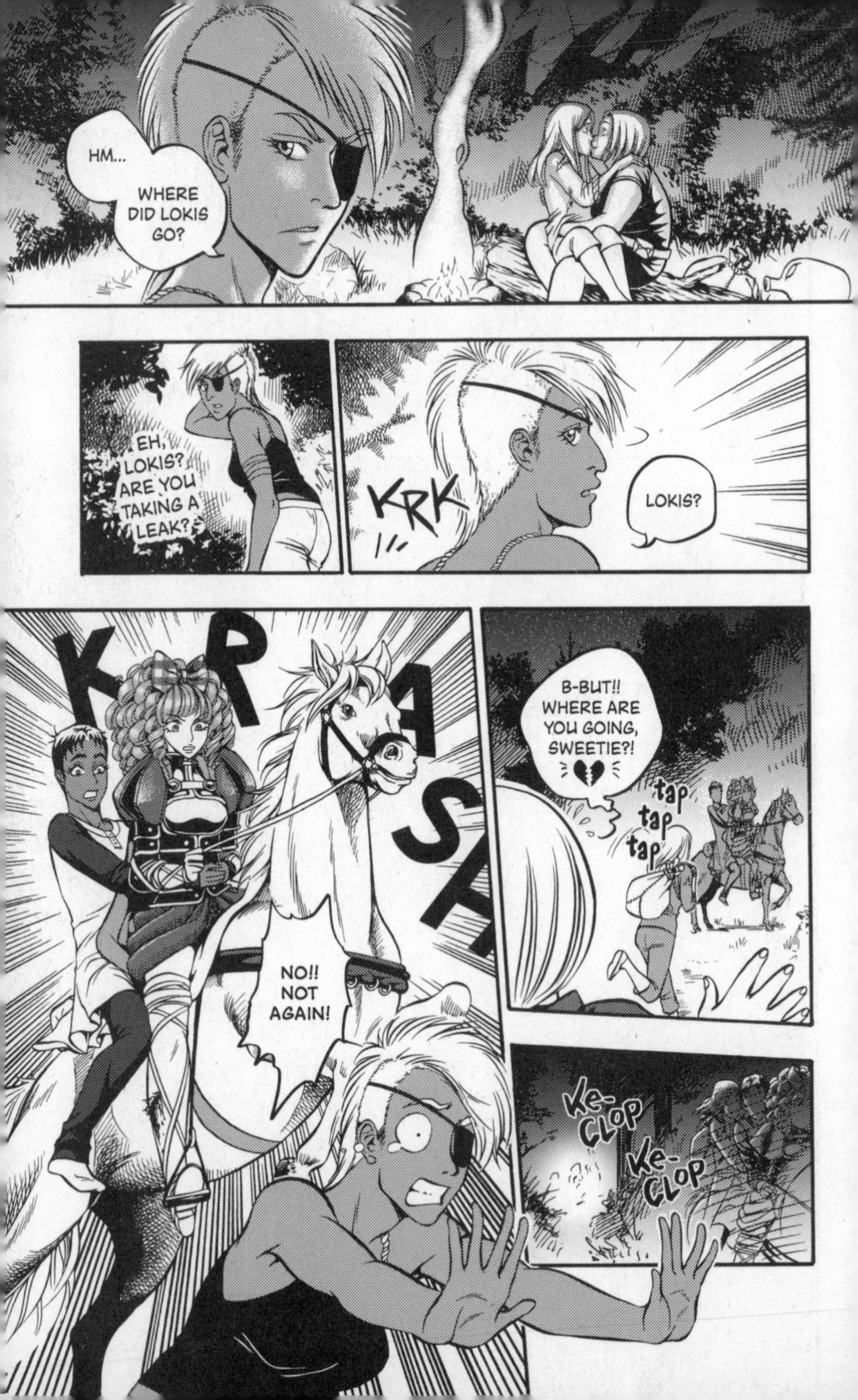
HM...
WHERE DID LOKIS GO?
EH, LOKIS? ARE YOU TAKING A LEAK?
KRK
LOKIS?
KRASH
NO!! NOT AGAIN!
B-BUT!! WHERE ARE YOU GOING, SWEETIE?!
tap tap tap
KE-CLOP
KE-CLOP

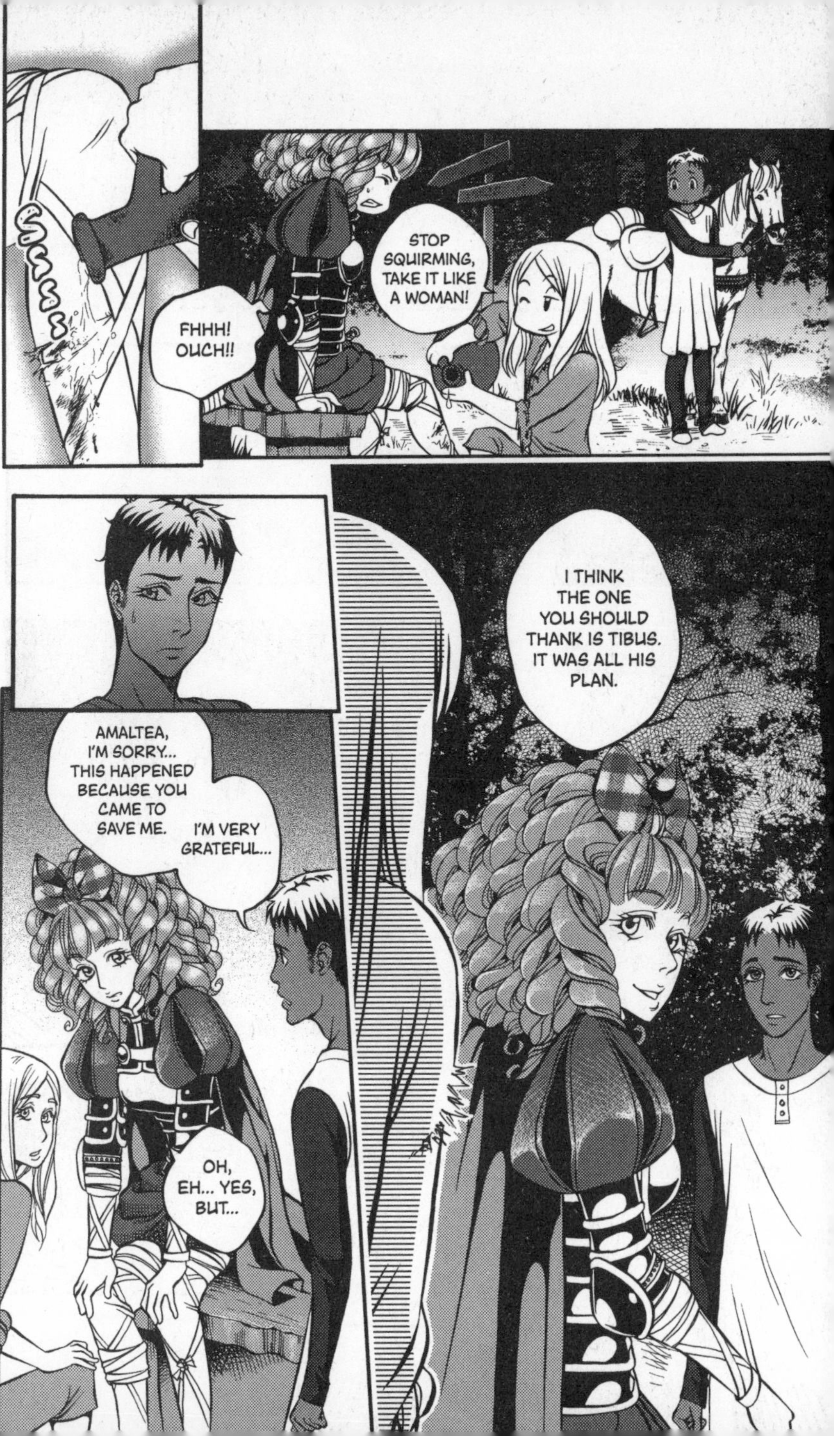
SSSSS
FHHH! OUCH!!
STOP SQUIRMING, TAKE IT LIKE A WOMAN!
AMALTEA, I'M SORRY... THIS HAPPENED BECAUSE YOU CAME TO SAVE ME.
I'M VERY GRATEFUL...
OH, EH... YES, BUT...
I THINK THE ONE YOU SHOULD THANK IS TIBUS. IT WAS ALL HIS PLAN.

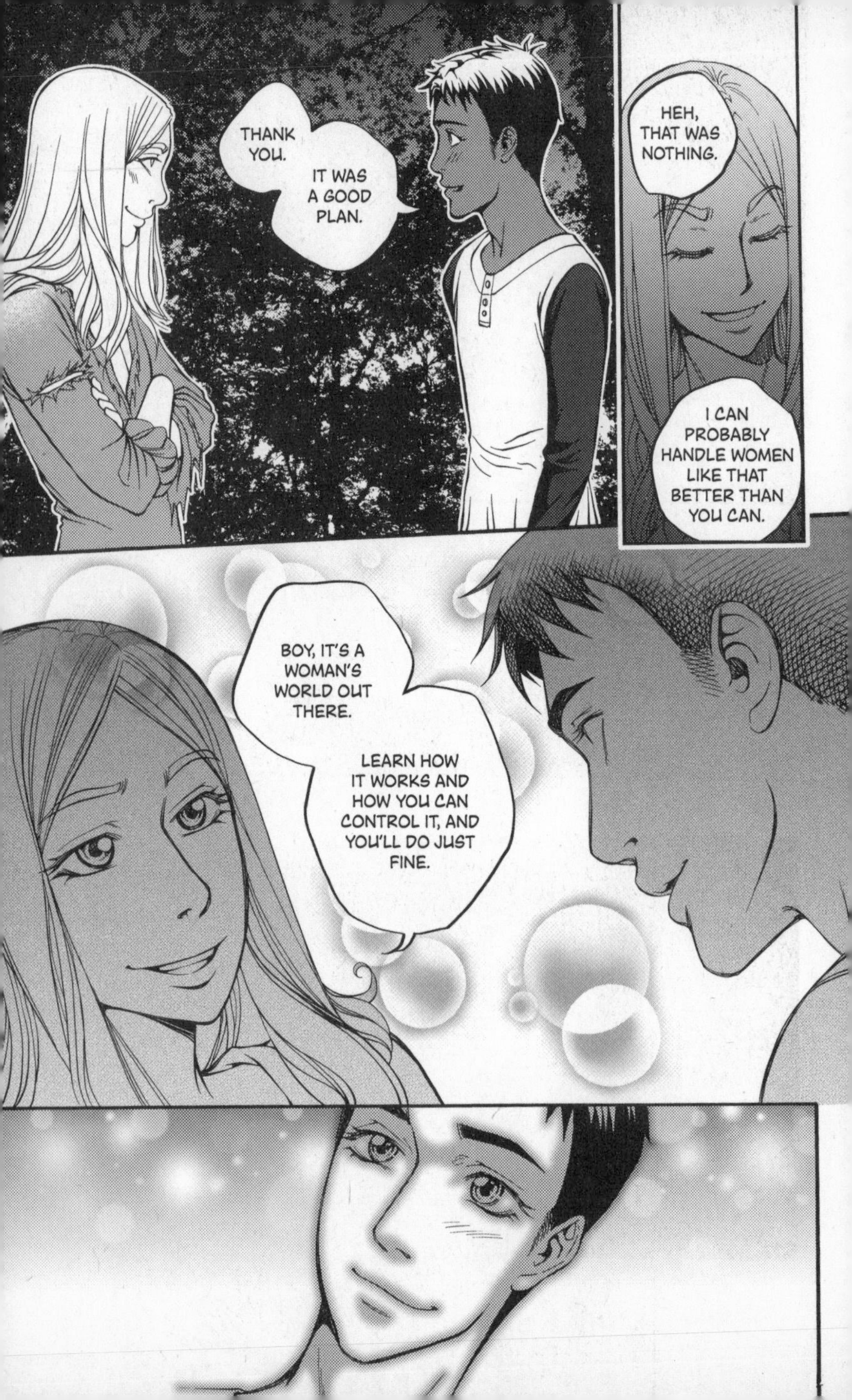
THANK YOU.
IT WAS A GOOD PLAN.
HEH, THAT WAS NOTHING.
I CAN PROBABLY HANDLE WOMEN LIKE THAT BETTER THAN YOU CAN.
BOY, IT'S A WOMAN'S WORLD OUT THERE.
LEARN HOW IT WORKS AND HOW YOU CAN CONTROL IT, AND YOU'LL DO JUST FINE.

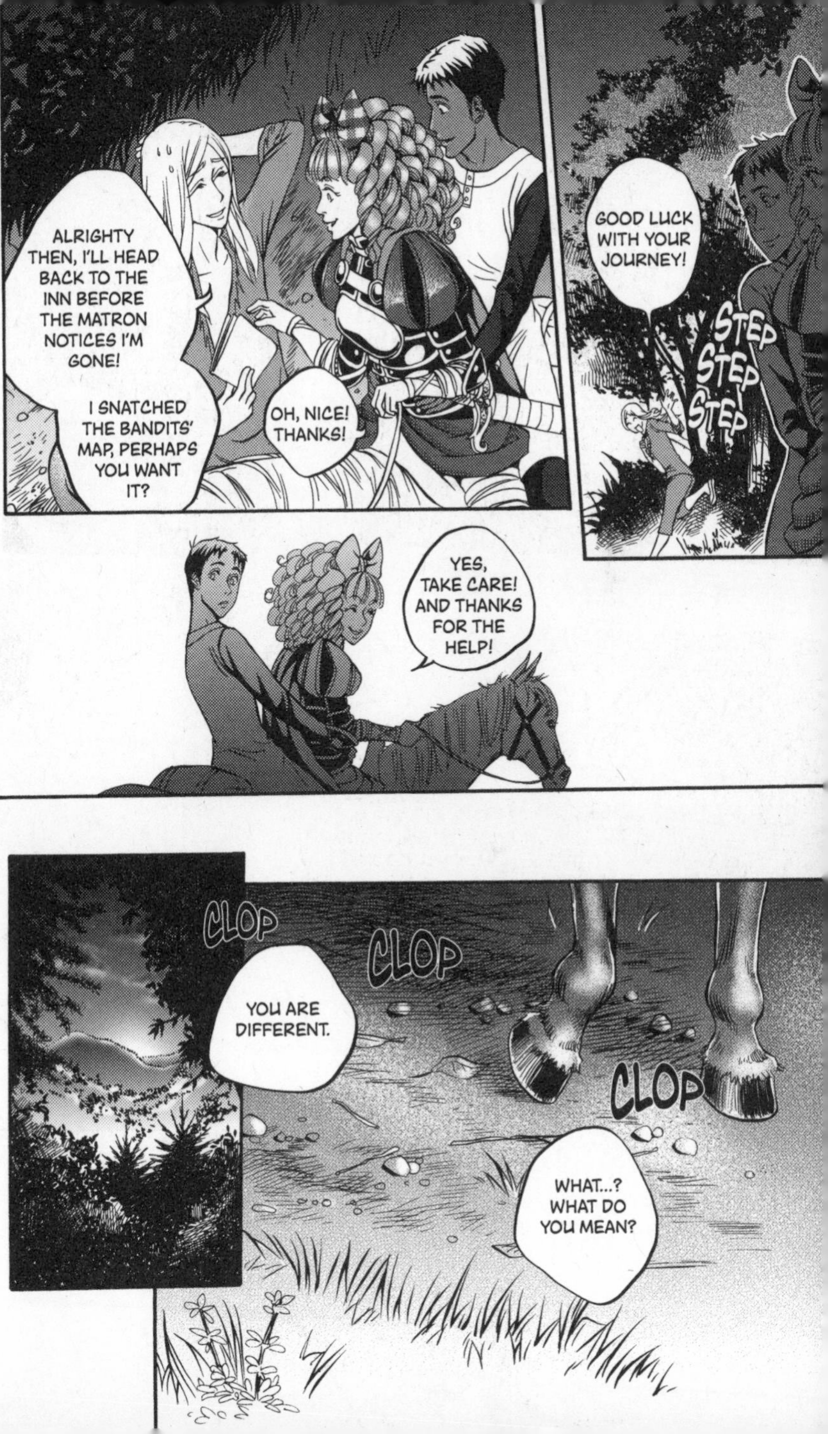
ALRIGHTY THEN, I'LL HEAD BACK TO THE INN BEFORE THE MATRON NOTICES I'M GONE!
I SNATCHED THE BANDITS' MAP, PERHAPS YOU WANT IT?
OH, NICE! THANKS!
GOOD LUCK WITH YOUR JOURNEY!
STEP STEP STEP
YES, TAKE CARE! AND THANKS FOR THE HELP!
CLOP
YOU ARE DIFFERENT.
CLOP
CLOP
WHAT...? WHAT DO YOU MEAN?

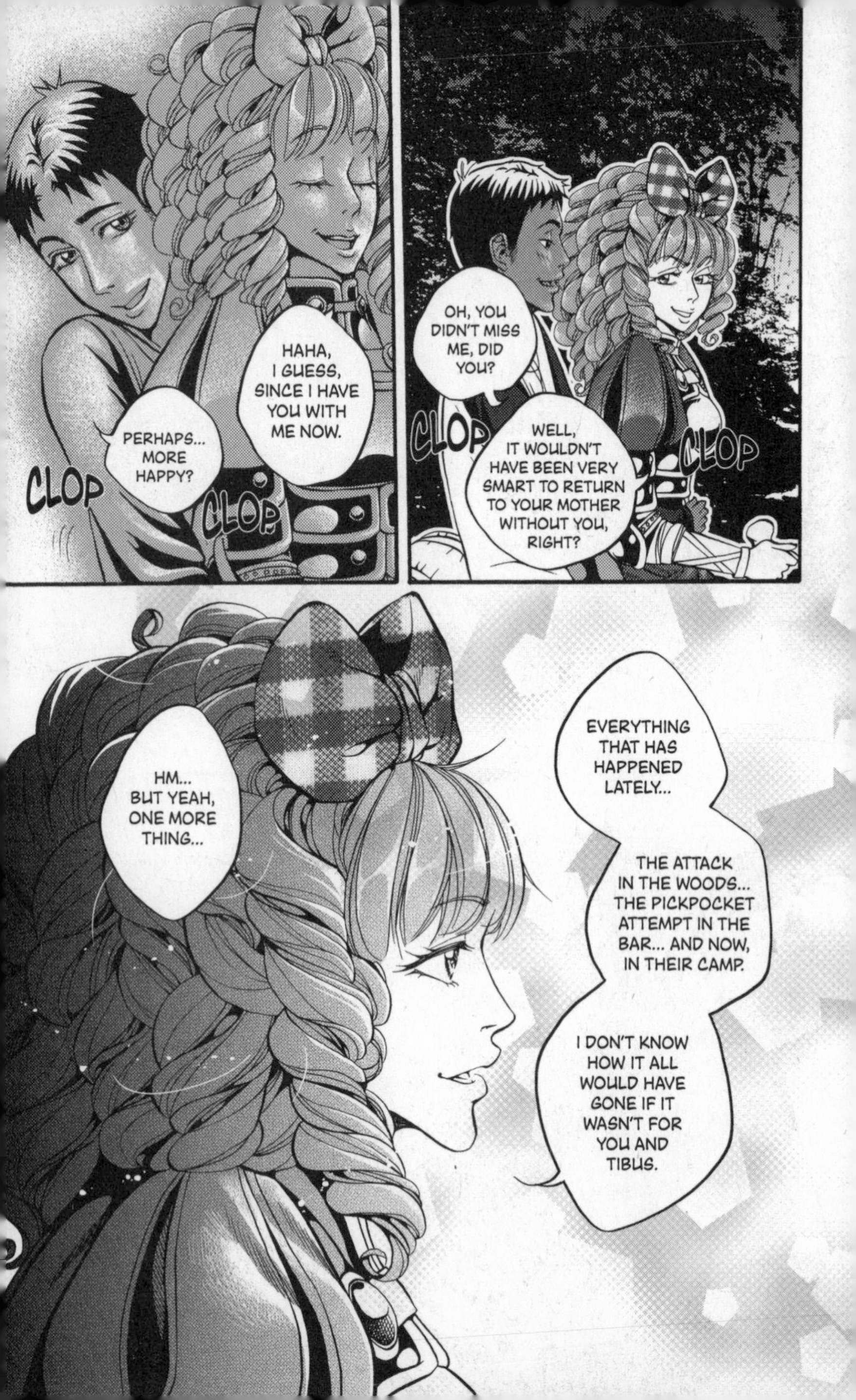
PERHAPS... MORE HAPPY?
HAHA, I GUESS, SINCE I HAVE YOU WITH ME NOW.
CLOP
CLOP
OH, YOU DIDN'T MISS ME, DID YOU?
CLOP
WELL, IT WOULDN'T HAVE BEEN VERY SMART TO RETURN TO YOUR MOTHER WITHOUT YOU, RIGHT?
CLOP
HM... BUT YEAH, ONE MORE THING...
EVERYTHING THAT HAS HAPPENED LATELY...
THE ATTACK IN THE WOODS... THE PICKPOCKET ATTEMPT IN THE BAR... AND NOW, IN THEIR CAMP.
I DON'T KNOW HOW IT ALL WOULD HAVE GONE IF IT WASN'T FOR YOU AND TIBUS.

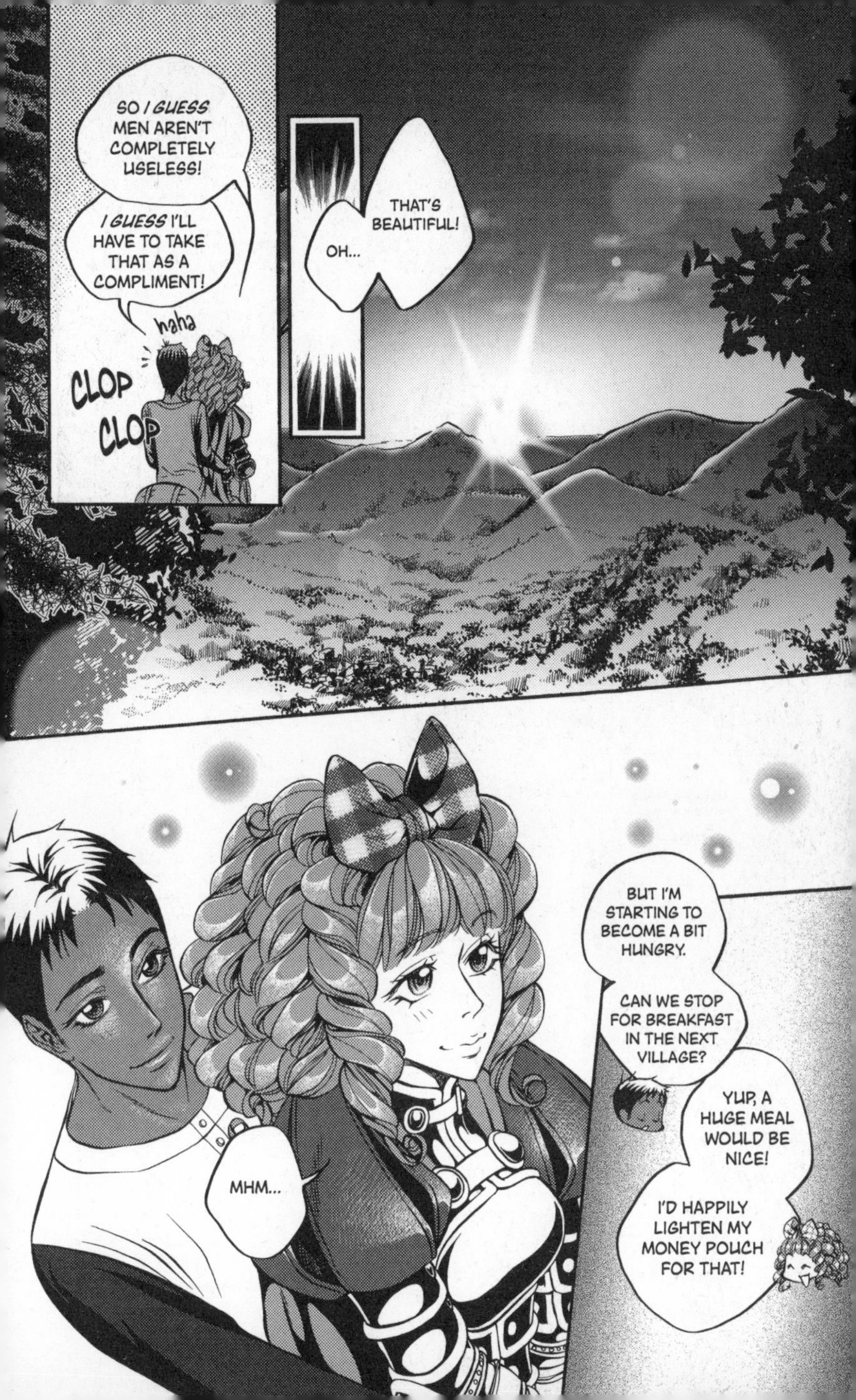
SO I GUESS MEN AREN'T COMPLETELY USELESS!
I GUESS I'LL HAVE TO TAKE THAT AS A COMPLIMENT!
haha
CLOP
CLOP
OH...
THAT'S BEAUTIFUL!
MHM...
BUT I'M STARTING TO BECOME A BIT HUNGRY.
CAN WE STOP FOR BREAKFAST IN THE NEXT VILLAGE?
YUP, A HUGE MEAL WOULD BE NICE!
I'D HAPPILY LIGHTEN MY MONEY POUCH FOR THAT!

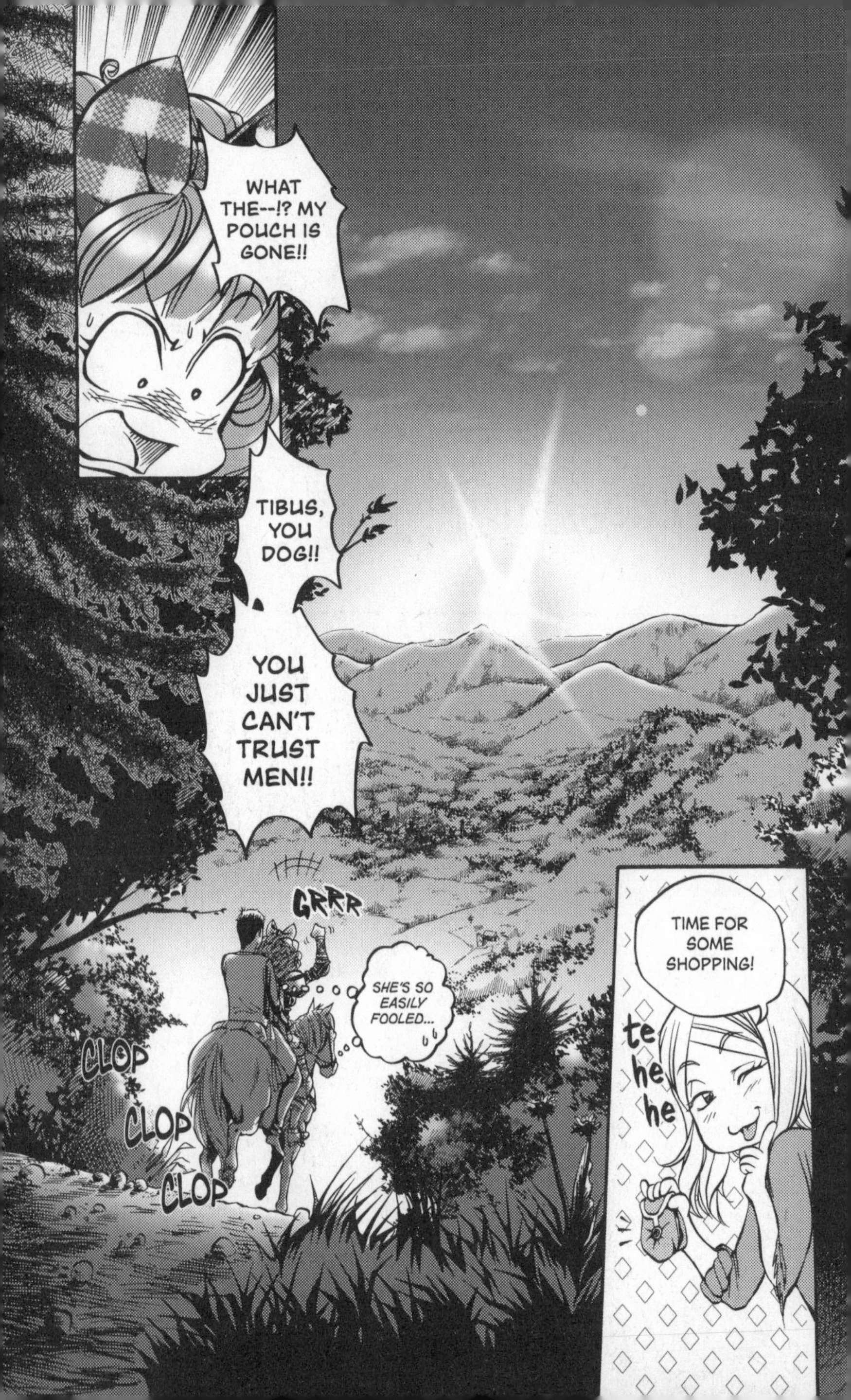
WHAT THE--!? MY POUCH IS GONE!!
TIBUS, YOU DOG!!
YOU JUST CAN'T TRUST MEN!!
GRRR
SHE'S SO EASILY FOOLED...
CLOP
CLOP
CLOP
TIME FOR SOME SHOPPING!
te he he

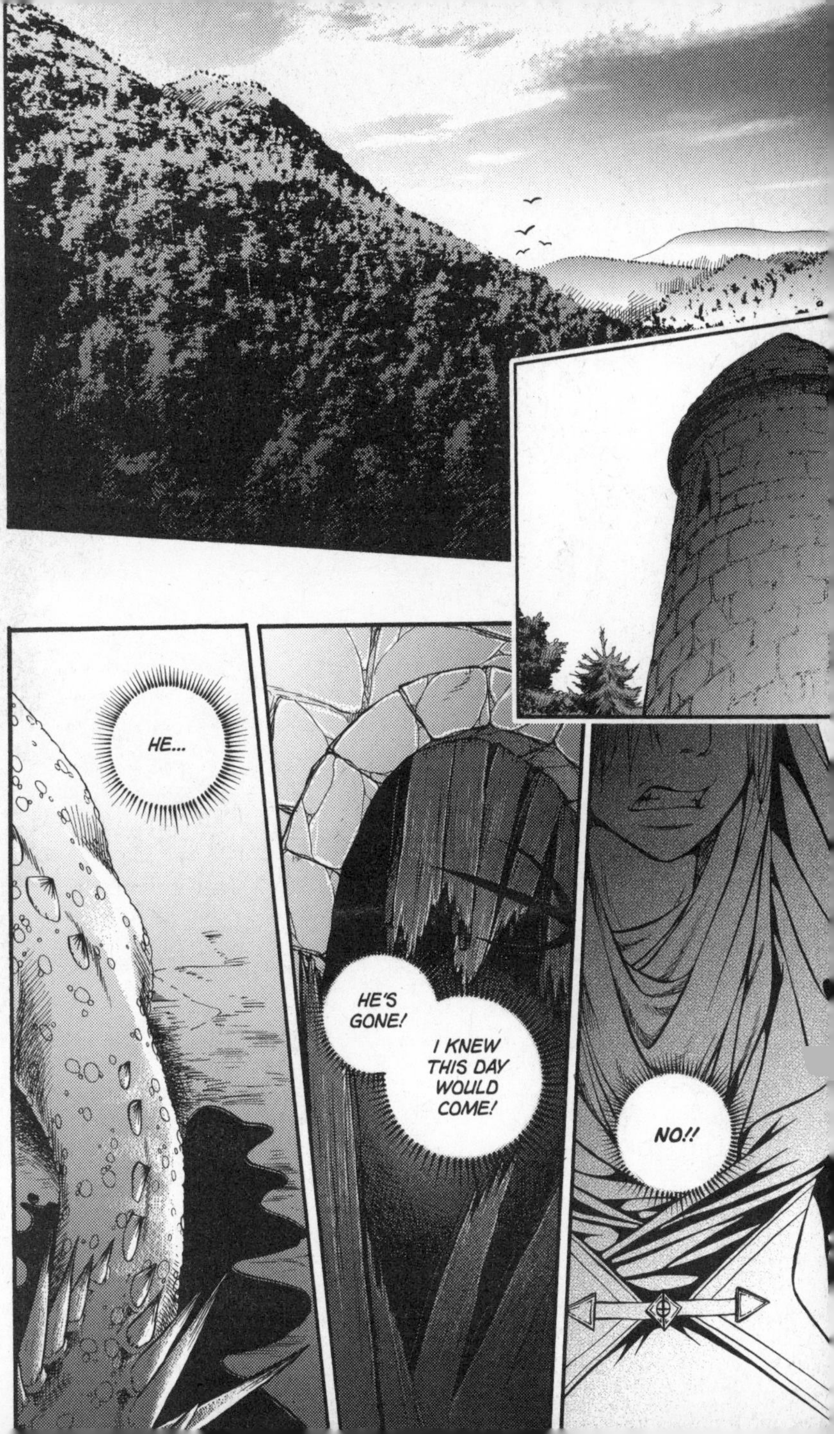
HE...
HE'S GONE!
I KNEW THIS DAY WOULD COME!
NO!!

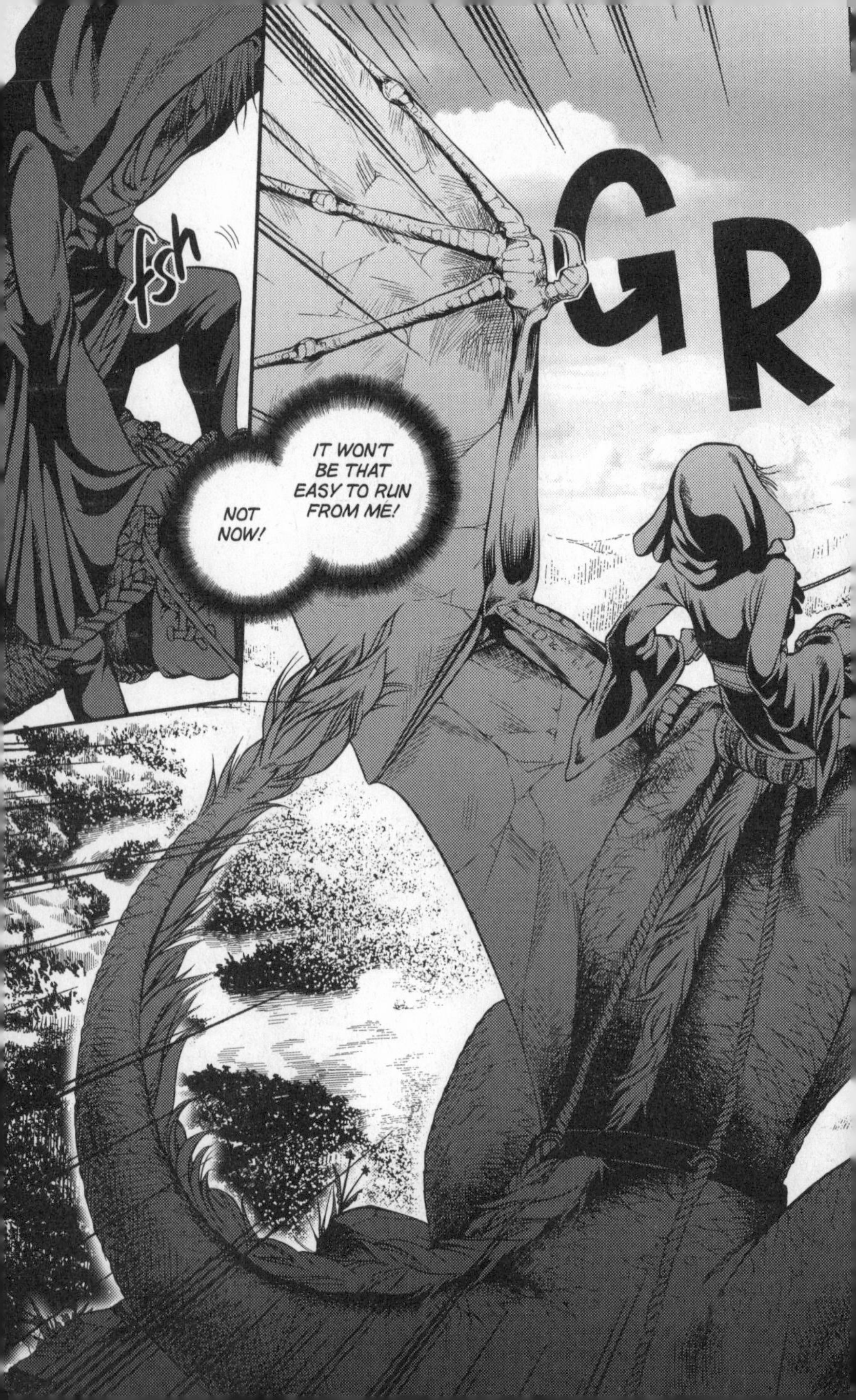
fsh
IT WON'T BE THAT EASY TO RUN FROM ME!
NOT NOW!
GR

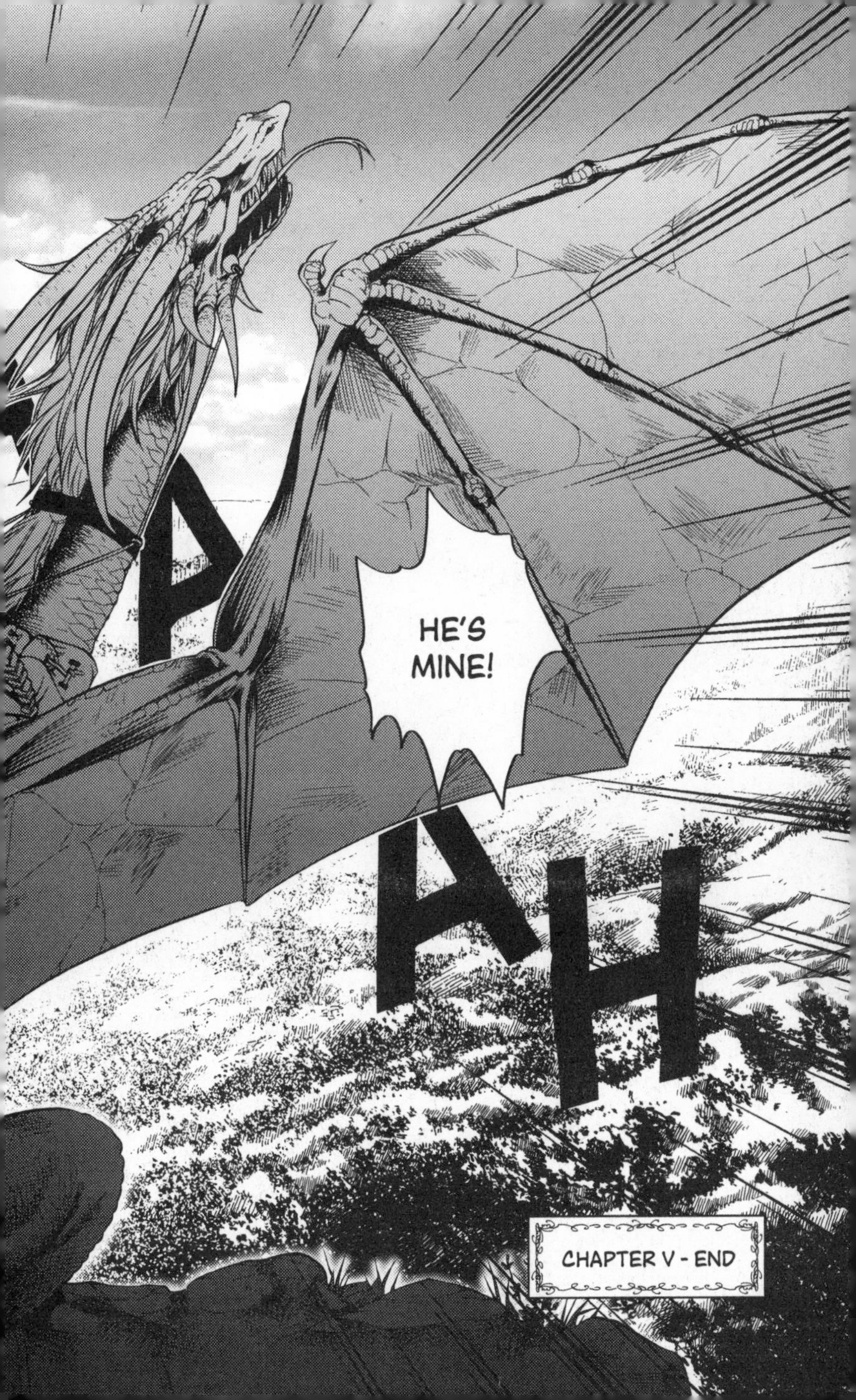
PAH
HE'S MINE!
CHAPTER V - END

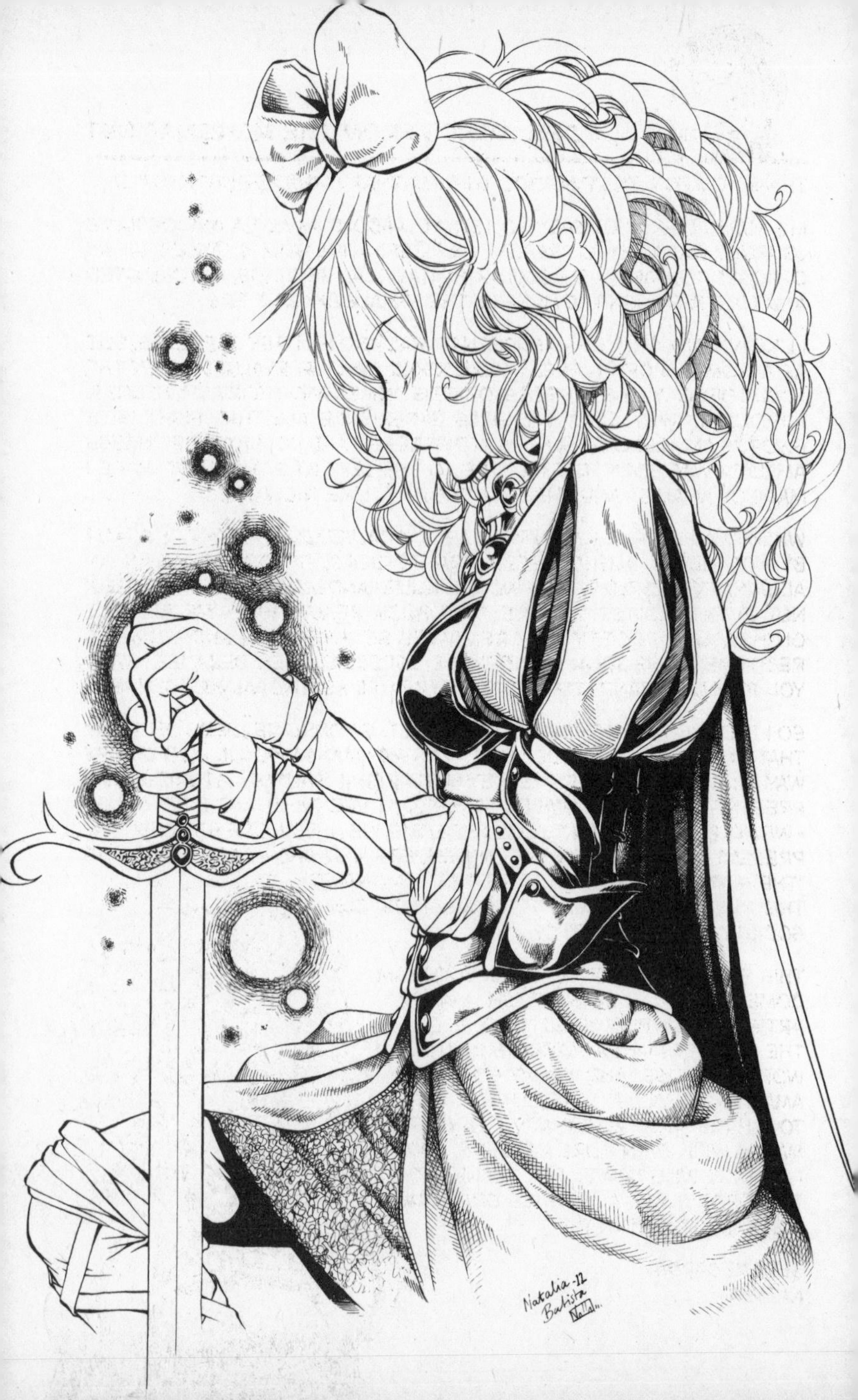
Natalia -12
Batista

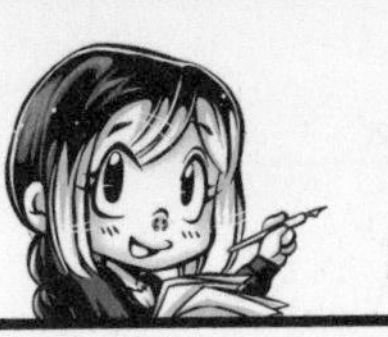

SOME WORDS FROM THE MANGA ARTIST

THANK YOU FOR STEPPING INTO THIS IMAGINARY UPSIDE-DOWN WORLD!

MY HOPES WERE NOT ONLY TO TELL YOU ABOUT AMALTEA AND OSSIAN'S JOURNEY, BUT ALSO TO PRESENT AN ALTERNATIVE FANTASY TALE THAT, AS OPPOSED TO MANY WITH SIMILAR FANTASTICAL SETTINGS, IS DOMINATED AND TOLD THROUGH THE LIVES OF THE FEMALE CHARACTERS.

I LIKE WHEN A STORY HAS SUPERNATURAL AND FANTASY ELEMENTS. BUT, AS A WOMAN, I OFTEN FEEL OVERLOOKED OR UNDERVALUED WHEN THE FOCUS OF SO MANY OF THESE STORIES IS ON MEN AND THEIR ADVENTURES. I THOUGHT, "WHY CAN'T WE GIRLS EXPERIENCE ALL THAT, FIGHT WITH SWORDS AND RESCUE PRINCES IN DISTRESS?" AND SO, SWORD PRINCESS AMALTEA WAS BORN. THE PICTURE TO THE LEFT WAS THE FIRST IMAGE I MADE OF AMALTEA AND IT IS STILL THE ONE I LIKE THE MOST.

WHEN I WAS 15 YEARS OLD, I READ A BOOK CALLED *DAUGHTERS OF EGALIA* BY NORWEGIAN AUTHOR GERD BRANTENBERG. IT TOOK PLACE IN AN ALTERNATIVE WORLD WHERE WOMEN RULED AND MEN WERE OPPRESSED, NOT EVEN ALLOWED TO VOTE. THIS BOOK REALLY MADE ME REFLECT ON HOW OUR SOCIETY DIFFERENTIATES BETWEEN MEN AND WOMEN. I RECOMMEND THE BOOK TO EVERYONE, ESPECIALLY MEN, BECAUSE I WANT YOU TO UNDERSTAND HOW IT IS TO BE TREATED AS "THE WEAKER GENDER."

SO I THOUGHT ABOUT HOW I COULD GIVE THE YOUNG READERS OF TODAY THAT SAME FEELING AND DECIDED A FANTASY MANGA WOULD BE THE BEST WAY. OUR WORLD NEEDS MORE MATRIARCHAL FANTASY STORIES THAT PRESENT WOMEN AS CAPABLE, STRONG, INDEPENDENT AND EVEN CRUEL - WITHOUT BEING SO ON THE MEN'S TERMS. WE NEED MORE STORIES THAT PRESENT A DIFFERENT VIEW ON GENDERS AND SHOWCASE WOMEN AS "THE NORM." WE NEED STORIES THAT CAN START THE KINDS OF IMPORTANT DISCUSSIONS OUR SOCIETY IS IN DIRE NEED OF.

THIS ENGLISH EDITION IS TRULY A DREAM COME TRUE. AS A SWEDISH MANGA ARTIST, BEING PUBLISHED IN ONE OF THE BIGGEST MANGA MARKETS IN THE WORLD IS HUGE, AND TO DO SO WITH AMALTEA MEANS A LOT TO ME. I GET TO SHARE THIS ALTERNATIVE FANTASY MANGA WITH EVEN MORE READERS, AND I KNOW IT WILL TRAVEL FAR THANKS TO TOKYOPOP. I WILL ALWAYS BE GRATEFUL FOR THIS OPPORTUNITY!

BEST REGARDS,
NATALIA

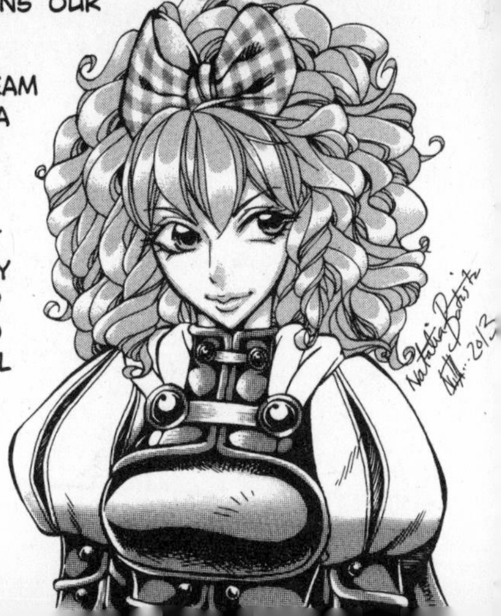

IN THE NEXT VOLUME OF

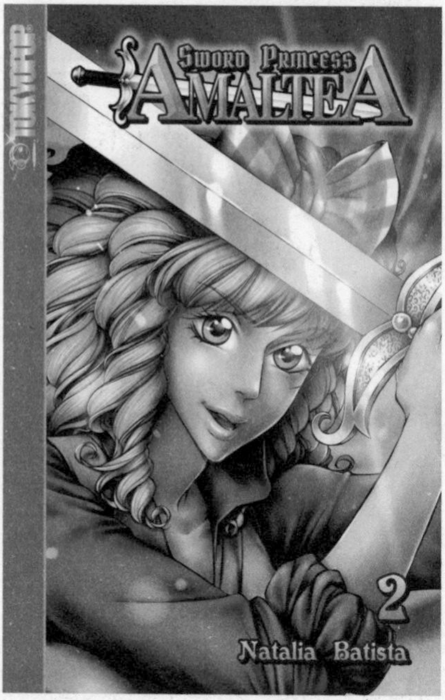
TOKYOPOP
Sword Princess
AMALTEA
2
Natalia Batista

AFTER – RELUCTANTLY – FOLLOWING THE QUEEN'S ORDERS TO EMBARK ON HER SOLO COMING OF AGE JOURNEY, BATTLING A DRAGON, RESCUING THE BEAUTIFUL PRINCE OSSIAN AND GETTING ATTACKED BY BANDITS, PRINCESS AMALTEA IS BEGINNING TO SEE THAT MAYBE THE WORLD ISN'T AS SIMPLE AS SHE ONCE THOUGHT.

NOW THE FATED PAIR HAVE A LONG JOURNEY AHEAD OF THEM, AND WITH PRINCESS DOROTEA HOT ON THEIR TRAIL THEY'LL NEED TO MOVE QUICKLY IF THEY WANT TO MAKE IT TO THE GREY MOUNTAINS QUEENDOM BEFORE SHE CATCHES UP TO THEM. THAT'LL TAKE COOPERATION, BUT WITH AMALTEA TOO STUBBORN AND ARROGANT TO LISTEN TO HER FELLOW TRAVELER, PERHAPS SHE'LL NEED TO SPEND A DAY IN HIS SHOES...

THE AUTHOR

NATALIA BATISTA IS A SWEDISH
MANGA ARTIST, ILLUSTRATOR AND COMIC ART
TEACHER AT SERIESKOLAN IN MALMÖ, THE MOST
PROMINENT COMIC ART SCHOOL IN SWEDEN. HER
WORKS INCLUDE THE KIDS MANGA *MJAU!*, PUBLISHED
IN SWEDEN, PORTUGAL AND THE US. NATALIA WAS
A FOUNDING MEMBER OF THE SWEDISH MANGA
ARTIST COLLECTIVE AND PUBLISHER
NOSEBLEED STUDIO.

NATALIA LOVES LISTENING TO PODCASTS,
COOKING VEGAN FOOD AND FARMING HER OWN
VEGETABLES. SHE'S GOT TWO CATS WHO LIKES
HANGING OUT NEAR HER WHEN SHE DRAWS, AND
OCCASIONALLY SPILL HER WATER CUPS.

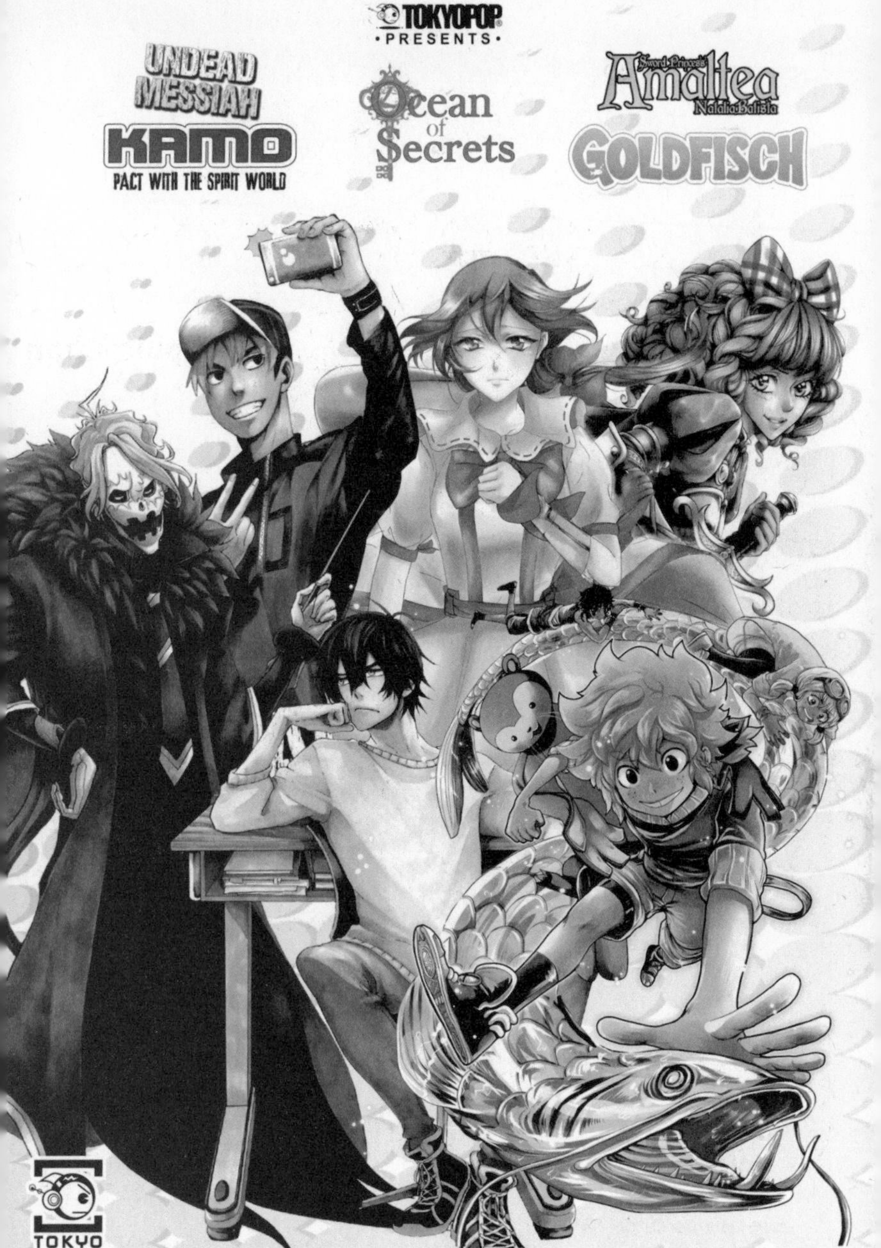
TOKYOPOP
PRESENTS
UNDEAD MESSIAH
KAMO
PACT WITH THE SPIRIT WORLD
Ocean of Secrets
Sword Princess Amaltea
Natalia Batista
GOLDFISCH
TOKYO POP

Check out the back of the book for some exclusive sneak peeks!

How do you read manga-style? It's simple! Let's practice -- just start in the top right panel and follow the numbers below!

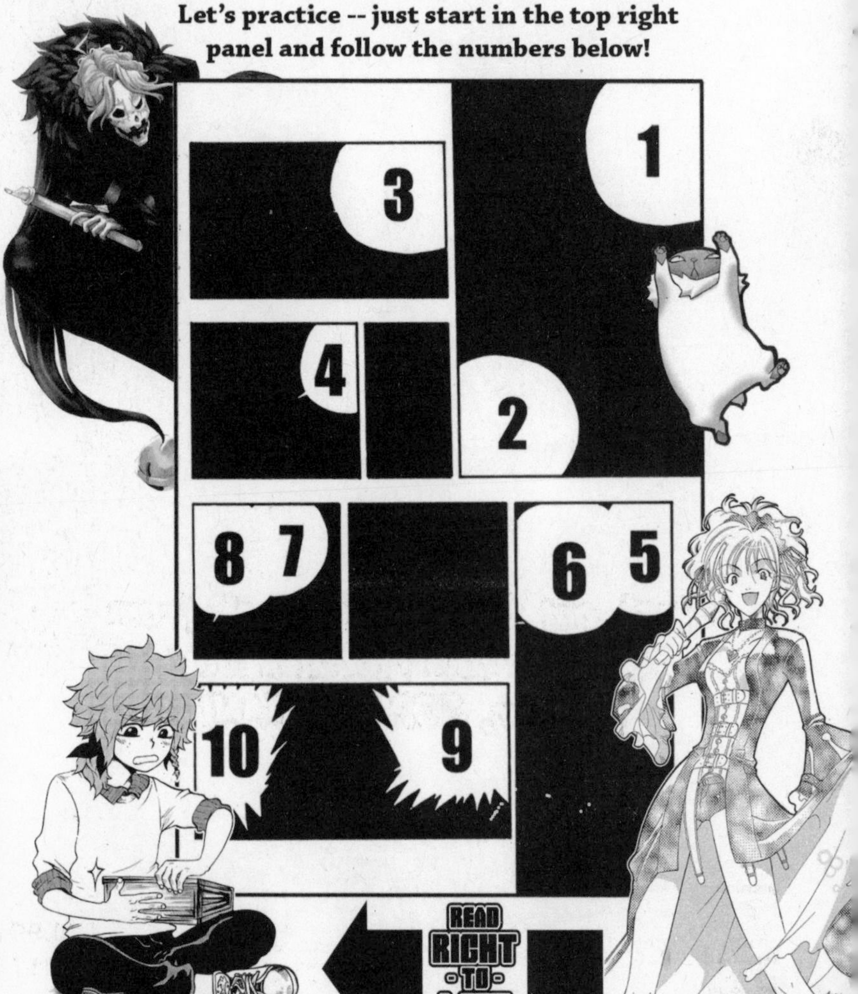
1
2
3
4
5
6
7
8
9
10
READ
RIGHT
-TO-
LEFT

Crimson from *Kamo* / Fairy Cat from **Grimms Manga Tales**
Morrey from ***Goldfisch*** / Princess Ai from ***Princess Ai***

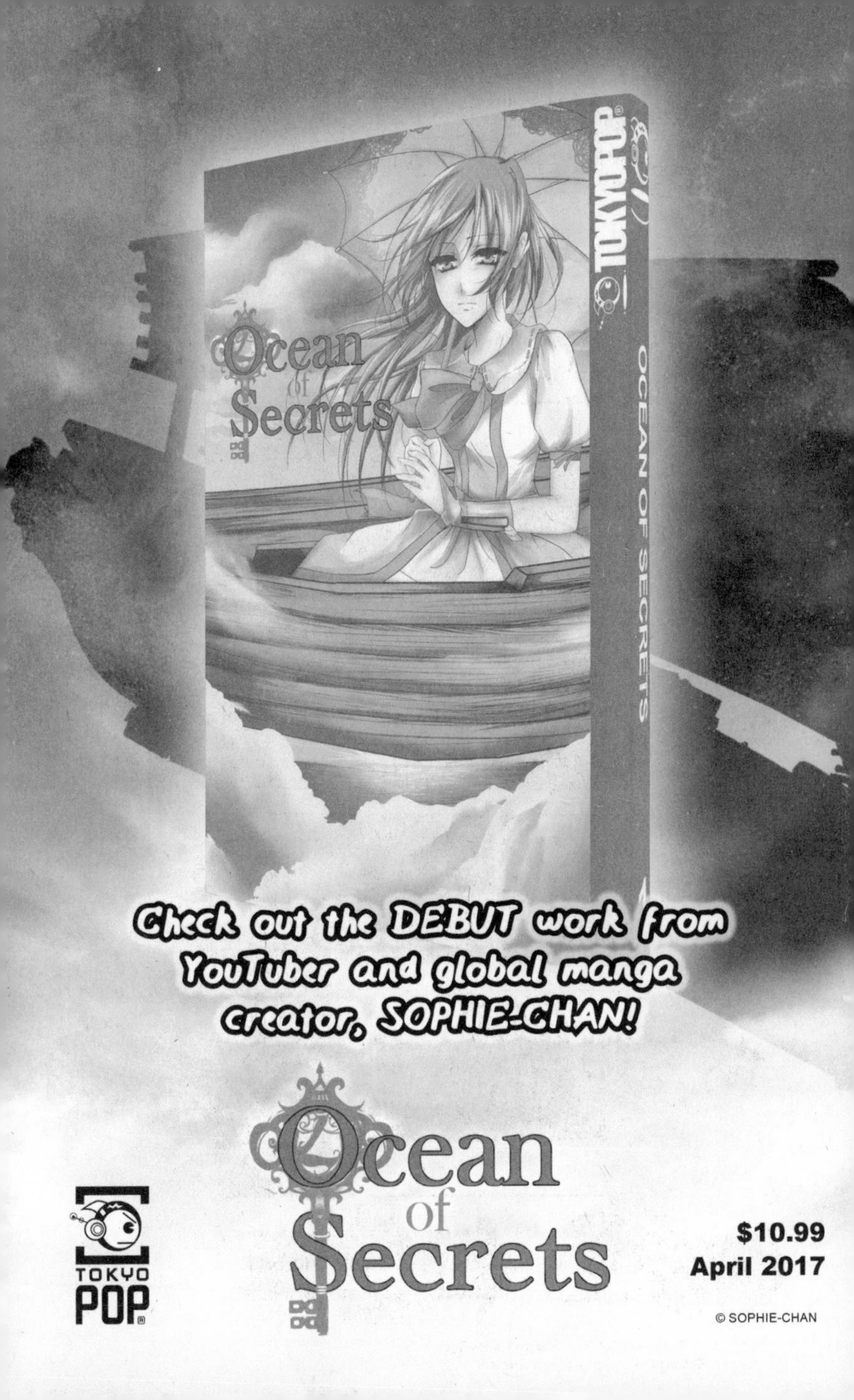
Ocean of Secrets
TOKYOPOP
OCEAN OF SECRETS
Check out the DEBUT work from YouTuber and global manga creator, SOPHIE-CHAN!
Ocean of Secrets
TOKYO POP
$10.99
April 2017
© SOPHIE-CHAN

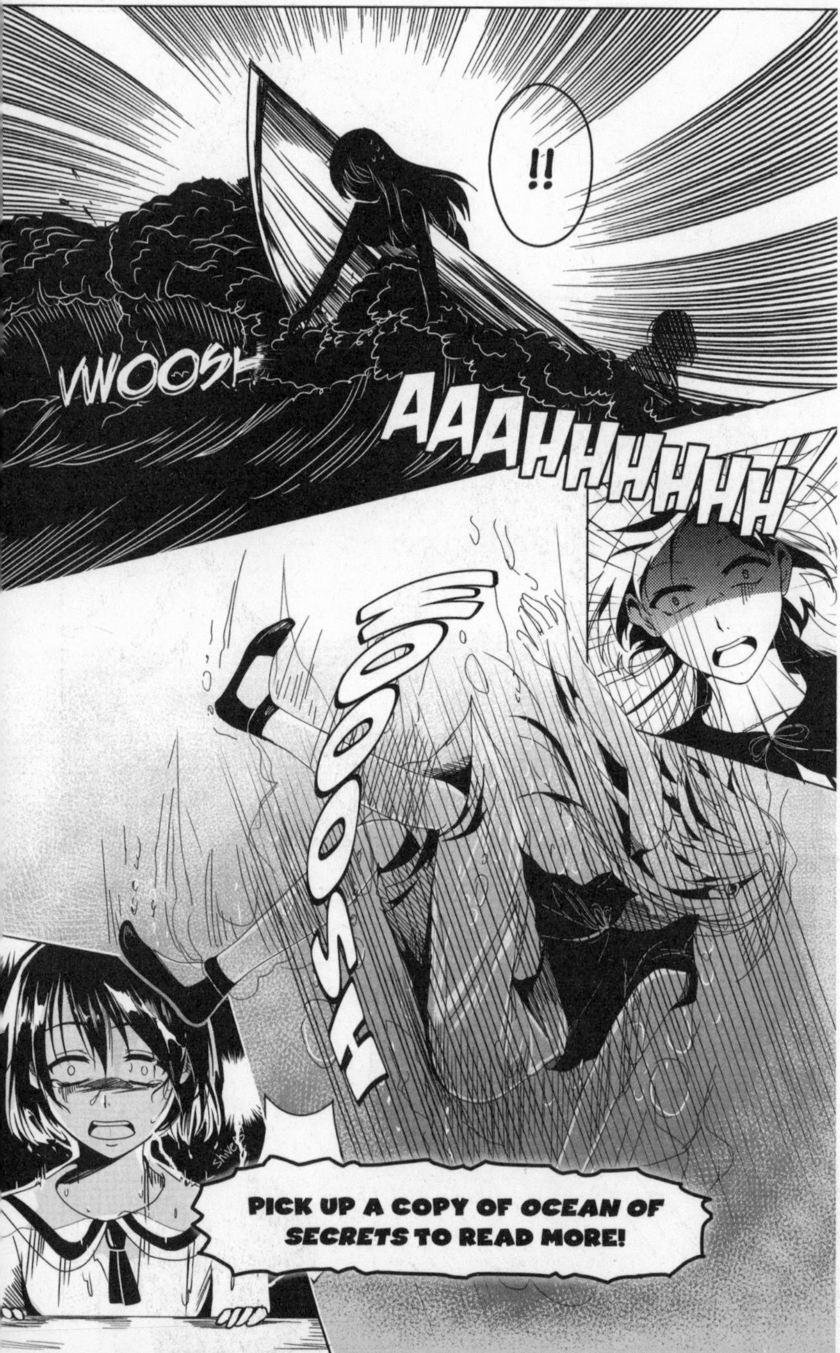
!!
VWOOSH
AAAHHHHHH
WOOOSH
shivers
PICK UP A COPY OF *OCEAN OF SECRETS* TO READ MORE!

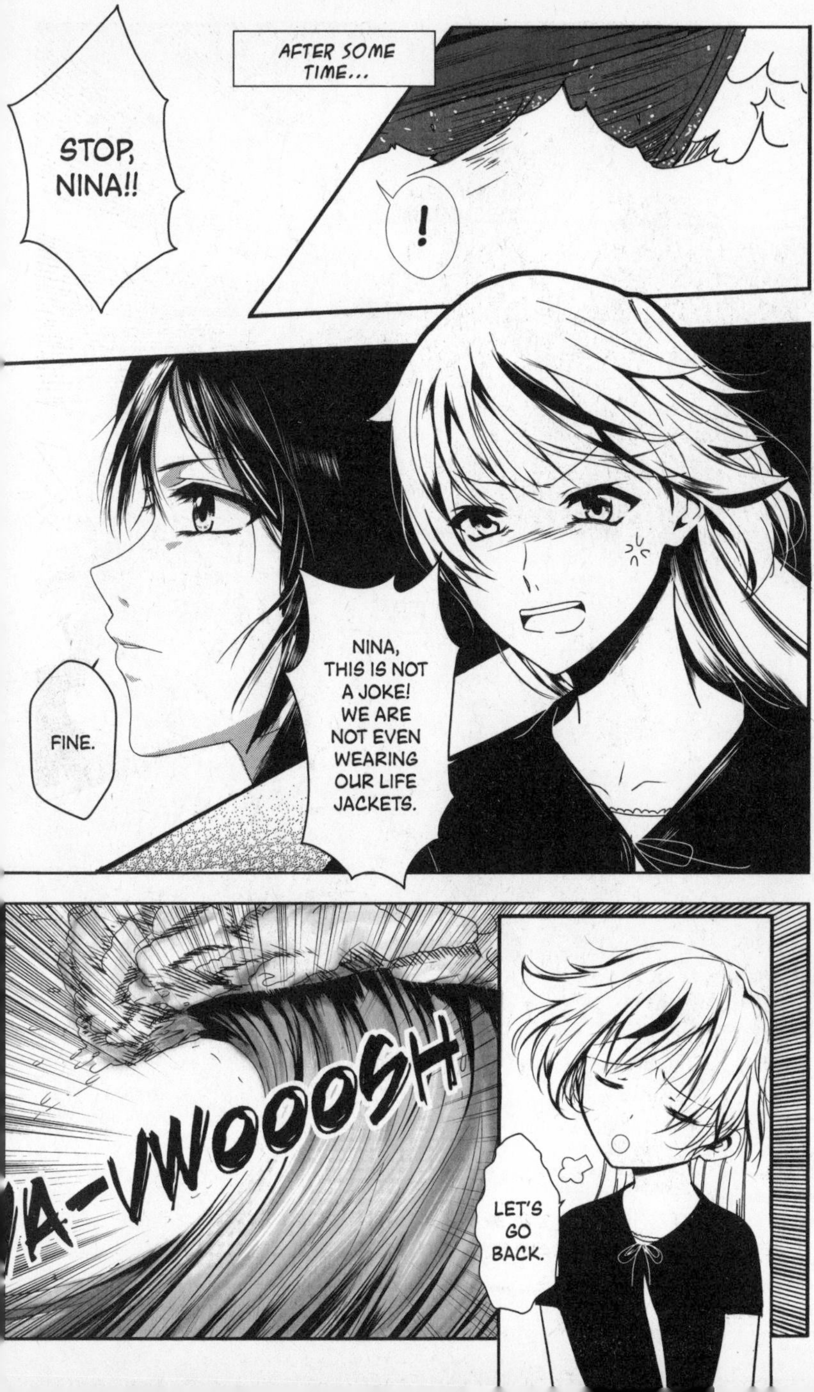
STOP, NINA!!
AFTER SOME TIME...
!
FINE.
NINA, THIS IS NOT A JOKE! WE ARE NOT EVEN WEARING OUR LIFE JACKETS.
A-VWOOOSH
LET'S GO BACK.

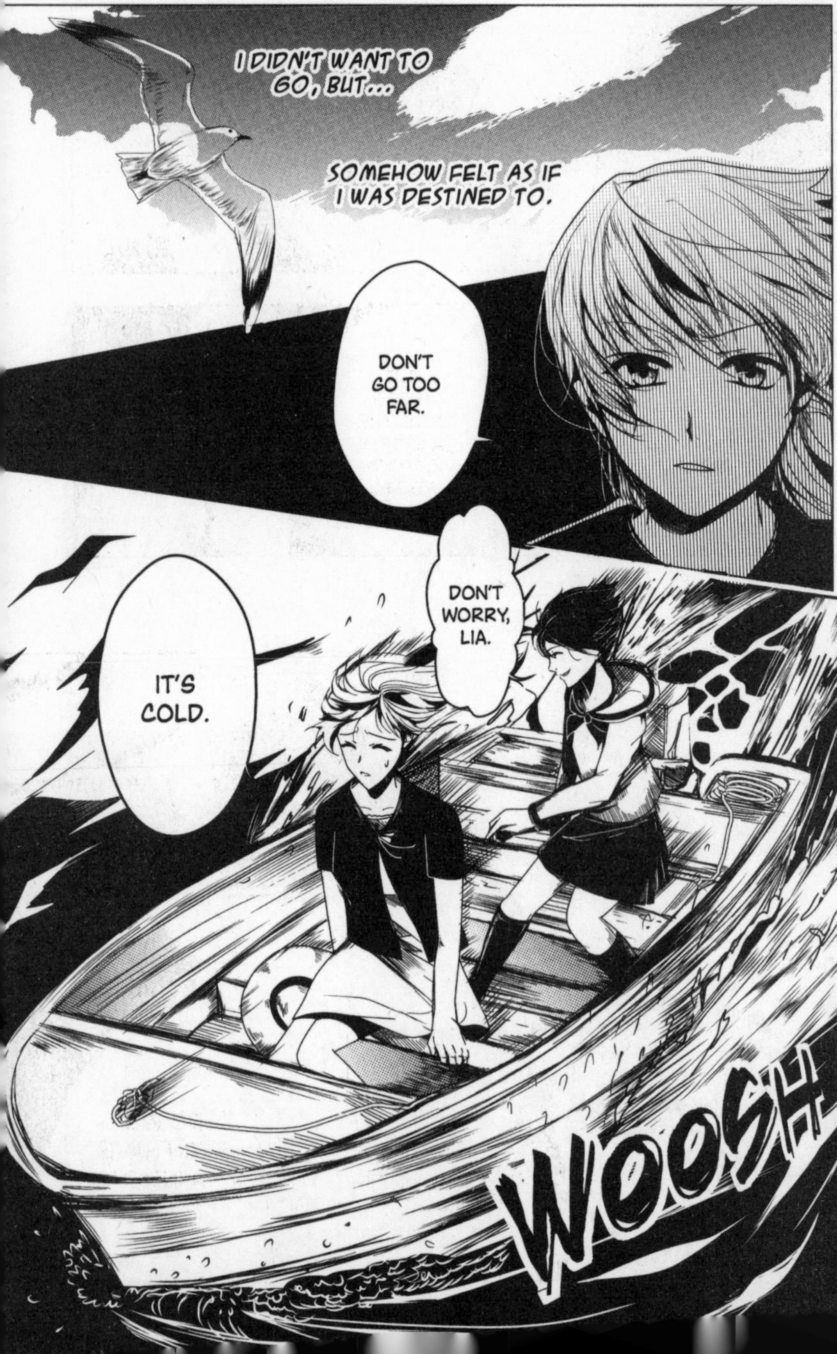
I DIDN'T WANT TO GO, BUT...
SOMEHOW FELT AS IF I WAS DESTINED TO.
DON'T GO TOO FAR.
IT'S COLD.
DON'T WORRY, LIA.
WOOSH

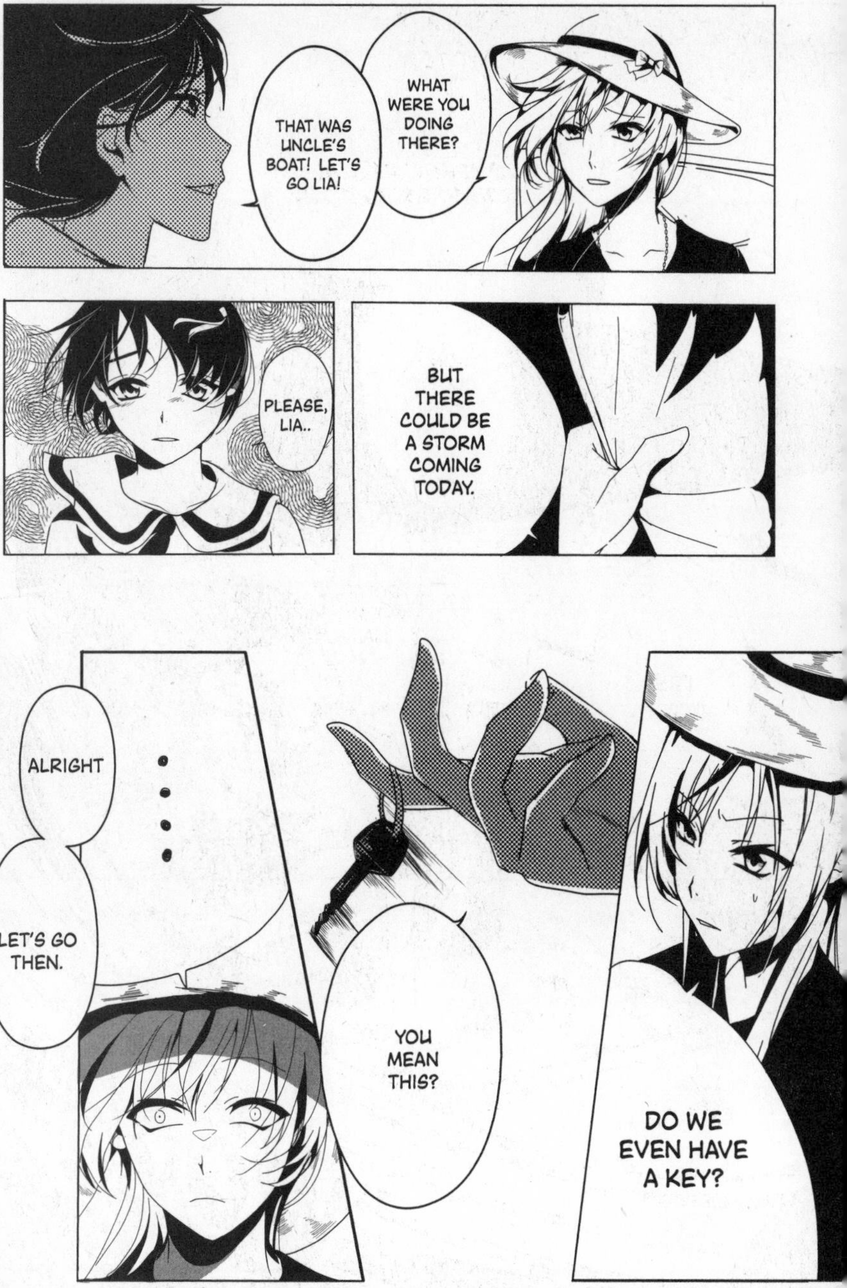

THAT WAS UNCLE'S BOAT! LET'S GO LIA!
WHAT WERE YOU DOING THERE?
PLEASE, LIA..
BUT THERE COULD BE A STORM COMING TODAY.
ALRIGHT
....
LET'S GO THEN.
YOU MEAN THIS?
DO WE EVEN HAVE A KEY?

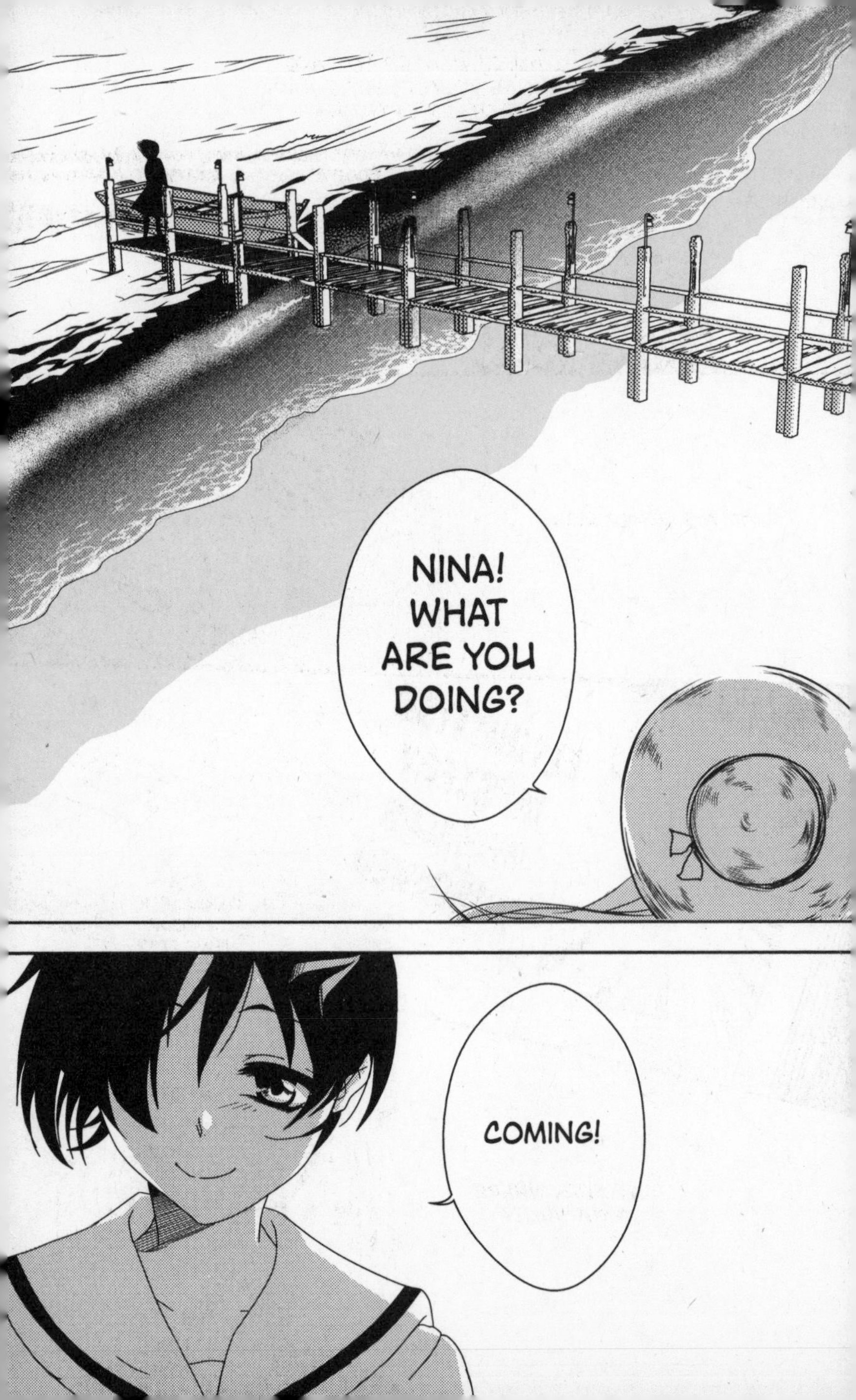
NINA! WHAT ARE YOU DOING?
COMING!

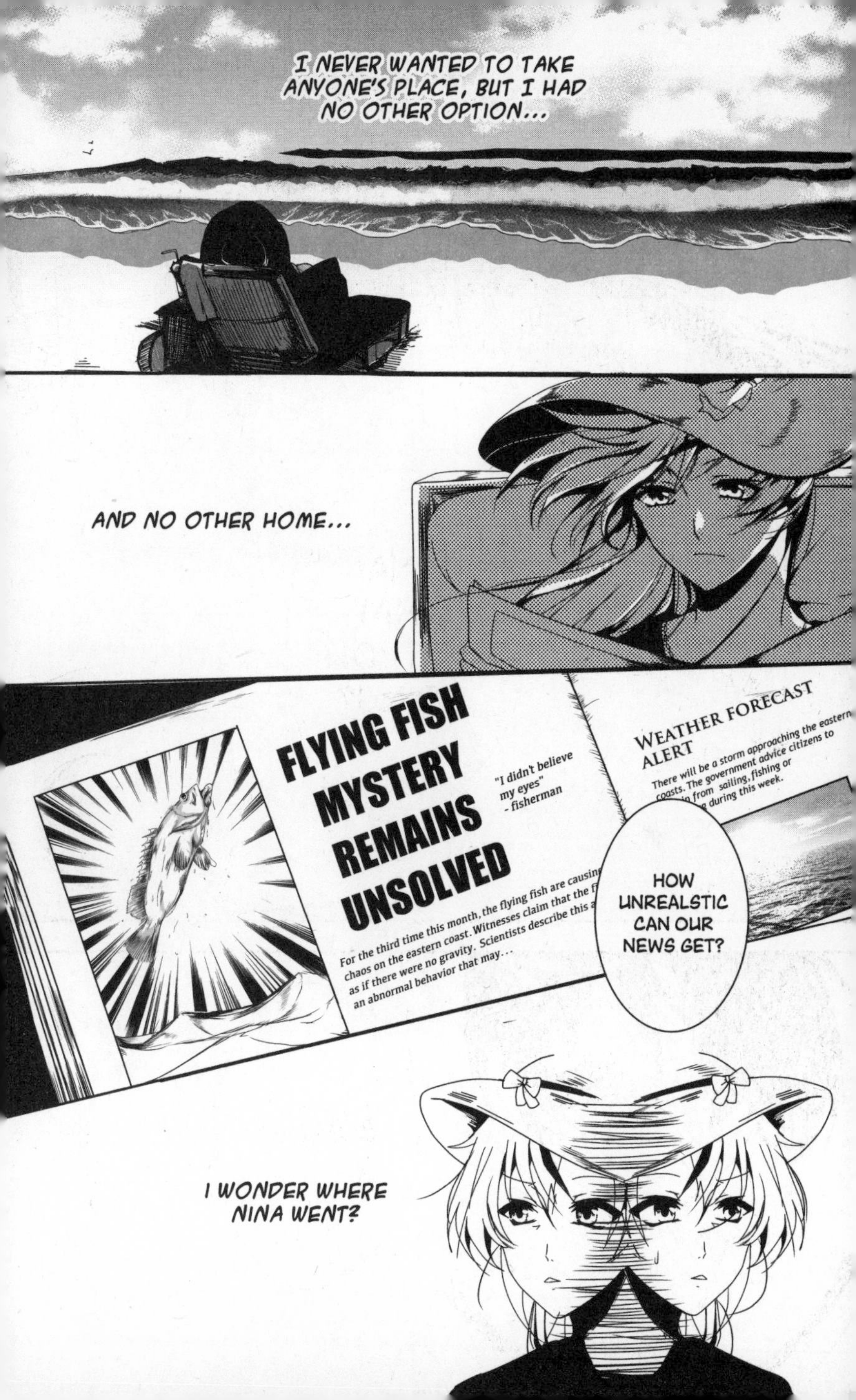
I NEVER WANTED TO TAKE ANYONE'S PLACE, BUT I HAD NO OTHER OPTION...
AND NO OTHER HOME...
FLYING FISH MYSTERY REMAINS UNSOLVED
"I didn't believe my eyes" - fisherman
For the third time this month, the flying fish are causing
chaos on the eastern coast. Witnesses claim that the f
as if there were no gravity. Scientists describe this a
an abnormal behavior that may...
WEATHER FORECAST ALERT
There will be a storm approaching the eastern
coasts. The government advice citizens to
from sailing, fishing or
during this week.
HOW UNREALSTIC CAN OUR NEWS GET?
I WONDER WHERE NINA WENT?

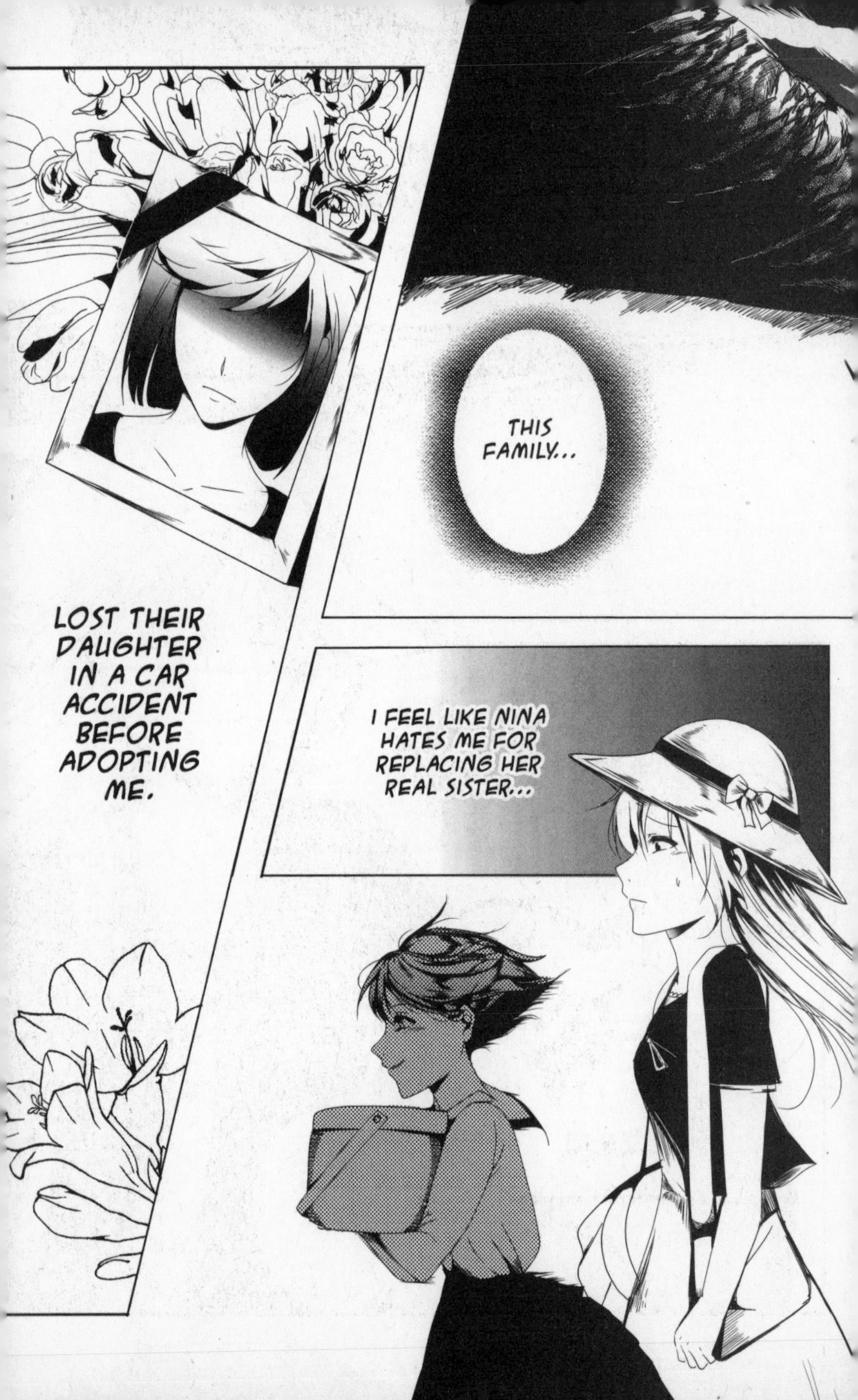
THIS FAMILY...
LOST THEIR DAUGHTER IN A CAR ACCIDENT BEFORE ADOPTING ME.
I FEEL LIKE NINA HATES ME FOR REPLACING HER REAL SISTER...

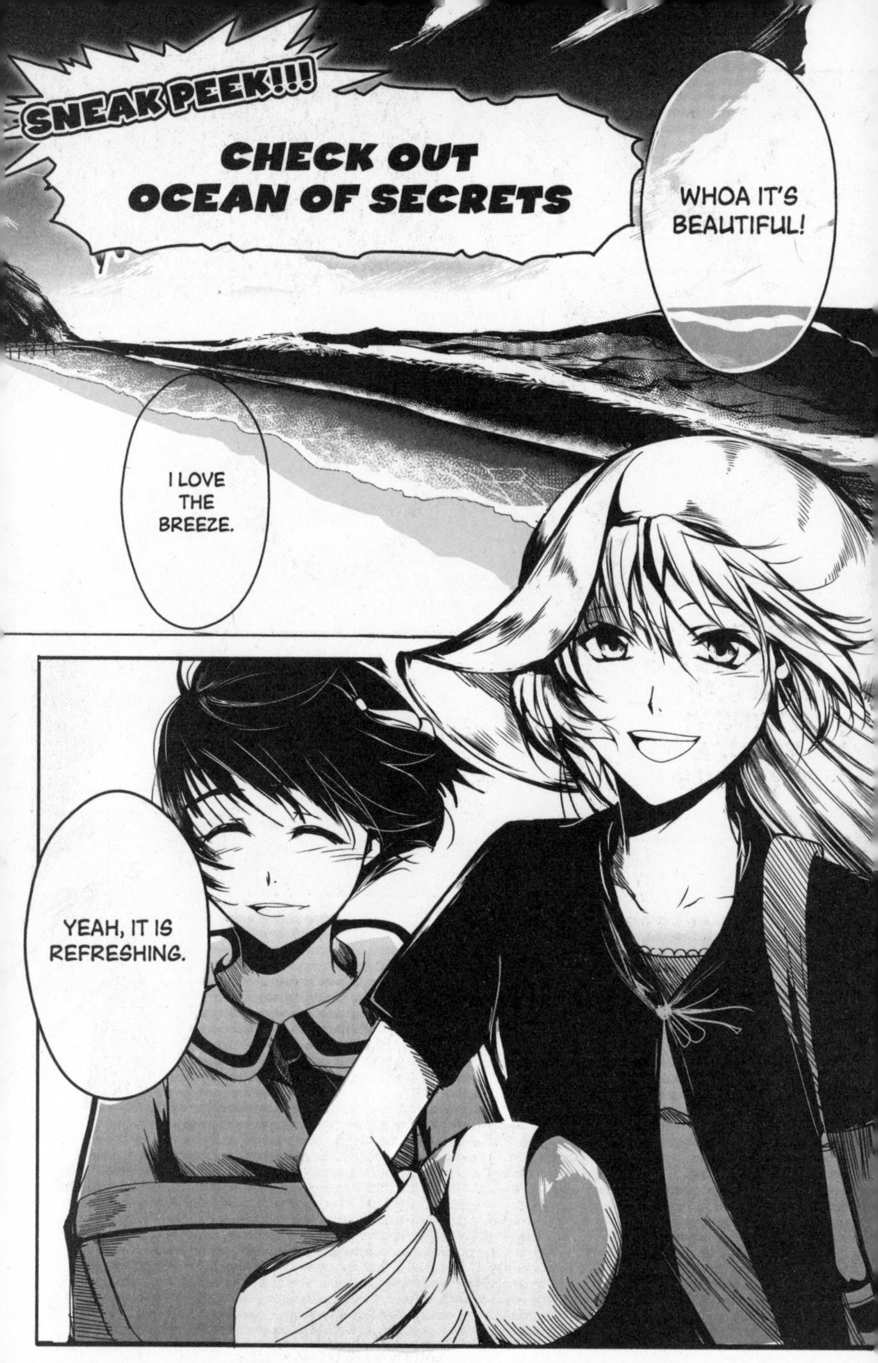
SNEAK PEEK!!!
CHECK OUT OCEAN OF SECRETS
WHOA IT'S BEAUTIFUL!
I LOVE THE BREEZE.
YEAH, IT IS REFRESHING.

GRIMMS manga Tales

The Grimm's Tales reimagined in manga!

Beautiful art by the talented Kei Ishiyama!

Stories from Little Red Riding Hood to Hansel and Gretel!

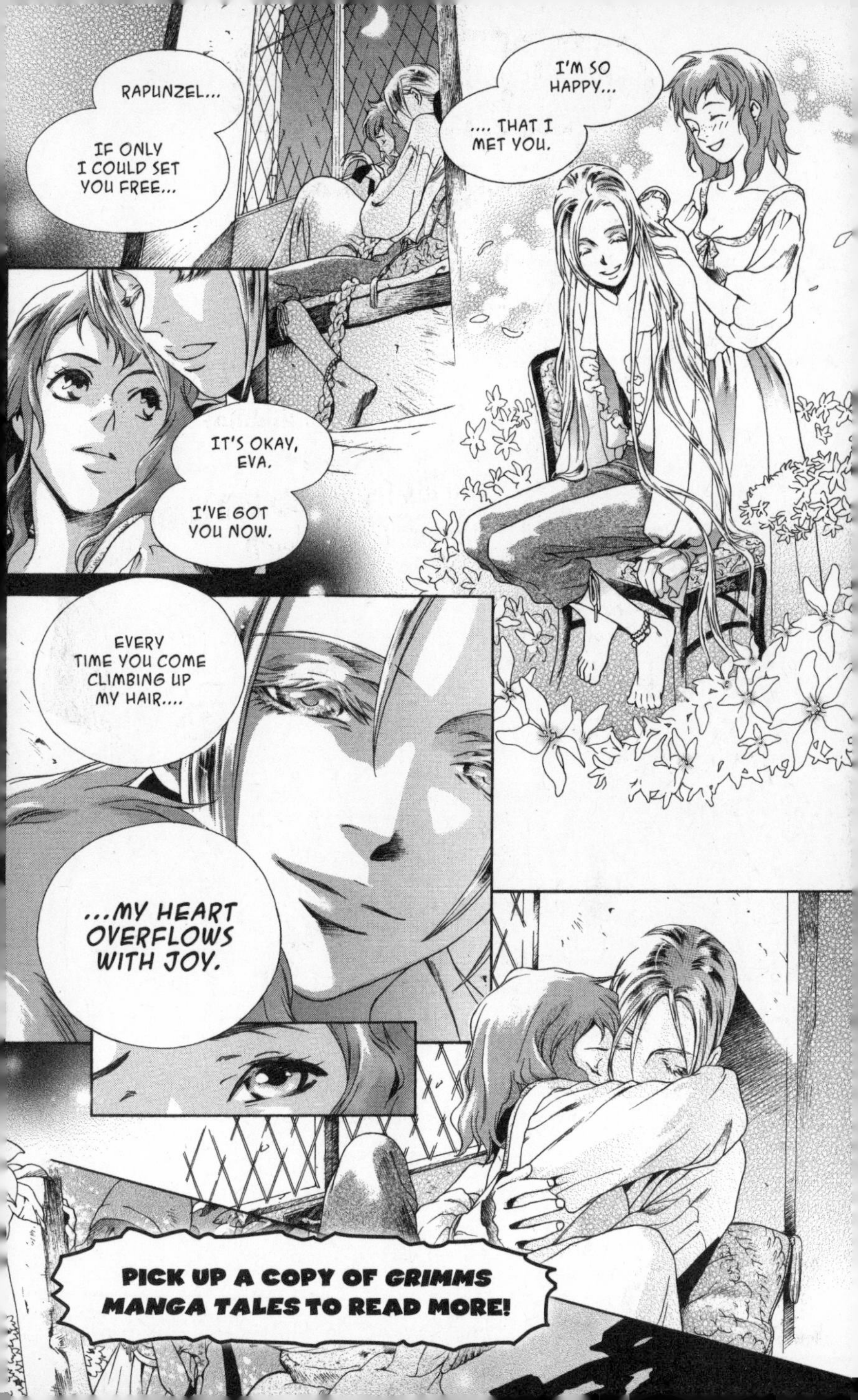
RAPUNZEL...
IF ONLY I COULD SET YOU FREE...
I'M SO HAPPY...
.... THAT I MET YOU.
IT'S OKAY, EVA.
I'VE GOT YOU NOW.
EVERY TIME YOU COME CLIMBING UP MY HAIR....
...MY HEART OVERFLOWS WITH JOY.
PICK UP A COPY OF GRIMMS MANGA TALES TO READ MORE!

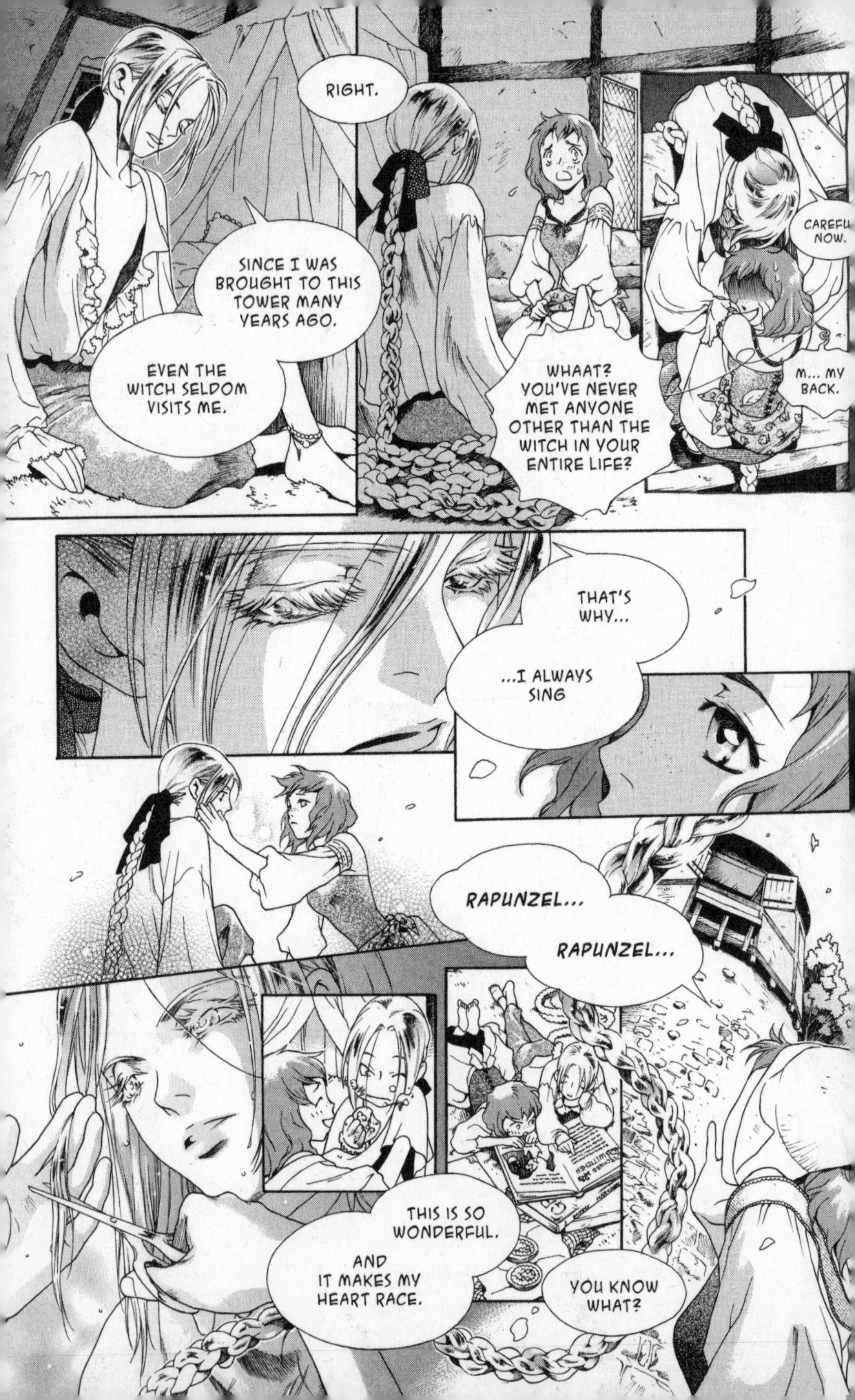
SINCE I WAS BROUGHT TO THIS TOWER MANY YEARS AGO.
EVEN THE WITCH SELDOM VISITS ME.
RIGHT.
WHAAT? YOU'VE NEVER MET ANYONE OTHER THAN THE WITCH IN YOUR ENTIRE LIFE?
CAREFU NOW.
M... MY BACK.
THAT'S WHY...
...I ALWAYS SING
RAPUNZEL...
RAPUNZEL...
THIS IS SO WONDERFUL.
AND IT MAKES MY HEART RACE.
YOU KNOW WHAT?

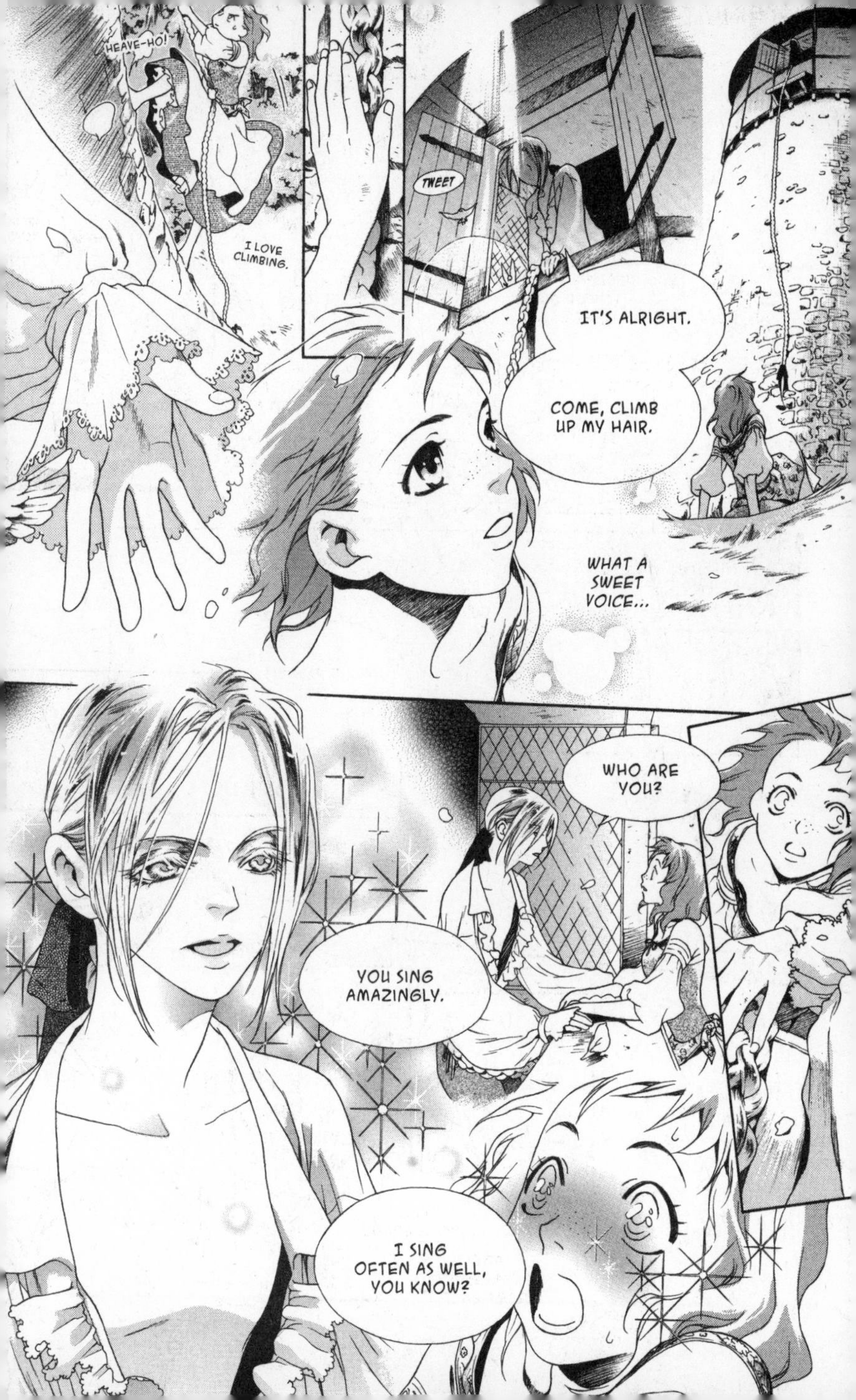
HEAVE-HO!
I LOVE CLIMBING.
TWEET
IT'S ALRIGHT.
COME, CLIMB UP MY HAIR.
WHAT A SWEET VOICE...
YOU SING AMAZINGLY.
WHO ARE YOU?
I SING OFTEN AS WELL, YOU KNOW?

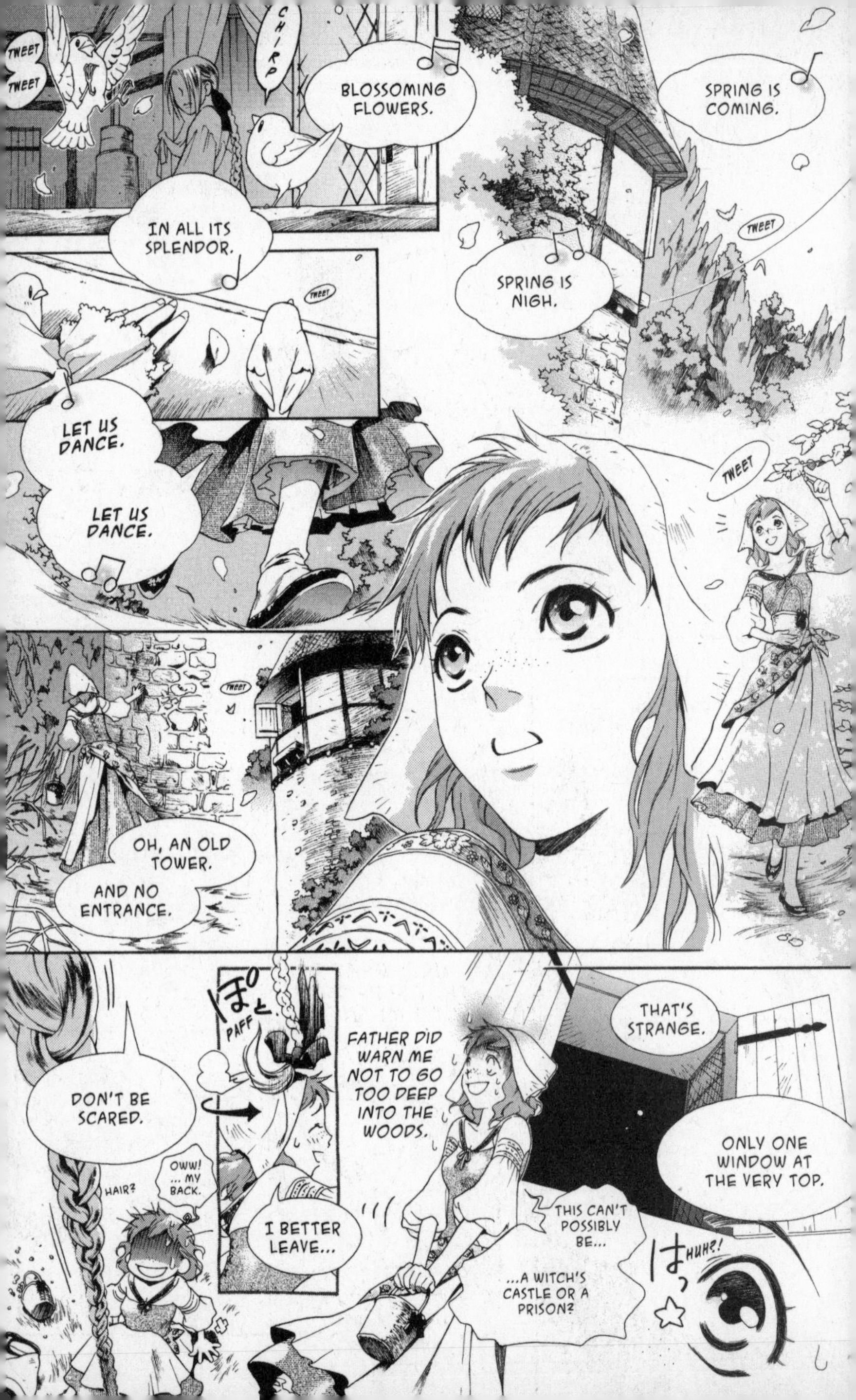
TWEET
TWEET
CHIRP
BLOSSOMING FLOWERS.
SPRING IS COMING.
IN ALL ITS SPLENDOR.
TWEET
SPRING IS NIGH.
TWEET
LET US DANCE.
LET US DANCE.
TWEET
TWEET
OH, AN OLD TOWER.
AND NO ENTRANCE.
THAT'S STRANGE.
ONLY ONE WINDOW AT THE VERY TOP.
はっ HUH?!
THIS CAN'T POSSIBLY BE...
...A WITCH'S CASTLE OR A PRISON?
FATHER DID WARN ME NOT TO GO TOO DEEP INTO THE WOODS.
I BETTER LEAVE...
ぽと PAFF
DON'T BE SCARED.
HAIR?
OWW! ... MY BACK.

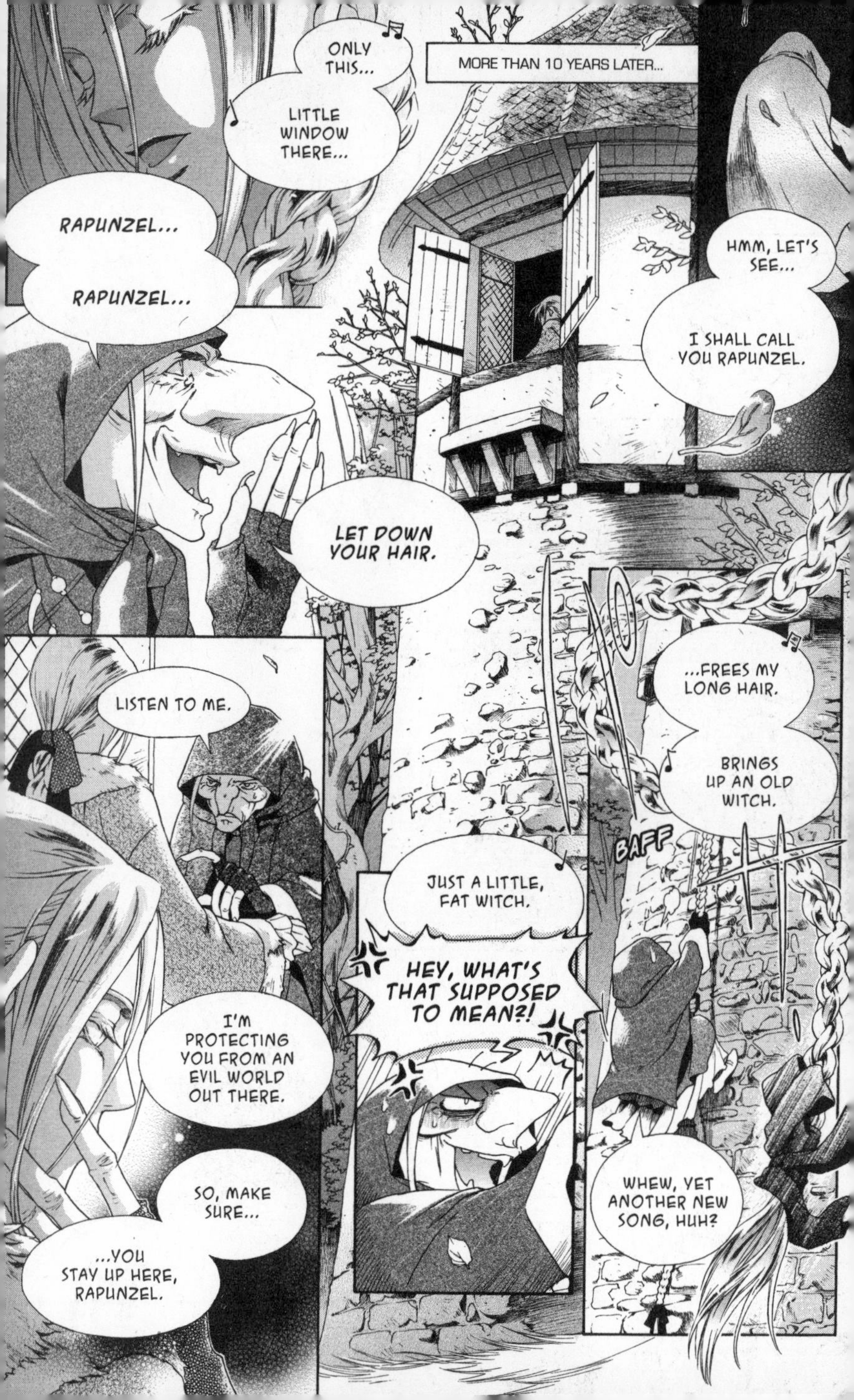
ONLY THIS...
LITTLE WINDOW THERE...
MORE THAN 10 YEARS LATER...
HMM, LET'S SEE...
I SHALL CALL YOU RAPUNZEL.
RAPUNZEL...
RAPUNZEL...
LET DOWN YOUR HAIR.
LISTEN TO ME.
I'M PROTECTING YOU FROM AN EVIL WORLD OUT THERE.
SO, MAKE SURE...
...YOU STAY UP HERE, RAPUNZEL.
...FREES MY LONG HAIR.
BRINGS UP AN OLD WITCH.
BAFF
JUST A LITTLE, FAT WITCH.
HEY, WHAT'S THAT SUPPOSED TO MEAN?!
WHEW, YET ANOTHER NEW SONG, HUH?

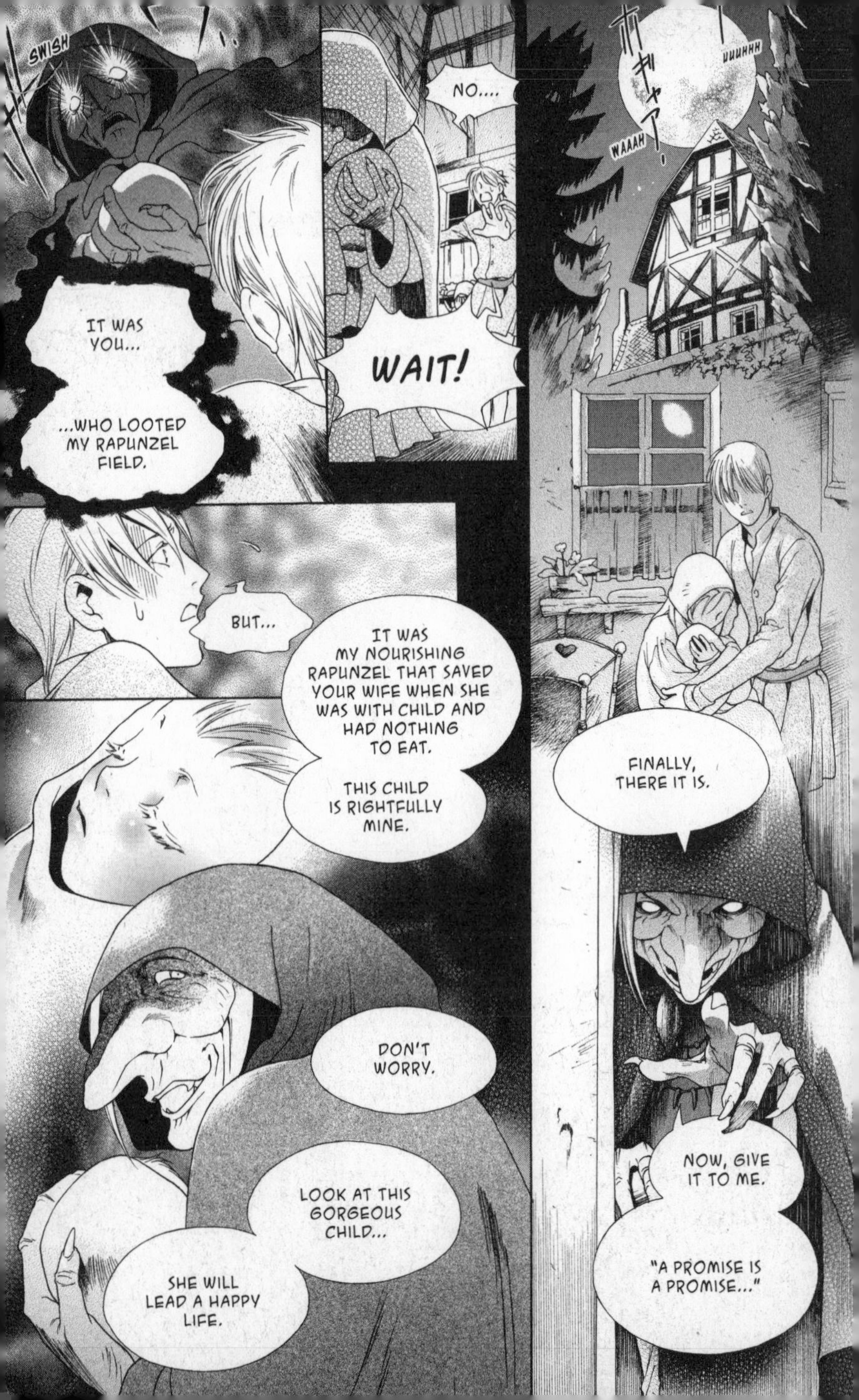
SWISH
IT WAS YOU...
...WHO LOOTED MY RAPUNZEL FIELD.
NO....
WAIT!
BUT...
IT WAS MY NOURISHING RAPUNZEL THAT SAVED YOUR WIFE WHEN SHE WAS WITH CHILD AND HAD NOTHING TO EAT.
THIS CHILD IS RIGHTFULLY MINE.
DON'T WORRY.
LOOK AT THIS GORGEOUS CHILD...
SHE WILL LEAD A HAPPY LIFE.
ホギャア!
WAAAH
UUUHHH
FINALLY, THERE IT IS.
NOW, GIVE IT TO ME.
"A PROMISE IS A PROMISE..."

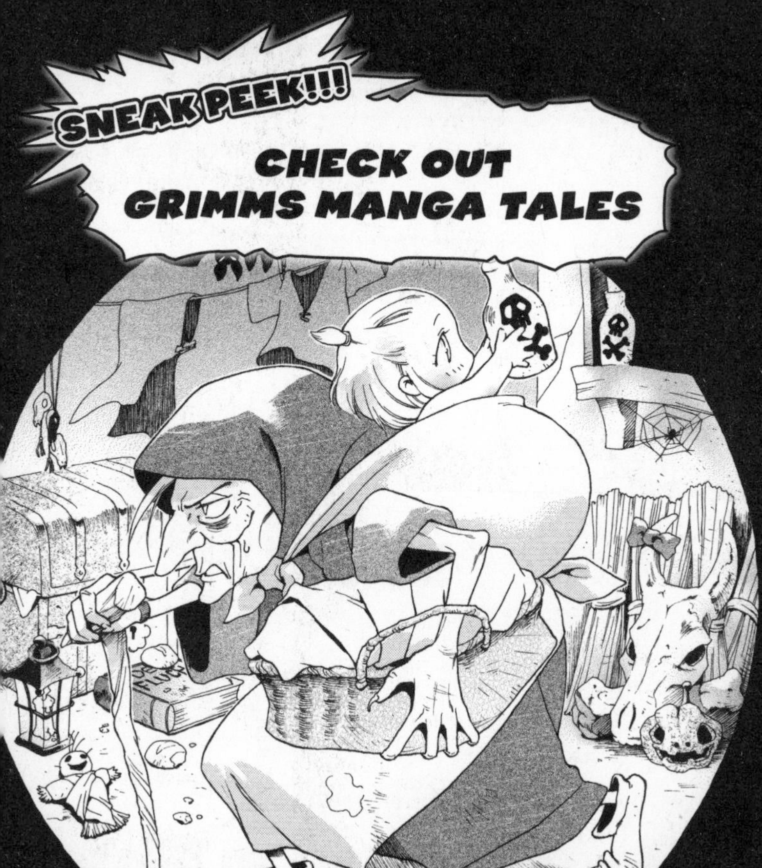
SNEAK PEEK!!!
CHECK OUT GRIMMS MANGA TALES

RAPUNZEL

Sword Princess Amaltea Volume 1
Manga by: Natalia Batista

Book One Assistants	-	**Catarina Batista, Emil Johansson, Joakim Waller, Yossra El Said and Elise Rosberg**
Editorial Associate	-	Janae Young
Marketing Associate	-	Kae Winters
Technology and Digital Media Assistant	-	Phillip Hong
Digital Media Coordinator	-	Rico Brenner-Quiñonez
Licensing Specialist	-	Arika Yanaka
Copy Editor	-	M. Cara Carper
Graphic Designer	-	Phillip Hong
Retouching and Lettering	-	Vibrraant Publishing Studio
Editor-in-Chief & Publisher	-	Stu Levy

A  Manga

TOKYOPOP and ⊙ are trademarks or registered trademarks of TOKYOPOP Inc.

TOKYOPOP inc.
5200 W Century Blvd
Suite 705
Los Angeles, CA 90045 USA

E-mail: info@TOKYOPOP.com
Come visit us online at www.TOKYOPOP.com

f www.facebook.com/TOKYOPOP
🐦 www.twitter.com/TOKYOPOP
▶ www.youtube.com/TOKYOPOPTV
📌 www.pinterest.com/TOKYOPOP
📷 www.instagram.com/TOKYOPOP
t. TOKYOPOP.tumblr.com

ISBN: 978-1-4278-5917-4

First TOKYOPOP Printing: April 2018
10 9 8 7 6 5 4 3 2 1
Printed in CANADA